AF539498

Impact of Economic Reform Policies on Dalit and Weaker Sections

IMPACT OF ECONOMIC REFORM POLICIES ON DALIT AND WEAKER SECTIONS

Edited by

ANIL KUMAR THAKUR

and

R.N. THAKUR

Published on behalf of
ECONOMIC ASSOCIATION OF BIHAR

DEEP & DEEP PUBLICATIONS PVT. LTD.
F-159, Rajouri Garden, New Delhi-110027

IMPACT OF ECONOMIC REFORM POLICIES ON DALIT AND WEAKER SECTIONS

ISBN 978-81-8450-063-9

Typeset by SHRI GANESH COMPOSERS,
R-3/120, Balaji Chowk, Mohan Garden, New Delhi.

Printed in India at NEW ELEGANT PRINTERS, A-49/1, Phase I,
Mayapuri, New Delhi-110064.

Published by DEEP & DEEP PUBLICATIONS PVT. LTD.,
F-159, Rajouri Garden, New Delhi-110027. Phones: 25435369, 25440916.
E-mail: ddpbooks@yahoo.co.in • ddpubs@gmail.com
Sales Showroom: 2/13, Ansari Road, Daryaganj, New Delhi-110002
Phone: 23245122, 65479462 • Fax: 011-23245122

Contents

Preface

The book "Impact of Economic Reform Policies on Dalit and Weaker Sections" is based on the deliberations made under the IXth Annual Conference of Economic Association of Bihar and Jharkhand (EABJ). The themes of this book include the concept, various analysis of policies made under the globalisation suited and not suited for the dalit and weaker sections of Society. The dalits, adivasis, minorities, women and backward castes are seen and treated as second class citizen still now. Though empowerment of dalits SCs, STs, OBCs, Women and minorities are being held but still they are far behind in the stream of development. The policies are made for their upliftment, but they become unable to be real beneficiaries of those policies. Reservations are made for them. But in one hand jobs markets are shrinking, employment opportunities are reducing and in another hand vast giants of corruption are there to divulse their shares. The awareness is highly essential apart from all these laws and enactments meant for them. They have to be safeguarded not only politically and to make them toys for the sake of snatching votes from those Sections. They have to be safeguarded socially, academically and all the most economically. They are not untouchables. They are the persons of main stream.

We think, this book will be fruitful for those oppressed, depressed and down-trodden Sections of Society as well as for them who show their real or mechanical sympathy for them. They will flourish and develop in this century along with all. They need share, right and power, not sympathy and tears.

ANIL KUMAR THAKUR
RAM NARESH THAKUR

Introduction

The book "Impact of Economic Reform Policies on Dalit and Weaker Sections" is the outcome of the deliberations made under one of the four sessions in IXth Annual Conference of Economic Association of Bihar and Jharkhand (EABJ) held in A.N. College, Patna on 29-30 March, 2006. There are twenty-nine articles altogether in this book. The number of authors is forty-six. Fourteen articles are written by the single author each separately, thirteen by double authors each and rest two are written by three authors each. All these articles are the unique research works made by the learned authors on the impact of economic reform policies on dalit and weaker sections of the society. This book is scholarly edited by Dr. Anil Kumar Thakur, Honorary Secretary and Treasurer, Indian Economic Association and Prof. R.N. Thakur, Ex-Executive Committee Member, IEA. They have rich ideas and grand vision. The twenty-first century has to face the challenges for the development of dalits and weaker sections of society including women and depressed minority class. This book will focus on the views, ideas and principles for the upliftment of dalit and weaker sections.

The first article 'India's Economic Reform and its Social Dimension' is written by S.K. Singh. In this article Singh has discussed the concept, the need and problems faced by the economy during 1990s, objectives of reform, reform package, implications of reforms and the content of the economic reforms as well as the analysis of the various aspects of social dimension relating to economic reforms in India. Kumar Ratnesh and Binay Kumar Singh have stressed on the impact of economic reforms on poverty and workforce structure among social groups with reference to rural

India. According to them the post-reform period was expected to provide greater flexibility in employment opportunities for all the social groups. R.N. Singh, Upendra Sharma and Chitranjan Ojha in their article have also emphasised on the impact of reform policies on the Indian economy. The poverty and unemployment remain great problems of the Indian economy and it is worsening day-by-day. The country requires the policies with 'human soil' and not only with 'human face'. B.K. Jha and R.K. Marandi have analysed the prospects of economic empowerment of Tribals through value addition of minor forest produce in Jharkhand. Thus the unemployed labour force would be able to get employment throughout the year. This will check the migration of tribals from forest villages to the cities within and outside the State in search of job and it will emancipate them from the Socio-economic and other types of exploitation. S.P. Saha and B.K. Chaudhary have dealt in detail the subsequent result of globalisation policy of the government and the failure of dalits to approach the access of benefits made for them. They plea for more government intervention for real gain of reform policies meant for them. Rashmi Akhoury presents the unpleasant picture of globalisation on dalits and minorities. According to her the rise of Hindutva, demolition of Babari Masjid structure, review of constitution, degradation and harassment of minorities, saffronisation of education and generally communalisation of the polity are not to be taken as accidental or chance factors (events). They are very much complementary to globalisation and its linkages. Hindutava or fundamental Islamism strengthen feudalism and regressive values. It in *de facto* promotes untouchability and whips up caste hatred against the lower castes in general and dalits in particular. These are the abstacles in the way of balanced progress (development) of society. Sanjay Kumar and Bipin Prasad Singh have vividly expressed the changing pattern of 'Kamioti' system with special reference to Mushahar Community of Gaya district. Kamia System as a traditional labour form of this region has changed into wage labour. Mushahars initiated to pay cash wage as well as they are migrating from there due to this system. Ranju Ranjan Kumari and Krishna Nand Yadav are of opinion that the development strategies which simply increase women's access to resources do not necessarily ensure their empowerment, but women's control on resources is necessary for their empowerment. They on the basis of their indepth study pave the ways for women's empowerment. In their views the real way of empowering women is to provide them human rights, protection and participation in property, to safeguard their entitlement and to honour them with equal status for executing effective role in shaping and modeling the development of nation and destiny of India in future. Ram Naresh Thakur in his article 'Empowerment of Women in Bihar' has stressed the conditions, factors, issues and policies for the empowerment of women specially in Bihar. He, by analysing the various aspects of demography of Bihar, has compared the relative positions of women in different regions. He is of the opinion that women of Bihar are less empowered and backward in comparison of other States. The sex ratio is low and literacy rate is the lowest. It has direct bearing on the fertility rate, population growth, health care, education, orthodoxy and so many related issues of development. Women have to face various obstacles and hurdles in the way of their progress. The government is required to take effective steps sooner to change their destiny and to bring them on the equal footing with men. H.N.P. Singh relates the depressed condition of dalits socially and economically. Untouchability still knocks the door of institutions like marriage, caste, Hindu temples, etc. The cultural hegemony of 'dwija' remains intact and dalitness remains physical reality. S.K.L. Das has dealt with the reverse effects of reform on dalits. In his opinion Karl Marx's proletarian revolution only can destroy all kinds of exploitation and to establish the greatest human democratic society where weaker sections and common man can improve their lot. Hence, new policies will be needed to reduce the insecurity of the weaker sections as well as the large number of dalits, who are living a life of misery and destitute. Sukhmani Das and Meera Ranjan Lal enquired the attention paid to discrimination with children in the society. He opined that the children, being the hope of future also, are suffering a lot and are subjected to endless toil and hard work without having any corresponding opportunities to grow. The authors have praised the role of I.L.O. in this contest and suggested to adopt measures accordingly. B.K. Jha studies that child labour along with large number of vulnerable groups in India may have to bear the costs of globalisation and liberalisation.

Md. Reyazuddin tells that child labour cannot be weeded out despite several welfare legislations enacted by the government from time to time. It is every one's responsibility to protect these flowers from the damaging effects of excessive exposure of heat, cold and rains. They should be put on the right track always as they are the seeds of future national growth. According to P. Roy and S.P. Sah the phenomenon of child labour is a symptom of disease and is a consequence of exploitative system, operating at the national and international level, lopsided development, uneven resource ownership correlating of large-scale unemployment and object poverty among the nations. It cannot be eliminated voluntarily in any case. Umesh Prasad and B. Chaudhary have shown their views that this human problem, the problem of child labour, has closed the future development of the country. J. Prasad and Rajesh Kumar have dwelt upon the view that it is an undeniable facts that the long-run solution of the problem requires medical reforms in property relations. Serious and honest land reforms along with sufficient provision of credit and other infrastructure facilities are also very much essential. Mridula Kumari highlighted the issues, prospects and problems of female child labour specially in the post-reform era. In her opinion the decay of public production system and privatisation emerged due to globalisation have made the situation worse and painful. R.K. Devi discussed in detail the various dimensions, issued and policies of child labour in India. She has suggested that it is essential to tackle this issue simultaneously from all related angles, so that as a whole the impact may be transparent, impartial, visible and useful. According to the macro-economic study of Nageshwar Sharma and A. Kumar the women empowerment requires their emancipation from dependency. The implementation of liberalisation policies lead to the continuous decline in the employment opportunities, specially in the organised sector. This causes the displacement of women. They are compelled to depend upon informal sector where women are exploited in many respects. C.P. Azad and C.P. Singh discusses women empowerment after fifty years of independence. Overall women have been subjected to exploitation, atrocities, male dominance and gender-bias. Manoj Shankar Gupta explains the various different legal and government-based approaches in India for empowering women. He has focussed the fact that how women's empowerment is basically groomed by the men behind the curtain as Indira Gandhi by Pt. Nehru, Jay Lalitha by M.G. Ramchandran, Mayavati by his master Kansi Ram and Smt. Rabari Devi by her husband Laloo Yadav, etc. He has explained in detail the various articles of Indian constitution, Sections of I.P.C., C.P.C., Cr. P.C. and many Acts anuncted by the legislature for empowering women in India. As per the review of Padmini Prasad the women can be empowered by the economic means and ways properly as increasing individual income, developing habit of saving, access to market and alternative credit delivery system, etc. By those means the rural women can maximise their contribution to the economy. In the eyes of Md. Imeteyaz Hassan the backwardness of Muslim women has increased in lack of literacy and for prevailing orthodoxy. Orthodoxy within the Muslim Society has suppressed the identity of Muslim women. He feels that the efforts should be made by the women themselves towards their own education as well as their daughters and other girls of the family. For it awareness is highly required. The effort of the author is praiseworthy. M. Alamgeer has dealt the Socio-political analysis for the empowerment of Dalits. In his study, 'Dalits are the group of people who face social discrimination in worst form including untouchability. He has explained various social and educational policies to improve the situation. He has made distinct difference between *de-jure* discrimination and *de-facto* segregation with the dalits. The study is appreciable. S.K. Jha and Nand Kumar have stressed the state of despair of the State of Bihar. In Bihar there is income inequality, poverty and unemployment. They have suggested many remedial measures for increasing agricultural produces for the upliftment of weaker section of society. Sheela Sharan Singh has discussed elaborately about the child labour eliminating policy of the government along with the serious conditions of child labour in India. According to him poverty and illiteracy are the main causes which are required to be eliminated. Sabita Kumari and Suresh Kumar have highlighted the problems and prospects of women's empowerment through Panchayati Raj Institutions. According to their view by involving women, delivery of services in the sectors of education, health, credit and governance will become effective. Enhancing women's rights, access to resources and participation in decision-making will not only benefit the women's segments but also the whole community. Anil Kumar Thakur, Ashwani Kumar and K.B. Padamdeo have analysed in detail the impacts of economic reforms on dalits. They plea for many safeguards for dalits as: (i) Social, Educational, cultural and religious safeguards, (ii) Economic safeguards, (iii) Political

Safeguards, and (iv) Safeguards for employment, etc. In their view benefits of the reservation policy to the dalit community have been more indirect than direct. Unemployment and poverty are endemic in the country and the new economic policy will aggravate them further. Leaving the public sector to fend for itself, the private sector will thrive where reservations of employment will have no room. Dalits fear that they manage to get reserved jobs in the government, but the liberalisation and privatisation snatch them from their hands soon.

This book will be fruitful for the scholars, students, the researchers and the policy-makers and show the path for proper development of dalits and weaker sections of India.

ANIL KUMAR THAKUR
RAM NARESH THAKUR

List of Contributors

1. **Anil Kumar Thakur,** Secretary & Treasurer, Indian Economic Association.
2. **Anirudh Kumar,** A.S. College, Deogarh, Jharkhand.
3. **Ashwani Kumar,** Department of Economics, Dalmiya Nagar Mahila College, Dehri-on-sone.
4. **B.K. Jha,** University Professor & Head, Department of Rural Economics & Co-operation, T.M. University, Bhagalpur, Bihar.
5. **Binay Kumar Singh,** Lecturer, Deptt. of Economics, Y.N. College, Dighwara (Bihar).
6. **Binod Choudhary,** Department of Economics, Patel Trimurthy College, Patna.
7. **Binod Kumar Chaudhary,** Lecturer, Department of Rural Economics, M.L.S.M. College, Darbhanga.
8. **Bipin Prasad Singh,** S.K.M. College, Nawada, Bihar.
9. **Birendra Kumar Jha,** Reader & Head of Economics Department, D.B.K.N. College, Narhan, Samastipur, Bihar.
10. **Chandra Prakash Azad,** Madan Ahilya Mahila College, Naugachia.
11. **Chandra Prakash Singh,** Centre for Regional Studies, T.M. Bhagalpur University, Bhagalpur.
12. **Chitranjan Ojha,** Lecturer in Commerce, Kisan College, Soh Sarai, Nalanda, Bihar.
13. **Hari Narayan Prasad Singh,** Department of Economics, Kisan College, Soh Sarai, Nalanda.

14. **Jagdish Prasad,** Department of Commerce, College of Commerce, Patna.

15. **K.B. Padamdeo,** Department of Commerce, College of Commerce, Patna.

16. **Krishna Nand Yadav,** Department of Economics, R.L.S.Y. College, Aurangabad (M.U.), Bihar.

17. **Kumar Ratnesh,** Lecturer, Deptt. of P.G. Studies & Research in Economics, Pt. Jawaharlal Nehru P.G. College, Bundelkhand University, Banda (U.P.).

18. **M. Alamgeer,** Head, Department of Political Science, Samastipur College, Samastipur.

19. **Manoj Shankar Gupta,** Department of Commerce, R.K.D. College, Magadh University, Patna.

20. **Md. Imeteyaz Hassan,** Lecturer, Department of Commerce, College of Commerce, Patna.

21. **Md. Reyazuddin,** Reader in Commerce, Vanijya Mahavidyalaya, Patna University, Patna.

22. **Meera Ranjan Lal,** Department of Economics, J.D. Women's College, Patna.

23. **Mridula Kumari,** Lecturer in Economics, College of Commerce, Magadh University, Patna.

24. **Nageshwar Sharma,** Principal, A.S. College, Deogarh, Jharkhand.

25. **Nand Kumar,** Department of Humanities, Delhi College of Engineering, Delhi.

26. **Padmini Prasad,** Department of Commerce, College of Commerce, Patna.

27. **Pashupati Ray,** Department of Political Science, A.S. College, Deoghar.

28. **R.K. Marandi,** Hon. Director, Research Associate, Respectively, Agro-Economic Research Centre for Bihar and Jharkhand, T.M. Bhagalpur University, Bhagalpur.

29. **R.N. Singh,** Lecturer in Economics, Kisan College, Soh Sarai, Nalanda, Bihar.

30. **Rajesh Kumar,** Department of L.S.W., Magadh University, Bodh Gaya.

31. **Ram Kumari Devi,** Lecturer in Economics, G.J. College, Rambagh, Bihta, Patna.

32. **Ram Naresh Thakur,** P.G. Centre of Economic Studies, Samastipur College, Samastipur, Bihar.

33. **Ranju Ranjan Kumari,** Centre for Universal Research Development Studies, Patna.

34. **Rashmi Akhoury,** Lecturer, Department of Economics, College of Commerce (M.U.), Patna.

35. **S.K. Jha,** Department of Economics, T.N.B. College, Bhagalpur.

36. **S.K.L. Das,** Head, Department of Economics, P.K. Roy Memorial College, Dhanbad (Jharkhand).

37. **Sabita Kumari,** Research Officer, Centre for Universal Research and Development Studies, Patna.

38. **Sanjay Kumar,** Secretary, Deshkal Society, New Delhi.

39. **Shambhu Prasad Sah,** Department of L.S.W., A.S. College, Deoghar.

40. **Sheela Sharan Singh,** Department of Economics, S.M.D. College, Punpun, Patna.

41. **Shrawan Kumar Singh,** Formerly Professor of Economics, IGNOU, Jagan Institute of Management Studies, Rohini, New Delhi.

42. **Sukhmani Das,** Department of Economics, I.S.T.G. College, Aungari Dham, Nalanda (Bihar).

43. **Surendra Prasad Saha,** Head, Department of Commerce, J.M.D.P.L. Mahila College, Madhubani.

44. **Suresh Kumar,** Department of Public Administration, Patel Trimurti Evening College, Kumhrar, Patna.

45. **Umesh Prasad,** Department of Economics, J.N.L. College, Khagaul, Patna.

46. **Upendra Sharma,** Reader in Economics, Kisan College, Soh Sarai, Nalanda, Bihar.

1

India's Economic Reform and its Social Dimension

SHRAWAN KUMAR SINGH

This paper is concerned with India's Economic Reforms and its Social Dimension. For the sake of analysis the paper has been split into two broad sections. Section-I is concerned with the concept, the need, and problems faced by the economy during 1990s, objectives of reform, reform package, implications of reforms and the content of the economic reforms. Section-II analyses the various aspects of social dimension relating to economic reforms in India.

In any discussion on economic reforms, there ought to be three strands: (i) why were reforms necessary and what was wrong with the earlier system? (ii) what reforms have been introduced?, and (iii) what remains to be done?

The new policies placed overwhelming reliance on private initiative and enterprise to achieve the objectives. Public investment expenditures would over time, play a secondary role. There are essentially two aspects to economic reform, relating to internal and external economic policies. Each, in turn, has two aspects. In internal policy-making, one aspect is debureaucratisation and easing of controls; the other pertains to privatization of public enterprises, following the neo-liberal philosophy of *laissez-faire* and reliance on the market for all investment decisions, with minimum government intervention in the economy.

The New Economic Policy is a set of policies and administrative procedures introduced in July, 1991 to bring about changes in the economic direction of the country. Though these policies and procedures have a macro-economic thrust, their impact on micro-level economic activities cannot be ignored. From this point of view, the New Economic Policy will have its repercussions on the entire gamut of economic development.

There is a feeling that the earlier development model was wrong. Socialism has failed because it could not generate wealth on a sustained basis. Yet, basic socialist concerns about poverty and inequalities have still not disappeared. India's basic objectives have not changed but the need to change the strategy of growth has been increasingly accepted. There is a passive consensus in favour of the strategic shift in the development strategy. So the real question in the process of environment reforms is not the *"sterile debate"* between *"the state and a pure market,"* but the question of "how to manage the transition (i) from excessive to reduced state intervention; (ii) from intervention in the wrong areas to those in previously neglected important ones; and (iii) from one form of reliance on quantity controls to another form of reliance on prices of policy".

The strategy of self-reliance based on import substitution followed so far, has to be combined with the strategy of export promotion. The phase of rapid industrial growth, from the 1950s till about 1965, was characterised by government stimulus in the form of public investment. The boom of the Eighties was supported by public consumption in the form of government expenditure. This was not sustainable and resulted in the government slipping into a fiscal crisis and the economy suffering from balance of payments problems. But the basic point is, that all the expansionary phases have so far been either based on public investment or public expenditure. The economic reforms and policy changes in India have focussed on two methods of increasing the aggregate demand:

(i) private investment-led, and
(ii) private consumption-led expansion, including exports.

There has been a lot of debate on the behaviour of private investment-domestic and foreign—in the context of reforms. Economic reforms reflect a review of the role of government, or more general of the State *vis-a-vis* the market. By early 'nineties' most, if not all, economies launched on a policy of redefining and reducing overall, the role of the State. This phenomenon clearly signifies the new trade-off between *'State failures'* and *'market failures'* or what may be termed as the new realities in the relationship between the State and the market.

Problems Faced by the Economy in 1990

Before considering the various steps for restructuring the economy, it is important to be clear as to what were the most serious problems facing the Indian economy in 1990. The situation that the nation and the economy had to face in mid-1991 was grim. The balance of payments situation had deteriorated so sharply and the foreign exchange reserves had fallen so low, that the possibility of default in payment was imminent. On the domestic side, while the Indian economy had done extremely well in terms of real growth between 1985 and 1990, the fiscal situation had also deteriorated sharply. The budget deficit as well as the overall fiscal deficit had sharply increased contributing on the one hand, to large increase in money supply and on the other, to sharp increase in interest payments. Fiscal deficit of the centre and the states taken together, which was about 7.5 per cent of the GDP in the late Seventies, had increased to about 11 per cent by 1991. The fiscal deficit of the central government alone which was below 6.0 per cent in the late '70s had increased to 8.5 per cent during the same period. Consequently, interest payments in the central government's budget had become the single largest expenditure item rising from 2 percent of GDP in 1980-81 to nearly 4 per cent of GDP in 1990-91. The country thus entered the '90s with a fiscal deficit that was simply unsustainable.

Need for Economic Reforms: The reforms were imperative for the following reasons:

1. The downgrading of India's credit rating made commercial loans difficult.

2. Funds flow from West Asia dried up following the Kuwait crisis. There were large withdrawals of NRI deposits during the early part of 1991, and foreign direct investment was low.
3. Aid for poorer countries was getting scarce because of larger claims by the former Soviet States and increased demands in the United States for domestic spending. Compulsions of efficient use of aid made the case for reforms stronger.
4. Following the collapse of old attitudes worldwide and the emergence of a global market, India had no *other alternative but to initiate economic policy reforms.*

However, reforms cannot be wholly attributed to these economic compulsions. The necessity for macro-economic reforms had been steadily gaining credence in the 1980s. The control system under the *'permit raj'* had become unpopular. The timing was, therefore, ripe for an assault on the system and would be greeted with a sense of relief. It is well known, that structural adjustment involves hard choices. The choices are described as being hard because they often have implications that find disfavour with the populace at large, at least in the short run.

For the Indian economy, 1991 was an *epoch-making year*. Bold measures were taken to resurrect the economy from the brink of a fiscal and balance of payments crisis. Sweeping market-oriented reforms in industry, foreign trade, and investment were introduced to liberalise the economy from the shackles that were binding it for decades. Economic reform has many dimensions. To be worth its name, radical reform programme must cover all the major aspects of the economic regime. Since June, 1991 the Indian economy is going through a stabilisation programme. Being essentially a shock therapy to meet certain contingencies, it is a short term affair, to be completed within a year or two. The crucial test for its success is: *does it create conditions for durable growth*? The crisis underlined the need to set in motion *a series of structural changes in the trade, industry, and finance sectors so* as to provide the necessary springboard for the economy to take-off for self-sustaining growth.

Objectives of Economic Reforms: Reforms intended to achieve the following:

1. stabilisation and macro-economic balance through fiscal, monetary and exchange rate policies;
2. a liberalised trade regime with no import licensing and tariff rates comparable to other industrialising developing countries;
3. an exchange rate system which makes the rupee convertible, at least for current account transactions of the balance of payments;
4. a competitive financial system with sound regulations;
5. an industrial sector free of many controls; and
6. autonomous, competitive, and streamlined public enterprise sectors.

There is a common thread running through all these measures. The objective is simple and that is to improve the efficiency of the system. The regulation mechanism involving multitude of controls has fragmented capacity and reduced competition even in the public sector. The thrust of the economic reforms or *New Economic Policy (NEP)* is towards *creating a more competitive environment in the economy as a* means to improving the productivity and efficiency of the system. This is to be achieved by removing the barriers to entry and the restrictions on the growth of firms.

The Economic Reforms Package: It is important to understand clearly what the economic reforms package is and equally important, what it is not. Economic reforms can be briefly summed up as a package consisting of three separate sets of policies: (*Arun Ghosh*, 1992).

The stabilisation of economy meaning thereby, the bringing into balance the aggregate demand and supply, the imbalance being in the main caused by large and endemic deficits in the central government's budget during the Eighties, which got reflected in the spiral of inflation at home and deficit in external payments abroad. The policies adopted in this context relate to budgetary and credit policies.

(i) A *restructuring* of the Indian economy with a view to making The Indian industry internationally competitive. The policies adopted in this context range from industrial and foreign trade policies to issues like the lending policies of financial institutions (including banks), the pattern of government expenditure and public investment, including the policy relating to the public sector, and the approach on sick units and in regard to *subsidies generally and the subsidisation of small business and farms in particular.*

(ii) *The globalisation of the Indian economy*, throwing open (in stages) the import of all commodities (including consumer goods), reducing the customs tariffs allowing free inflow of foreign capital (including short-term capital), opening up the service sector to foreign capital (especially in the matters of banking, insurance, and shipping) and full convertibility of the rupee.

Implications of Reforms: According to Dr. Arun Ghosh the three-pronged approach has major implications for the functioning of the economy and its future direction. They imply a complete and a sudden break from the past, and several issues arise relating to:

(a) the desirability of the pattern of development sought;
(b) the timing of the various policies and, more importantly, their sequencing (and in fact the wisdom of the frequent changes in policy which has the effect of creating uncertainties, in the Indian economy),
(c) The relative importance attached to the different aspects of policy, in as much as domestic priorities relating to the provision of education, health, and employment globalisation of the economy; and
(d) The likely impact of the package of policies.

It must be noted, that while the stabilisation policies are intended to correct the lapses and put the house in order in the short term, the structural reform was intended to accelerate economic growth over the medium term. Structural reform policies cannot succeed, unless a degree of stabilisation has been brought about. But stabilisation by itself will not be adequate unless structural reforms are undertaken to avoid the recurrence of the problems faced in the recent period. Basic needs approach does not address the broader fundamental issue of why there are poor and how they should utilize whatever little they have. Then there is the question why should the government decide the priorities for the poor. Focusing on what one perceives to be external environmental constraints and ignoring what is feasible or what is not feasible within one's own society is a wrong way of thinking about it. It is more of an excuse for not doing things that one should do. There is no escape from reforms if the country has to attain higher growth rate to eliminate poverty and destitution. Reforms have been top down so far. Public participation is low. It is extremely necessary to educate the people on positive aspects of economic reforms. It is the political economy that frustrates reforms. Economic principles do not work differently in different places. The trouble is that these universal principles are not self-executing: they do not automatically translate into clear-cut institutional arrangements or policy prescriptions. There is a call for a redefinition of the role of the government from being a provider of goods and services to being a regulator and a facilitator ensuring fair play. The government needs to reflect seriously on the disconcerting gap between promise and performance on socio-economic and especially mass livelihood issues—and undertake a first mile course correction.

What has been the content of economic reforms? We present below list of major economic policy decisions announced so far since the programme was initiated.

(a) External Sector—Devaluation of the Rupee: Full convertibility of the rupee on current account since August, 1994. Substantial liberalisation of rules and procedures for foreign private investment. Foreign Exchange Regulations Act (FERA) was liberalised to allow 50 per cent equity participation in most industries; the FERA has now been replaced by Foreign Exchange Management Act (FEMA). Reforms in Gold Policy; and imports of gold are allowed under baggage rules. Substantial de-compression of imports, with only a short negative list to become shorter.

(b) Domestic Sector: Industrial licensing scrapped except for 6 industries primarily those of strategic importance, or producing hazardous goods; The whole chapter in the

Monopolies and Restrictive Trade Practices Act (MRTPA), which was ostensibly meant to curb the concentration of economic power, is scrapped; The convertibility Clause abolished; this clause hitherto enabled the term-lending financial institutions to convert industrial loans into equity at the price and time chosen by the lending institutions, and the exclusive domain of the public sector has been pruned. Only five industries are now reserved (i.e., Defence-related industries, Atomic Energy, Mineral Oils, Mining) for public sector. But the private sector is welcome to apply even in respect of these. Besides, partial privatisation of some of the profit making public enterprises has been initiated, to develop a *safety net* for workers who are likely to be retrenched as a result of measures were to close down sick units or rationalisation of the staffing pattern of PSUs. The problem of *black money* started being attacked at the root; some measures adopted to curb the generation of new black money (the flow), some others to mop up the black money generated (stock), and for productive purposes.

(c) Fiscal Policy Reforms: (a) resolved to cut on government expenditure, (b) reduced rate, and (c) simplification in respect of individual income tax, corporate tax, excise and customs duties.

(d) *Financial Sector Reforms* initiated so far are: (a) Mutual funds allowed in the private sector; (b) foreign institutions permitted in pension funds, portfolio investments in Indian companies; (c) Deposit interest rates liberalized; (d) for the first time ever the SLR (the Statutory Liquidity Ratio) is reduced, and that too drastically; banking sector thrown open to private enterprise; insurance sector also opened to private enterprise; Steel industry deregulated; and Policy announcement made regarding small and tiny sector.

However, it must be noted that the process is by no means complete. The unfinished tasks are numerous, and can be divided into three broad categories. They are: (i) whatever has been done is only the start. The process needs to be carried further and consolidated in each of the above areas; (ii) *there are several areas, which have not been touched as yet*, and (iii) the introduction of reforms has brought to surface some relatively *unanticipated problems* that need to be considered and addressed.

Altogether, the above package constitutes a sharp turn-around in policy thinking, compared to the *license permit raj* built up during the 1960s and 1970s. Some measures were taken to relax controls during the late 1970s and 1980s but these moves were a pale shadow of what is underway now. Observers of the Indian scene were very impressed by the dispatch with which government issued one policy statement after another. This speed of taking decisions was indeed remarkable. If, however, relevant policy moves are assessed against what is required to be achieved under the fundamental aims of the reforms, then the record of policy decisions does not appear to be all that impressive. What has happened so far is surely a good start but it leaves many gaps to be filled up. The agenda of issues, which will have to be tackled, is very long indeed.

II

Social dimension: The important consideration is not whether the economic reforms measures are anti-poor or not, but whether they are in fact *"pro-poor"*. In other words, is there an explicit *"equity"* dimension to the economic reforms or is the "human face" merely an attempt to neutralise the negative impact that the reform measures would have on the extant and structure of income and asset distribution? The very fact that the social sector spending policies, including the creation of the *National Renewal Fund (NRF)* for retrenched workers, is defined as a *"safety net,"* such policies are meant to compensate for equity losses and would not necessarily improve the existing structure of incomes and asset inequality in the country.

There are areas in which government intervention is specifically required to ensure that apart from efficiency gains, the economic reform measures would have a positive impact on equity as well. These areas are: (i) employment, (ii) food security, (iii) health, (iv) education, (v) technology, and (vi) environment. While *"equity"* is not an explicit goal of the economic reforms measures, it is necessary that this is so and a clear definition of what equity should imply in the Indian context should be developed.

Another important consideration relates to the fact, that while we are assessing the social impact of the reforms measures, a distinction be made between the direct *"transitional costs"* of reform measures in terms of equity losses, and the already pre-existing equity loss that occurs due to the inquitious nature of the extant economic regime. One should not confuse between the inegalitarian consequences of the existing social and economic order and what might be the specific product of the economic reform measures.

In measuring government's support for greater equity, it would not be correct to look only at budgetary allocation, but one should also look at the efficiency of resource utilisation. Have the economic reforms helped better utilisation of existing resources, even if fiscal stabilisation required a squeeze on total allocation?

The economic reform measures should not imply a retreat of government from all spheres of the economy and society. While in some areas there would have to be reduced governmental intervention/support, in others like health care, education, and social welfare, they ought to be more purposive and better targeted, in terms of equity, and intervention by the government.

The broad thrust relating to education, health, and the public distribution system is that public provisioning of these services is still important and inadequate attentions being paid to improving the quality of these services in the public sector. On the other hand, the increasing privatisation of these services has created a dualistic structure in which *a high value, high quality private sector is growing while a low value low quality public sector is stagnating*. Unless the government invests more money and improves the quality of the services rendered, the retrogression in these sectors would have adverse social externalities resulting in a national loss.

If financial allocations are no measure of public support, there is no evidence either to suggest that the government is any more committed today than before, to improving the efficiency of resource utilisation. The real challenge before the government today is, therefore, not *so much to reduce the role of the government in the social sectors but in fact to make government more responsive to the needs of the people.*

Indeed, *the popular base for economic reform can only be built when ordinary people perceive an improvement in the quality of their life.* Deregulation, debureaucratisation, decontrol, disinvestment and so on are only ways to wind down the involvement of the government in the economic life of the people. While much of this is popular with the business community, most consumers of public services are desperately seeking a more efficient and humane government, rather than just less government. For less government is no substitute for good government. (*Sanjay Baru, 1993*).

Prof. V.S. Vyas has cautioned the central government against resorting to *"unmindful cut in government expenditures"* on sectors like education and health, besides infrastructure and human resource development to reduce deficit. In our enthusiasm to reduce deficit, we must not curtail the expenditure vital for development. Fiscal adjustment and economic reform is not simply a matter for the drawing room. In the period of transition, it imposes a burden of adjustment that is distributed in an asymmetric manner. Without correctives, the burden of adjustment is inevitably borne by the poor. Whatever we might say about social safety nets, we do not have the resources for this purpose. It cannot and will not suffice to assert, that the burden of such adjustment would have to be borne by the affluent and the middle class, simply because the rich in our society have the incomes to immunise themselves from the burden of structural adjustment.

There can be no adjustment without pain, but we must do everything possible to minimise the social costs of the transition, in particular the burden on the poor. Restructuring on the supply side, which follows structural reform, will inevitably impose a burden on wage-labour. The phrase *'adjustment with a human face'* could then become hollow and deceptive (*Deepak Nayyar, 1992*).

In this context, one is inclined to agree with the view that "the agenda for sound macro-economic policies has to be harmonised with legitimate social objectives and the removal of longer-term constraints on growth. While no simple tune produces this harmony, there is no doubt that we need a radical departure in policies as well as popular attitudes and political behaviour. Indeed, all these are inextricably linked." [*Patel, 1991*].

The policy makers should not ignore the fact, that any

experiment with India, no matter how well-intentioned, has to take into account the well-being of 1000 million people and not just the top 20 per cent, given that the creamy layer is attractive enough for the marketing needs of the Western world. Thus, even if high tech does come to the country, even if industrial systems are upgraded and even if exports pick up; unless reforms seek to wipe the tears off the face of the lowliest in the land, the bottom line will continue to suggest failure. *The concept of globalisation has no provision for the poor except for the safety nets.*

Assessing the human face of structural adjustment and fiscal stabilisation in India, one may ask the question what is the share of food subsidy in our gross domestic product? It would be over one per cent of GDP, then, why bother about it when nearly 40 per cent of our population lives below the poverty line? Don't touch the food subsidy, but target it better. The public distribution system (PDS) should supply food at realistically affordable prices, especially because inflationary expectations seem to be strongly linked to PDS issue prices in India.

Prof. V.S. Vyas has highlighted the inconsistency of the government's approach to the PDS. On the one hand, the government is of the view that it wants to target the PDS to the poor and on the other hand, it increases food prices. Dr. Vyas is concerned about the inflationary impact of the price hike and says, "a more courageous and desirable course would have been to reduce subsidies on inputs. In the quest for reducing fiscal deficits, the government is becoming unmindful of the social consequences". This goes against the government's desire to keep the rate of inflation within limits. The hike in food prices will serve some purpose, if the government is really serious about fiscal discipline and can curb revenue expenditure sharply. If non-productive government spending does not come down, this can only have an inflationary impact. Food prices are very sensitive subjects and history reveals that stabilisation and adjustment programmes have been given a bad name by rising food prices.

By announcing that the grain distributed in tribal and some other backward areas will be sold at a cheaper price, the government has made an attempt to target the PDS at the poor. It might also exclude better-off classes in urban areas, something more often recommended by economists but resisted by politicians of all hues. It remains to be seen whether such targeting succeeds, and does not fall a prey to leakages and corruption. The contents of the PDS basket need to be changed if the aim is to target the poor. There is no reason why superior foods like sugar and edible oil should be subsidised by the PDS. Coarse grains could form a good proportion of grains distributed in backward areas. Since inferior foods are disliked by better off sections; leakages will be fewer. A better way of targeting the poor is to expand rural employment programmes at low wages, which will attract only the needy.

Fiscal adjustment, which sought to reduce the wide gap between the income and expenditure of the government, constituted the core of the macro-economic stabilisation programme.

According to Professor *Deepak Nayyar*, the quality of adjustment leaves much to be desired. There are three reasons underlying this concern: (a) it cannot provide a sustainable solution to the fiscal crisis; (b) it is likely to constrain economic growth; and (c) it is disturbing the burden of adjustment in an unequal manner. In a period when we are imposing a substantial burden on the poor through expenditure adjustment, the equity principle demands, that the rich and the better-off share this burden through their contribution to direct taxes.

Thus, as has been pointed out by Professor *Deepak Nayyar*, it seems that the fiscal adjustment embodied in the budgets has lost sight of why the adjustment was necessary in the first place. The budget-makers have been *concerned with form rather than substance and quantity rather than quality*. What is more, the adjustment has been regressive in its impact. The rich, who derived much of the benefit from the profligacy of the 1980s when the government and the country lived beyond their means, have been spared the burden of adjustment, while the cost is borne by the poor.

Professor A.M. Khusro is of the view, that the new policy has so far impacted only the elite industrial and commercial society—the importers, the exporters, the traders, some manufactures, and the NRIs. The logic of the policy is that once these elements are allowed freedom to perform and begin to produce competitively with improved efficiency, the output in various sectors will expand rapidly. The labour force required for expanded production would increase and improvement in production and supplies will restrain the rate of inflation and benefit the masses at large. In other words, if the policy does get implemented, the production and employment will trickle down of course, with a time lag. *Eventually, the masses will judge the policy through its effects on employment, prices, availability of output and a noticeable decline in the rate of inflation.* But all this will depend upon whether the first stage of implementation does or does not go through. That is why implementation is more important.

Recent Thinking: There is no escape from reforms, if the country has to attain higher growth rate to eliminate poverty and destitution. Reforms have been top down so far. Public participation is low. It is very necessary to educate the people on positive aspects of economic reforms. It is the political economy that frustrates reforms.

India may be among the fastest-growing economies, but the HDR 2005 says, the country's record in human development continues to remain less than impressive. The report notes, that the incidence of poverty in India has fallen from 36 per cent in 1990 to 25-30 per cent and appears to be on track to achieve the Millennium Development Goal (MDG) of reducing by half the proportion of people living on less than a dollar a day by 2015. However, on most other indicators, especially health (reducing child and maternal mortality), achieving universal primary education and gender equality, it may reach the MDG goals only some time between 2015 and 2040. Painting a grim picture, the HDR points out that one in every 11 children dies in the first five years of life and that India alone accounts for 2.5 million child deaths annually, i.e., one-fifth of the world total. Inadequate public health provision exacerbates vulnerability. Not surprisingly, four states—Bihar, Madhya Pradesh, Rajasthan and Uttar Pradesh—account for more than half the child deaths. These States are also marked by some of the deepest gender inequalities. Explaining the conundrum of why accelerated income growth has not propelled India into a faster poverty reduction track, the HDR says, that extreme poverty is concentrated in the rural areas of the northern poverty-belt states including *Bihar, Madhya Pradesh, Uttar Pradesh and West Bengal*, while income growth has been most dynamic in other states, urban areas, and service sectors. At a national level, rural unemployment is rising, agricultural output is increasing at less than two per cent a year, farm incomes are stagnating and growth is virtually *"jobless"*.

Successive governments have stressed reforms with a human face but the country's report card on human development indicates, that the policies have failed to improve the living conditions of the poor. Worse, the growth post-reforms has been characterized by a further widening of inter-state disparities and the growing urban-rural divide in India. The disparities are in respect of both per capita income and social indicators.

The World Development Report 2006, titled *'Equity and Development'*, raises important issues about the nature of inter-linkages between inequality and the effectiveness of any development strategy.

Dealing with inequality with brute force, will simply not work. The main focus of anti-inequality policies must be on creating access to health, education, credit and a host of other productivity enhancing services, and opportunities for employment and commerce and investment, rather than narrowing the income gap between The rich and poor. It argues that, the experience of the developed world suggests that societies can deal with inequality of outcomes as long as there is perceptible equality in access and opportunities. "As sage as this advice is, it is probably cold comfort to ruling political parties facing re-election with a far shorter time horizon than it takes development policies to show results." [*Business Standard*, September 23, 2005]. India might be booming economically, but the WDR slams the country's labour laws, caste system, and gender inequities. Greater equity can underpin even faster growth. It has come out with a three-pronged strategy to combat inequity and promote development:

(i) Investing in people, by expanding access to quality health and education services, and providing safety nets for vulnerable groups;

(ii) Expanding access to justice, land, and economic infrastructure such as roads, power, water, sanitation and telecommunications; and

(iii) Promoting fairness in financial, labour, and product markets, so that poor people have easier access to credit and jobs and are not discriminated against in any market.

The World Bank Report has also praised pro-equity land reforms undertaken by the West Bengal government. It pointed out, that the land tenancy reforms in the West Bengal increased security of tenure for sharecroppers while guaranteeing them at least 75 per cent of output. Land productivity, it added, rose by 62 per cent as a result. Increasing poor people's access to credit and insurance also proved to be an effective way of leveling opportunities to increase prosperity. The Report also calls on nations to promote greater equity in the global arena, notably in the international markets for labour, goods, ideas, and capital. To achieve this, the report urged the rich countries to allow greater liberalisation under the *Doha Round at the WTO*, to allow poor countries to use generic drugs, and to develop financial standards appropriate to developing countries. The report also reiterated the importance of increased and more effective developmental aid. While drawing a fine *distinction between equality and equity*, the report said, "Equity is not the same as equality in incomes or health status or any specific outcome. Rather, it is the quest for a situation in which opportunities are equal, that is, where personal effort, preferences and initiative—and not family background, case, race or gender—account for the differences between people's economic achievements".

Workers in the unorganised sector have low earnings and poor working conditions, and lack social security protection. It is being realised that there is a need for social security programmes, particularly for neutralizing some of the negative consequences of the liberalisation reforms. Besides, the case for any sort of changes to labour laws can be strengthened, if all workers have at least a minimum of social security. The state has a role in helping the poor in times of insecurity and in ensuring minimum security for those unable to gain from the post-liberalisation economic growth process. The term social security in the developing countries is used in a much broader sense than in the developed countries. *Amartya Sen and Jean Dreze* distinguish between two different aspects of social security—*protection and promotion*. The protective-type programmes such as old age pension, widow pension, and survivor benefits provide a certain degree of support to persons facing specified adverse contingencies. India has so far relied on promotional measures such as self-employment and wage employment programmes, general health, and education [*Dev*, 2005].

Any economic reform agenda that neglects, sidelines or rides roughshod over the deprivations and basic livelihood concerns of the vast majority of Indians will fare ill in the mass political arena. There is a very high degree of popular consensus on this matter that cuts across class and party lines. On test will be the new government's ability to bring about a more equitable growth of the economy while persisting with the reform agenda. Since global capital never looks kindly upon efforts to pursue independent economic policies, will this government be able to address the needs of all, not just a few classes, of people? [*The Hindu*, May 21, 2004]

In its critique of the current process of globalisation, the Report of the '*World Commission on Social Dimension of Globalisation*' underlines, the "deep-seated and persistent imbalances in the current workings of the global economy, which are ethically unacceptable and politically unsustainable". The report calls for good national governance built on a strong democratic political system and social equity. It calls for state provisioning of public goods, social protection, and human capabilities. While calling for the support and supervision of markets, it also calls for prudent management of the process of integration into the global economy. Employment creation should be a priority in national policies it emphasises. Empowering local communities and local governments is also seen as strengthening national capacity in a globalizing world [*Kannan*, 2004].

There is a disjunction between the concerns of policy-makers and the concerns of the voters. Such disjunction does not augur well for the future of reforms. Reformers of an academic mould tend to underplay the economic significance of the political fact, that the votes of the poor and the backward regions far outweigh the votes of the rich and the relatively advanced areas. Reforms in agricultural policy must translate into high growth in rural areas. Employment, both rural and urban, must rise exponentially. So must the incomes of the poor. There must be a tangible sense of equity in the receipt of the benefits of reforms. Fifty years of experience have taught us—or ought to have taught us—that the main constraint on development is the delivery mechanism. Development delivered through the bureaucracy has failed. We now have the constitutional means of delivering economic reforms through political reforms. An entire gamut of policies, ranging from agricultural growth and rural diversification to the buckling of urban growth to the immediate rural hinterland, rural industrialization with the focus on food-processing, a massive programme of rural connectivity, the empowerment of women in rural and urban India, guaranteed and affordable food supplies to the poor, village grain banks, employment assurance preferably, employment guarantee schemes, environmental upgradation, particularly through afforestation and watershed development, rural housing, rural education (with quality upgradation through distance education techniques), rural health, massive public investment in agriculture and irrigation, true cooperation based on the sacrosanct principles of voluntary association, autonomy, and democratic functioning, above all, quick affordable justice beginning with *Nyaya Panchayats*—all these are far more pressing priorities for reform than the urban, middle class preoccupations of the present generation of reformers. A democratic polity requires a people responsive economic policy [*Aiyar*, 2003].

Do policies promoting equity lead to faster reduction in poverty or is economic growth the more effective means? The WDR provides empirical evidence to show that equity and growth are complementary to each other. The pursuit of one makes possible a more effective achievement of the other. Public policy must therefore intervene to check inequality both on considerations of equity and for negative impact it has on development. These strong linkages have been recognized for long. No government anywhere in the world professes to shun the equity dimension in public policy. The key question has always been one of priorities. Should equity-oriented policies come first in a scheme of poverty reduction or should economic growth be furthered at all costs?

In the era of coalitions, the parties that actually support the government have the biggest clout. Since it can actually influence the government's policies and programmes. A growth-oriented mindset is not only compatible with, but a necessary pre-requisite for better social justice in the future?

This is precisely where the WDR comes out with a strikingly revolutionary concept—revolutionary from the point of view of orthodox practitioners of development. WDR 2006 emphasises that equity and growth are complementary, not contradictory in nature. Equity increases—in the sense of reduction of inequality—can, in fact, directly contribute to increased economic efficiency and growth. Everyday, the policy-makers in a developing country are faced by the choice of equity vs efficiency. It is to be hoped that the revolution heralded by the WDR will be a more sustainable one, leading to benefits all round.

India is now embarking on a bolder programme of providing 100 days of guaranteed wage employment to an adult member in every rural household, in 200 districts to begin with, and it is intended to cover the entire country within five years. If the lessons of earlier employment schemes have been learnt, and right choices are made on selection of works, and there is adequate social and political mobilization at the levels of implementation, the *National Rural Employment Guarantee Scheme* can bring some tangible benefits. How the picture unfolds remains to be seen.

China has enjoyed eight straight quarters of annual growth of 9 per cent or more, but Beijing has grown increasingly worried about social discontent stemming from rising income inequality and huge gaps in the health care and retirement systems. China's priority will be to deliver better lives to people left out of the country's economic boom and push for a 'harmonious society'. A policy shift could have far-reaching impact since the country has become a major engine of global economic growth.

References

Aiyar, Mani Shankar (2003), "Economic Policy in a Democratic Polity," *Economic and Political Weekly*, November 29.

Baru, Sanjay (1993), "NEP: The Equity Dimension," *The Economic Times*, March 25.

Datta, Bhabatosh (1992), "Alternative Strategy: The Basic Issues," *Business Standard*, August 26.

Dev, S. Mahendra (2005), "Social Security for Unorganised Workers," *The Hindu*, September 26.

Ghosh, Arun (1992), "Self-reliance, Recent Economic Policies and Neo-Colonialism," *Economic and Political Weekly*, April 25.

The Hindu (2004), "Reform with a Human Face", Editorial Comment, *The Hindu*, May 21.

Kannan, K.P. (2004), "For a Fair Globalisation," *Economic and Political Weekly*, September 18.

Khusro, A.M. (1991), Old Order Changeth Yielding Place to New, First VKRV Rao Memorial Lecture delivered at the 74th Annual Conference of the *Indian Economic Association at Anantapur* (AP), December, 15.

Naik, S.D. (2005), "HDI: Conundrum of Rising Income, Growing Poverty," *The Hindu, Business Line,* September 27.

Nayyar, Deepak (1992), "Perceptions (interview column)," *The Economic Times,* February 18 and 25.

—— (1994), "Fiscal Adjustment: Why and For Whom?" *Times of India,* February 27.

Patel, I.G. (1991), "New Economic Policies: A Historical Perspective," *IIMB Foundation Day Lecture 1991,* Bangalore, October 21.

Sen, Chiranjib (1998), "The Budget, Government Style and Sustainability of Economic Reforms in India," *Economic and Political Weekly,* November 7.

Singh, Ajit Kumar (1993), "Social Consequences of New Economic Policies," *Economic and Political Weekly,* February 13.

Vyas, V.S. (1993), "New Economic Policy and Vulnerable Sections—Rationale for Public Intervention," *Economic and Political Weekly,* March 6.

World Bank (2005), *World Development Report, 2006,* New Delhi.

2

Impact of Economic Reforms on Poverty and Workforce Structure Among Social Groups with Reference to Rural India

KUMAR RATNESH AND BINAY KUMAR SINGH

INTRODUCTION

In the early 1990s, the Indian government initiated a series of economic reforms which have now come to be known as the 'New Economic Policy' (NEP). These measures are new in so far as they reverse the main, if not all, policy instruments used by the government since the beginning of the planning in the early 1950s. The NEP comprising 'stabilisation'[1] and 'structural adjustment programmes'[2] were introduced in tune with the theoretical framework of IMF and World Bank, at least initially as response to overcome the crisis due to a steep fall in the foreign exchange reserve, galloping inflation, large public and current account deficit and mounting of domestic and foreign debt. Indian reforms, thus, were essentially of a 'crisis driven' variety. They did not represent strategic choice with a vision of long-term development of Indian people. A number of scholars have, therefore, expressed their concern about the possible adverse impact of these measures on the poor and some have provided empirical evidence in support of this argument. There is, however, much less realization about the adverse impact of new measures on the main rule set of the general poor, i.e. scheduled castes, scheduled tribes, and other backward classes (called Social Groups). Some of the changes in economic policy of the government are going to affect this section (i.e. social groups) more significantly than the other groups in the society. This paper intends to highlight the impact of these far reaching economic reforms on economic conditions of social groups in India. This is done by looking at the changes in two important aspects namely (a) poverty, and (b) workforce structure.

SOCIAL GROUPS

The Scheduled Castes and the Scheduled Tribes are the socially and economically most disadvantaged sections of the Indian society and various forms of affirmative actions have been provided for in the Constitution as well as by the Legislature.

Scheduled Castes are at the bottom of the Hindu Caste hierarchy. Also known as 'untouchables' they were treated as outcasts. It is still difficult for persons belonging to Scheduled Castes, living in rural areas, to access employment opportunities other than the one in which they are born, which is most of the time the lowest occupation in social hierarchy and also the least productive. Persons belonging to the Scheduled Castes are also deprived in regard to their access to education and skills. As a result, very few have skills and ability to move to other forms of employment opportunities, even if they can beat the social rigidities. Even though the nature and severity of caste-based occupational rigidities is not the same in different areas within the country, they are still at the bottom of traditional rural society, finding employment in the lowest occupation, and having little access to education. Their share in the country's total population is quite substantial as the SCs account for 179.7 million representing 17.5 per cent in 2001 (projected on the basis of the trend of their decadal growth rates, in absence of the Data of 2001 Census, see Table 1). According to the 1991 census, SCs account for 138.2 million, of whom 81 per cent live in rural areas, but spread all over the country, except in the state of Nagaland and the two UTs of Andaman and Nicobar Islands and Lakshadweep (Planning Commission, 2002, II, p. 405). However, with the urbanisation and the entry of market and forces their age old rigidities are being broken down on moderated to a great extent.

TABLE 1

Population and Decadal Growth Rate of SCs & STs and Total Population (1971, 1981, 1991 & 2001)

(Number in Millions)

Census	*Population*			*Decadal Growth Rate*		
	Total	*SCs*	*STs*	*Total**	*SCs*	*STs*
1971	548.1	80.0 (14.6)	38.0 (6.9)	24.8	24.2	26.
1981	683.4	104.7 (15.3)	51.6 (7.6)	24.7	30.9	35.8
1991	846.3**	138.2 (16.5)	67.8 (8.08)	23.9	32.0	31.4
2001	1027.0	179.7# (17.5)	88.8** (8.6)	21.3	30.0 (estd.)	31.0 (estd.)

Notes: * Includes SCs and STs.

** Includes the projected population of Jammu & Kashmir.

#Estimated Population based on the trend of the decadal growth rate of SCs & STs between 1961 & 1999.

Figures within the brackets indicates percentages of the total.

Source: Planning Commission, Tenth Five Year Plan, 2002-07, Vol. II.

Scheduled Tribes, on the other hand, are mostly traditional societies and tribes that have been left out of the modern growth process because of geographic and cultural isolation. According to the 1991 census, they account for 67.76 million and represent 8.08 per cent of the country's total population. Of these, 1.32 million (1.95 per cent) belong to the Primitive Tribal Groups (PTGs) whose conditions are even worse than those of the rest of the tribals. In the absence of the data of 2001 Census, population of STs is estimated to have reached 88.8 million by 2001, representing 8.6 per cent of the country's total population (projected on the basis of the trend of the decadal growth rate of the STs, refer to Table 1). Lack of access to mainstream development has led to their economic backwardness and exploitation by the other groups.

The third category, which is the rest of the rural population other than Scheduled Castes and the Scheduled Tribes, is not a homogenous entity. In the 55th Round of NSSO, further classification segregated into 'Other Backward Classes' (OBC) and the rest. The share of other groups in rural population constitutes 71 per cent in 1999 (NSSO, 55th Round CD ROM, GOI). Since they form part of the mainstream Hindu society and are distinctly different from the Scheduled Castes and the Scheduled Tribes, they have been clubbed together into one group.

IMPACT OF ECONOMIC REFORMS ON THE POVERTY AMONG SCs AND STs

While the economic scenario of the country has taken striking strides registering change, growth and development, the situation of SCs, STs and other groups continued with not much a change as reflected in their high poverty ratio when compared to the general population, as pointed in the Table 2.

TABLE 2

Population Living Below Poverty Line (1993-94 and 1999-2000)

(In Per cent)

Category	*1993-94*		*1999-2000*		*Percentage Change (1993-94 to 2000)*	
	Rural	*Urban*	*Rural*	*Urban*	*Rural*	*Urban*
Total (1)*	37.27	32.38	27.09	23.62	(-) 10.18	(-) 10.04
SC (2)	48.11	49.48	36.25	38.47	(-) 11.86	(-) 11.01
GAP (2-1) (3)	10.84	15.82	9.16	14.85	(-) 1.68	(-) 0.97
ST (4)	51.94	41.14	45.86	34.75	(-) 6.08	(-) 6.39
GAP (4-1) (5)	14.67	7.48	18.77	11.13	(+) 4.10	(+) 3.65

* Includes SC & ST Population.

Source: Tenth Five Year Plan, Vol. II, Planning Commission (2002), New Delhi.

From Table 2 it can be seen, that poverty ratio is declining over the years (1993 to 2000, i.e. after NEP years) both in rural and urban areas. The rate of decline in respect of the percentage of SCs living below the poverty line was marginally higher than that of the total population between 1993-94 and 1999-2000. The gap between the total population and the SCs also decreased during the same period in both urban and rural areas. However, the incidence of poverty among the SCs still continue to be very high with 36.25 per cent in rural areas and 38.47 per cent in urban areas, when compared to 27.09 and 23.62 per cent respectively, in respect of total population in 1999-2000. This is primarily because of the fact, that a large number of SCs who are being below the poverty line are landless with no productive assets, and with no access to sustainable employment.

Alongwith the general population, the percentage of ST families living below the poverty line has also shown a declining trend between 1993-94 and 1999-2000 (Table 2). However, it is discouraging to notes that the rate of decline in respect of STs is much lower than that of the general population. Also, the gap between the poverty rates of the general population and of the STs has increased to 4.10 per cent and 3.65 per cent rural and urban areas respectively during the period 1993-94 to 1999-2000. Further, the incidence of poverty amongst STs still continues to be very high with 45.86 and 34.75 per cent living below the poverty line in rural and urban areas respectively, when compared to the figures of 27.09 and 23.62 per cent, in respect of general population in 1999-2000. This is, also, primarily because a large number of STs are landless with no productive assets and with no access to sustainable employment.

The characteristics of poverty among these two social groups can also be seen on the basis of some relevant indicators comprising their monthly per capital expenditure and value of land assets owned by them.

MONTHLY PER CAPITA EXPENDITURE OF SCs AND STs

Monthly per capita expenditure (MPCE) is defined by the household consumer expenditure over a period of 30 days divided by the household size. The 55th round survey of NSSO formed 12 MPCE classes for the rural areas, starting from the lowest

Rs. 0-225 to the highest Rs. 950 plus. In Table 3, average MPCE of SCs and STs families alongwith other backward classes, and other than SC/ST families are given. The table is given for getting a comparative view of vulnerability of SC/ST families.

TABLE 3

Average MPCE of SC and ST Families vis-a-vis Other Social Groups

(as in 1999-2000)

State	*Scheduled Tribes*	*Scheduled Castes*	*Other Backward Classes*	*Others*	*Ratio of MPCE of ST/others*	*Ratio of MPCE of SC/others*
Andhra Pradesh	382.96	381.68	438.76	564.35	0.68	0.67
Assam	437.39	414.19	435.57	421.58	1.04	0.98
Bihar	337.16	329.32	384.66	457.59	0.74	0.72
Gujarat	438.21	459.46	530.09	655.44	0.67	0.70
Haryana	–	534.24	641.26	834.48	–	0.65
Karnataka	404.28	419.39	507.45	560.08	0.72	0.75
Kerala	674.11	597.03	724.28	870.77	0.77	0.68
Madhya Pradesh	325.38	374.74	417.54	516.20	0.63	0.72
Maharashtra	384.33	429.45	489.74	569.99	0.67	0.75
Orissa	284.55	351.10	394.96	480.04	0.59	0.73
Punjab	548.08	581.66	652.45	909.19	0.60	0.64
Rajasthan	456.89	501.41	560.04	621.50	0.75	0.80
Tamil Nadu	384.46	427.01	547.56	651.01	0.59	0.65
Uttar Pradesh	425.38	399.13	441.94	562.78	0.75	0.71
West Bengal	375.68	439.38	516.33	463.14	0.81	0.95
All India	387.69	418.51	473.65	577.22	0.67	0.72

Source: NSSO Report No. 472.

Table 3 shows low MPCE for tribal families in most of the states. At the all India level, MPCE of tribal families is 7.95 per cent less from that of SC families, 48.89 per cent less from that of other social groups and 22.17 per cent less from OBC families. From the Table 3, it can be noticed that only in five states e.g., Andhra Pradesh, Assam, Bihar, Punjab, and Uttar Pradesh the average MPCE, tribal families have to spend major portion of their income on food items. For example, at all India level share of food consumption expenditure in total expenditure of tribal families is found to be 62.08 per cent whereas for SC families it is 60.40 per cent, and for others it is only 57.97 per cent (NSSO Report No. 472). In states like Assam (68.87%), Bihar (68.31%), Orissa (68.29%), and West Bengal (68.84%), share of food consumption expenditure is very high in tribal families. In spite of high share of food consumption expenditure in total expenditure, 6.8 per cent of tribal families reported, that they are not getting adequate food (NSSO Report No. 466). The corresponding percentage for SC is 5.5 per cent. This inadequacy of food intake among SC and ST families can corroborated by lack of consumption of nutritions food by women of these families (National Family Health Survey II). The consumption of a wide variety of nutritious food is important for women's health. Adequate amounts of protein, fat, carbohydrates, vitamins, and minerals are essential for a well balanced diet. But due to low income, women from scheduled tribe families have a relatively poor diet that is particularly deficient in fruits and milk or curd (NFHS 2 Report). Thus, poverty has a strong negative effect on the consumption of nutritious food. Consumption of some nutritious food by women of different social groups is given in Table 4.

TABLE 4

Percentage of Ever Married Women Consuming Specific Food at least Once in a Week: All India

Type of food	*ST*	*SC*	*OBC*	*Others*
Milk or curd	34.4	44.9	57.8	62.1
Pulses or beans	80.6	85.6	89.4	89.0
Green leaf vegetables	81.5	84.5	84.7	86.9
Other vegetables	87.6	93.2	93.9	93.6
Fruits	20.9	24.5	33.5	39.7
Eggs	21.9	27.5	29.8	27.8
Chicken, meat, or fish	25.7	32.6	31.8	33.4

Note: All figures are in percentage.
Source: National Family Health Survey-II 1998-88, Survey report.

It can be seen from Table 4, that of the tribal families 52.4 per cent women do not have the opportunity to get eggs, chicken, meat or food while are rich in protein. The corresponding percentage for SC families is 39.9 per cent, for OBC 38.4 per cent, and for others 38.8 per cent. This aspect is sufficient to present the case of deprivation of tribal and scheduled caste families, in particular their women.

HOLDING OF LAND

One of the main factors behind the causes of poverty among the SCs and STs is poor land holdings. According to NSSO definition, household assets are all assets which include all physical assets, financial assets and dues receivable on loans. In definition the assets, NSSO identified land, building, livestock, agricultural implements and machinery, transport, equipments and household durable goods are physical assets. Since land is the significant asset in the rural areas to sustain livelihood, the distribution of households of different social groups according to the size and class of land possessed is shown in Table 5. The data available for the 50th and 55th round of NSSO are presented side by side for getting a comparative view and the changes that occurred during the post-reform period, i.e., from 1993-94 to 1999-2000.

From Table 5, it is evident that though the share of marginal farmers is increasing in all the social groups and the share of small farmers and above size class groups is declining in all the groups, increase in the case of, above 10 acres size class, in respect of other groups can be noticed. In comparison to the land possessed indicator, amount of land actually cultivated by a household is a better indicator of the economic status, than the amount of land possessed. For this reason, NSSO collects information on this item during their quinquennial survey on consumer expenditure, during 50th and 55th round. The results from these two rounds are given in Table 5(a) for having a comparative view.

It can be noticed from the Table 5 and 5(a) that the proportion of households owning and cultivating (operating) larger holding size of land above 5 acres was found to be in social groups other than SC and ST. This testifies that SC and ST groups are comparatively land-poor because they are poor; one factor reinforcing the other and sustaining contributing towards their wretched condition. The NSSO Report No. 432 shows that, at and all India level the average value of assets in a tribal family is

Rs. 52,660 only against Rs. 1,34,500 in case of other social groups. Average value of assets in a SC family is found to be Rs. 49,189.00 only.

TABLE 5

All India Distribution of Households by Size, Class of Land Possessed

Size, Class of land (In acres)	*ST*		*SC*		*Others*	
	50th	*55th*	*50th*	*55th*	*50th*	*55th*
Land less	13.3	7.2	18.1	10.0	11.2	5.8
Up to 2.5	51.3	63.4	68.5	79.7	57.4	65.4
Above 2.5 to 5.00	18.7	16.5	8.0	6.5	15.1	12.8
Above 5.0 to 10.00	11.9	9.9	3.9	2.8	9.9	9.3
Above 10.00	4.8	3.0	1.5	1.1	6.4	6.7

Notes: Figures are in percentage.
Sources: NSSO Report No. 469 for 55th Round.
NSSO Report No. 425 for 50th Round.

TABLE 5 (A)

All India Distribution of Households by Size, Class of Land Cultivated

Size Class of land (In acres)	*ST*		*SC*		*Others*	
	50th	*55th*	*50th*	*55th*	*50th*	*55th*
Less them 0.025	30.1	32.1	52.8	55.5	35.7	35.3
0.025 to 1.00	18.0	20.8	22.5	23.7	17.7	21.3
Above 1.00 to 2.50	20.6	22.4	12.7	12.0	17.9	17.6
Above 2.5 to 5.00	17.8	16.2	7.7	5.8	14.6	12.6
Above 5.00 to 10.00	9.5	6.5	3.2	2.1	8.7	8.1
Above 10.00	4.0	2.0	1.2	0.7	5.4	5.1

Notes: Figures are in percentage.
Source: NSSO Report No. 469 for 55th Rounds NSSO Report No. 425 for 50th Rounds, Size Class of land (In acres) ST, SC, Others.

Having had an overview of the distribution of SC and ST population and impact assessment of reforms on their poverty within relevant indicators (i.e., comprising low monthly per capital expenditure and low land assets) in India, we now turn to the next section, i.e., to the impact of the new economic policies on the work-structure among social groups in rural India.

IMPACT OF ECONOMIC REFORMS ON THE STRUCTURE OF RURAL WORKFORCE AMONG SOCIAL GROUPS IN INDIA

The poor cannot afford the luxury of remaining unemployed for long. Poverty forces men and women to accept any job they come across. Workers belonging to the STs and SCs were economically more active compared to the others in 1990s. The workforce participation rate (WPR) for male in rural India was the highest among STs (55.90%), followed by SCs (53.10%), and then others (52.70%) in 1999-2000. Similarly, the WPR for rural female was most sustained among STs (43.90%) followed by SCs (32.40%), and others (26.60%) in the same year [*Himanshu*, 2003]. One possible reason suggested by some authors for this could be the difference in the proportion of population attending educational institutions (*Sundaram*, 2001). This is the lowest for the 'Scheduled Tribes' group followed by 'Scheduled Castes', and 'Others'. So, though men and women in these groups are economically more active than those in the general population, because of their illiteracy they could not escape from their poverty.

In a country like India, where incidence of poverty and illiteracy among STs and SCs are high, it was feared that NEP would adversely affect workforce structure of the most vulnerable groups, as SCs and STs can neither complete nor sustain in the liberalised market economy, wherein the national/multinational companies with their cost effective products are causing a serious threat to the tradition-based economy of SCs and STs. Workers in the SCs and STs categories were likely to be affected through these policies, as agriculture is not brought within the purview of reforms in the early period. Again since majority of the SCs and STs work in rural India and are predominantly engaged in agricultural works, they are likely to be affected much more. To understand the impact, therefore, we need to know to what extent, the as pattern or structure of employment, occupational distribution, and industrial distribution of work force has changed in the post-reform period.

Occupational Distribution of Workforce

The pattern or structure of employment in terms of occupational distribution of workers as self-employed, regular, or casual labourers is shown in Tables 6, 7, and 8. Although these categories by themselves do not tell us much about the quality of employment without some indicator for earnings, they do provide some idea about the working conditions of the rural population. For example, a shift, towards casual employment may not be bad if it is a part of diversification of the economy, and provides better real wages than self-employed or regular employment. But, in general, regular employees have better working conditions and security of tenure than casual employees.

Among Scheduled Tribes nearly 50 per cent of the workforce are self-employed, around 5-6 per cent are regular employees, and around 44-45 per cent are casual labourers. Over the years, there has been casualisation of the labour force with proportion of workers employed as casual labourers increasing from 34.5 per cent in 1983 to 45 per cent in 1999-2000 for rural males, and 39.8 per cent in 1983 to 45.3 per cent in 1999-2000 for rural females. This increase is seen across all the rounds for both rural males and females. The increase in percentage of casual labourers has been at the cost of a decline in both the self-employed and the regular categories. In the self-employed category the decline is from 56.5 per cent in 1983 to 49.4 per cent in 1999-2000 for rural males, and 58 per cent in 1983 to 52.6 per cent in 1999-2000 for rural females. While the decline in self-employment among males is sharper during the 1980s, among females this decline is much sharper in the 1990s. In the case of regular employment it constitutes only 2 per cent of the total rural female workers and 6 per cent of the rural male workers in the 1990s. The proportion of workers employed in regular employment has declined by around 3 percentage points since 1983 for rural males while for rural females there has not been any significant change.

This trend at the all-India level is, however, not shared by all the states. The increase in casualisation is seen mostly in Madhya Pradesh and Orissa. But, unlike the national trend where self-employment is declining and casual labour is increasing, in

TABLE 6

Self-employed as Percentage of Total Workers for Rural Population by Social Groups

Rural Males	*Scheduled Tribes*				*Scheduled Castes*				*Others*			
	1983	*1987-88*	*1993-94*	*1999-00*	*1983*	*1987-88*	*1993-94*	*1999-00*	*1983*	*1987-88*	*1993-94*	*1999-00*
1	*2*	*3*	*4*	*5*	*6*	*7*	*8*	*9*	*10*	*11*	*12*	*13*
Andhra Pradesh	44.77	57.64	54.94	54.55	23.53	25.55	20.06	22.98	59.43	56.88	55.98	54.49
Assam	76.06	69.35	72.02	75.51	64.31	67.04	58.80	57.79	61.77	60.04	57.88	55.45
Bihar	54.45	52.68	55.98	64.35	20.35	22.59	19.25	23.53	67.14	64.42	66.80	62.61
Gujarat	52.96	36.10	28.18	40.17	29.21	19.29	25.27	24,23	65.49	56.65	56.20	58.08
Haryana					21.18	23.99	28.92	28.02	77.97	81.47	74.52	71.31
Karnataka	47.73	37.79	40.00	50.70	30.47	28.99	35.84	23.12	65.47	60.84	65.47	60.77
Kerala					16.47	20.12	14.23	12.54	48.33	48.51	43. S2	41.58
Madhya Pradesh	64.84	60.74	60.13	48.13	48.61	47.36	42.55	44.44	72.94	72.28	70.16	66.04
Maharashtra	36.53	35.11	39.07	33.97	33.81	33.39	29.50	21.26	60.11	57.43	52.64	51.30
Orissa	50.00	44.53	47.23	38.87	44.90	38.27	44.90	38.56	58.68	61.10	64.23	57.41
Punjab					27.30	23.71	21.50	24.85	81.46	78.60	74.42	75.74
Rajasthan	81.17	52.50	56.01	58.33	59.35	54.37	55.00	60,20	86.48	76.49	80.34	81.06
Tamil Nadu					20.00	20.14	17.81	16.11	52.46	52.71	49.50	43.75
Uttar Pradesh					53.99	50.86	48.89	50.10	82.77	80.85	80.46	77.96
West Bengal	33.97	43.95	30.64	32.37	39.85	47.13	46.36	43.22	55.97	59.08	61.38	54.44
All-India	56.48	52.03	50.59	49.37	37.55	38.10	36.46	35.03	67.84	65.42	64.90	62,05

(Contd.)

TABLE 6 (*Contd.*)

1	2	3	4	5	6	7	8	9	10	11	12	13
Andhra Pradesh	42.28	53.76	56.26	52.81	16.61	21.08	17.74	16.98	53.35	55.14	52.33	49.67
Assam	72.46	92.26	75.82	85.58	61.48	74.85	48.45	48.84	45.16	59.88	45.00	^5.32
Bihar	61.36	62.73	55.03	64.31	24.50	19.66	14,02	20.38	68.78	61.11	55.20	5.96
Gujarat	54.87	42.45	34.67	45.92	30.26	18.27	34.71	32.45	67.93	56.68	67.21	69.25
Haryana	—	—	—	—	33.70	37.22	37.65	59.59	89.91	93.03	90.97	93.53
Karnataka	38.44	34.56	45.73	42.40	25.39	24.44	26.29	19.86	58.09	51.39	61.94	57.38
Kerala	—	—	—	—	32.91	31.22	23.66	18.15	63.70	63.20	60.71	59.56
Madhya Pradesh	66.67	63.86	60.31	48.22	45.82	47.11	41.51	43.16	72.70	71.67	69.28	61.16
Maharashtra	34.69	34.69	34.11	35.92	28.29	32.86	25,51	19.46	61.86	61.64	52.45	53.27
Orissa	47.44	52.99	54.32	46.67	49.25	46.11	40.86	43.65	59.52	64.52	66.50	57.22
Punjab	—	—	—	—	76.10	69.16	68.78	80.95	96.25	94.19	93.81	55.35
Rajasthan	89.36	75.00	84.30	86.42	71.02	68.71	76.42	75.35	94.74	88.81	93.01	93.89
Tamil Nadu	—	—	—	—	21.43	22.54	17.15	16.59	52.07	54.34	52.32	50.00
Uttar Pradesh	—	—	—	—	57.63	59.79	58.61	55.64	91.21	89.23	90.58	87.85
West Bengal	30.49	39.94	37.77	23.23	57.92	55.76	45.85	50.30	71.05	73.33	72	86.92
All-India	58.07	57.71	55.60	52.62	40.68	42.13	38.03	37.04	69.81	68.03	66.67	66.17

TABLE 7

Regular Workers as Percentage of Total Workers for Rural Population by Social Groups

Rural Males	*Scheduled Tribes*				*Scheduled Castes*				*Others*			
	1983	*1987-88*	*1993-94*	*1999-00*	*1983*	*1987-88*	*1993-94*	*1999-00*	*1983*	*1987-88*	*1993-94*	*1999-20*
1	*2*	*3*	*4*	*5*	*6*	*7*	*8*	*9*	*10*	*11*	*12*	*13*
Andhra Pradesh	8.53	6.73	6.10	4.46	14.22	11.75	8.74	7.44	11.11	10.07	7.97	7.97
Assam	10.55	7.66	6.58	6.54	12.64	11.99	8.43	15.58	19.11	16.76	15.19	18.74
Bihar	10.10	13.21	5.07	3.13	5.57	12.57	4.34	2.66	6.53	7.36	4.80	4.83
Gujarat	7.11	14.92	6.87	6.72	9.28	16.85	10.68	11.03	7.79	10.61	10.82	10.82
Haryana	—	—	—	—	25.86	12.74	13.45	13.23	13.56	10.32	13.16	15.85
Karnataka	4.90	9.04	5.53	5.63	4.03	8.33	5.59	6.65	6.50	8.39	6.87	7.68
Kerala	—	—	—	—	11.43	7.37	6.58	12.02	16.04	12.87	12.92	13.37
Madhya Pradesh	6.86	5.46	2.94	3.91	11.83	13.84	8.16	4.98	8.96	11.05	6.87	5.47
Maharashtra	15.32	10.29	7.67	8.21	12.16	13.07	9.46	12.40	13.72	14.31	12.75	12.83
Orissa	8.87	5.47	4.23	2.57	9.35	7.05	4.65	5.86	13.16	11.38	7.66	8.15
Punjab	—	—	—	—	21.10	24.45	13.63	19.61	9.35	14.56	12.79	15.00
Rajasthan	4.17	3.39	3.21	4.92	8.17	8.33	7.04	8.60	6.48	7.77	8.70	8.35
Tamil Nadu	—	—	—	—	10.25	10.86	8.99	11.33	12.39	14.75	13.83	17.60
Uttar Pradesh	—	—	—	—	7.24	5.57	3.52	5.34	6.06	5.80	6.58	7.69
West Bengal	16.90	4.98	15.98	13.49	8.65	7.53	7.99	5.79	12.13	10.64	10.75	7.56
All-India	9.04	8.11	5.92	6.08	10.07	10.22	7.04	7.72	9.85	10.28	9.51	9.68

(*Contd.*)

TABLE 7 (*Contd.*)

1	2	3	4	5	6	7	8	9	10	11	12	13
Andhra Pradesh	0.88	0.73	0.48	1.81	2.21	1.81	1.57	3.58	3.38	1.53	2.23	4.01
Assam	12.32	9.68	1.96	3.72	19.67	7.19	12.42	28.49	29.84	14.81	21.88	25.18
Bihar	1.89	4.99	2.07	1.01	1.42	9.31	0.38	1.13	1.06	3.47	1.60	1.49
Gujarat	1.11	4.53	1.80	1.72	5.20	6.35	0.83	2.18	1.01	2.37	1.63	1.81
Kerala	—	—	—	—	9.11	6.85	7.89	.38	9.90	10.04	9.82	14.67
Madhya Pradesh	1.75	2.05	0.39	2.52	4.60	5.31	1.89	1.84	3.24	5.00	1.45	0.92
Maharashtra	1.66	2.24	1.94	1.02	2.33	2.03	2.04	2.04	1.11	2.44	2.56	1.69
Orissa	1.07	1.03	0.75	0.63	0.90	4.67	1.08	0.62	2.86	3.23	2.43	2.58
Punjab	—	—	—	—	5.35	5.09	5.37	2.38	1.56	2.58	1.77	3.65
Rajasthan	0.33	0.89	0.18	0.62	2.40	3.76	1.53	1.42	0.46	1.40	1.17	0.83
Tamil Nadu	—	—	—	—	2.70	3.62	3.65	6.33	3.92	8.24	5.96	7.18
Uttar Pradesh	—	—	—	—	2.18	3.44	0.6	1.17	0.42	1.54	1.05	1.66
West Bengal	12.14	5.03	7.86	11.33	3.33	7.83	7.32	4.19	4.61	4.85	5.71	4.62
All-India	2.10	2.64	1.45	2.05	3.15	4.49	2.25	3.09	2.60	3.74	3.03	3.38

Note: Figures for Haryana, Kerala, Punjab, Tamil Nadu, and Uttar Pradesh have been excluded for the Scheduled Tribe Category because of the negligible proportion of Scheduled Tribes in these states.

Source: All the figures have been extracted using unit record data supplied on CD-ROM by NSSO, GOI.

TABLE 8

Casual Labourers as Percentage of Total Workers for Rural Population by Social Groups

Rural Males	*Scheduled Tribes*				*Scheduled Castes*				*Others*			
	1983	*1987-88*	*1993-94*	*1999-00*	*1983*	*1987-88*	*1993-94*	*1999-00*	*1983*	*1987-88*	*1993-94*	*1999-00*
1	*2*	*3*	*4*	*5*	*6*	*7*	*8*	*9*	*10*	*11*	*12*	*13*
Andhra Pradesh	46.7	35.63	38.95	40.99	62.25	62.25	71.2	69.59	29.46	33.03	36.04	37.54
Assam	13.39	22.99	21.4	17.94	23.05	20.97	32.77	26.63	19.11	23.2	26.92	25.81
Bihar	35.45	34.11	38.95	32.52	74.09	64.83	76.42	73.81	26.33	28.22	28.40	32.56
Gujarat	39.93	48.98	64.95	53.11	61.51	63.86	64.06	64.74	26.72	32.73	32.98	31.10
Haryana	—	—	—	—	52.96	63.27	57.62	58.75	8.47	8.21	12.31	12.85
Karnataka	47.38	53.16	54.47	43.66	65.50	62.68	58.57	70.23	28.03	30.77	27.66	31.55
Kerala	—	—	—	—	72.90	72.51	79.18	75.44	35.63	38.61	43.26	45.05
Madhya Pradesh	28.30	33.80	36.93	47.96	39.56	38.80	49.29	50.57	18.10	16.67	22.97	28.49
Maharashtra	48.15	54.60	53.31	57.82	54.03	53.54	61.04	66.34	26.17	28.26	34.61	35.87
Orissa	41.13	50.00	48.53	58.56	45.75	54.67	50.45	55.58	28.15	27.52	28.10	34.44
Punjab	—	—	—	—	51.60	51.84	64.88	55.53	9.18	6.84	12.79	9.26
Rajasthan	14.67	44.11	40.78	36.74	32.49	37.30	37.96	31.20	7.04	15.74	10.96	10.59
Tamil Nadu	—	—	—	—	69.75	69.00	73.20	72.57	35.14	32.54	36.67	38.65
Uttar Pradesh	—	—	—	—	38.78	43.57	47.59	44.56	11.17	13.35	12.96	14.35
West Bengal	49.14	51.07	53.38	54.14	51.50	45.34	45.65	50.99	31.90	30.28	27.87	38.00
All-India	34.47	39.86	43.49	44.54	52.38	51.67	56.50	57.25	22.30	24.30	25.59	28.27

(Contd.)

TABLE 8 (*Contd.*)

1	2	3	4	5	6	7	8	9	10	11	12	13
Andhra Pradesh	56.84	45.50	43.26	45.37	81.18	77.11	80.70	79.43	43.24	43.33	45.44	46.33
Assam	15.22		22.22	10.70	18.85	17.96	39.13	22.67	25.00	25.31	33.13	29.50
Bihar	36.74	32.28	42.90	34.68	74.07	71.03	85.61	78.49	30.16	35.42	43.20	39.55
Gujarat	44.03	53.02	63.53	52.36	64.54	75.38	64.46	65.38	31.06	40.95	31.17	28.94
Haryana	—	—	—	—	52.75	59.31	60	38.34	8.26	5.23	8.3	4.98
Karnataka	59.41	61.27	53.08	56.91	72.36	72.42	70.91	78.96	38.99	46.39	35.7	40.11
Kerala	—	—	—	—	57.97	61.93	68.45	66.46	26.4	26.77	29.46	25.78
Madhya Pradesh	31.58	34.09	39.31	49.27	49.58	47.58	56.6	55.00	24.05	23.33	29.28	37.92
Maharashtra	63.65	63.06	63.95	63.06	69.38	65.11	72.45	78.51	37.03	35.92	44.99	45.04
Orissa	51.50	45.98	44.92	52.71	49.85	49.22	58.06	55.73	37.62	32.26	31.07	40.21
Punjab	—	—	—	—	18.55	25.75	25.85	16.67	2.19	3.23	4.42	1
Rajasthan	10.31	24.11	15.52	12.96	26.58	27.53	22.05	23.23	4.81	9.79	5.83	5.28
Tamil Nadu	—	—	—	—	75.87	73.84	79.20	77.07	44.01	37.42	41.72	42.82
Uttar Pradesh	—	—	—	—	40.19	36.77	40.73	43.19	8.37	9.23	8.38	10.50
West Bengal	57.36	55.03	54.37	65.44	38.75	36.41	46.83	45.51	24.34	21.82	21.43	18.46
All-India	39.83	39.65	42.95	45.33	56.17	53.37	59.72	59.88	27.60	28.23	30.30	30.45

Note: Figures for Haryana, Kerala, Punjab, Tamil Nadu and Uttar Pradesh have been excluded for the Scheduled Tribe Category because of the negligible proportion of Scheduled Tribes in these states.

Source: All the figures have been extracted using unit record data supplied on CD-ROM by NSSO, GOI.

Andhra Pradesh. Bihar and Karnataka, self-employment has increased and casual labour has declined, especially in the 1990s. The extent of casualisation also varies among different states. While in Bihar, only 32.5 per cent of all rural male ST workers are casual labourers, this proportion is as high as 58 per cent for Maharashtra and Orissa. Similarly among rural females the proportion of casual labourers in total workers is more than 60 per cent in West Bengal and Maharashtra, while only 13 per cent of rural female workers in Rajasthan are casual labourers.

The largest proportion of Scheduled Caste rural workers are casual labourers, followed by those who are self-employed and regular employees. Unlike the Scheduled Tribe category in which more than 50 per cent were self-employed, among the Scheduled Castes, the self-employed constitute only 35 per cent. Across states, there is wide variation in the proportion of casual labourers. This proportion is highest in Kerala, Bihar, Tamil Nadu, and Andhra Pradesh where the share of casual labourers among the rural male SCs is more than 70 per cent and is close to 80 per cent for rural females. The share of casual labourers is low in Assam (27% for males and 23% for females), Rajasthan (31 and 23%) and Uttar Pradesh (45 and 43%). Further, casualisation among Scheduled Castes has increased for both rural males and rural females and this increase was from 52 per cent in 1983 to 57 per cent in 1999-2000 for males, and from 56 to 60 per cent for females, and the cost of decline in both self- and regular employment, was sharper during the 1990s. Among females, this was mainly a result of decline in self-employment, but among males the decline was more in regular employment.

More than 60 per cent of rural workers belonging to the 'Others' category are employed as self-employed. And like other social groups, this group has experienced increased casualisation. Among rural males in this category, the percentage of casual labourers has increased from 22.3 per cent in 1983 to 28.3 per cent in 1999-2000, and among rural females, there has been an increase from 27.6 per cent in 1983 to 30.5 per cent in 1999-2000. However, in spite of this increase, the proportion of casual labourers is significantly lower in this category when compared to the Scheduled Tribe, and Scheduled Caste categories, where it is close to 50 per cent for STs and close to 60 per cent for the SCs. Further, the increase in casualisation is mainly at the cost of self-employed workers, with the regular employees maintaining their share at around 10 per cent for rural males and around 2-3 per cent for rural females during all the rounds. The share of regular employees has declined in Andhra Pradesh, Bihar, Kerala, Madhya Pradesh, Orissa, and West Bengal, while it has increased in Gujarat, Haryana, Karnataka, Punjab, Rajasthan, Tamil Nadu, and Uttar Pradesh. The proportion of self-employed workers, on the other hand, is declining in all the states for rural males and in all states except Gujarat and Haryana for females.

Unlike the other two categories, where not much variation was seen in terms of level of casualisation of the workforce across states, in the case of the 'Others' category, a large variation among states is seen for both rural males and females. Also, though the share of casual labourers has increased, the increase is not shared to the same extent by all the states. The share of casual labourers in this category is as low as 10 per cent in Punjab and Rajasthan, and as high as 45 per cent in Kerala. In fact, the north-western states show the least level of casualisation. The states with high casualisation in this category are Kerala (45%), Tamil Nadu (38.7%), West Bengal (38%), Andhra Pradesh (37.5%), and Maharashtra (35.8%). In terms of increase in casualisation, the top five states are Madhya Pradesh (10.4%), Maharashtra (9.7%), Kerala (9.4%), Andhra Pradesh (8.1%), and Assam (6.7%). The trend is similar for females.

As seen above, the decline in self-employment as a proportion of total employment among all the three categories indicates a drop in the various opportunities available for self-employment. This fall in the proportion of the "Self-employed" category over the last two decades is most probably due to the decline in the size of landholdings. Among rural males in the 'Others' group, a majority are working as self-employed in the northern and western states where agriculture is still the major occupation. These states are also the states with the least casualisation for this group, suggesting that the upper castes still prefer to remain in agriculture as self-employed. It is quite possible that many of these are under-employed but staying in agriculture for want of better employment opportunities outside the agriculture field. Since the Scheduled Castes belong to the lowest section of the rural society with very little assets in their hand, casual employment seems to be the refuge of first and last option. For the Scheduled Tribes, their lack of access to mainstream development also means, that they still find employment primarily in agriculture. Lack of employment opportunities in the non-farm sector and primitive nature of agriculture also translate into the pattern of employment. A majority of them continue to stay in self-employment and casual employment. However, in the last two decades, there is a definite shift towards casualisation of labour. Casualisation is a good index of the distressingly poor conditions pertaining to the availability of employment opportunities as well as the phenomenon of under-employment. For a well-off farmer, the availability of cheap casual labour not only reduces his wage cost but also makes him free from any labour laws. For some, the increase in casualisation may not be as bad, as it may prove to be a sign of free mobility of labour in a developed labour market (*Bhalla*, 1997a; 1997b). But such an assumption in the Indian case, will be too premature. In fact, this category is found to have the highest poverty headcount ratio among all household types (*Sundaram and Tendulkar*, 2003).

INDUSTRIAL DISTRIBUTION OF WORKFORCE

A look at the industrial distribution of workers suggests, that a majority of the rural male and female workers are still employed in agriculture and though over the years, the proportion engaged in agriculture is declining. It is still more than 70 per cent for the 'Others' group and more than 80 per cent for the STs, with the SC category, falling in between as evident from Table 9.

Even though the share of non-agricultural employment has increased during the six-year period between 1993-94 and 1999-2000, this shift is nowhere close to what was achieved during the four and half year period between 1983 and 1987-88. This is true for all the categories and for both rural males and females. In fact the comparative figures for the three groups for the 1980s (1983 to 1987-88) and 1990s (1993-94 to 1999-2000) is 6.2 per cent for the 1980s, and 1.3 per cent for the 1990s for ST males, 4.1 per cent for the 1980s, and 3.4 per cent for the 1990s for SC males, 4 per cent for the 1980s, and 2.3 per cent for the 1990s for 'Other' males. The corresponding figures for females are 6.5 per cent for 1980s, and –0.2 per cent for the 1990s for STs, 5.4 per cent for the 1980s, and

TABLE 9

Percentage of Total Workers Employed in Agriculture and Non-Agriculture for Rural Population by Social Groups

Category	*Scheduled Tribes*				*Scheduled Castes*				*Others*			
	1983	*1987-88*	*1993-94*	*1999-00*	*1983*	*1987-88*	*1993-94*	*1999-00*	*1983*	*1987-88*	*1993-94*	*1999-00*
Agricultural Rural males	87.7	81.5	83.3	82.0	78.8	74.7	75.5	72.1	75.6	71.6	71.6	69.3
Non-Agricultural Rural males	12.3	18.5	16.7	18.0	21.2	25.3	24.5	27.9	24.4	28.4	28.4	30.7
Agricultural Rural males	92.7	86.2	90.6	90.8	86.9	81.5	87.0	86.4	86.5	80.7	84.3	84.3
Non-Agricultural Rural females	7.3	13.8	9.4	9.2	13.1	18.5	13.0	13.6	13.5	19.3	15.7	15.7

Source : CD ROM by NSSO, GOI.

0.6 per cent for 1990s for SCs, 5.8 per cent for the 1980s, and 0 per cent for the 1990s for 'Others'.

The need for a structural shift of the workforce towards the non-farm sector has been emphasised by both academics and policy makers (*Chadha*, 2002; *Chadha* and *Sahu*, 2002). But what seems to emerge from the data on industrial distribution of employment among different social groups is that, though the process of shift towards non-agricultural employment has continued in the 1990s, and even recovered the losses suffered during the early years of reforms, the pace of growth has actually slowed down as compared to the 1980s.

SUMMING UP

A few points emerge from the above exercise of looking at the impact of economic reforms on the incidence of poverty and workforce structure among social groups. The incidence of poverty among the SCs and STs still continues to be high during 1990s, in comparison to total population mainly due to the fact that a large number of SCs and STs who are living below the poverty line are landless with no production assets and lack have a access to sustainable employment. Poverty has also found to be negative impact on the consumption of adequate food intake among SCs and STs families corroborated by lack of nutritious food for women of these families.

The employment characteristics as well as the structural changes in them are distinctly different for the socially backward household groups such as, the SCs and the STs. The STs' employment pattern is characterised by high workforce participation rate mainly as self-employed and casual and predominantly in the agrarian sector. On the other hand, the SCs' employment pattern is characterised by a very high proportion in casual labour. The 'Others' group finds employment mainly as self-employed in agriculture. Although there is evidence of diversification towards non-farm sector in the 1980s as well as the 1990s, the process seems to have slowed down during the post-reform period. However, the worrying trend is the increasing casualisation of labour for all the household groups and more so for the Scheduled Castes. Being the lowest group in traditional rural society, it adds to their vulnerability in the employment market also. The post-reform period was expected to provide greater flexibility in employment opportunities for all the social groups. A look at the trends reported above, does not suggest any significant improvement over the pre-reform period and in many cases, the structural retrogression suffered in the early years of reforms is yet to be neutralised.

Notes and References

1. Stabilization programmes has the main objectives of balance of payment at least in short-run by reducing deficit on current account and second to curb inflation. The main instrument for stabilisation programme are fiscal policy and monetary policy, both are applied in a manner so as to reduce the level of aggregate demand.
2. The main objectives of structural adjustment programme was to shift resources (a) from non-traded goods to trade goods sector and within, later from import substituting activities to export activities, (b) from government sector to private sector, (c) from such reallocation of resources the SAP seeks to improve resource utilisation by increasing the degree of openness of economy, and changing the structure of incentives and institutions in favour of private initiative and against states (see Bhadauria & Nayyar, 1996).

References

Bhaduri, A. and Nayyer, D. (1996), *The Intelligent Persons Guide to Liberalisation*, Penguin.

Bhalla, Sheila (1997a), "Trends in Poverty, Wages and Employment in India," *Indian Journal of Labour Economics*, Vol. 40, No. 2.

Bhalla, Sheila (1997b), "The Rise and Fall of Workforce Diversification Process in Rural India," in Chadha, Sharma (eds.).

Chadha, G.K. (2002), "Rural Non-farm Employment in India: What Does Recent Experience Teach Us?," *Indian Journal of Labour Economics*, Vol. 45, No. 4.

Chadha, G.K. and Sahu, P.P. (2002), "Post-reforms Setback in Rural Employment," *Economic and Political Weekly*, May 25.

Chadha, G.K. and Sharma, Alakh N. (eds.) (1997), *Growth Employment and Poverty: Change and Continuity in Rural India*, Vikas Publishing House, New Delhi.

Deshpande, Sudha (2000), 'Structural Adjustment and Its Impact on Poverty and Female Workers Among Scheduled Castes and Scheduled Tribes' in Joganand, P.G. (ed.), Rawat Publications, Jaipur.

Ghosh, D.K. (2003), *"Scheduled Castes and Scheduled Tribes: Some Reflections on Poverty Characteristics & Poverty Alleviation Programmes"*, IEA 86th Conference Volume.

GoI (1997), "Employment and Unemployment Situation among Social Groups in India, 1993-94," NSS Report No. 425, NSSO, New Delhi.

GoI (1999), "Results on Employment and Unemployment Situation among Social Groups in India 1993-94: NSS 50th Round (July 1993-June 1994)," *Sarvekshana*, Vol. 22, No. 4.

Himanshu (2003), "Changes in Workforce Structure Among Social Groups in Rural India", *Indian Journal of Labour Economics*, Vol. 46, No. 4, 2003.

Planning Commission (2002), *Tenth Five Year Plan*, Vol. II, Govt. of India, New Delhi.

Sen, A. (2002), "Agricultural Employment and Poverty: Recent Trends in Rural India," in Ramachandran, V.K. and Swaminathan, Madhura (eds.), *Agrarian Studies*, Tulika Books, New Delhi.

Sen, Abhijit and Himanshu (2003), "Poverty and Inequality in India: Getting Closer to the Truth," Proceedings, Centre for Economic Studies and Planning, Jawarharlal Nehru University, New Delhi.

Sundaram, K. (2001), "Employment and Unemployment in the 1990s," *Econnmic and Political Weekly*, March 17.

Sundaram, K. and Tendulkar, S.D. (2003), "Poverty among Social and Economic Groups in India in the 1990s," Working Paper No. 118, Centre for Development Economics, Delhi School of Economics, New Delhi.

Thorat, S.K. (2000), "New Economic Policy and its Impact on Employment and Poverty of Scheduled Castes", in Jogannad, P.G. (ed.), Rawat Publications, Jaipur.

3

Impact of Economic Reform Policies on the Indian Economy

R.N. SINGH, UPENDRA SHARMA AND CHITRANJAN OJHA

Looking at the scenario of the Indian economy, it seems that the impact of reforms and policies are not encouraging. Even today poverty and unemployment remain great problems of the Indian economy and it is worsening day-by-day. The situation is problematic. The problem of financial crisis has made the procedure of globalisation more serious. Unemployment itself appears as the outcome of this gigantic development and poverty is the progeny of progress. In this context we can say that the country requires the policies with 'human soil' and not only with 'human face'.

India's economic reforms began in 1991 when a newly elected Congress government under the leadership of P.V. Narasimha Rao facing exceptionally severe balance of payments crisis, embarked on short-term stabilization combined with a long-term programme of comprehensive structural reforms. Rethinking on economic policy had begun earlier in the mid-1980s by which time the limitations of a development strategy based, on import substitution, public sector dominance, and pervasive government control over the private sector were clear. But the policy response at the time was limited to liberalizing particular aspects of the control system without changing the system itself in any fundamental way. The reforms initiated in 1991 were different precisely because they recognised the need for a system change, involving liberalisation of government control, a large role for the private sector, and greater integration with the world economy.

The impact of economic reform in India is illustrated by the narrowing of the 'growth gap' *vis-a-vis* East Asian countries during the period 1930 to 1990. Post-1990, Indian Economy has fared very well in terms of economic growth rate. Economic growth in India averaged 6 per cent per annum during the decade of the 1990. In this context, we can see that the Common Minimum Programme (CMP) document of the NDA Government (1996) showed its complete commitment to maintain the tempo of reforms launched in 1991.

India's New Economic Policy is driven by growth-centered development. Its major emphasis is on privatisation, liberalisation, increased competition, and reduction in regulation of foreign trade, increased exports, and enhanced foreign investment. It is argued, that this shall enable free flow of goods, information technology, and capital. Thus globlisation is a motivating force for developing nations to develop at a faster pace. It has opened access to new markets and new technologies. There have been definite deep seated impacts as well increased growth rate, tremendous expansions of information technology sector, foreign direct investment (FDI), and increased exports. India's economic reforms programmes since the 1990s have involved two basic sets of policy measures. The first set aims to achieve macro-economic stabilization by reducing both fiscal/budgetary deficits and the balance of payments deficits. Reducing fiscal deficits involves a cut in public expenditure and also an attempt to raise public revenue to bring about a balanced budget overtime. The medium-term objective was to progressively reduce the public sector deficit from the high of 12.5 per cent of GDP to about 4 per cent of GDP, in the next 10 years. To reduce the BOP deficit, the economic reforms programme in India has heavily relied on currency devaluation to boost exports and reduce imports.

Reforms are means to achieve the ultimate goal of economic development of the country, and the well-being of its people. in the words of the World Bank Report on India as cited in Kumar (2000), "Reform is not needed for its own sake but for the sake of India's poor and in the interest of having them both contribute to the growth process and benefit from it." In this context, the present paper reviews the impact of economic reforms on Indian economy and we shall concentrate on the achievements and failures of these reforms and their implications for Indian economy, and the Indian people. Economists do not have any agreement on the desirability and implications of the reforms. They are divided between pro and anti-reforms. But one thing is very clear, that the Indian economic crisis of the late 1980s was the consequence of partial liberalisation of the early Eighties, and the treatment suggested, adopted, and implemented was complete Liberalisation, Privatisation, and Globalisation (LPG).

Growth, unemployment, poverty, inequality, balance of payments, etc., had been the major problems faced by the Indian economy. Here, we shall evaluate the performance of Indian economy on these fronts.

ECONOMIC REFORMS AND GROWTH RATE

Although economic reforms were introduced under the Rajiv Gandhi regime, it got a logical and consistent shape only from 1991 when the Narasimha Rao government initiated a programme of macro-economic stabilisation and structural adjustment with the support of the IMF and the World Bank. These reforms led the economic growth to rise to over 7 per cent in 1996–97, but it declined subsequently in 1997–98. In Table 1 we see that the growth rate of India's GNP at factor cost at constant prices.

The growth rate of the Indian economy has considerably decelerated in 1997–98 over the previous years. To some extent, this slowdown could be on account of the contagion effect of the East Asian crisis on India indirectly, and economic sanctions imposed on India in May, 1998 following Pokhran II by major industrial countries. The macro-economic impact of reforms can also be judged from the sectoral performance of the economy. The sectoral rates of growth have been summarised in Table 2.

TABLE 1

Annual Growth Rate of GNP at Factor Cost

Year	*Growth Rate (per cent of 1980–81 Prices)*
1981–82	5.8
1985–86	4.1
1990–91	5.2
1993–94	6.2
1994–95	7.8
1995–96	7.4
1996–97	7.7
1997–98	5.1
1998–99	6.0
1999–2000	4.8

Source: *Economic Survey* (various issues) and *Report on Currency and Finance* (various issues).

TABLE 2

Annual Rates of Growth of Real GDP at Factor Cost by Broad Sectors (%)

Year	*Agriculture and Allied*	*Industry*	*Services*
1985-86	0.5	6.6	6.0
1990-91	4.2	7.0	6.4
1992-93	5.8	4.4	4.6
1993-94	3.6	6.9	5.6
1994-95	5.7	9.3	5.6
1995-96	0.8	12.5	8.3
1996-97	8.7	6.5	7.9
1997-98	-0.07	6.2	8.4
1998-99	7.6	4.6	6.2
1999-2000	4.6	3.2	5.7

Source: *Economic Survey* (various issues) and *Report on Currency and Finance* (various issues).

The annual rate of growth of real GDP at factor cost has declined in industry and services sector in the post-reform period as compared to pre-reform period. However, in case of agriculture and allied activities, this rate fluctuates because of the vagaries of the nature. The key reason for a slowdown in industrial growth has been the significant fall in public investment levels that have occurred during the 1990s especially since 1995. Recent trends and surveys do indicate that the industry may finally be coming out of the recession in the second half of 1999-2000. The index number of industrial production showed the growth of industrial production during 1999-2000 as compared to earlier period and is given in Table 3.

Table 3 depicts that, the index numbers of industrial production registered a significant-growth which might be suggestive of the impending recovery of industrial growth. There are many dimensions in which performance has lagged behind expectations. Faster growth has not reduced poverty as much as it should have, nor has it created the number of high quality jobs needed to satisfy the aspirations of the country's increasingly educated youth. Growth has not been as regionally balanced as it should have been. Deficiencies in social development indicators have also continued and became a major constraint for achieving a growth rate of 7 to 8 per cent.

TABLE 3

Index Numbers of Industrial Production

Year	*General Index*	*Manufacturing*
1993-94	1000.0	100.0
1994-95	108.4	108.5
1995-96	122.3	123.5
1996-97	129.1	131.8
1997-98	137.6	140.5
1998-99	143.1	146.7
1999-2000	146.4	150.4

Source: *Report on Currency and Finance* (various issues).

The results of the first-phase of the reforms programmes have, however, been visible only in big cities and towns. Mobile phones, E-commerce, swanky cars, motor bikes, availability of international brands in most of consumer durables, trendy dresses, plastic money, and 24-hours banking through automated teller machines have all become a reality in the country today. But on the other hand, the poor and the middle classes in the lower segment of the salary bracket have been left untouched by the reform process. The plight of the senior citizens can be mentioned in this regard. Retired employees of public and private organisations, who do not have a pension cover, are realising that the returns on their investments are not enough to fetch them a decent lifestyle in the consummerism-driven economy. Though, the inflation rate has dropped dramitically since reform process yet, the effect of consumerism has left more people dissatisfied today than in the past.

Economic Reforms and Employment

The comparison of employment situation between the pre-reform decade and post-reform decade depicts a dismal picture. It is clear from Table 4.

TABLE 4

Pre-reform and Post-reform Employment Position in India (Annual Compound Growth Rate)

Activities	*1980-90*		*1990-98*	
	Urban	*Rural*	*Urban*	*Rural*
Activities allied to agriculture	2.93	5.62	3.15	1.80
Non-agricultural activities	2.88	2.81	-1.08	-2.15
Economy as a whole	2.99	3.13	-1.27	-1.58

Source: Government of India, Economics Census, 1980, 1990 and 1998, C.S.O. as given by G.K. Chadha (2001).

Table 4 depicts that the annual compound growth rate of urban employment in Indian economy dwindled from 2.99 per cent during 1980-90 to –1.27 per cent during 1990-98. The annual compound growth rate of rural employment decreased from 3.13 per cent during 1980-90 to –1.58 per cent during 1990-98. The growth rate of employment in rural allied agricultural activities during corresponding period were 1.80 per cent and 5.62 per cent, whereas in the non-agricultural activities the corresponding growth rates were –2.15 per cent and 2.81 per cent, respectively. The annual compound growth rate of urban employment was 2.88 per cent and –1.08 per cent respectively. The employment growth rates in urban allied agricultural activities during the corresponding period was 2.93 per cent and 3.15 per cent, whereas in the non-agricultural activities, it was 2.88 per cent and –1.08 per cent respectively. The employment in the rural and urban areas grew at 2.03 per cent and 3.99 per cent between 1987-88 and 1993-94, where the corresponding growth rates between 1993-94 and 1999-2000 were 0.67 per cent 3.4 per cent respectively. We can see the scenario of unemployment rates during 1993-94 to 1999-2000 from Table 5.

TABLE 5

Unemployment Rates During 1993-94 to 1999-2000 in india

NSS Round (year)	*Male*			*Female*		
	US	*CWS*	*CDS*	*US*	*CWS*	*CDS*
Rural						
50 (1993-94)	2.0	3.1	5.6	1.3	2.9	5.6
55 (1999-2000)	2.1	3.9	7.2	1.5	3.7	7.0
Urban						
50 (1993-94)	5.4	5.2	6.7	8.3	7.9	10.4
55 (1999-2000)	4.8	5.6	7.3	7.1	7.3	9.4

Source: NSSO, Key Results of 50th Round and 55th Round (1999-2000).

Table 5 depicts the unemployment rates during 1993-94 and 1999-2000. The rural unemployment rate (Usual Status) did not show any significant change in 1999-2000 compared to 1993-94. The current weekly status (CWS) and current daily status (CDS) unemployment rates in the rural area, however, increased during this period. Almost similar is the position in the urban area, except for female unemployment rate. The usual status urban unemployment rate however decreased from 5.4 per cent in 1993-94 to 4.8 per cent in 1999-2000.

The growth rates of employment in the organised sector both, public and private, witnessed a declining trend from 1.44 per cent in 1991 to 0.04 per cent in 1999. The decline was more sharp in the public sector, from 1.52 per cent in 1991 to –0.19 per cent in 1996, and zero growth in 1999 than the private sector from 2.21

per cent in 1992 to 0.11 per cent in 1999. Evidently, the Indian organised sector is of late, experiencing a jobless growth. In the liberalised regime the takeovers of Indian firms by the MNCs, merger of Indian firms with foreign companies, the substitution of foreign capital for Indian capital, sharing of Indian markets by foreign companies and flux of imports in Indian market, etc. is likely to result in more and more shrinkage of employment opportunities. Compared to the organised sector, the share of unorganised sector in employment under total employment category increased to 92.46 per cent in 1997 from 91.88 per cent in 1990. The share of informal/unorganised sector (non-agricultural activities) employment increased from 64.5 per cent in 1992 to 68.1 per cent in 1997. Clearly, there has been a shift towards informal production and employment in Indian economy. Such a shift has caused increase in income inequality with higher wages paid in the tradeable skill-intensive sector and lower wages in the informal low-skill sector. The gap between skilled and unskilled wages widened in a India during the reforms period. India, being inhabitant of large population of unskilled and illiterate workers, would suffer rather more from such inequalities. Moreover, the quality and nature of informal sector employment is far more inferior and insecure than that in the organised sector.

ECONOMIC REFORMS AND POVERTY

Conceptually, the notion of poverty is a complex phenomenon in content and scope. It is both widespread and intensive, and intrinsically related to socio-cultural, socio-political, and socio-economic factors which indicate the contemporary ideologies and policies followed by society. In this context the Planning Commission data indicates that the incidence of poverty climbed down from 30.57 per cent in 1993-94 to 26.10 per cent in 1999-2000, a fall of 4.41 per cent point in six years period. It cannot be boasted upon as a great success of reforms because the percentage point declined in poverty incidence from 36.20 per cent in 1987-88 to 30.51 per cent in 1993-94. The total number of peoples below the poverty line remained almost the same in 1999-2000 as it was in 1993-94. Contrary to the statistical jugglery by the Planning Commission, the estimates of NSSO show that the incidence of rural poverty increased from 37.27 per cent in 1993-94 to 42.25 per cent in 1998 and that of urban poverty increased from 32.36 per cent to 34.58 per cent in the same period. Keeping in view the decline in employment, growth rate of the economy in general, and that the agriculture and allied activities and rural employment in particular, the NSSO estimates seem more near reality. But the inequality has also increased during the reform period.

ECONOMIC REFORMS AND EXTERNAL SECTOR

Balance of trade, foreign exchange reserves, exchange rate, external debt, and FDI are the main indicators of the external health of any economy. The deficit balance of trade increased from $3345 millions in 1992-93 to $9613 millions in 1999-2000. The share of Indian exports in the world exports was 0.6 per cent in 1990 and remained exactly 0.6 per cent in 1998 also. The average annual rate of growth of exports was 9.8 per cent. However, it was higher during 1991-2000 than that of 8.3 per cent during 1981-90. Nevertheless, it was much lower than that of 15.6 per cent during 1971-80.

The burgeoning foreign exchange reserves of nearly $38 billion in March 2000, compared to $19 billion in 1993-94, is termed as a great success of reforms. The net private remittances played a much more significant role in it. The short-term capital flows, a fair weather friend, accounted for 62.7 per cent of the foreign exchange reserves on an average during 1991-92 to 1999-2000.

The extent of India's debt burden rose from Rs. 1630 billion (US $83.8) in 1991 to Rs. 4293 billion (US $ 98.4 billion) in 2000. The per capita debt-burden on India rose from Rs. 1926 in 1991 to Rs. 4208 in 2000. The World Bank has put India among the top 15 indebted countries and is classified as moderately indebted. The exchange rate of Indian rupee depreciated from Rs. 17.94 in 1990-91 to Rs. 46.75 per dollar in December, 2000. Clearly, the reforms have exposed Indian economy to greater external vulnerability.

CONCLUSION

The present decade is the decade of economic reforms. The policies of Liberalisation, Privatisation, and Globalisation (LPG) were given top priority and were made basic factors for the development of the economy. Under this policy the basic infrastructure sector was opened for private sector. Except 15 industries, the private sector was allowed enterance in all industries.

As the economic reforms were in progress, the number of forces causing unemployment increased simultaneously thus, increasing the number of poor. The present and future generations will have to be built on these foundations. Unemployment itself is the out come of this gigantic development and poverty is the progeny of progress. Unless we eliminate the vicious circle of bottlenecks, sustainable development is not possible in future. The fundamental objective of economic reforms is to bring about rapid and sustained improvement in the quality of life of the people of India. The only durable solution to the curse of poverty is sustained growth of income and employment, in agriculture, in industry, and in services. Such growth requires investment in farms, in roads, in irrigation, in industry, in power, and above all in people. In this context, the present government has taken a praiseworthy step by passing the Rural Job Guarantee Bill in which a hundred days assured employment every year for a member of every rural household, and it has been implemented in the beginning in 200 districts of the economy. This programme was aimed at providing jobs during the lean period in rural areas, where agricultural is the main source of livelihood.

Liberalisation, Privatisation, and Globalisation (LPG) in its present form and at its present pace, is not the appropriate choice for Indian economy and its people. In fact, it is not the only alternative. There are many other alternatives. Efforts must be made to mobilise internal resources, not by disinvestment but through vigorous fiscal management and tax collection. Instead of giving fiscal concessions to corporate sectors and the other upper income groups in the name of encouraging, private initiative they should be checked from large amount of tax-evasion, misappropriation and wastage.

The salvation of Indian economy and people, thus does not lie in LPG led growth, as it would not solve the pressing problems of unemployment, poverty, inequality, and deprivation. In fact, LPG is being suggested, implemented and perpetuated by the rich and for the rich. The larger interest of the economy and people demands judicious and rigorous management of the economy and good governance as Bimal Jalan has written in his book "The Future of India." Again he has said in his book, that the corruption is not only a moral issue. It distorts priorities of investment, lowers growth, and thus contributes to the continuation of poverty. In view of this, the people of developing and less developed countries in general and that of India in particular would have to organise themselves and fight out the prevailing partial and unjust globalisation.

The role of faster economic growth in poverty reduction cannot be discounted. But growth needs to be complemented with social development, such as, improvement in literacy, skill, health, status, life expectancy, etc. so that the growth and development process becomes shared one and the benefits percolate down to the poor. Economic reforms without clear rules and policies may not be in the interest of any country. International institutions have to frame such rules and policies and oversee their implementation. There is urgent need for huge investment. The country should immediately start targeted programmes for the bottom 20 per cent and the worst off amongst these. The government should start more and more programmes, which directly benefit the poor. Therefore, the country requires the policies with 'human soul' and not only with 'human face'.

REFERENCES

Arya, P.P. and Tandon, B.B., *Economic Reforms in India; From First to Second Generation and Beyond*, Deep & Deep Publication, New Delhi.

Dutt, Gaurav (1999), "Has Poverty Declined since Economic Reforms? Statistical Data Analysis," *Economic and Political Weekly*, Vol. XXXIV, No. 50.

Jalan, Bimal, *The Future of India: Politics, Economics and Governance*, Penguin Books India Pvt. Ltd., New Delhi.

Kumar, Nagesh (2000), "Economic Reforms and their Macro-Economic Impact," *Economic and Political Weekly*, March 4-10.

Rao, C.H. Hanumanta, *Agriculture, Food Security, Poverty and Environment; Essays on Post-reform in India*, Oxford University Press, New Delhi.

Sachs, D. Jeffery, *The End of Poverty; Economic Possibilities for Our Time*, Penguine Books India Pvt. Ltd., New Delhi.

Srivastava Madhuri (2004), *Economy of Uttar Pradesh—Emerging Challenge*, BHU, Deptt. of Economics, Organising Committee, 87th Annual Conference of the Indian Economic Association, BHU, Varanasi.

4

Prospects of Economic Empowerment of Tribals Through Value Addition of Minor Forest Produce (MFP) in Jharkhand

B.K. Jha and R.K. Marandi

"Yet if he is deprived of security in employment he became the prey of a mental and physical servitude incompatible with the very essence of liberty. Nevertheless economic security is not liberty though is a condition without which the liberty is never effective. . . . Without economic security, liberty is not worth having. Men may be free and will yet remain unable to realize the purpose of freedom."

— Harold J. Laski in *Liberty in Modern State*

BACKGROUND

The socio-economic life of the tribals is intimately interrelated, intermingled and intertwined, with the forests. The tribals have dwelt and are still dwelling mainly within the forests and on the outskirts of the forests. Forests are an important adjunct to tribal culture. The pockets of tribals are mostly located in certain remote interior parts of this country, which are usually hilly and forested. As a matter of fact, the plateau, hilly, and forested topography of these areas with their typical endowments, distinct ethnic composition, and peculiar socio-cultural settings possesses special potentials and places specific problems in the upliftment of these people. These tribals are very poor, backward, and do not have gainful employment. Even farming of agricultural crops has limited scope owing to poor land, and lack of water resources due to plateau topography. But at the same time, they have also been gifted by nature with the abundance of diversified flora, perhaps as a compensation *(Srivastava & Tripathi, 1987).*

With the passage of time, the tribal economy was shattered on account of its limited agricultural potentiality and various types of restrictions from time to time as well as their peculiar way of life being sober and simple. They supplement their economy by making Dona (made of leaves), Patals (made of leaves), collecting datum (small plant twigs needed for cleaning teeth), etc. Some of them are also engaged in making baskets, cloth weaving, carpentry, and pottery, but majority of them work as labourers and are even now sometimes exploited for their simplicity. Their greatest asset is labour *(Sahay and Sahay, 1987).*

So far as the tribal economy of Jharkhand which has a geographical area of 79,714 sq. kms and the population of 2.69 crores in Census 2001 is concerned, it is predominantly agro-based. Out of total population of Jharkhand, tribals constitute about 23 per cent. Tribals living in the forest tracts of Jharkhand earn their precarious livelihood from innumerable fragments of limited cultivable land to feed themselves. More effective ways and means have to be found to generate more income and employment opportunities for them. The ways and means that will economically and socially empower them to fight against their hunger and deprivation must be found.

Economic empowerment is not a business of a day or two. It is a process of enabling an individual to think, behave, take action, and control work in self-sustainable ways. It is the state of feeling of self-employment to take control over one's own destiny. Empowerment is the process by which the powerless gain greater control over the circumstances around their lives. It includes both controls over resources like physical, human, intellectual, and economic *(Batliwala, 1994)*. It is not merely a feeling of greater extrinsic control, but also intrinsic capacity, greater self-confidence, and an inner transformation of one's consciousness that enables one to overcome external barriers to accessing resources or changing traditional vocation *(Pinso, 2001)*. In the light of a brief review on empowerment, one best example can be explored by way of undertaking primary processing and marketing of Minor Forest Produce (MFP) by the tribals for gainful income and employment. This paper confines itself to the analysis of the prospects of economic empowerment of tribals through value addition of minor forest produce available in the forest tracts of Jharkhand state. The analysis is based on secondary data collected from various sources in the area of study.

MINOR FOREST PRODUCE (MFP) AND TRIBALS

Forest produce, as such, not only plays an important role in the tribal economy, but is also important as it generates employment opportunities during the non-agricultural season. It is broadly grouped in two categories:

(i) Wood-Based Forest Produce (WFP), i.e., major forest produce, which comprises timber, small wood, and the firewood, and

(ii) Non-wood Based Forest Produce (NWFP), i.e., minor forest produce, classified by the National Commission on Agriculture (NCA) as: (a) fibres and flosses, (b) grasses, bamboo, seeds, and canes, (c) essential oils (including oil yielding grasses), (d) oil seed, (e) tans and dyes, (f) gum and resins (g) drugs, spices, poisons and insecticides, (h) leaves, (i) edible products, (j) lac, (k) tassar silk, (l) wax, (m) honey, and (n) other products.

Tribals, at large, depend on the collection of Minor Forest Produce (MFP) for their livelihood. They collect various items of MFP from the forest to supplement their income from agriculture. It serves as employment and income cushion for them, usually, as a secondary occupation. Several studies related to MFP have brought out the share of income earned from the collection of MFP to their total income and also the creation of work mandays. A study *(Srivastava & Sharma, 1994)* in Rajasthan has found that Kendu leaves, the highest revenue earning MFP, employ 50,000 tribal people for 40-50 days, generating about 20 lakh mandays of work. A similar study *(Tiwary, 1986)* has also indicated that agricultural production from tribal land is inadequate to maintain a household at subsistence level. Households having less than 5 acres of land mainly depend on MFP collection and the percentage of income to their total income realized through the sale of MFP varies from 10.00 to 53.03 in Andhra Pradesh, 7.00 to 41.07 in Bihar, 34.00 to 35.00 in Madhya Pradesh and 5.04 to 13.04 in Orissa. In the Panchamahal district of Gujarat it has been found that 35 per cent of the total earnings of tribal were from MFP. Yet another study conducted in the Bastar district of Madhya Pradesh indicated that an average household earns about Rs. 500 a year (against a total income of Rs. 1,750) from the sale of MFP without any initial input of risk.

In Jharkhand the Birhors, the Hill-Khariyas, the Pahariyas, the Birjias, and the Korwas are some of the tribal communities who largely eke out their subsistence from the extensive forest surroundings inhabited by them. Their individual as well as community life is organised to procure food by hunting, collecting roots, tubers, fruits, nuts, flowers, leaves, and raw materials such as fibres, tree skins, bamboo, wax, etc. for preparing ropes, and basketry items. From the economic point of view, the Birhors of Bihar state like those are of special significance as they are nomadic and colonized. They exploit the forest for chops and fibres apart from roots, fruits, leaves and hunt animals. They go in groups for collecting fibres and other MFPs which they sell in the weekly local markets. In recent times, the Pahariyas and Karwas, the traditionally forest hunting tribes of Jharkhand are shifting from their forest economic activities to shifting agriculture or settled agriculture. In Singhbhum, the local tribals have a great liking for and dependence on the Sal trees. Its hard, durable timber is used for making village carts, roof beam, the soft kernel of the fruit is eaten by the tribals in lean times and also used in making chocolates. Sal leaves are also used in the form of drinking cups in tribal villages and for making plates *(patta)*. The sal seeds' oil has many industrial uses. The sal tree is also worshipped by the tribals, may be for its traditional importance in the life of the tribals, and their economic life. The forest supplement even the agriculturist tribes with its produce such as fire wood, leaves, fruits, honey, grasses, etc. Forest dwelling tribes like Birhor depend on the forest to the extent of 90 per cent, the hill cultivator Malers get 60 per cent of their livelihood from the forest and the agriculturist tribes like Munda, Oraon, and Ho depend on it to the extent of 45.00 per cent *(Jha, 1998)*. Thus, it can be held that the forests give tribals food and provide material to build homes and in fact, their economy revolves around the forest.

Most of the MFPs occur in widely scattered areas making economic exploitation difficult: With the large scale of deforestation, the search of MFPs is becoming more intense, backbreaking, and unremunerative. These MFPs are usually brought to the haats (local markets) to be sold or bartered for certain the essential consumer goods. Their poverty and unorganized character force them to sell their produce at very low prices to the local traders who are in liaison with the wholesale dealers. The produce changes a number of hands and thereby the intermediate functionary appropriates the most. There has always been a wide gap between the price or wages paid to primary collectors and the final consumers'/user price of the produce. More or less similar is the situation for nationalised MFPs, whose marketing is done by the forest department. It is also evident from the study conducted in Andhra Pradesh, that the price realised by the tribals for their produce ranged between 11.07 per cent to 47.47 per cent of the consumer prices indicating the extent of exploitation of the tribals by the marketing agencies, be it public or private traders.

In terms of value contribution, MFPs account for about 30 per cent of the total value added by the forestry sector in the country but it does not contribute much to the tribal economy. Besides, there is also lack of attitude and awareness of value orientation among tribals, which has been affecting the adoption of the techniques needed for value addition to forest produce, after primary processing at village or local level. Thus, if the tribals are encouraged to undertake some primary processing instead of selling the raw MFP, it will add more value to the produce, which further enables them to get a higher price and gain work mandays too.

MFPs IN FOREST TRACTS OF JHARKHAND

(i) Kendu Leaf

The prospect of value addition to Kendu leaf is to manufacture bidi, gul, and gudaku. It is a major revenue earner and employment provider to the tribals. Its annual collection was estimated at 7,18,000 standard bags, valued at Rs. 1615 lakh in 1997-98.

(ii) Oil Seeds

Prominently found in forest tracts of Jharkhand oils and fats can be easily processed, which are used for making soaps, paints, glycerin, etc.

(a) Mahua Seeds

Mahua trees (Madhuka indica) grow throughout in tribal areas of Jharkhand especially in Santhal Parganas regions of Jharkhand. These seeds have considerable importance in the economic life of the tribals. During 1995-96, 704 MT of Mahua seed was procured by the Bihar State Forest Development Corporation (BSFDC) which has now been replaced by JSFDC.

(b) Sal Seed

Now-a-days by using different and advanced technology of value addition, filtration, and chemical treatments, the oils of sal seed are used for manufacturing lubricants for aeronautics, chocolate making, biscuits of khalli, soap making, greases, etc., and also used as food by tribals after boiling it in salt mixed water mixed with salt. In 1997-98, 4700 MT was procured from Jharkhand region.

(iii) Medicinal Herbs and Plants

Extracts from roots, leaves, flowers, seeds, etc. of different medicinal plants are used in almost all system of treatment. The main MFPs of the forest of Jharkhand region possessing medicinal value are: Karanj, Myrobalans, etc.

(iv) Gum

Gum is one of the most important MFP, constituting 10 per cent of the total value sold by the tribals in Jharkhand region. There are 34 forest tree species in the state, which yield Gum.

(v) Mahua Flower

It is used mainly as a raw material for the preparation of country liquor and its name is almost synonymous with tribals.

(vi) Tamarind

It is one of the edible products which has gained importance in the tribal economy since centuries.

Gum, Lac, Tasar, Honey, Wax, Tamarns, Agava sistane, etc. are the other products, traditionally contribution substantially to the tribals' livelihood in the region.

PROSPECTS OF VALUE ADDITION OF MFPS

The above product profile analysis indicates, that the most marked prospect of value addition in Jharkhand is to kendu leaf at collector's level which is primarily used in bidi rolling, manufacturing of gul, and gudaku. The value addition in kendu leaf can increase the income of tribals many times. The wages for collection of kendu leaf of one standard bag, i.e., one thousand pola (one pola containing 50 leaves) was Rs. 225 in 1997-98 which is almost unchanged now-a-days. The total annual collection of kendu leaf during the year 1997-98 was 7 lakh 18 thousand standard bags. An amount of Rs.16 crores for 15 lakh of wages was disbursed to the collectors. If value addition is made possible at the collectors level by ways of processing, scientific storage, transportation and above all credit provisions, the above amount may increase many times.

The value addition of Sal seed may prove difficult at collector's level due to complicated process, high technology, costly machinery, and quality control. However, if such facilities could be provided to collectors on co-operative or SHG lines, the tribal collectors would then be benefited enormously. The SFDC sells most of the collected oilseeds by auction to the private traders, who in turn sell it to oil and soap making industries. No value addition is done either by the FDC except for drying in the sun. Traders transfer the seed to the expelling unit where value is added by extracting oil and supplying to the manufacturing units. If this value addition is done at the local level, involving the tribals they can earn more money and profit.

Tasar culture, the traditional culture having deep roots and conventional expertise of tribals is extensively practiced in Jharkhand. Though Tasar culture in the area is endowed with rich manpower and natural resources, the challenge is to utilise these factors imaginatively. Even if 35 per cent to 40 per cent of existing food grain wealth is exploited, the tasar industry may generate meaningful and remunerative employment to over a million tribals in Jharkhand.

Amla (Emblica officinalis) trees are very common in the forest of Chotanagpur, but its fruits which are eaten raw or cooked do not seem to have been exploited. Large quantities of fruits fall on the ground and go waste and consumed by the tribal folk at immature stage. Amla is very rich in Vitamin C, the ingredient which helps to resist disease and infection. Fresh juice of Amla is reported to contain 20 times as much Vitamin C as orange juice. Since the diet of tribals is deficient in Vitamin C use of Amla should be popularised among them. Nutrition experts have calculated that the average individual needs 75 mg. of vitamin C per day. Amla contains much tonic acid and dried Amla fruits have good market as products of amla have medicinal use and also used in preparation of ink with the fruit of Terminalia chebula, iron slag, hair dyes, shampoos, hair oils, etc., and fruits along with bark are also employed for tanning.

Tamarind collected by the tribals of the state are mostly sold to the Corporation without any processing. Most of the produce is neither de-fibered nor deseeded before it is offered to sell to the TCDC, therefore, collectors are getting very low prices. If proper awareness is created among the tribals and facilities are provided to them, the may get remunerative prices which would certainly increase the income and employment of the tribal households in the study area. Besides adding value to main produces, by-product is also being put to use in the manufacturing of commercial starch which is used by weavers for sizing the cloth and adding stiffness to the cloth *(Jha, 1998)*.

Therefore, it may be concluded that if proper facilities for value addition of MFPs are provided to collector households in the forest tracts of Jharkhand, the collectors in general and tribals in particular would get longer benefit of value addition, which will ultimately empower them on economic and social fronts. The unemployed labour force would get employment throughout the year, which would check the migration of tribals from forest villages to cities within and outside the state in search of the job during lean season where they are the easy prey to exploitation, economic, social, cultural, sexual and what not?

> *"[Equality in rank and fortune wealth without which equality in rights and authority (legal) could not long subsist" — Rousseau]*

REFERENCES

Batliwala, S. (1994), "The Meaning of Empowerment: New Concepts for Action in Gita Sen *et. al.* (eds)," *Population Policies Reconsidered: Health Empowerment and Right*, Cambridge, Mass: Harvard University Press.

Jha, A.K. (1998), Report on Prospects of Value Addition of Forest Produce in Tribal Areas, A.E.R. Centre, T.M. Bhagalpur University.

Pinto, A. (2003), Referred in an article the Empowerment Benefits of Cooperation, *Kurukshetra*, November Issue.

Sahay, Umapati and S. Sahay (1987), *Forest in Socio-Economic Development of Tribals, Tribals & Forest* (eds.), Bihar Tribal Welfare Research Institute, Ranchi.

Srivastava, D.C and R.L. Tripathi (1987), *Prospects of Agriculture in the Tribal Area of Chhotanagpur, Tribals & Forest* (eds.), Bihar Tribal Welfare Research Institute, Ranchi.

Srivastava, S.K. and V.D. Sharma (1994), Management of Forest Resources for Sustainable Development of Tribes in Rajasthan, Wasteland News, August-October.

Tewari, D.N. (1986); Forestry in National Development.

5

Economic Reforms and Status of Dalits

SURENDRA PRASAD SAHA AND BINOD KUMAR CHAUDHARY

Since the adoption of New Economic Policy (NEP) based on Liberalisation, Privatisation, and Globalisation, several measures have been initiated to reinvigorate the Indian economy. No doubt, it has led to faster economic growth but both poverty and unemployment among Dalits have increased. The nature of jobs created in the present modernised and globalised economy demand relatively more technically skilled professionals which are not available among Dalits due to their poor economic and educational status. Due to the growing importance of MNCs and Contracting Public sectors, Dalits are not getting the benefits of reservation and governments' protectionist policy. Hence, again more government intervention is needed.

INTRODUCTION

When India became an independent nation, it was confronted with the social and economic backwardness of some sections of its people among several other problems. Dalits known, as scheduled castes under Indian constitution are one of the groups, which are most backward. The term 'Dalit' is inclusive of all the oppressed and exploited sections of society. Etymologically the term is inclusive of meanings such as; downtrodden, disadvantaged, underprivileged, dispossessed, deprived, and is subject to untouchability, and of impure occupation. Other determinants are the low economic, political, and educational conditions. It does not, however, confine merely to economic exploitation in terms of appropriation of surplus but also relate to suppression of culture-ways of life and value system and more importantly the denial of dignity.

With the attainment of independence, various government measures such as reservation, anti-untouchability and abolition of caste based discrimination have widened the scope for economic, cultural, and social mobility in such areas as education, employment, industry, accumulation of wealth, acquisition of land, extent of political participation, etc. Economic status is perhaps the most important among them. It is mainly through economic status that there has been dignity of self among others in the society which is manifested as recognized part in any developed society.

Over 58 years, one thus expects a great deal of social, economic, and cultural change to have taken place among Dalits. However, it is a task for national leaders and other economic scientists to examine from time to time the extent and obstacles to such desired economic changes. In this context, a question may be raised: Have various economic policies significantly contributed to real economic and social status among Dalits? If so, what impact do economic policies have on the population of Dalits? To what extent the new economic policy of Government of India has affected the economic and social status of Dalit population or Dalit masses? This article tries to examine these questions.

A PREVIEW

According to the 1991 Census, there were 138 million persons belonging to the Dalit communities, constituting 51.8 per cent of total population of the country. Though Dalits are found in most states, they are largely concentrated in Uttar Pradesh and Bihar in the North, West Bengal in the east, Tamil Nadu and Andhra Pradesh in the South, Rajasthan, Gujarat and Maharashtra in Western India. A vast majority of Dalits, i.e., 84 Per cent live in rural areas and occupationally they are agricultural labourers, share croppers or self-cultivators. Nearly 13 per cent of households, as against 11 of the others are landless. And among those who own land a vast majority nearly 86 per cent, are small and marginal farmers. Thangaraj and S.R. Sankran have argued that participation of Dalits in Indian economy before economic reforms has not been satisfactory and in 1987-88 half of the Dalit's population was living below the poverty line. A section of Dalits, some times along with agriculture pursue traditional caste occupations such as leather, weaving, fishing, scavenging, basket making, etc.

Since July 1991, India has adopted the New Economic Policy, which constitutes a major break with the economic policy pursued since independence. The main thrust of the economic reforms is on liberalisation, privatisation, and globalisation (LPG). Further, the LPG Policy is composed of two parts: (i) short-term 'stabilisation' measures such as devaluation of the Indian rupee by about 20 per cent, and (ii) long-term 'Structural Adjustment Programme' (SAP, so christened by IMF/IBRD) which, as the name suggests is intended to restructure the Indian economy. Obviously, the scope of SAP is so wide and comprehensive, that it seeks to alter, in a major way, policies with respect to monetary and fiscal management, trade and prices, location ownership, structure, management, and control of industrials belts, foreign capital, multinational corporations (MNCs) and technology, agriculture and other activities, investment in social sectors such as health, education and other infrastructure services. Being a member of WTO, the economic reforms of Indian economy was based on the principles of the beginning of the justification of state intervention in natural working of the market. Functioning of a free market was considered as an essential factor for evaluation of efficiency.

The New Economic Policy is based on the following three basic premises:

(i) The process of competition, both internal and external

would help to achieve optimum allocation of resources and secure their efficient utilisation.

(ii) Opening up of the economy would enable the country to have greater access to modern foreign technology, which on the one hand, would strengthen the forces of competition and efficiency; and on the other to help the promotion of import and exports.

(iii) The above together would help the country or a region to achieve a higher rate of economic growth.

As we know that a large number of Dalits are agricultural labourers small, and marginal farmers, entrepreneurs or workers in informal sectors and as far as the impact of economic reforms on these classes are concerned with, two striking arguments have taken place. First through dismantling of the welfare state, the NEP in all probability is set to affect adversely the social and economic interests of all the weaker sections, but most of all of the Dalits. Second, relevant empirical information, wherever available is provided about the Dalits with a view to representing the condition of Dalits as a whole. The Paper is divided into three sections:

In section I, the Issues, Strategies and Tasks Ahead are presented. Among other things, it will discuss the issues on Ambedker's contribution towards the economic policy and Dalits, which proclaims the Ambedkar's economic theory in the context of economic reforms.

Section II will examine the impact of dismantling of the economic welfare state on the advancement of these communities with specific reference to the prospective erosion of reservation policy and process of co-modification of social services.

The last section III will highlight the conclusions of paper.

ISSUES, STRATEGIES AND TASKS AHEAD

Although economic reforms have completed one decade and social and economic equality is still a distant dream. Sincere commitment to equality and the much needed economic status among Dalits is lacking. Moreover, economic reforms have put a lot of status on the state intervention for improving the economic condition of Dalit masses.

A programme of structural adjustment inevitably creates transitional difficulties, and the government is deeply conscious of the need for social safety to the Dalit communities to ensure that the burden of transition does not fall disproportionately on the downtrodden or deprived classes of the society who are struggling against the state and dominant sections of the society; they are still too weak to make a decisive impact on the ruling classes. With this objective under New Economic Policy, Social Safety Net Programme (SSNP) with the support of the World Bank and some bilateral donors is fabricated. The SSNP is focusing on the needs of the most vulnerable sections of our society; particularly the Dalit workers affected by industrial pollution, agricultural labourers and small and marginal farmers. Dr. B.R. Ambedkar was one of the leading proponents of the 'Theory of the Stage of Economic Traditionalism' in his writing. The Problem of the Rupee and Evolution of Provincial Finance in British India, which gave strong anti-imperialist but fairly orthodox liberal economic assessment of British rule. Ambedkar dealt with the devaluation controversy of his day. Strikingly at that time, it was the Indian bourgeoisie, who wanted a low rupee against the pound while British bureaucracy wanted a high rupee first, undoubtedly because they were primarily in an industry which had been a world leader from the very beginning (the textile industry) the second, at least partly because of interests which would have preferred to be able to buy more pounds from their salaries in rupee when they retired.

Ambedkar's own position was to argue for a moderately low rupee, which became the central theme in New Economic Policy in 1991. He gave a class analysis of the effects of devaluation saying that entrepreneurs and self-employed (from businessmen to farmers) would benefit from a low rupee, while wage and salary owners (from bureaucrats to daily labourers) would benefit from high one which would keep consumer goods cheaper. Ambedkar's recommendation was therefore one, which he consciously saw as a compromise between workers and capitalists; a devalued rupee but not quite as much as the Indian bourgeoisie would have liked.

Ambedkar advocated the need for morality in the economic and political order of the society which was one of the crucial points of his criticism on closed economy. Ambedkar's moral economy was the subject for arguing for market economy; he considers them (values of liberty, equality and fraternity) as universal ideals and as necessary for the welfare of the Bahujan Samaj (Dalit community). Ambedkar never accepted the equation of morality with suffering, poverty, asceticism or renunciation of money and consumption. He pointed out three basic elements:

> (i) the role of the state was seen to be in providing protection and removal of poverty in Bahujan Samaj, (ii) the role of the market was to be in the production and accumulation of wealth by individual householders (modified by moral concerns), and (iii) the role of community, which would give equality as seen in the development of voluntaristic equalitarian communism in the Bhikku Sangha.

On the basis of the above discussions, it is clear that a large part of his approach, finally would have been pragmatic looking for the most effective combination of state, market, and community roles; that he would have been clearly for the kind of globalisation that would aid the Dalits and other downtrodden to establish their full place in a world heritage that he would have been concerned both with all-round economic growth and its impact on Dalits. He would clearly have given an overriding power to the state than many of those speaking in his name and referring only to his period of advocacy of state socialism and though he would not deny the occasional need to use state power to override property rights, he would see acquisition not as an evil but as a part of a process of wealth creation and would look to voluntary sharing in a community of concern (Dalits) as primary means of achieving equality.

As far as economic reforms and Dalits are concerned, it would be too simplistic and populist to say that nothing has changed in the last fifty years. However, the fact remains that the economic status has marginally improved since economic reforms commenced. Ambedkar's views on economic reforms are now striking positive changes. Self-assertion by the Dalits, the following factors have contributed in bringing about changes:

First, there is an overall acceptance of equality as desirable norm, thanks to the perception of the liberal and radical philosophical discourse, capitalist development, and technological advancement including communications changes in society. Treating Dalits on an equal footing and enabling them to avail of opportunities in the non-traditional sectors implies sharing the cake (of the country's resources) with them. And that cake is not big enough to meet the needs of everyone. However, there is a microscopic minority among them which adheres to a liberal ideology with decaste mental frame and behaviour and as supportive of the Dalit cause.

Second, Capital development, nonetheless sluggish, has weakened the traditional functioning of the caste system. Though caste remaining in its form and content are different from what prevailed in earlier time, caste is a limiting rather than the determining factor in choice of occupation (*Gough,* 1960). Occupational diversification, albeit to a limited extent has taken place within the Dalit community. Those Dalits who have some assets for investment and for marketable skills have received university education, and has become professionals, entre-preneurs, white-collar employees, professionals, politiciations, etc. The recent agenda of economic reforms comprising economic liberalisation, globalisation and privatisation may to some extent accelerate the process of diversification of occupations in society including among the Dalits. New non-traditional occupations particularly in the informal sectors could increase, which may provide opportunities to Dalits for livelihood. But the present context of second-generation economic reforms with unlimited market and competition, the potential for representation of Dalit, is widely ushered in social and economic equality. The reservation policies for the job have created the new opportunities for Dalits and has non-bloody competition as we witnessed in the period 1995-2003 between Dalits and ruling classes, Dalits and middle class OBCs are now entering into the Government Sectors.

Third, protective discrimination through reservations in government jobs and admission to educational institutions has paved the way for Dalits to enter the middle class. Upward mobility has created hope and given them confidence that there is scope for improving their condition and be at par with others. However, the recent process of retreat of the state has begun to affect them adversely. As such educated unemployment in general and among Dalits in particular is increasing by leaps and bounds. Most of the first generation educated Dalits seeking employment don't have the capital and skills to enter and survive in the market. Such a state of affairs leads to frustration among middle class Dalits. Nonetheless, middle class Dalits occupy an important position in the community by functioning as its vocal section. *Fourth,* various legislations prescribing punitive action against the practice of untouchability sociability, though not implemented very effectively have checked to some extent, blatant discrimination against the Dalits. It is more so in public the than private spheres.

IMPACT OF THE NEP (NEW ECONOMIC POLICY) ON DALITS

As we find that the role of the state in the economic affairs to have adverse consequences for the Dalits. In the Indian context ruling class further implies the so-called upper castes, having greater command over the material and non-material resources. Consequently, the intervention of state in favour of the ruling class which who also happens to belong to upper castes is bound to affect adversely the interests of the poor in general and the Dalits in particular. However, even in an unequal society, the ruling classes cannot remain totally neutral towards the minimal requirement of the vast majority of the poor. Thus, they have to take care of these socio-economically disadvantaged sections of the society through devising some economic and other policies and programmes intended to create some purchasing in their hands. They have to do this for three reasons. *First,* maintenance of social stability requires that all socio-economic groups in the society develop a feeling that they stand to benefit from the overall development process in the state. *Second,* in a competitive democratic system, the ruling class (and castes) is always constrained to obtain as large a support and section as possible with a view to widening their social base. *Third,* in a capitalist economy, creation of additional purchasing power is one of the objective conditions for sustaining, if not enlarging the size of the market; so vital for maintaining the rate of economic growth. The reservation policy meant for the Dalit communities is a case in this direction.

One of the major consequences of the economic reforms is the contraction of the public sector. Whatever rewards such reforms may bring to the economy, it is most likely to have an adverse effect on the fortunes of the Dalit communities. This is because the contraction of the public sector is certainly going to restrict the scope of the reservation policies, which, in turn is going to result in the erosion of job opportunities for the Dalits. In this context, three pertinent questions may be raised. *First,* will the overall process of privatization of the economy and all the attendant policies create enough jobs to compensate for the loss of jobs arising due to the contraction of the public sector? *Second,* assuming for a while that private sector does so, what is likely to be the nature of these prospective jobs? *Third,* and most important, what chance do the Dalit communities stand for getting a fair share of these jobs to compensate for the adverse consequences of the erosion of reservation policies?

The reply to these questions can be given in the present context of job prospects for Dalits as below:

First, it is a matter of grave concern that since economic reforms began, the overall growth of the economy has been raised but the level of employment for Dalits has proportionately not increased. This may mainly be the wrong implementation of the policies of economic reforms (*Mundie,* 1992; *Kundu,* 1993; *Mungekar,* 1994; *Gupta,* 1995; *Sengupta,* 1998 and *Das,* 2001). Earlier agriculture was the last resort of employment; but over the years there is a growing tendency among the better off landowners to substitute labour with machinery and other technological devices. As a consequence, the labour-absorption capacity of our agriculture is declining (*Tyagi,* 1981; *Vaidynathan,* 1992; *Bhalla,* 1997; *Sen,* 2001 and *Singh,* 2003). The organised sector as a whole is a great failure in contributing to employment generation. For instance, the total estimated employment in the organised public and private sectors rose from 2673 million in 1991 to 32.37 million in 2001, i.e., by a mere 5.64 million within a period of one decade. Again, within the organised sectors, the performance of manufacturing sector (both public and private) is just deplorable. The multi-national companies (MNC) that are entering into Indian economy are most likely to adopt capital intensive techniques of production as they are/will be increasingly catering to the conception requirements of the employment prospects of Dalits because of slackness in the strict enforcement of reservation policies. Not only it is the phenomenon in manufacturing sector, but also the banking, insurance, and telecommunication. These three major areas of service sector are being computerised, again leading to a trade off between efficiency and employment. How much the employment prospects for Dalits in the country are becoming gloomier is demonstrated in following table:

Employment Scenario at a Glance (1992-2002)

(Figures in Million)

(I) The backlog of unemployment at the outset of 8th Plan	230
(2) Addition to the labour force during plan period	36.0
(3) Total employment to be provided	59.0
(4) Likely employment generation during the Plan Period	31.5
(5) Backlog of unemployment in the middle of Ninth Plan	27.5

Source: Govt. of India, 2002, Planning Commission, Draft Mid-Term Appraisal of the Ninth Five Year Plan, 2000-01, New Delhi.

The above table makes clear that the economic reforms will not create more opportunities for Dalits. Far from this, what is germane is that the jobs that will be created will not be proportionate either to the prospective post-reforms rate of the the economic growth or to the number of job-seekers among downtrodden classes that will be demanding them. Second, regarding the nature and quality of the jobs, it seems logical to argue that the jobs, which the economy may create, will demand relatively more technically skilled professional competence. But the number of such personnel among Dalit communities is marginal and far behind in possessing these capabilities due to their poor economic status. This answers the third question, viz., how are these jobs going to be shared by the Dalits? The chances of their sharing of these jobs are indeed bleak. This is so when job interests of these depressed and disadvantaged groups are less than adequately protected even in the presence of a constitutionally prescribed (and hence obligatory) reservation policy, how will their interests be protected with the erosion of the very same reservation policy? In other words, prospective erosion of reservation policy on the one hand and the prejudiced caste-ridden social arrangement on the other are more likely to create an unfavourable situation in the labour market even for the meritorious among Dalits.

What then is the prospective scenario with respect to their job opportunities in the era of economic reforms? The answer seems to be inescapable. The Dalits will crowd themselves still more into the unorganised and informal sectors of the economy than are today. This in turn, will result in the economic marginalisation of Dalits.

In The New Economic Policy, the government has taken the responsibility of making available the jobs for relatively poor sections of society by Special Drive Scheme. The rationale for such scheme stems from the future on the part of a large sections of society to enter the job market for the want of alternative jobs. Since the market is guided solely by the consideration of private sector or MNCs, it does not care for those who are unable to get them. Thus, the economic reforms are useless for Dalits and Dalits are not into the consideration of private management. This makes it obligatory for the welfare state to take special care of the relatively vulnerable sections of society through implementing specially designed policies and schemes such as: (i) Reservation of Dalits in private sectors and MNCs as well as (ii) Special drive for Dalits to fill the backlog vacancies. Since the Dalits constitute the bulk of the poor and unemployed, they have to suffer in NEP regime. The number of Dalit employees in government services declined from 6,28,000 in 1991 to 6,04,000 in 1992 but marginally increased to 6,90,250 in 2003, while those in the public sector dropped from 4,32,000 in 1991 to 3,98,000 in 2003 (*S.K. Throat*, 2003:04). Thus, the burden of the NEP has fallen most heavily upon the Dalits.

CONCLUSION

The central argument of this article is that India's Economic Reforms on liberalisation, privatisation and globalisation may enable the country to secure economic growth perhaps at a relatively high rate but the highly iniquitous social system creating and sustaining an unequal opportunities structure will deprive the socio-economically and culturally disadvantaged and dispossessed groups. So, the Dalits will not get any opportunity of sharing meaningfully the benefits of this prospective economic growth. This will be essentially due to erosion of the reservation policy on the one hand and the growing process of realisation of jobs under special drive on the other. It is therefore imperative for the Dalits and along with them all sections of Dalits in the country to wage a united battle to see that welfare state is not dismantled by the ruling classes.

REFERENCES

Ambedkar, B.R., (1979), *Babasaheb Ambedkar: Writings and Speeches*, Vol. II, Bombay, Government of Maharashtra, Education Department.

Bara, J.S., (1983), *The Political Economy of Rural Development: Strategies for Poverty Alleviation*, New Delhi, Allied Publishers.

Galantar, Mare, (1991), *Competing Equalities: Law and the Backward Classes in India*, Delhi, Oxford University Press.

Gupta, S.P., (1994), Recent Economic Reforms and their Impact on Poor and Vulnerable Sections of Society: NCAER, Mimeo, New Delhi.

Omvedt, Gail, (1997), *'Dalits and Economic Policy; Contribution of Dr. B.R. Ambedkar, Fourth World* 4(i)—Education Department, Government of Maharashtra, Mumbai, pp. 22-26.

Thorat, Sukhdeo, (1997), "New Economic Policy and its Impact on Employment and Poverty of Scheduled Castes; Occasional Paper Series 2, Pune, pp. 27-29.

6

Impact of Globalisation on Dalits

RASHMI AKHOURY

INTRODUCTION

The historical experience of the countries which have adopted the package of economic stabilization and structural adjustment programme, indicates a fall, in many cases quite significant, in the standards of living of large sections of the population, mostly the working classes, as a result of slowing down of employment opportunities, increase in open unemployment as well as underemployment, fall in real wages, withdrawal of food subsidies, rise in the prices of public services, contraction of social expenditure by the government, and a decline in capital expenditure. It also reveals that the burden of SAP has fallen more severely on the urban as compared to the rural areas and on the unorganized sectors of the economy as compared to the organized ones.

Globalization is also considered an important element in the new economic policies. The Dalits are being threatened by the process of globalization. With the advent of market economy, where consumerism is flourishing, the Dalits are bound to be affected adversely. Needless to mention, the market economy is geared to meet the consumerist aspirations of the business and other classes and the poor are getting marginalized more and more. "The guarantee of employment in all spheres of life, as was available in pre-globalization period, no longer exists and the threat of starvation among the Dalits is increasing. Unfortunately, the nexus between the fast deteriorating socio-economic conditions of the Dalits—Bahujans and globalization has not been seen by many commentators" (*Kanchallaiah*, 1997). A closer analysis shows that the Dalits may not get any entrepreneurial space in the market structure which survives on social connections in India. Though the experts have been taking pride in the export performance of India. The World Development Report (1996) data provided a very gloomy picture of our exports share in the world during the four years of reform.

P.G. Jogdand, in his article, "Impact of New Economic Reform Policy on Dalits: Some Observations" puts forth his views regarding the negative impact of NEP on Dalits. Within the given socio-economic structure of India, the NEP will definitely aggravate the hardships of the Dalits. It is on the basis of outcome where these reforms were implemented he is trying to show the same results the reforms will produce in our society also.

Anand Teltumbde, in his article on "Impact of New Economic Reforms on Dalits", gives a detailed account of empirical evidence from the international as well as Indian experience in the implementation of these reforms. He has also delineated the areas in which the Dalits are going to be hit by these reforms. He says the economic reforms have a pro-rich bias and wherever they were implemented, they have worsened the situation of the masses of poor people. He points out that Indian reforms were essentially 'crisis driven' and not 'strategy driven' when they were adopted.

DALITS IN AGRICULTURE SECTOR

Dalits are mostly agriculture workers. About 75 per cent of Scheduled Caste workers and about 87 per cent of Scheduled Tribe workers are agricultural workers while about 60 per cent of non-SC/ST categories are agricultural workers. Out of the total

Scheduled Caste agricultural workers, about 50 per cent are agricultural labourers as per 1991 censu . Land concentration continues even today despite land reforms. As per 1985-86 agricultural census, the top 10 per cent of the holdings of more than 10 acres control about 50 per cent of the total land under cultivation while the bottom, (marginal and small holdings) 76 per cent of holdings control only about 28 per cent of total land under cultivation. This unequal distribution of land is also associated with caste as land is mostly in the hands of upper castes, to the exclusion of Dalits, and other backward castes.

The position of Dalits deteriorated in terms of their access to land in 1980s despite significant improvement in economic growth at an all-India level. It can be seen from NSSO data in Table 1 that Scheduled Caste households with absolute landlessness and without homestead increased from 2.48 per cent in 1983-84 to 15.5 per cent in 1987-88, while it increased from 2.5 per cent to 9.8 per cent only in case of other households. Scheduled Caste households possessing 0.01 to 0.40 hectare (near landlessness) declined from 60.98 per cent to 49.7 per cent while it declined from 39.3 per cent to 34.4 per cent in case of others. That is, landlessness increased by 13.02 per cent, near landlessness declined by 11.48 per cent among Scheduled Caste households during 1983-84 to 1987-88, despite significant improvement in per capita net state domestic product from 1,697 to Rs. 1,933 at 1980-81 prices during the same period at an all-India level (Table 2). In case of Scheduled Tribe households absolute landless increased by 6.4 per cent and near landlessness declined by 2.65 per cent during this period. On the other hand, landlessness increased by 7.3 per cent and near landlessness declined only by 4.86 per cent in case of others during the same period.

Food production at an all-India level rose from around 48 metric tonnes for a population of 363 millions in 1951 to 176 metric tonnes for a population of 830 million in 1990. State intervention at various points and heavy public sector investment in agriculture and irrigation, research and development, subsidies for fertilizers, electricity, irrigation, high quality seed, and generous support prices played significant role in increasing food production. But, after dip in foodgrain production in 1991-92, the growth rate picked up, and started decelerating from 1993-94. In 1995-96, there was a negative growth rate of 3.4 per cent. The

TABLE 1

Distribution of Households by Size/Class of Land Possessed by Household Groups in Rural Areas at All India Level

Year	*Scheduled Tribe Households*			*Scheduled Caste Households*			*Other Households*		
	With-out own homestead (0.00 ha)	*With-own home-stead (0.00 ha)*	*0.01 ha to 0.40 ha*	*With-out own homestead (0.00 ha)*	*With-own home-stead (0.00 ha)*	*0.01 ha to 0.40 ha*	*With-out own homestead (0.00 ha)*	*With-own home-stead (0.00 ha)*	*0.01 ha to 0.40 ha*
1983-84	3.90	4.27	29.65	2.48	5.28	60.96	2.50	2.86	39.30
1987-88	10.30	2.30	27.00	15.50	4.90	49.50	9.80	2.70	34.40

Source: *Sarvekshana* (NSSO), Vol. XIII No.1, 38th Round, Jan.-Dec. 1983, No. 40 (July-Sept. 89), p. 5 and *Sarvekshana* (NSSO) 43rd Round (July 1987, June 1988), Vol. XV, No. 2, No. 49, Oct.-Dec. 1991, p. 35.

decline in the growth rate of food production in 1995-96, coupled with high level of open market sales have reduced public food stock from a record level of 30.3 million tonnes in January 1995 to 28.56 million tonnes in January 1996. In the Eighties, the annual growth rate of foodgrains was 2.8 per cent which was higher than the annual population growth rate of 2.14 per cent. But, in the post-liberalization period, that is, from 1990-91 to 1996-97, the annual growth rate of foodgrains was only 1.7 per cent, which was lower than the current rate of population growth.

Capital formation in agriculture has a crucial role in agricultural development. During 1990-91 to 1995-96, the share of public investment in total investment in agriculture went down from 25 per cent to 20.8 per cent. There has been a decline in the central assistance to states in early 1990s leading to decline in the state plan. This causes concern as state plan expenditure is usually spent on agriculture, irrigation, and social services. These kind of policies followed in early 1990s would decelerate the growth of agriculture to less than 2 per cent a year.

Agricultural labourers particularly Dalits who are mostly landless labourers, would be more adversely affected not only due to low growth rate of agricultural production but also due to shift in the production from food crops to non-food crops. The index of food production (1981-82=100) increased from 143.7 in 1990-91 to 150.4 in 1995-96, while the index of non-food production increased at a faster rate, i.e., from 156.3 to 187.7 during the same period. The area under foodgrains cultivation fell from 100.7 million hectares in 1990-91 to 97.3 million hectares in 1995-96, while the area under non-foodgrains increased from 120 million hectares to 132.6 million hecares, during the same period. The net per capital availability of food per day has declined from 510 grams in 1990 to 490 grams in 1996.

It should also be noted that the average monthly per capita consumer expenditure of Scheduled Castes and Scheduled Tribes for 30 days were Rs. 94.31 and Rs. 87.15 respectively, while it was 120.42 in case of non-SCs/STs, in 1983 in case of rural areas and the corresponding figures for urban area were Rs. 128.95, Rs. 133.11 for SCs and STs, and Rs. 172.11 for non-SCs/STs. This clearly shows that per capita expenditure of Dalits was much lower than that of non-Dalits.

There were trends of increase in the incidence of poverty in

TABLE 2

Per Capita Net State Domestic Product at 1980-81 Constant Prices

1982-83 PC NSDP Rank	*State*	*Amount (Rs.)*	*1987-88PC NSDP Rank*	*State*	*Amount (Rs.)*
1.	Delhi	4019	1.	Delhi	4601
2.	Goa	3152	2.	Goa	3493
3.	Pondicherry	3088	3.	Punjab	3310
4.	Punjab	2875	4.	Pondicherry	3309
5.	Haryana	2475	5.	Maharashtra	2813
6.	Maharashtra	2473	6.	A & N Islands	2695
7.	A & N Islands	2414	7.	Sikkim	2678
8.	Gujarat	2025	8.	Haryana	2598
9.	Sikkim	1746	9.	Arunachal Pradesh	2184
10.	Arunachal Pradesh	1744	10.	Nagaland	2016
11.	Himachal Pradesh	1673	11.	Gujarat	1942
12.	J & K	1671	12.	Karnataka	1909
13.	Karnataka	1665	13.	West Bengal	1828
14.	Nagaland	1616	14.	Tamilnadu	1821
15.	West Bengal	1571	15.	Himachal Pradesh	1818
16.	Andhra Pradesh	1545	16.	Manipur	1693
17.	Tamilnadu	1527	17.	J & K	1575
18.	Manipur	1485	18.	Andhra Pradesh	1530
19.	Kerala	1482	19.	Assam	1521
20.	Tripura	1443	20.	Meghalaya	1485
21.	Assam	1367	21.	Tripura	1470
22.	Meghalaya	1361	22.	U.P.	1455
23.	U.P.	1360	23.	Kerala	1413
24.	Rajasthan	1276	24.	Orissa	1320
25.	Orissa	1133	25.	Rajasthan	1241
26.	Bihar	873	26.	Bihar	979
27.	M.P.	536	27.	M.P.	649
	All-India	1697		All-India	1933

Source: Estimates of State Domestic Product and Gross Fixed Capital Formation, 1991, CSO, Department of Statistics, Ministry of Planning, Government of India, pp. 12-13.

early 1990s. It raised from 34 per cent in rural areas and 36 per cent in urban areas in 1989-90, to 41.7 per cent in rural areas, and 37.8 per cent in the urban areas in 1992-93. But some economists who supported liberalization dismissed it by saying, that it is based on the thin sample of NSSO, It was also found that there was significant deterioration in the consumption share of individuals in the lowest three deciles while the top three deciles gained since 1990-91. In 1990-91, the share of consumption of bottom three deciles was 15.96 per cent as against 49.24 per cent for the top three deciles in rural areas, while it was 13.74 per cent as against 53.85 per cent in urban areas. But, in 1992, the corresponding figures were 15.60 per cent as against 50.48 per cent in rural areas and 13.17 per cent as against 55.15 per cent in urban areas.

Real wages in agricultural sector after price correction made by the consumer price index for agricultural labour, showed a significant decline and even became a negative for the unskilled labour. The real wage annual rate of growth for unskilled agricultural labour declined from 3.3 per cent from pre-reform period (1986-87 to 1990-91) to 0.7 per cent in the post-reform period (1990-91 to 1995-96). The general prices were rising at the annual average rate of 10 per cent (on the basis of WPI) while food prices doubled during 1990-91 to 1995-96. It is also to be noted, that the food prices were raising at a faster rate than general prices. As a result, dalits would have been more adversely affected as most of them are agricultural labourers.

The position of Dalits would deteriorate further under liberalization, as serious attempts are being made to remove the land ceilings and induct the national or transnational corporations into agricultural sector. This would lead to de-peasantation. In a labour surplus agrarian economy, this kind of policy would be not only detrimental to the development of economy but also to the stability of the state.

Some economists argue, that under WTO there would be ample scope for promoting agricultural exports particularly food products like rice. If these items are allowed to be exported freely to the world market, the top 25 per cent of farmers, who control 75 per cent of land, would definitely benefit substantially and become richer but the bottom 75 per cent of the farmers, who control only about 25 per cent of land, cannot gain anything, as they do not have any marketable surplus. Moreover, it raises the domestic food prices in line with world prices and hits the poor particularly Dalits. India's rice exports rose from 505 thousand tonnes in 1990-91 to 4,914 thousand tonnes in 1995-96. That is, nearly an increase of ten times for six years. However, in terms of value, rice exports rose from $160 million in 1990-91 to $1,366 million in 1995-96, i.e., an increase of about eight times only. The exports of cereals increased from 1,151.81 thousand tonnes to 6,157.86 thousand tonnes during the same period. This may be one of the important reasons for rise in foodgrains' domestic prices as domestic food supply declines due to increased exports of the same, while the average growth rate of food production during liberalization period was declining.

The rural poor, particularly Dalits, are handicapped in terms of labour, land, and credit markets. In the post-Green Revolution period, although agricultural production increased tremendously, the real wages at the all-India level remained almost stagnating due to raise in labour force and decline in employment elasticity. Employment elasticity in primary sector at all-India level declined from 0.99 per cent during 1961-65 to 0.63 per cent during 1981-91. In addition to this, the labour also could not move as labour market is segmented. Workforce cannot cannot casually move from low paid areas to high paid areas. This is also due to the fact that some labour generally depends upon employer in more than one market, what is known as interlocking of markets (credit or land). The degree of this kind of dependence is more in case of Dalits because of their weak economic base and social discrimination. In the product market also Dalits are discriminated against particularly in rural product markets. They do not have equal access to product markets to sell their products and as a result, they do not get remunerative prices for their products. Under these circumstances, if state limits its role in the process of economic development and leaves the matters to the market in the context of liberalization, the economic conditions of poor, particularly Dalits would further deteriorate. To make these markets poor-friendly, the state has to play an active and crucial role in improving their employment opportunities and income generating assets position.

In case of Dalits, the role of state has to be not only economic but also protective to enable them to overcome the problems of poverty and social discrimination. Their skills have to be improved through expansion of educational facilities. It enables them to shift to non-farming economic activities and reduces their excess dependence on agriculture. Effective implementation of land reforms is essential, given the skewed distribution of land, to reduce the inequalities. Land concentration in few households is the main reason for rural poverty and social tensions. Land reforms and educational reforms played a very important role in countries like South Korea and Taiwan in reducing inequalities and in raising land and labour productivities.

EFFECTS ON DALITS

(1) This stage is establishing a new industry based on knowledge which can be seen in software computer programming, knowledge, and information consulting companies, research and development wings of various industrial houses, industry financed research programmes in universities, and the importance of "intellectual property rights". In the Indian situation, which already shows signs of development of this sector, the caste division of labour is going to have a marked effect. The majority of Dalits despite reservations, scholarships for education, have remained and will remain part of the unorganized labour. With increasing commercialization of education, the freedom to get educated is already becoming meaningless, particularly for highly specialized educational branches through which alone people can be enrolled in the knowledge-based industry sector. A tiny section of Dalits which has already gotten into the high echelons of the educated population, might find a miniature niche in this industry, but the majority is going to get pushed out of even traditional unorganized sector jobs.

(2) The new division of labour which this stage is bringing forward is a division between pure knowledge-based industry and applied technology-based industry, and applied technology-based industry. In pure knowledge-based industry, the main entrants are going to be Brahmans and other upper castes like Banias, and Khatris and Kayasthas, and the lower rungs of the applied technology industry will be filled up in the majority by Dalits.

(3) This stage is going to do away with many of the existing unorganized sector jobs, like rag-picking, sweeping of today's kind, bidi-making, tobacco-processing, etc. Everywhere it is going to bring clean and automatized work process. Jobs in these restructured sectors are not going to go to the unskilled unorganized workers of today. Sections of these unorganized

workers will have to get training and become skilled to be able to work in these work processes. Those sections who cannot get trained will become redundant and unemployed, which will have a majority of Dalits. Unless and until there is a rapid development of fifth stage capitalism in agriculture, these unemployed sections are not going to find any jobs. In India if we look towards the pace of development on the basis of this stage, in coming years increasing unemployment is going to be the result.

(4) In agriculture, also changes based on this stage of capitalism have started taking place. The beginning of horticulture based on modern techniques of biotechnology, growing vegetables and flowers with green-house technology, growth of precooling centres for fruits and vegetables, etc. in rural areas, production of specified agricultural products for export, modern organic farming techniques are examples of these changes. The pace of these changes is very slow even in states like Maharashtra, Karnataka, Andhra Pradesh, and Kerala where agriculture has already capitalistically developed. In states like Bihar, Orissa, and (eastern) Uttar Pradesh, the pace of these changes is going to be negligible. Indian capitalism has to have a big programme of education for the workers in these new agriculture processes and it has to increase the pace of changes tremendously. Otherwise, these changes will have the effect of throwing unskilled agricultural labourers out of jobs. Even if these changes acquire a fast pace, cultivating castes like, OBCs and Dalits are not going to be in control of these processes. People coming from castes like Brahmans, who for generations never participated in the development of agriculture, are going to control these processes. All others are going to be workers using applied technology. Even jobs in these processes which are related to higher education are going to go to upper castes.

(5) There are two ways through which this stage of capitalism can bring about complete change in agriculture. One is to lift the Ceiling Act and go for big farming houses or companies. (This is being tried everywhere and the ceiling acts are being evaded through forming trusts). The second way is to keep small cultivating farmers as they are and control the

production process by dictating methods of cultivation, controlling processing, and marketing, whether nationally or exports. The effects of the first method would make OBCs (including peasant castes) and Dalits as semi-skilled and unskilled workers working for farming companies and farm houses. This would in effect require a rapid development of non-agricultural capitalism. If this development does not take place then there will be tremendous unemployment. By the second method rapid generation of unemployment will not occur but unskilled Dalit, adivasi, and agricultural labourers would still become unemployed.

(6) The public sector has already started shrinking and this will go on. At the same time, there is going to be a shrinkage of the vastly developed and bloated state bureaucratic structures. This shrinkage is going to put many men and women coming from OBCs castes and Dalits out of jobs. At the same time, reservations in these sectors will lose their importance because of their small size.

Dalits are part of exploited castes. The majority of these are part of the exploited classes in the modern world. This section can either fight for a better share of the pie of the new stage of capitalism (new economic policy for India) or they can have their alternative movement which, along with giving them a better and respectable stake would them towards an alternative socialist society. Accepting the existing society and trying to gain a better share is a thing which exploited sections have been doing and will continue to do so. But that doesn't end their exploitation or do away with the basic miseries they suffer under the system, and that is why they should have an alternative which they could implement through the movement which could give them both – a comparatively better life and take them towards a liberated society.

(1) In agriculture sector, the development of science today has already invented higher productivity of biomass-based sustainable organic agriculture. The new economic policy would base itself on this along with some aspects of chemical

agriculture in a centralized manner. But this kind of agriculture is most suitable for decentralized production processes in agriculture which can give more power to the cultivators, artisans of a new kind, and other producers. For example, rather than falling prey to the propositions of processing and marketing companies, toiling peasants along with men and women from different types of agricultural labourers can start their own efforts to establish highly modern decentralized process of organic agriculture. They can demand infrastructural facilities and credit to start the new process. Production of bio-fertilizers, growth of earthworms, and useful organisms like rhizobium, production of organic pesticides, plant growth-promoting materials, selection and development of seeds could be done at the level of the village or cluster of villages. This can generate a lot of employment in the form of producer controlled cooperative industries.

(2) New technologies of replacement of steel with small timber can open up another sector for decentralized agro-industries which could take away centralized control over material production at the infrastructural level. Construction of roads, small dams, buildings could be done on this basis. In the same way, natural fibers could be used for various infrastructural purposes.

(3) In the energy sector, this stage of capitalism is going towards a renewable base, but in a centralized manner. Here also Dalits and other exploited castes and classes should demand centralized energy generation on the basis of solar, biomass and wind power. It has been experimentally proved by some of the pro-people technologists that it is possible to have decentralized production of such kind. This then can come under the decentralized collective control of exploited castes and classes.

(4) Water as a crucial means of production could be thought about in the same manner. Today, the control over water is becoming more and more privatized for the use of agriculture and industry. Delinking control over water from property holding and demanding equitable rights to use the sight an amount of water necessary for crucial basic necessities of the family can prove at least partially liberating. Through this

Dalits, women, and toiling peasants including OBCs can have crucial resource under their control.

In industrial sectors environmentally sound and productive disposal of solid degradable waste linking it with the agricultural sector on the fringes of industry, can generate meaningful employment with control over important resources. This can also be linked with the reconstruction of slums in an alternative way by the slum-dwellers themselves.

Today, the new economic policy is not to nationalize industries which are becoming sick but to give it again into private hands. This could be used by workers themselves as an opportunity to organize such industries in worker controlled alternative ways. But for doing this, workers should not try to run these industries as they were run by capitalist owners. They should go for finding out alternative ways, in which these industries could be reorganized, their production modified, and their market modified, etc.

For doing all this, all old concepts of the movement have to be radically changed. The majority of the Dalits, OBCs, and peasant castes who now are part of organized and unorganised workforce, toiling peasants, etc. should not go on thinking themselves as being at the receiving end of the system. Unless and until these sections start thinking and practicing in their role of producers (and not just wage-labourers) and as future controllers of their own destiny (and not just as praja), they cannot launch such a movement. The stage of the movement now should go from demanding reservations to have control over political, economic, cultural, and social destiny. This not only requires re-educating the masses, but reorienting the intellectuals too, particularly in social and natural sciences and technology. It is high time that the educators must be educated.

CONCLUSION

Dalits, at the lowest end of the economic and social ladder, are quite obviously at the receiving end of the elitist culture promoted by globalisation. Economically, the small gains made through reservations have been, in essence, reversed; and socially the elitist culture, which marginalizes the poor generally, will have a double impact on Dalits, due to the Hindutva (Brahminical) wave during this period.

More than 75 per cent of the Dalit workers are still connected with land; only 25 per cent of which are marginal and small farmers, while the remaining are landless labourers. In the urban areas, they work mainly in the unorganised sector. Out of the total dalit population of 138 million, the number of Dalits in services falling in the domain of reservations does not exceed 1.1 million; a mere 0.8 per cent. As per the Rural Labour Enquiry Report of 1987-88, over 63.14 per cent of the total rural households were wage labour households as compared to 31.16 per cent for others. In the same year, half of the Dalit population was below poverty line as against 39.06 per cent for others. The incidence of poverty was 55.12 per cent for the neo-Buddhists among them. It was 60.5 and 50 per cent for the agriculture labourer and for the non-agriculture labourer respectively.

The economic dimension of the caste question is intimately connected with land reforms, as the bulk of Dalits are without land. Land reforms is therefore, a key question for their development. But, globalisation has not only eclipsed this agenda of land reforms but it has substituted it with corporatisation of farming for the global agricultural market. The policy thrust of the World Bank-IMF-WTO combine has always been clearly for the abolition of the land ceiling laws and for liberalizing investment in agriculture. Land reforms have openly been opposed.

If we turn to the sphere of education, we find that as a result of various reform movements and particularly because of Ambedkar's role, many dalits took to education. Fundamentally this is now negated under globalisation, which has given impetus to the 'human capital' understanding, that measures the education system exclusively in economic terms particularly in responding to market needs. The new Policy Framework for Reforms in Education, drafted by a committee convened by Mukesh Ambani with Kumarmangalam Birla as members, seeks to drive privatisation and introduce rampant commercialisation of higher education along the lines of the USA. It envisages foreign direct investment in education, progressive reduction of government funding for universities and making them adopt the route of self-sufficiency, and concurrent development of a credit market for private finance to meet the cost of higher education. The latter is a clear smoke screen to diffuse its elitist intentions; as everyone knows that more than half the population of this country are just not creditworthy. Higher education, thus, is to be entirely market-oriented and clearly out of bounds of the commoners, not to talk of dalits. The commercial ethos that entered the education field through globalisation has further created a divide between haves and have-nots. The pay sets in the educational institutions have fortified the class basis of education. Dalits who have been barely able to afford schooling with the aid of freeship and scholarship are now being squeezed out from both ends. Firstly, education has become increasingly inaccessible and unaffordable to them. Even if they persist with it, they have to face several hurdles on the way to secure education that would get them gainful employment. The increasing opportunity cost of schooling is dissuading many dalits from education resulting in increasing numbers of dropouts. Even if they crossed all the hurdles as an exception, they would face a far bigger hurdle in the job market that tended to value your family background more than your scholastic performance. The economic globalisation has brought in a fundamental change in the composition of a major section of the job market. The manufacturing sector that valued the formal educational inputs has been shrinking whereas the service sector that required such attributes as one's looks, mannerisms, 'communication', connections, relationships, etc., that could be summed up as one's class attributes, did not value educational qualification. This class divide cannot be easily crossed by dalits.

In the sphere of jobs the wholesale privatization of the public sector taking place and the massive retrenchment of government jobs the question of reservation in the sphere of jobs has become irrelevant. And as the private sector has no job reservation policy the job opportunities that had been available to dalits during the past three decades will now totally dry up. The general population is facing the horrors of unemployment; this will be more deeply felt by dalits.

In addition, the government, which has been systematically cutting expenditure on the people's welfare at the behest of the World Bank/IMF, has also cut its expenditure on Schedule Castes and Scheduled Tribes. The outlay for SC, ST, and OBC welfare has declined from 8 per cent in 1990/91 to 6.7 per cent in 1994/95.

If we turn to the sphere of social oppression, untouchability, which is intrinsic to the brahminical order of Hindu religion, has been strengthened in this period. Globalisation in India, took a leap in 1991, with the SAP conditions imposed by the taking of the IMF loan. Hindutva took a leap in 1992, with the destruction of the Babri Masjid and the anti-Muslim programs that followed. The phenomenon of emergence of religious fundamentalism in many countries and particularly in our country in the era of globalisation is not a chance happening. It is the imperative of globalisation that the large multitude of masses is held in a conformist mode. The rise of Hindutva, demolition of the Babri Masjid, review of the constitution, denigration and harassment of minorities, saffronisation of education and generally communalisation of the polity, are not to be taken as unconected events. They are very much complementary to globalisation. Though the minorities, and particularly the Muslims, may have been the main target of this wave, Hindutva strengthens feudal values in all spheres of life, and so it, *defacto*, promotes untouchability, and whips up caste hatred against the lower castes in general, and dalits in particular.

So, we see Dalits too are victims of globalisation in both the economic and the social sense. So they too constitute an important force in the anti-globalisation, anti-imperialist struggle in the country.

REFERENCES

Alagh, Y.K., "National Economic Growth with Distributive Justice," *Mainstream*, Feb. 12, 1994, p. 29.

Bandyopadhyay, D. (1995): "Impact of SAP: Finger and Jobless Growth," *Mainstream*, May 13, 1995, p. 12.

Dev, S. Mahendra (1995): "Economic Reforms and Rural Poor," *Economic & Political Weekly*, Aug. 19, p. 2085.

Government of India, *Economic Survey*, 1996-97, pp. 524-25.

Gupta, S.P., "Economic Reforms and its Impact on Poor," *Economic and Political Weekly*, Vol. XXX, No. 22, June 3, 1995, p. 1298.

Nan Chariah, G., *Land and Caste*, Himalaya Publishing House, Bombay, 1988, p. 20.

Pathy, Jaganath, "The Consequences of the New Economic Policies on the People of India: A Sociological Appraisal", *Sociological*, Vol. 44, March, 1995.

Singh, Ajit Kumar (1993), "Social Consequences of New Economic Policy," *Economic and Political Weekly*, Feb. 13, 1993.

Tendulkar, Suresh and L.R. Jain, 1995, "Economic Reforms and Poverty," *EPW*, June 10.

Vyas, V.S., "New Economic Policy and Vulnerable Sections, Rational for Public Intervention," *Economic and Politic Weekly*, Vol. XXVIII, No. 10, March 6, 1993, p. 407.

7

Changing Pattern of 'Kamioti' System with Special Reference to Musahar Community

SANJAY KUMAR AND BIPIN PRASAD SINGH

This paper is an outcome of the study undertaken by Deshkal Society. The objective of the study was to understand the changing nature of the kamioti social system prevalent among the Musahar community members. The geographical coverage area of this study comprises of those villages of Gaya district of Bihar, where Musahars are living in large numbers for centuries. It is basically an ethnographic study, which uses the methodology of interview and observation extensively. The essence of the study is that the kamia system as a traditional labour form of this region has changed into wage labour. It reflects two major trends. First, Musahars have integrated themselves to the rural labour market and hence they demand wages cash in for their labour. Second, Musahars in large numbers are migrating from the region.

Govind Manjhi is an inhabitant of Pattharkatti *tola* which is located in Katari village of Gaya district. He is around 65 today. He is a sharecropper and has got a plot of three *bighas* assigned to him by his landowner-master. On this plot of land, he grows different crops. Earlier his occupation was *Kamioti*. He used to be a ploughman of his landowner and in lieu of his service he got five *katthas* of land. For every working day that he devoted to the service of his master, he would get two *sers* of raw food grains as the fixed amount of daily wages in kind. These food grains would be either *Khesari* (a kind of pea in the form of a pyramid) or any other coarse grain. About *Kamioti,* he says, "When there were nuptial ceremonies of any of the progeny, we had to be attached to the *Kamioti* with some of our *galla-pati* (goods and chattels) as well as any *nagadi* (cash) that we had. All the money that we had saved up for times of crises was put into the pool of *Kamioti* and we were left with nothing substantial to take care of our needs. Drawn in the month of *Jeth* (the third month of the Hindu calendar), the amount taken could be returned in the coming *Jeth* (after an interval of one year) only. The landowner, once he gave the money for this purpose, would not be willing to get it back normally." He used to say, "I had given you the money to work as a ploughman in my field, not to return it to me". When some other strong-headed, haughty landowner used to press his opinion into his ears that "If you don't get it back, he (*Kamia* or worker) will never return it to you", the landowner would be ready to get back his money. But this would hardly make any difference in our condition for we were trapped anyway, anyhow. If we refused to attach ourselves to the *Kamioti,* the landowner would threaten to disallow us from cutting grass for our cattle from grazing in the fields owned by them. They also used to say that they wouldn't let us collect the cow dung".

Sidheshvar Manjhi also stays in the same *tola*. He has been associated with the *Kamioti* for thirty-five years. As the landowner himself is not capable of pursuing farming on his own, he has started giving his land for sharecropping. Drawing substantial benefit from this situation, Sidheshwar has also become a sharecropper with five *bighas* at his disposal. He is illiterate but wants his sons and daughters to get education and be literate: "If our boys somehow get education, our colony will certainly see the light of development and reform. Our children will go to school, but due to our financial constraints, we can't afford to give them higher education." Aju Manjhi is a son of this man, who makes *khal* (pestle), bricks, *kundi* (latches), *diya* (lamps), *malava*, etc., by stone cutting. In Pattharkatti, there are hundreds of Musahars who are engaged in making stone-idols and other goods from stone. Thin womenfolk do the work of polishing. Sadhu Manjhi is a 20-year-old lad. He is Siddheshvar Manjhi's son. He makes stone idols of Lord *Ganesha, Parvati, Hanuman, Kartikkeya, Sai Baba, and Gautam Buddha*. He has received the training of stone carving in the company of other sculptors. He is also preparing for his matriculation examinations.

Patharkatti is now known as Shilpipuram. People belonging to all castes are sculptors. There are no caste restrictions on anyone taking up the occupation of sculpting whether he/she is a *Ravidas, Pasi, Koiri, Yadav, Nut, Nai*, Musahar, *Gaud*, etc. All of them usually sit together to accomplish their task. Mohan Manjhi says, "Earlier, people from our caste did not mix up and hobnob with others. Now the situation has undergone a change." He makes the idols of *Basaha Bail* (humped bull, considered the vehicle of Lord *Shiva*). Asked whether he has even been to the temple of *Thakur Jee* (Lord *Shiva*), he says with a little bit of hesitation, "No. I never felt the need of doing so."

Musahar artisans from Shilpipuram are willing to start a business of idol-makings, sculpting and architecture on their own, but dearth of capital is presenting the biggest hurdle to their aspirations. There are some *Gaud Brahmin* and *Teli* (oilmen) families in the village who get the services of these artisans and sell the stonework made by them to traders and dealers from outside. There is a branch of the State Bank of India, which provides loans for such artistic pursuits, but intermediaries and brokers usually eat up these loans. Substantial amounts of loans have been released from the Bank in the name of many Musahars, but they have not yet reached the beneficiaries.

There is an *Udyog-Bhavan* (industrial premises), in the village as well. Here costly machines and instruments pertaining to stone-craft are lying unused for several decades. The sales promotion centre and all the other functional units of this *Bhavan* exist merely on paper. No official, nobody from among the staff ever goes there and the only faces that can be seen are those of watchmen. Villagers used to get training in stone-craft from 1955 to 1990. There were two types of curricula prescribed for this purpose: one of them was half-yearly and the second one was triennial. Trainees also got a stipend of Rs. 150 every month. Now whatever training the craftsmen get, is from the society itself and in the course of their work.

Musafir Manjhi presents the phenomenon of Musahar turning into an artisan in these words: "In 1973, Fuji *Guruji* got an idol of the Buddha constructed from stones found in the adjacent hills. In order to facilitate the process of bringing stone-blocks down the hills, Musahars got the job of labourers for the construction of a road. Later on 40-50 people belonging to the Bhuiyan community were involved in mine cleaning. They used to blast rocks with the help of dynamite. Through *Sabbals* (boring tools) they would make holes in stones. At that time they used to get eight *annas* per *bitta* for boring. Now stones are exported from outside. There are hundreds of Bhuiyans today, who are involved in the occupation of idol-making and sculpting."

Aishakhi Manjhi who hails from the Katari Panchayat of Naranni village has been a *Kamia* from 1956 to 1966. His son is a wage-earning labourer. While the contractor gives him forty rupees and meal wages in addition, a peasant farmer pays only twenty-five rupees including the meal wages. Aitwari Manjhi says, "Rich land owners do not like the idea of our settlements on a piece of public land. They want to capture it. But we shall not go back."

Pravesh Manjhi is a twenty-year-old who has lost both his legs due to polio. He had schooling up to standard II. He says, "I want to continue my studies but the condition of my family does not allow me to do so. In order to enhance the income base of my family, I do different kind of jobs including paddy harvesting, bricklaying, etc. As my legs can't function properly, I am unable to do jobs that involve the tasks of carrying burdens on my shoulders. I am learning to drive tractors and have also developed some skill in it".

Chandreshwar Manjhi occupies a land of two *bighas*, which includes his homestead. He also takes two *bighas* for sharecropping. He is a non-matriculate, but his daughter has already done her matriculation. One of his sons is in the seventh standard. Two sisters of Rajkishore Manjhi are educated up to the seventh standard. He pursues farming on one *bigha* of homestead and two *bighas* on the sharecropping basis. He is also a fitter of diesel engines. Whatever time is saved from farming is devoted to other secondary pursuits, including the job of a building mason as well. Among those Musahars who don't have occupations akin to farming, there are many who go out of the village (often to other states) in the month of October to work at farms and mills. When there are rains in June, they come back again.

Shyamdeo Manjhi is an inhabitant of Dashrath Nagar (Gehlor Panchayat). He does *Kamioti* at the service of Avadhesh Singh from Sonara village. He has worked for seven years in the Forest Department as a daily wage earner. His job there included; digging the earth, sowing seeds, running *lattha*, looking after plants, etc. He used to get forty rupees for all these tasks. He never got a permanent job. He is also the President of the Primary School Committee of Dashrath Nagar. About *Kamioti*, he says, "Every *Kamia* gets two kilograms of food grains whereas other labourers get two kilograms and a quarter. The *Kamia* gets six *Kattha ghevari*'. For this, the master (landowner) provides seed, water and manure, and the produce from this land goes to the household of the *Kamia*. During the paddy harvest season, he gets one *gahi* out of 12 *gahis* and in *Rabi Seasons*, he has a share of one *bojha* (stack) in 12 *bojhas*. For *Davani-pitni*, he gets the same two kilograms. Any landowner, who wants to raise some *Rabi* crop in his field or wishes to employ some other labourer, cannot take a decision without the consent of the *kamia*. If his master breaks the promise, the *Kamia* can also put pressure on the latter. For instance, if the master does not have any work for the *Kamia* to engage in, he can go over to someone else for work. But as long as his master has some work in his own field, he cannot go elsewhere only for the sake of more wages. As Many as 66 Musahars have got land under land ceiling in the Chhibra *mauja*. The landlords of Bela village earlier owned this land. It had bushes and thickets in plenty including *Kamaula, Ditehari*, etc. Musahars cleared this tract and made it arable. Now, they raise coarse grains like *madua* as well as maize and lentil, etc.. Some traces of paddy are also visible. Agriculture is essentially based on rainfall. If there is no rain, crops die out. Fifteen years ago, a total of thirty-three wells were dug in this land by the government. But there is no water in any of them. Sometimes, they contain scant amounts of rainwater. Pots, if they are shaken with this water inside, have thick layers of filthy mud at the bottom.

Every Musahar has got around one and a half acres of land. If there is a proper system of water management, positive changes can be brought about in the prevailing conditions of the land and it can be very productive as well. Musahars do not have enough money to make alternative arrangements for water.

Recently, fifteen families from Bundela Bigha village have forcibly infiltrated and settled in this place. Local *Rajputs* have been instrumental in getting them settled all over during one *Ashadh* midnight this year and have captured their Bundela Bigha land for themselves. Shyamdeo Manjhi says, "We contacted everyone ranging from the B.D.O. and Tehsildar to the *Daroga* (Police Sub-Inspector). We also gave them some bribes. But our land was never measured, nor was any action taken against the culprits."

The piece of land under the Forest Department lying adjacent to the hills spread out from Bodh Gaya to Rajgir, thousands of Musahars from nearby villages have infiltrated and settled. This has slackened the grip of their traditional masters over them. Now they are capable of pressing for the maximum possible wages. Pano Devi from Karjani says, "As we have got so close to the hills, we have to face an acute water crises. We have still to fetch water from the same old place from where we used to. We have to go as far as a mile to fetch water. Let alone the livestock, even humans are unable to get adequate quantity of water. Nevertheless, we have one advantage; now we go over to Kanjani-Pithroa to earn our wages and get three kilograms of rice, wheat or flour for our work. Till a year ago, we used to go to work after eating at our homes. Then, we got just a *ser* and a quarter of raw grains. This is something quite remarkable." Government works are done on paper and they have nothing to do with the problems of real life —this is precisely the conclusion drawn by the Musahar society. Nanhak Manjhi from Naranni complains, "Six thousand rupees have been drawn in our name, but we have absolutely no idea of it. Thirty-two landless *Harijans* have got sanctions of land, but nobody knows where that land is." Old people are unable to get old-age pension in time. If one or two among them get it, they are unable to get the whole amount. Akali Devi, Sugia Devi, Suvasi Devi – all of them unanimously complain that they are not getting the old-age pension in spite of repeated applications they have sent to the authorities.

Rampati Manjhi says, "There is a provision for twenty thousand rupees under *Indira Awas Yojana.* I have received seventeen thousand only. Someone else got the cheque encashed in my name and gave the amount to me. Only those who had their own capital got their houses completed whereas those of many others are still incomplete."

Mahani Devi says, "I could not get the whole amount due to be paid to me under *Indira Awas Yojana.* An intermediary took money for bricks and cement. He gave five stacks of cement and put down ten in the account book".

Jhapasi Manjhi got a loan from the Bank for purchasing buffaloes. We can have an idea of his plight in his own words: "We got a buffalo that cost only twenty six hundred whereas its estimated price was rupees five thousand. Actually, only brokers select buffaloes. They get the price limits determined forcibly. The buffalo that was purchased for me could give just two glasses of milk. I took that milk with me and went over to the Bank Manager. The Manager asked me to present a written account of it to him. After a few days' interval, the buffalo died. I had a clash with the broker. Eventually its cost was estimated at twenty-six hundred rupees on account of this clash only. As the subsidy was fifty per cent, I had to return thirteen hundred. The Manager was honest and so, my life was somehow spared". Anke Bazar Block is located in Gaya district. Binova Nagar is a small rural settlement in this block lying adjacent to Jhumrahi Hills. It is a settlement of Musahars. All its inhabitants have their own land ranging between 30 to 45 *Dismil* to each one's share. They have proper documents that testify their acquisition and ownership of land. There are 15 wells in this village that have been dug under *Shramdaan* programme. Each of these wells has a water level up to four-five feet. There is sufficient water in these wells for Musahars to pursue their farming occupation. In the month of January, potato, wheat, chilli, *Mangrela, Ajavain,* garlic, lentil, tomato, etc., are produced in these fields. With the help of *lattha-kundi,* water is drawn from these wells for irrigation.

Goats, cows, oxen, buffaloes are among the major livestock of these people. There are plants of *Shyama tulsi, tulsi, Van tulsi* at different places. *Tulsi Beer* is the hero of Musahar folk-tradition. They consider themselves his descendents. These plants trace the relevance of their abundance in the collective popular memory of that very *Tulsi Beer*. Moreover, those plants also serve medicinal purposes. Trees of palm, papaya, mango, plum, guava, *pipal*, *pakad*, *bel*, banyan, etc., can also be seen here in plenty. Musahars have a special kind of respect for trees. They look after all the vegetation all over the hills or on the piece of land acquired by the Forest Department. With their mutual cooperation they have built beautiful mud-houses and have been able to construct many things that fulfil their needs.

There is a residential girls' school in Banke Bazar. Girls belonging to the *Harijan* communities study in this school. Of them, 80 per cent girls are from the Musahar community. Inside the premises of this school, there is a proper arrangement of boarding and lodging facilities for these girls. *Jayantis* (birth anniversaries of great personalities) are celebrated in this school, but there are no holidays on such occasions. When harvesting and sowing seasons approach, there are vacations for two-three months. Girls are imparted practical education and training in this school. They are taught to sow paddy seeds, milk cows, implant trees and vegetation, make *rakhis*, cook food, etc.

This school is basically run on the means of resources mobilised by the local population. Since people belonging to the Musahar community selflessly contribute their labour to different construction works including the building of embankments, roads, etc., villagers reciprocate through grain donations and financial assistance for the education of these girls.

Surendra Pathak of Bhaluhar plays the role of a real source of inspiration in giving an organised form to these activities. He says, "I only tell people to do things, but it is the people who actually perform or 'act'. I tell them that you have to do your work yourselves. Waiting for the government or any other agency to do things for you amounts to obstructing the free flow of progress."

CREDITORS' NOTE

I Sohan Bhuiyan, resident of mauza Diha, pargana Pahra, in the district of Bihar, do hereby acknowledge to have taken an advance of Rs. 24–14–0 for agreeing to work as a kamia and menial servant from Jainu Singh, by caste Rajput, of Diha. In this document which I execute, I willingly and voluntarily bind myself to plough on nakdi and bhaoli lands of Jainu Singh, and to grow cotton, sugarcane, etc., for him, and to work wherever the lands of Jainu Singh may be located. My descendants and I forever bind ourselves to be ready to perform any work given to us, and to perform all the duties of a menial servant without objection. If at any time I abscond I shall be liable to be brought back by the said Jainu Singh by force and shall offer no objection, and if I refuse to return or offer resistance I shall be liable to pay the nakdi and bhaoli produce of one plough and Rs. 100 in cash and then I and my descendants can be released from our obligations. I shall be paid the same diet allowance or wages as is customary in this village and around. If I cause any other work of the aforesaid Jainu Singh to suffer he shall have authority to administer justice, as he thinks proper. For the above this document is executed by way of Sewaknama so that it may be of use where occasion requires.

Dated 15 Asarh 1262 (1855)

[Gyan Prakash: 1990, *"Bonded Histories: Genealogies of Labour Servitude in Colonial India,"* p. 226]

This tale is one hundred and fifty years old. We realise from this contract how this horrible custom has been weakening in the hundred and fifty years since its inception. The process of its breaking has become possible thanks to the everyday struggle of the *Kamia* people and the larger movement from outside. Although we understand that this community is defined through its passiveness, its rat eating habits and the fact that it is standing on the margins of progress, but we also need to know that it has been struggling incessantly to gain respect and freedom and has been constantly striving to find a way out of bondage.

This example illuminates yet another fact that the *Kamias* are not mere agricultural labours. It is a different thing altogether that both before and after Independence, the Government has placed it either under the bonded labour category or named it as agricultural labourers. This kind of categorisation has not remained confined to the likes of bureaucrats and policy-makers alone. Those who have sought to work amidst them for the sake of their upliftment—whether it is the ultra left or the rightists—have also tried to understand their problems and stand up for them from within the same framework. They haven't given much thought as to who a *Kamiya* is or what the custom and practice of *Kamiauti* represents?

8

Economic Reform and Empowerment of Women: Issues, Options and Concerns

Ranju Ranjan Kumari and Krishna Nand Yadav

INTRODUCTION

In recent years the empowerment of women has emerged as an important issue in Indian society and also on a global basis. There has been an increasing realisation and recognition that empowerment of women is absolutely essential for familial, societal, national, and global development. Empowering women is the goal to eliminate discrimination against women and girl children, strengthen women in leadership and decision-making, increasing access to education, and increasing women's access to and control over economic resources.

Women as an independent target group, account for 495.74 million and represent 48.3 per cent of India's total population, as per the 2001 Census. The issues of women have been receiving the attention of the government right from the First Five Year Plan (1951-56), and the same has been treated as a subject of 'welfare'. But from the Sixth Five Year Plan (1980-85) and onwards there has been a marked shift in the approach to women's issues from welfare to development. Accordingly, the Sixth Plan adopted a multi-disciplinary approach with a special thrust on the three core sectors of health, education, and employment. In the Seventh Plan (1985-90), the development programmes continued with the major objective of raising the economic and social status of women and bringing them into the mainstream of national development. The Eighth Plan it was promised to ensure that benefits of development from different sectors do not by-pass women. And, the Ninth Plan (1997-2002) made two significant changes in the conceptual strategy of planning for women. Firstly, "Empowerment of Women" became one of the nine primary objectives of the Ninth Plan. Secondly, the plan attempted "convergence of existing services" available in both women-specific and women-related sectors.

It is in this backdrop, the decentralised-planning programme attempted a gender planning exercise in the local self-government and massive training programmes were conducted for gender sensitisation of women elected representatives of local governments. In the wake of above facts, it is necessary to know the meaning of "Women's Empowerment." The UNICEF in 1993 provided a women's empowerment framework, which argues that women's development can be viewed in terms of five levels of equality, of which empowerment is an essential element at each level. The levels are welfare, access, conscientisation, participation, and control. In her study of female tree plantation workers of Sri Lanka, Samar Singhe (1993) reveals that the "development strategies which simply increase women's access to resources do not necessarily ensure their empowerment." Women's control of resources is necessary for their empowerment. From their research in Bangladesh, Schuler and Hashemi (1993) hypothesized that "the process of empowerment should weaken the systemic basis of women's subordination". They identified six layered hierarchy of domains in which women have traditionally been subordinated such as:

- Sense of self and vision of a future;
- Mobility and visibility;
- Economic security;
- Status of decision-making power within the household;

- Ability to interact effectively in the public sphere; and
- participation in non-family groups.

Batliwala (1994) defined empowerment as "the process of challenging existing power relations, and of gaining greater control, over the source of power". According to her, women's empowerment is seen as 'the process and the result of the process' of:

- Challenging the ideology of male domination and women's subordination;
- Enabling women to gain equal access to and control over resources (material, human, intellectual); and
- Transforming the institutions (family, education, religion, media and so on) and structures (legal, political, economic and social) through which the ideology and practice of subordination is reinforced and reproduced.

According to the World Bank (2004), empowerment is the process of enhancing an individual's or group's capacity to make choices and transform those into desired actions and outcomes. We still, however, do not have consistent analytic framework on how to operationalise empowerment in different contexts, or how to track empowerment activities, or effects. The World Bank (2004) has, however, developed an analytical framework for measuring empowerment which includes concepts, context, and the framework in practice.

Empowering women has become the stated goal of many development interventions. But in spite of a framework and perspective for women's empowerment, it is imperative that these initiatives and strategies are translated into social, political, economic, educational, and cultural empowerment of women. Hence this paper makes an attempt to analyse the various dimensions of empowerment of women. These dimensions are Economic empowerment, Social empowerment, Political empowerment, and Empowerment through education.

STATUS OF INDIAN WOMEN IN THE PRESENT SCENARIO

The world has entered the new millennium but it is a harsh

reality that the women in India have been ill-treated for ages almost all. In our male dominated society, women are discriminated in sectors of the society and even in their families. Sometimes, even their neighbours, friends, family members and their relatives sexually humiliate them. The social values dramatically decreased for various reasons. Currently women are always experienced trauma in all the sectors of society. The position varies from religion to religion, society-to-society, environment, as well as culture of the country. It starts from the birth of a baby girl, her education, health, profession, married life, and social status as well.

While the various developmental policies, plans, and programmes that have been implemented over the last few decades in India have brought forth a perceptible improvement in the socio-economic status of women. Even then, the problems like illiteracy, ignorance, discrimination, and violence continue to persist even today. Although there happens a constant debate among the development sectors, women's organisations, key professionals, and the academic fields to fight for the issues of women empowerment. But unless we are able to change our attitude towards women, no law, society or individual would be able to achieve desired goal. We can easily understand the status of Indian women through different tables.

India witnessed continued decline in sex ratio (see Table 1) since 1901 to 1971 from 972 to 930 women per thousand men respectively. In 1991, it became the lowest in the history of Census, i.e. 927. Again, in 2001 the sex ratio of total population was 933. The number of missing girls shows the existances of discrimination between boys and girls. Many social scientists have narrated several reasons for the missing girls. Impoverished parents' reluctance to raise large sums of money for girls' dowry is often cited as a reason for preferring a son. But preference for son cannot be blamed on poverty alone, since the drop in the number of girls is sharpest in prosperous states like Maharashtra and Punjab. Some wealthy communities even go for genetic manipulation to select male fetuses. In such families the reason for preferring son is that they want someone to take care of their family business and keep their heads 'high' in the society.

TABLE 1

Sex Ratio in India

Year	*Sex Ratio/000 males*
1901	972
1911	964
1921	955
1931	950
1941	945
1951	946
1961	941
1971	930
1981	934
1991	927
2001	933

Thus, firstly either the girls are murdered in the wombs of their mothers or in case they get an opportunity to open their eyes in this world, then also certain traditions of killing female babies (custom of DUDHAPITI) by putting opium on the mother nipples and feeding the baby, by suffocating her in a rug, by placing her after birth or over the face or simply by ill-treating the daughters and do not let them live. Few villages of Punjab are notorious as 'Kudimaar' (girl killers).

"India is catching up with other sexist, modern societies like south Korea and China in sex selective abortions". Noble prize winning economist Amartya Sen has said, "It is a technological revolution of reactionary kind."

The Census of 2001 mentions the following as the major causes of declining sex ratio: 1. Female Foeticide, 2. Female Infanticide, 3. High child mortality rate due to low premium accorded to girl child, and 4. Increase in Maternal Mortality Rate.

Internationally also the picture of India (see Table 2) appears quite gloomy. As per Table 2, India is having one of the world's lowest ratio for women to men. Although MMR has been declining from 4.68 in 1980 to 4.7 in 1998. Table 3 shows that it is still very and therefore, a matter of great concern.

Though the female work participation rate has increased from 19.7 per cent in 1981 to 25.7 per cent in 2001 as seen in Table 4, it is still much lower than the male work participation rate in both urban and rural areas. Hence, study of above tables reveals that women are still far lagging behind the men in all fronts.

TABLE 2

Comparative Sex Ratios
(Number of Females per 1000 Males)

Country	*Sex Ratio*
China	944
India	933
USA	1029
Indonesia	1004
Brazil	1025
Russian Federation	1140
Bangladesh	953
Japan	1041
Nigeria	1016

Source: Census 2001.

TABLE 3

Maternal Mortality Rate (1980-98)
(Per one lakh live births)

Year	*Maternal Mortality Rate*
1980	468
1993	437
1998	407

Source: Sample Registration System Bulletins for respective years, Registrar-General and Census Commissioner, GoI, New Delhi.

VIOLENCE AGAINST WOMEN IN INDIA

It is necessary to examine the status and position of Indian women in terms of wanton violence and crimes committed against then. The term violence against women refers to many types of harmful behaviour directed at women and girls because of their sex and unequal status as compared with men in society. According to Article 1 of the UN Declaration of the Elimination of Violence Against Women, "Any act of gender-based violence that results in, or is likely to result in, physical, sexual or psychological harm or suffering to women, including threats of such acts, coercion or arbitrary, deprivations of liberty, whether occurring in public or private life". The phenomenon of violence against women within the family in India is complex and deeply embedded.

TABLE 4

Work Participation Rates by Sex (1981 to 2001)

(In Per cent)

Census	*T/R/U*	*Female*	*Male*	*Persons*
1981	Total	19.7	52.6	36.7
	Rural	23.1	53.8	38.8
	Urban	8.3	49.1	30.0
1991	Total	22.3	51.6	37.5
	Rural	26.8	52.6	40.1
	Urban	9.2	48.9	30.2
2001	Total	25.7	51.9	39.3
	Rural	31.0	52.4	42.0
	Urban	11.6	50.9	32.2

Source: Census of India, 1991, Series I and Census of India, 2001: Provisional Population Totals, Registrar General & Census Commissioner, GOI, New Delhi.

According to National Crime Records Bureau Report 1998, 2371 cases of suicides were related to dowry disputes. According to reports out of every 100 rape cases in India only 5 or 10 offenders are convicted. According to another report in 1999, every day in India 42 women are raped, 18 cases of dowry related cruelty incidents at home, and 4 molestation cases were reported. It would be important to study the crimes against women with the help of tables on the basis of comparative data. National level Table 5 and State-wise Table 6 are presented here.

These Tables highlight a very dangerous and increasing trend of crimes and violence in all forms against women. It is striking here that Bihar, which ranks 30 and 18, in dowry deaths and rapes respectively, Deep-rooted ideology about the superiority of males enables them to exercise control on women and violence is one of the weapons that is used to enforce this authority. Violence against women is increasing day-by-day in spite of progressive legislations and active women's organisations. The new social order with its emphasis on consumerism is fuelling the demand for more dowry and hence leads to more gender related violence.

TABLE 5

National Level Crimes against Women

Crimes	*1988*	*1989*	*1990*	*1991*
Dowry deaths	2209	4006	4836	5121
Rape	6025	7895	10068	12096
Kidnapping	11126	14169	16235	19539
Molestation	15613	20497	10198	21138
Sexual harassment	7856	9934	8620	10711
Burning Housewives	180	132	153	678
Suicide due to torture in Husband's House	858	784	788	1032
Total	43867	57417	60898	70315

Sources: (i) Asgar Ali Engineer, *Women, Fundamentalism and the Role of the state; Understanding Society and Politics*, G.U. 1992. (ii) Prabhash P. Singh, *Women in India: A Statistical Panorama*, Inter-Alia, New Delhi, 1991, pp. 461-69.

The key factors, which can be considered to improve the women's status in the society, would come from our routine behaviour which starts from our families, neighbours, society and work environment and above all with the community we belong to once all sectors of the society have a deep understanding and internationalization of respect for women and women's welfare, security, development and recognize them as their partners with the equal right only then, women will be more empowered and real progress could be seen.

CONSTITUTIONAL SAFEGUARDS FOR WOMEN

The constitution of India, undoubtedly, has provided better safeguards to women. India's concern in safeguarding the rights and privileges of women found its best expression in the constitution of India. While Article 14 confers equal rights and opportunities on men and women in the political, economic, and social spheres, Article 15 prohibits discrimination against any citizen on the grounds of sex, religion, race, caste etc. and Article 15(3) empowers the State to make affirmative discrimination in favour of women. Similarly, Article 16 provides for equality of opportunity in the matter of public appointments for all citizens; Article 39 stipulates that the State shall direct its policy towards providing men and women equally the right to means of livelihood and equal pay for equal work; Article 42 directs the State to make provisions for ensuring just and humane conditions of work and maternity relief; and Article 51(A)(e) imposes a fundamental duty on every citizen to renounce practices derogatory to the dignity of women. To make this *de-jure* equality into a *de-facto* one, many policies and programmes were put into action from time to time, besides enacting/enforcing special legislations, in favour of women.

Many other legislative supports are also available to women. A few of them are as such: (a) The Immoral Traffic (Prevention) Act, 1956, (b) The Dowry Prohibition Act, 1961 (28 of 1961), (c) The Indecent Representation of Women (Prohibition) Act, 1986, (d) The Commission of Sati (Prevention) Act, 1987 (3 of 1988), (e) Indian Penal Code, 1960, (f) The Muslim Personal Law (Shariat) Application Act, 1937, (g) The Hindu Marriage Act, 1954, (h) The Hindu Adoptions & Maintenance Act, 1956, (i) The Hindu Minority & Guardianship Act, 1956, (j) The Hindu Succession Act, 1956, (k) The Maternity Benefit Act, 1961 (53 of 1961), (l) The Medical Termination of Pregnancy Act, 1971 (34 of 1971), (m) The Family Courts Act, 1984, (n) Juvenile Justice Act, 1986, (o) The Child Labour (Prohibition & Regulation) Act, 1986, and (p) The Pre-Natal Diagnostic Technique (Regulation and Prevention of Misuse) Act, 1994.

The need for linkage between programmes oriented to women and national policy towards weaker sections has come to be increasingly realized. Several commissions have been appointed by the Central and the state governments to suggest measures for protecting womens' rights in various fields. Two such commissions were appointed by the central government in 1971 and 1992 respectively. The National Commission for Women (NCW), set-up in January, 1992 was directed to look into women-

TABLE 6

Ranks of Selected States According to the Average Rate (1998-2000) of Crimes Committed against Women (Per Lakh)

States	*Rape*		*Dowry Deaths*		*Cruelty by Husband and Relatives*		*Molestation*		*Sexual Harassment*		*Total Crime against Women*	
	Rate	*Rank*	*Rate*	*Rank*	*Rate*	*Rank*	*Rate*	*Rank*	*Rate*	*Rank*	*Rate*	*Rank*
Andhra Pradesh	1.2	11	0.63	24	6.37	28	4.2	22	2.27	30	17	28
Assam	2.83	28	0.17	14	3.27	22	2.77	17	0.07	7	13.63	21
Bihar	1.53	18	1.07	30	1.47	14	0.5	3	0.1	9	6.8	8
Delhi	3.17	30	0.93	29	0.77	9	4.4	23	1.1	26	18.27	29
Gujarat	0.73	5	0.2	15	7.8	30	2.27	12	0.3	19	13.6	20
Haryana	1.97	23	1.47	32	6.2	27	3	19	1.87	29	16.2	26
Jammu & Kashmir	1.8	20	0.1	10	0.37	6	5.13	28	3.57	32	16.73	27
Karnataka	0.53	4	0.4	20	3.03	20	2.83	18	0.23	15	10.97	16
Kerala	1.63	19	0.1	10	7.33	29	5.3	29	0.23	15	15.2	24
Madhya Pradesh	4.5	31	0.8	26	3.77	24	10.1	32	0.97	24	21.5	31
Maharashtra	1.4	16	0.43	22	7.93	31	3.17	21	0.93	23	15.13	23
Orissa	2.1	25	0.73	25	3	19	4.43	25	0.5	21	12.97	19
Punjab	1.17	10	0.83	28	2.67	17	0.93	7	0.07	7	7.03	9
Rajasthan	2.33	26	0.8	26	9.93	32	5.73	30	0.1	9	23.97	32
Tamil Nadu	0.73	5	0.3	17	1.03	13	3.07	20	2.8	31	20.4	30
Uttar Pradesh	1.03	9	1.3	31	3.27	22	1.5	10	1.57	27	10.6	15
West Bengal	1	8	0.33	18	4.9	26	1.47	8	0.03	6	8.83	11
Total (All India)	1.57		0.7		4.43		3.27		0.93		13.8	

Note: *Analysis was done for all 32 states and UTs and the ranks are shown accordingly.

Source: National Crime Records Bureau: Crime in India, 1998-2000.

related issues, probe the status of women, examine various legislations and point out loopholes and gaps and assess the causes of discrimination and violence against women and suggest possible remedies.

COMPARATIVE STATUS OF WOMEN

Women's empowerment has been beset with problems even internationally, although women make up half of the world's population, produce 80 per cent of its food, labour for two-thirds of its working hours, are paid 10 per cent of income and own one percent of its property.

To be sure, the decade of the women (1976-85), the adoption of the Convention on Eliminating Every Form of Discrimination Against Women (1979), the key role of women in the development process, and their rights have created a global public demand for their empowerment. Moreover, their activities have got underway a reorientation of international policies on women. But, despite numerous progressive international moves in the area of formal legislation, the political debates on the legal status are in no way over.

It is necessary to mention here the Gorbachev Era and the Perestroika experience of The U.S.S.R. The Gorbachev era was quite significant as far as "woman's question" was concerned. The twenty-seventh Congress of the CPSU in 1986 constituted a landmark in the history of the Soviet Union as it introduced various reform measures like glasnost, perestroika and new thinking. Gorbachev believed that democratization and restructuring were not possible without the increased and active role of women. He noticed that women were not duly represented in governing bodies and emphasized their entry into governing bodies at all levels. So, he revived women's councils (Zhensovetys) in the twenty-seventh Congress. The concept was institutionalized under the Soviet Women's Committee in January, 1987 during the All Union Conference on Women. By 1987, Gorbachev had created 240,000 Zhensovetys across the country under the Soviet Women's Committee to work under the party to unite women for the cause of communist development. Further, women constituted over 50 per cent in the local government by 1988.

TABLE 7

Women Administrators and Managers

(As percentage of total)

Country	*Percentage*
Canada	42.4
USA	42
Singapore	34.3
Thailand	21.8
Sri Lanka	16.9
Malaysia	11.9
China	11.6
Bangladesh	5.1
Pakistan	3.4
India	2.3
Industrialized Nations	27.4
Developing Nations	10.0

Source: UNDP Report, 1997.

But recently the radical changes are taking place in many countries by way of opening up of new opportunities for policies on women. On the one hand, this is because the extent of the disadvantage and suppression of women is more visible. And on the other, because the fields of work for women have become wider, if mainly in urban centres. In some countries, women have been able to push through binding legal regulations (election laws, political party statutes, women's quota rules for local councils), in order to guarantee their stronger participation in parties and trade unions. With the programme and slogans of "empowerment" and "redistribution of power," women who are organized in self-help organizations, associations, networks and political parties are demanding participation in political decision processes and access to the political institutions. They are striving for social power in a bid to influence the factors which cause discrimination against them.

The transition from authoritarian to democratic forms of government in a great number of countries have placed women's organizations in a changed environment. There are now countless such bodies, and their combined clout is changing the status of women and helping to broaden their scope for social action. But in some countries women are still faced with considerable difficulties in organizing themselves with formal status.

It should not be out of place to mention here, that despite several efforts made for empowering women in India, the Indian women could not get equal status to men even in the age of globalisation which is evident from the comparative Table 7.

A recent study conducted by UNESCO in seven South-East Asian countries indicates, that in terms of awareness, party membership, contesting elections, voting or deliberate abstention from voting, and decision-making, women's participation has not been impressive. They remain in the periphery of power and influence, says the study. Mostly the leaders of different parties are interested in winning candidate. While more women are entering politics and winning elections, their representation in the Union Government as well as states continues to be abysmal.

TABLE 8

Literacy Rate by Sex (1981-2001)

(In %)

Census	*Females*	*Males*	*Persons*	*Male-female gap in literacy rate*
1981	29.76	56.38	43.57	26.62
1991	39.29	64.13	52.21	24.84
2001	54.16	75.85	65.38	21.69

Source: Census of India, 2001: Provisional Population Totals, Registrar-General & Census Commissioner, GoI, New Delhi.

PROCESS OF WOMEN EMPOWERMENT DURING REFORM ERA

Ever since India adopted the economic reform policies of globalisation and structural adjustment, women's empowerment has been a central concern in all the major discourses. Within the framework of a democratic polity, our laws, development policies, plans and programmes have been aimed at women's advancement in different spheres. In recent times, particularly from 6th Plan to 10th Plan, the empowerment of women has been recognised as the central issue in determining the status of women and the National Commission for women was set-up by an Act of Parliament in 1990, to safeguard the rights and legal entitlements of women.

The year 2001 was celebrated as Women Empowerment Year. During the year, various activities and programmes were taken up on different issues pertaining to women's social, political, and economic empowerment. The impact of action in the field of Social, Political, Economic, and others are discussed below:

(A) Social Empowerment

Social empowerment creates an enabling environment through adopting various affirmative developmental policies and programmes for development of women, besides providing them easy and equal access to all the basic minimum services, so as to enable them to realize their full potential through education, health, and nutrition etc.

Education

The bold decision to declare "education as the fundamental rights" reflects the government's concern and commitment to ensure that everyone born in India is literate and thus fulfils the constitutional commitment of "Education for All by 2007". The Sarva Shiksha Abhiyan launched in 2000 is playing key role in this direction. The partial gains in women's education as reflected in the female literacy shows an increase from 29.76 per cent in 1981 to 54.16 per cent in 2001 (Table 8). Also it is necessary to mention here that as per 2001 Census for the first time, the absolute number of female illiterates has come down from 200.07 million in 1991 to 189.6 million in 2001. Similarly, the gap between female and male illiterates and drop out rate has started to narrow down. But more efforts are needed because in The absence of proper education empowerment is meaningless. Status of women literacy is clear from Table 8.

Health and Family Welfare

Although there has been a significant reduction in infant mortality rate, there are several other reasons which causes deaths among poor women particular in rural areas. The highest number of maternal deaths in 1998 was due to haemorrhage (29.7%), followed by anaemia (19%) and sepsis (16.1%), which could have been prevented easily through better reproductive health care and nutrition. Despite the special sanction of the Medical Termination of Pregnancy (MTP) Act in 1971, illegal abortions continue to be performed by unauthorized persons like local quacks and untrained persons under unhygienic and unsafe conditions. In fact, abortions accounted for 8.9 per cent of the maternal deaths, which is quite high. Other causes of high morbidity amongst women are Reproductive Tract Infections (RTIs) and Sexually Transmitted Diseases (STDs), besides their higher vulnerability to cancer, malaria, and tuberculosis and other diseases due to their lower access to health care facilities (Table 9).

TABLE 9

Percentage Distribution of Cause-Specific Maternal Mortality Deaths—1998

Cause	*Percentage*
Haemorrhage	29.7
Anaemia	19.0
Sepsis	16.1
Obstructed Labour	9.5
Abortion	8.9
Toxaemia	8.3
Others	8.5

Source: Survey of Causes of Death (Rural), India, Annual Report, 1998, Registrar-General and Census Commissioner, GOI, New Delhi.

Although the government adopted the Life Cycle Approach in the Ninth Plan for meeting the health needs of target groups viz., women, mothers, and adolescent girls and the girl child. The Tenth Plan also commits to improve the accessibility and utilization of services of primary health care and family welfare with a special focus on under served and under-privileged segments of population through universalizing RCH services.

Food and Nutrition

In view of the critical link between the health and nutritional status of women, mothers and girl children, the Tenth Plan has laid down special emphasis on these two nutritionally vulnerable groups through ensuring intra household food security as the gender biases in the allocation of food have resulted in many nutritional deprivations amongst women and girls, perpetuating the vicious cycle of under mal-nourishment.

Besides, media has been considered as the best to portray the positive image of girls as well as women for their empowerment.

(B) Economic Empowerment

Economic dependency makes women weaker and helpless which compels them to be dependent on their husbands, family members, and parents. Hence, it is an urgent need for the women to be economically sound for their empowerment. Therefore, many poverty eradication programmes have been launched by the government particularly in rural areas to generate income among vulnerable groups in general and women in particular.

Therefore, the Tenth Plan has addressed the need for better targeting of benefits to women under various poverty programmes.

In fact, economic empowerment ensures provision of training, employment and income generation activities with both forward and backward linkages with the ultimate objective of making all women economically independent and self-reliant by organising women into Self Help Groups under various poverty alleviation programmes viz., Swarnajayanti Gram Swarozgar Yojana (SGSY), Swarna Jayanti Shahari Rozgar Yojana (SJSRY), Rashtriya Mahila Kosh (RMK), Support for Training and Employment Programmes (STEP) and Training-*cum*-Production Centre for Women, etc. and offering them a range of economic options along with necessary support measures to enhance their capabilities and earning capacities with an ultimate objective of making them economically independent and self-reliant.

In addition to above efforts, the government has taken special care for empowering women in various sectors such as micro-credit finance, agriculture, industries, small-scale industries, informal sector and services. Where women can earn for leading a sound and independent life which are discussed below.

Micro-Credit

The Tenth Plan has recognised the need for a comprehensive credit policy to increase women's access to credit either through the establishment of new micro-credit mechanisms, or micro-financial institutions, or strengthening the existing ones.

Micro-finance programmes are important for providing small credit to the rural poor and women in order to alleviate poverty. Micro-financing programmes through Self Help Groups (SHGs), introduced and expanded by non-governmental organisations (NGOs) in several parts of India, have the potential to minimize the problem of inadequate access of banking services to the poor women. They can also influence savings. The economic empowerment of women may be justified in terms of growing SHG-banks linkage programmes (see Table 10).

A striking feature appears when the number of deposit accounts per 1000 population is analysed on the basis of gender of the account holder (see Table 10). The analysis reveals that, on an average for the whole of India by the end of the year 2001, there were nearly 575 deposit accounts accruing to males per thousand females, which is above the national average (417 per thousand) of overall deposit accounts per thousand population. However, over the years this trend has been declining. In the year 1996 the number of deposit accounts per 1,000 males was as high as 598 but it gradually declined and came to a low of 575 by the end of year 2001. On the other hand, the number of deposit accounts per thousand females is increasing over the years. In the year 1996, there were only 192 deposit accounts per 1,000 females, which gradually increased to 205 in the year 1999, and went up to 216 accounts per 1,000 females by the end of year 2001. Though in absolute terms the deposit accounts per thousand males is much higher than it is for females, it is quite interesting to see that the deposit accounts per thousand males is decreasing, while that for females is increasing over the years.

The trend of increasing the number of deposit accounts per 1,000 population observed overall is on account of the increase in the trend of deposit accounts per 1,000 females. Since in India almost all SHG members under the micro-credit programmes are females.

TABLE 10

State/Regions	Deposit Accounts per 1,000 Males						Deposit Accounts per 1,000 Females					
	1996	1997	1998	1999	2000	2001	1996	1997	1998	1999	2000	2001
Northern region	794.5	776.4	764.55	757.88	751.37	737.29	269.8	280.4	289.3	295.7	303.3	308.1
Haryana	736.6	708.0	710.37	708.07	683.80	675.07	244.4	260.0	261.6	269.7	283.4	271.0
Himachal Pradesh	856.1	799.7	802.70	804.47	785.54	866.01	304.0	333.3	324.2	330.3	339.4	383.3
Jammu and Kashmir	630.5	652.5	635.93	637.24	656.00	641.63	200.6	218.8	231.7	232.2	226.8	262.5
Punjab	1110.6	1079.0	1071.21	1079.25	1060.83	1010.17	402.9	438.7	453.7	471.4	484.4	486.3
Rajasthan	420.1	411.5	419.26	423.35	421.69	412.40	106.7	110.9	118.0	123.7	127.9	130.9
Chandigarh	2555.0	2356.7	2335.51	2446.09	2445.59	2256.88	1073.1	1266.1	1190.9	1165.8	1124.7	1036.4
Delhi	1797.9	1762.5	1621.34	1510.07	1466.59	1534.86	755.1	639.9	712.9	694.7	700.3	766.3
North-eastern region	446.9	447.9	421.60	425.22	381.66	384.40	124.1	128.4	123.4	123.3	121.1	127.8
Assam	448.4	465.8	464.31	459.22	426.89	417.33	117.5	124.6	126.3	123.5	125.9	128.9
Tripura	470.9	477.9	410.10	425.50	386.51	446.17	131.9	138.2	126.5	131.8	123.5	155.6
Eastern region	494.4	508.3	496.89	492.39	481.60	476.70	135.6	134.7	135.2	137.0	142.9	136.8
Bihar	416.4	421.2	397.15	392.23	385.23	326.83	115.4	112.5	104.3	103.7	105.8	96.6
Orissa	390.7	407.3	400.09	409.13	400.76	411.55	76.9	82.0	88.8	92.6	97.5	102.9
Sikkim	342.4	315.8	316.36	302.82	315.07	364.31	104.8	117.6	129.0	132.3	97.5	99.1
West Bengal	639.1	663.4	666.41	657.00	640.98	666.44	188.5	187.0	195.4	199.3	112.4	194.0
Central region	495.9	498.6	499.90	498.94	479.80	495.22	148.7	148.3	155.6	157.3	210.4	170.3
Madhya Pradesh	385.1	395.6	387.01	380.27	362.92	387.01	110.0	92.4	97.0	95.1	165.3	123.1
Uttar Pradesh	546.9	546.0	551.92	553.48	533.32	535.06	167.6	175.6	184.1	187.4	191.7	191.1

(Contd.)

TABLE 10 (*Contd.*)

State/Regions	*Deposit Accounts per 1,000 Males*						*Deposit Accounts per 1,000 Females*					
	1996	*1997*	*1998*	*1999*	*2000*	*2001*	*1996*	*1997*	*1998*	*1999*	*2000*	*2001*
Western region	657.9	648.0	640.14	628.94	623.56	625.21	215.3	219.4	223.5	236.9	247.5	250.7
Goa	1926.1	1814.6	1739.71	1671.81	1774.72	2160.10	957.8	920.2	965.0	1011.7	953.6	1236.4
Gujarat	604.1	616.9	623.44	607.95	605.52	622.32	170.6	170.5	173.7	190.1	202.4	222.3
Maharashtra	666.2	645.2	629.70	622.23	613.25	606.03	226.2	233.0	236.7	247.9	258.5	250.8
Southern region	690.2	660.9	652.17	645.22	652.23	670.67	243.9	249.8	253.4	263.5	273.7	283.6
Andhra Pradesh	532.4	532.5	536.29	545.24	549.36	570.30	159.3	165.7	169.7	183.0	197.5	205.6
Karnataka	724.3	689.6	671.39	665.85	655.42	682.37	257.9	265.7	264.7	274.7	287.2	296.8
Kerala	885.0	854.2	862.37	856.89	844.20	842.99	367.4	381.0	389.3	402.4	406.8	410.5
Tamil Nadu	752.1	692.4	667.50	672.17	674.35	694.66	268.3	268.1	271.7	277.3	282.6	298.4
Pondicherry	888.4	842.3	843.93	807.84	784.03	906.09	262.5	294.0	309.6	286.5	330.4	400.3
All-India	598.3	591.8	584.01	580.81	569.71	574.96	191.8	195.1	199.2	205.0	212.8	215.6

Source: RBI, Basic Statistical Returns, 1996 to 2001.

TABLE 11

Growth Rates of SHGs and SHGs per 1,000 Females Across the States (1998-2001)

States	Growth of SHGs over the Years			Growth Rate	Growth of SHGs/1,000 Females over the Years			Growth Rate
	1998-99	*1999-00*	*2000-01*		*1998-99*	*1999-00*	*2000-01*	
Andaman and Nicobar	3	9	10	82.57	0.018	0.051	0.061	86.84
Andhra Pradesh	6579	29242	84939	259.31	0.179	0.786	2.258	255.39
Assam	10	46	156	294.97	0.001	0.004	0.012	288.79
Bihar	121	857	1846	290.59	0.003	0.018	0.046	324.17
Goa	4	14	27	159.81	0.005	0.018	0.041	180.97
Gujarat	879	1345	1375	25.07	0.038	0.057	0.059	24.70
Haryana	4	107	334	813.78	0.000	0.012	0.034	783.19
Himachal Pradesh	133	48	1166	196.09	0.041	0.014	0.390	210.24
Jammu and Kashmir	2	53	137	727.65	0.000	0.011	0.029	725.62
Karnataka	2002	3167	5627	67.65	0.079	0.124	0.217	65.51
Kerala	1291	1709	1826	18.93	0.079	0.104	0.112	18.59
Madhya Pradesh	461	1533	3174	162.39	0.012	0.040	0.110	200.29
Maharashtra	1058	3029	5509	128.19	0.024	0.069	0.119	121.14
Orissa	975	2021	3850	98.71	0.056	0.114	0.213	95.49
Pondicherry	15	144	150	216.23	0.028	0.257	0.308	233.26
Punjab	1	18	71	742.61	0.000	0.002	0.006	728.69
Rajasthan	465	526	2513	132.47	0.019	0.021	0.093	123.84
Tamil Nadu	2618	7671	16676	152.38	0.087	0.251	0.541	149.99
Uttar Pradesh	1464	7744	5457	93.07	0.019	0.097	0.069	92.59
West Bengal	554	2317	5351	210.79	0.015	0.061	0.138	205.40
All India	18639	61600	140194	173.97	0.039	0.128	0.283	167.91

Source: NABARD (2002).

We can easily observe the relationship between growth rate of SHGs and SHGs per 1,000 females across the states during the years 1998-99 to 2000-01. Table 11 clearly shows that though all listed states have a positive growth rate of SHGs, there is a wide variation among states. States such as Andaman and Nicobar, Gujarat, Karnataka, Kerala, Orissa and Uttar Pradesh have comparatively lower growth rates (below 100), whereas other states excel and have a SHG growth rate of above 100. However, it is not necessary that the states; that have a lower growth rate will have a lower number of SHGs. The states with lower growth rates might have begun their SHG-bank linkage programme at an earlier stage, so that it may already have sufficient linkages and further linking is quite difficult. Most of the states with lower growth rates will have a lower number of SHGs linked in the recent years compared to states that have a high growth rate. For example, we can observe from the Table 11 that, by the end of 2001, Kerala had 1,826 SHGs linked to banks but its growth rate was just 19. Goa has a comparatively lower number of SHGs linked to banks (27) in the same period, but its growth rate is as high as 160. Thus, one has to be careful in deriving inferences from this table. In the same table, the growth rate of SHGs per 1,000 females, a co-variate of growth rate of SHGs, is also given. We can observe a trend similar to that of the growth rate of SHGs level.

By linking SHGs with formal banks, both banks as well as SHGs will be benefited. The involvement of SHGs with banks could help in overcoming the problem of high transaction costs in providing credit to the poor by passing on some banking responsibilities regarding loan appraisal, follow-up, recovery, etc., to the poor themselves. In addition to that, the character of SHGs and the relationship between members offers a way to overcome the problem of collateral, excessive documentation, and physical access. By this, banks gain from the new risk-free credit market and a potential surplus sector (SHGs) and at the same time SHGs enjoy the advantage of larger and cheaper resources (Dasgupta, 2001). However, SHGs have to open a deposit account in the bank to get cheaper loans under the micro-credit programme.

NABARD (1999) advocated 'SHG-Bank Linkage' approach stresses the importance of links between commercial banks and NGOs as a mechanism for channelizing credit to the poor on a sustainable basis. In this model, rural women are expected to form groups and borrow from the banks as a group.

Agriculture

Women play an important role in agriculture but their position is pitiable in this sector. In view of the critical role of women in agriculture and allied sectors, as producers, concentrated efforts will be made to ensure the benefits of training, extension, and various programmes will reach them in proportion to their numbers. The programmes for training women in soil conservation, social forestry, dairy development and other occupations allied to agriculture like horticulture, livestock including small animal husbandry, poultry, fisheries, etc., will be expanded to benefit women workers in the agriculture sector.

Industry

The important role-played by women in the fields of electronics, technology, food processing, agro-industry, and textiles has been crucial to the development of these sectors. During the Tenth Plan, to increase the share of women in factories and industrial establishments, efforts will be made to remove the existing traditional bias that women are good only in stereo-type/ feminine jobs and encourage women to equip themselves with necessary professional/vocational skills and compete with men to make an entry into newer areas. Therefore, the Tenth Plan will consider initiating measures to facilitate women to work in the night shift in factories, if they so desire, as advocated by the National Policy for Empowerment of Women.

Employment and Income Generation

Employment and income generation for empowering women have become a matter of great concern for the Indian government. In this context, the on-going training-*cum*-employment-*cum*-income-generation programmes viz., SGSY, SJSRY, PMRY, STEP, NORAD, etc. will be further expanded to create more and more of employment-*cum*-income-generation opportunities and to cover as many women as possible living below the poverty line. In these efforts, priority will be given to female-headed households and women living in extreme/abject poverty. The programme of Swayamsidha will be further expanded to 2,000 additional blocks during the Tenth Plan. The micro-credit programme of RMK will be closely tied up with SHGs formed under Swayamsidha for financing various employment-*cum*-income-generation activities. Thus, Swayamsidha is going to emerge as a nation-wide integrated programme in order to provide a strong base for empowering women, both socially and economically, during the Tenth Plan and beyond.

Small-Scale Industry

The government has considered small-scale industries as a tool for empowering the women. The Tenth Plan will make special efforts to identify the traditional sectors that are shrinking due to advancement of technology, market shifts, and changes in the economic policies, and introduce necessary training programmes to re-train/upgrade the skills of the displaced women to take up jobs in the new and emerging areas of employment. Also, formulation of appropriate policies and programmes will be attempted to generate opportunities for wage/self-employment in traditional sectors like khadi and village industries, handicrafts, handlooms, sericulture, small scale and cottage industries. While attempting to bring forth the necessary structural adjustments in these sectors, women will receive priority attention.

Informal Sector

This sector provides employment to 92 per cent of informal labour in our country and women occupy a major share in the informal labour. In this regard, the government is making its best efforts to ensure both minimum and equal wages for women on par with men. The Tenth Plan will also endeavour to extend the important labour legislations to the informal sector, especially those legislations where the employers have a mandatory binding for providing basic minimum working conditions along with necessary welfare services for women workers. While formulating necessary policies and programmes for the betterment of women in the informal sector, the findings/results of the Fourth Economic Census (2001), as well as the un-attended recommendations of the National Commission on Self-Employed

Women in the informal sector (Shram Shakti), will be taken into consideration.

Opportunity in Services

Under the Tenth Plan the need to initiate affirmative action has been recognised is order to ensure at least 30 per cent reservation for women in services in the public sector as against the existing representation of 14.5 per cent in 1999. Therefore, several efforts like coaching and encouraging women to compete with men in competitive examinations are being made by the government during recent times. The government is also considering the proposal to provide support services for working women to ensure mobility in the employment market. Also efforts will be made to introduce special concessions and relaxations like multiple entries, increase in the upper age limit, hostel for working women and day care centres at working places as well as homes for the aged and disabled so that women can become independent and empowered.

EMPOWERMENT THROUGH IT AND ICT

Information technology has played a vital role in empowering the women in recent times. Although the impact of IT on the society has not been uniformly beneficial and the technology divide is being increasingly felt particularly in the developing countries like India. The IT revolution itself presents many avenues in a variety of fields for women to enter the workforce and thereby become empowered. Hence, IT strategies must be designed to enhance the capacity of women and empower them to meet the negative social and economic impacts, which may flow from the globalisation process.

The present experience of IT revolution shows that one of the most powerful applications of IT is in electronic commerce. This e-commerce, in the context of women's empowerment, refers not just to selling of products and services on line, but also aims at promotion of a new class of IT savvy women entrepreneurs. IT is capable of influencing the entrepreneurial behaviour of women by improving their innovativeness, decision-making ability and access to various services. There are significant opportunities for women in software. Network administration, education, and training, etc. are the important sectors of IT where women can be benefited enormously.

The given Table 12 presents the share of different sectors here women may be empowered through IT. Since, IT is penetrating every sector of the Indian economy, the relative position of sectors is likely to undergo a change during the next decade as well. Table 12 shows the market constitution of IT where we observe that share of IT in telecom, banking and finance, manufacturing and education has increased in 2002-03 in comparison to 1999-2000. In these sectors women can be benefited enormously and working nature of IT is also women friendly.

TABLE 12

Domestic IT Market Constitution (2002-03) (Percentage Share).

Sector	*1999-2000*	*2002-03*
IT/Telecom	10	22
Banking and Finance	18	21
Manufacturing	12	15
Government	34	14
Education	3	11
Small Office/Home	11	11
Energy, Transport	12	6
Total	100	100

Source: NASSCOM.

INFORMATION COMMUNICATION TECHNOLOGY AND WOMEN EMPOWERMENT

In India, the recent proliferation of Information Communication Technology (ICT) based service is perceived to have offered more employment opportunities for women. Call centres occupy prominent pace in ICT trade. A call centre acts as a focal point for web-based customer transactions, e-mail management and traditional phone calls. These jobs are considered to be more women friendly due to several counts including easy access and greater flexibility in work organisation perceived scope to combine family with career and apparent advantages in terms of equality and empowerment. As this job does not involve any physical exertion so it is considered conductive for women.

The jobs in Business Process Outsourcing (BPO) firms such as call centres were considered less demanding in terms of manual efforts and are found to be more appropriate for women. In developing countries, such new business is considered a good source of employment and looked at in terms of how well paid it is. India has been selected as a base for call centres because it lies in a time zone that makes it the preferred area for the UK, US, South East Asia, and Australia.

Call centres are concerned with e-business, which is expected to grow further and bring in more employment. The advantage of the time factor has provided employment to women but is also the source of most of women's family problems. Since call centre jobs have night duties and long-hours of work. Hence, it is expected that such employment would have an effect on her physical and mental health as well. But there is a greater acceptance of such non-traditional job by families across a larger segment of society.

It is important to know here the volumes and conditions of call centre jobs. Hence we are referring here to a survey of 100 women conducted by an agency at Delhi, Gurgaon, and Noida which is being reflected in Table 13.

Table 13 shows that 92 per cent women fall in the age group of 18-30 years while 92 per cent of the respondents are unmarried. This clearly shows that most working women prefer to remain unmarried for a longer period as they want to be economically sound and independent before their marriage. This table shows that 60 per cent of women in call centres are graduates while 79 per cent women are working as customer care executives and 10 per cent are senior executives. Table 13 also explains that 73 per cent women have a salary of less than Rs. 10 thousand per month. While 16 per cent women earn 10,000-15,000 and 7 per cent women earn 15,000-20,000, whereas only 4 per cent earn more than 20,000 per month. It is note worthy here that, out of 100 girls 87 girls belong to nuclear family while 65 of them are from service class family. Hence, we find that in call centres women have enough opportunities for employment.

TABLE 13

Women Working in Call Centres

		No. of Women
Age Group	Below 20 years	14
	21-25	67
	26-30	15
	31-35	Nil
	36-40	Nil
	41-45	3
	Above 45	1
	Total	100
Marital Status	Married	8
	Unmarried	92
	Total	100
Level of Education	School pass	22
	Bachelors degree	60
	Masters degree	18
	Total	100
Job Level	Customer care executives	79
	Senior executives	10
	Team leader	8
	Assistant manager	1
	Manager	2
	Total	100
Salary (Rs.)	Below 10,000	73
	10,000-15,000	16
	15,000-20,000	7
	Above 20,000	4
	Total	100
Family Status	Joint Family	13
	Nuclear family	87
	Total	100
Family Background	Business	30
	Services	65
	Professional	5
	Total	100

Source: EPW, February 12, 2005, pp. 685-86.

(c) Political Empowerment

Political empowerment provides ample opportunity to enjoy administrative power and this is the best way by which women can participate in the decision-making process of the nation. The greatest advantage of women's political participation in national life is that it brought them to the forefront. As women become more and more conscious about their identity, their very 'self' will persuade them to show their mettle in a male-dominated society. Although women have showed better efficiency and capability in Indian politics before and after independence but the paradoxical habits and nature of male dominated society have crushed the rights and efficiency of Indian women which resulted in the exploitation of women in various ways; economic, social, political, sexual and gender-based.

It is well known fact, that the main political parties of India don't regard women candidates as being much capable and efficient winning candidates as the male candidates. In India, women are considered to be good voters but not good "vote looters". Naturally, most women are becoming alienated from politics. That is why, realizing the reality of the fact, the policy makers and social scientists in India and abroad stressed women empowerment. In this regard, we cannot forget the efforts made by our former Prime Minister Rajiv Gandhi who dreamt of decentralised governance in rural India.

In India during reform era the 73rd and 74th amendments to the constitution have, no doubt, brought a million women into the public field for the first time. Ever since the enactment of the 73rd and 74th amendment in the constitution of India, empowerment of women at the grass-roots level has become a popular concept, which is used by many with varied meanings and explanations. (Batliwla, 1996, Batliwala *et.al.* 1998, Sharma, 1992). One third of the seats at the three levels of grass roots institutions of PRIs have been reserved for women of all categories.

But when we talk of overall participation of women in total political field, we observe a very dismal scenario on an all India basis. This scenario is evident from the women's representation in parliament after independence and even during globalisation era.

It is apparent from Table 14 and Chart 1, that representation of women in the Lok Sabha has not crossed 10 per cent. In the First Lok Sabha there were only 22 women constituting 4.4 percent of the House. It increased marginally over the years except in the Sixth Lok Sabha when the House had only 19

TABLE 14

Number of Women Elected to Lok Sabha

General Elections	*No. of Women Elected*	*Percentage*
First	22	4.4
Second	27	5.4
Third	34	6.7
Fourth	31	5.9
Fifth	22	4.2
Sixth	19	3.4
Seventh	28	5.1
Eighth	44	8.1
Ninth	28	5.29
Tenth	39	7.02
Eleventh	40	7.36
Twelfth	44	8.07
Thirteenth	49	9.02
Fourteenth	45	8.25

Source: Who's Who in Rajya Sabha.

Chart 1: Percentage of Women Elected to Lok Sabha

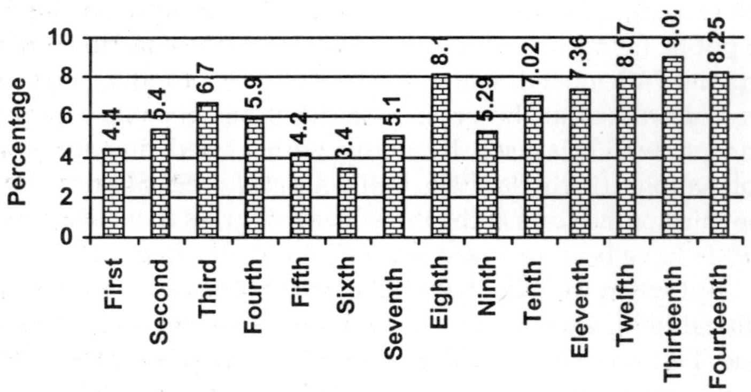

women members. In the 13th Lok Sabha there were 49 women members. However, in the 14th Lok Sabha, again the strength of women members has come down to 45. Similarly in the case of Rajya Sabha the percentage of women members has never crossed 12 per cent.

Table 15 gives quite a clear picture of women's participation in politics and regard given by national parties to them. In the Sixth General Elections, out of the total contestants of 2439, only 70 candidates were women, and in the Fourteenth General Elections, out of the total number of contestants, i.e., 59435 only 355 were women. Though the number of women participating in the elections is increasing gradually, the number of winning candidates are not increasing significantly. So far as the ticket distribution by the political parties is concerned, it is a harsh reality that these parties also abstain from giving their tickets to women candidates which is clear from Table 15. These national parties considered women candidates as "lost case." Hence, it is necessary to change the mindset of political parties towards women. These facts inevitably lead us to conclude, that there is need for positive action in favour of women.

TABLE 15

Gender-wise Break-up of Contestants to Lok Sabha in General Elections (Sixth to Fourteenth)

General Elections	*Total Contestants*	*Men Contestants*	*Women Contestants*	*Women from National Party*
Sixth	2439	2369	70	41
Seventh	4629	4486	143	77
Eighth	5492	5330	162	63
Ninth	6160	5962	198	87
Tenth	4831	4517	314	n.a.
Eleventh	13952	13353	599	125
Twelfth	4750	4476	274	107
Thirteenth	4648	4364	284	104
Fourteenth	5435	5081	355	110

Source: Election Commission of India.

Similar is the case of Bihar State Assembly where only 185 women could win the Assembly elections from 1952 to 2001. The regard and response given by different political parties is also clear from the Table 16.

TABLE 16

Women's Representation in Bihar State Assembly

Years	*Total Seat*	*Women*	*Congress*	*BJP*	*Janata*	*Left Party*	*RJD*	*Others*
1952	330	13	12	–	–	–	–	1
1957	319	34	31	–	2	–	–	1
1962	319	25	24	–	–	–	–	1
1967	319	10	8	–	–	–	–	2
1969	319	04	1	–	1	1	–	1
1972	319	13	10	–	–	3	–	–
1977	325	13	2	–	10	–	–	1
1980	325	14	11	–	1	–	–	2
1985	325	15	13	–	–	1	–	1
1990	325	13	7	–	4	1	–	1
1995	325	12	1	2	5	1	–	3
2001	243	15	–	3	–	–	6	6

Source: Bihar Insight/3/2005 and *Prabhat Khabar,* 31.12.2004.

The National Policy for the Empowerment of Women, 2001 has rightly admitted that exists a wide gap between the goals enunciated in the constitution, legislation, policies, plans, programmes, and related mechanisms on the one hand and the situational reality of the status of women in India, on the other hand. Noting that "... the empowerment of women has been recognised as a central issue in determining the status of women," the policy, sets among others, the objectives of promoting their advancement, development and empowerment and underlines the *de-jure* and *de-facto* enjoyment of all human rights and fundamental freedom by women on an equal basis with men in all spheres and their equal access to participation and decision-making in social, political and economic life of the nation. The need for strengthening legal systems aimed at elimination of all forms of discrimination against women has been emphasised. Thus, a broad framework and a perspective for empowerment of women exists only at the policy level in India. However, the need of the hour is to translate these ideas into actual numbers in legislative bodies and other representative institutions.

INITIATIVE TAKEN BY THE GOVERNMENT

The Government has taken several steps to empower the women. The government has set-up a National Commission for Women (NCW), a statutory body in 1992 to safeguard the rights and interests of women. The NCW, since its inception has investigated into a total number of 24,025 complaints wherein dowry deaths and dowry harassment cases accounted for the maximum number. The NCW has worked out on the Bill to ensure 33 per cent of reservations to women in Lok Sabha and Legislative Assemblies in future Elections in future. For this purpose the 81st amendment was introduced in the Lok Sabha on September 13, 1996 during the regime of H.D. Deve Gowda government but it could not be passed due to certain reasons. And recently it was introduced in the Lok Sabha but it could not take the shape of law on the basis of objections raised by some political parties like the RJD, Samajwadi Party, and other the likeminded parties. These parties demanded reservation for SC, ST, and OBC women within 30 per cent of total quota for women. Hence, it is still pending and under consideration before the parliament. Further, several important steps were taken by the Indian government during Ninth and Tenth Plan.

INITIATIVE UNDER NINTH PLAN

1. Adoption of Women's Component Plan (WCP) to ensure that benefits from other developmental sectors do not by-pass women and not less than 30 per cent of funds/benefits flow to them from all the women-related sectors. Review of the progress of WCP during the Ninth Plan reveals that funds flowing from one of the women-related departments (viz. Family Welfare) was as high as 70 per cent of its Gross Budgetary Support of the Ninth Plan (1997);
2. Launching of 'Swa-Sakti' to create an enabling environment for empowerment of women through setting up of self-reliant Self-Help Groups (SHGs) and developing linkages with lending institutions to ensure women's access to credit facilities for income-generation activities (1998);

3. 'Stree Shakti Puraskars' instituted for the first time in the history of women's development to honour 5 distinguished women annually for their outstanding contribution to the upliftment and empowerment of women (1999);
4. Setting up of a Task Force on Women under the Chairpersonship of Shri K.C. Pant, Deputy Chairman, Planning Commission to review the existing women-specific and women-related legislations and suggest enactment of new legislations or amendments, wherever necessary. The Task Force also suggested a thematic programme for celebrating the year '2001 as Women's Empowerment Year', besides reviewing 22 existing legislations (2000);
5. Introduction of Gender Budgeting to attain more effective targeting of public expenditure and to offset any undersirable gender-specific consequences of previous budgetary measures (2000-01);
6. Adoption of a National Policy for Empowerment of Women to eliminate all types of discrimination against women and to ensure gender justice, besides empowering women both socially and economically (2001);
7. Celebration of the Year 2001 as 'Women's Empowerment Year' to create awareness generation, remove negative thinking, besides building up confidence in women through the processes of concretization so that they can take their rightful place in the mainstream of the nation's social, political and economic life (2001);
8. Recasting of Indira Mahila Yojana as 'Swayamsidha',— an integrated programme for empowerment of women through a major strategy of covering the services available in all the women-related programmes besides organising women into SHGs for undertaking various entrepreneurial ventures (2001);
9. Launching of 'Swadhar' to extend rehabilitation services for 'Women in Difficult Circumstances' (2001);
10. Introduction of a Bill on Domestic Violence against

Women (Prevention) to eliminate all forms of domestic violence against women and the girl child (2002).

COMMITMENTS OF GOVERNMENTS UNDER TENTH PLAN

The following commitments have been made by the government to empower the women.

To adopt a sector specific Three-Fold Strategy for empowering women, based on the prescription of the National Policy for Empowerment of Women. They include the following:

1. Social Empowerment—to create an enabling environment through various affirmative development policies and programmes for development of women besides providing them easy and equal access to all the basic minimum services so as to enable them to realize.
2. Economic Empowerment—to ensure provision of training, employment and income-generation activities with both 'forward' and 'backward' linkages with the ultimate objective of making all potential women economically independent and self-reliant.
3. Gender Justice—to eliminate all forms of gender discrimination and thus, allow women to enjoy not only the *de-jure* but also the *de-facto* rights and fundamental freedoms on par with men in all spheres, viz., political, economic, social, civil, cultural, etc.

SUGGESTIONS FOR EMPOWERMENT

We can make women self-sustainable by ensuring opportunities for their education, employment, and economic independence in the following ways:

1. Strict Implementation of Law—All the policies and programmes that are meant for women must be implemented strictly. The areas may include health, education, legal aid, widows, nutrition, maternal health etc.
2. Free Education for Girl—The education of girls in the

rural sector is not possible as there is no education facility of secondary schools near the village. In such situation, the government should provide free transport to the girls for their study and should also open separate schools for girls.

3. Removal of Dowry System—Dowry is again a crime in the Indian society. Many parents consider girls as a curse of the God because they would have to generate huge dowry for their marriage. The girls are even killed during the pregnancy with sex determination female foeticide in the name of MTP. The statutes against the dowry related are not enough. The Dowry Act should be implemented which makes giving and taking dowry illegal.
4. Job Oriented Training—The girl's education should be job oriented and give priority to vocational training so that they are financially independent and may take care of them.
5. Health Care—The mental health of the women needs to be undertaken in all the sectors of the society. Depression amongst women is due to exogenous and indigenous factors. Exogenous factors arrive from the society in the form of want of son, dowry, loneliness, molestation, etc. Indigenous factors like depression could be caused through chemicals, unsafe abortion, taking unwanted medicines, sleeping pills, alcohol, tobacco, etc. The mental trauma disturbs a woman to live separately from her husband, leading to divorce, suicidal tendencies and sometimes even cause death. Counseling of women on their family and marital matters could be very useful.
6. Economic Independence—Economic dependency makes women weaker and helpless and they are compelled to depend on their husband, family, and parents. So, women should be maid financially independent by providing them jobs.
7. Provision of Social Security—The women now-a-days have to go for jobs to distant paces for which they have to use public transport. Sometimes women have to work upto late hours and they reach their homes late

in the night. The crime against women in the shape of molestation, rape, etc. has increased manifold. So there should be social security for women so that such incidents could be prevented.

8. Active Participation in Politics—The women should be encouraged to take active part in politics and the government should pass the Bill for women's reservation in politics soon as possible because the upper middle class women do not like to participate in the field of politics. The lower middle class women as well as women from SC, ST and OBC groups are too much occupied with their household works and they consider household works as their prime duty. Not only that the women from these vulnerable groups are not allowed to participate in the active politics by the male members even in age of economic reforms. So, the need is to motivate them towards politics.

CONCLUSION

In India, the empirical reality as well as the picture reflected in this paper regarding women tells a quite different story that women's conditions and human rights situation remains gloomy and still very marginal still, in our society. Men are in a very strong position and dominant, which women are in a powerless and subordinate position. Their subordinate position is manifested in male violence against women, sexual exploitation, and humiliation that erodes all human dignity and a very acute experience of vulnerability (Sarma, 1999:87). So, the women are still far lagging behind the men in all fronts. Be it politics, education, administration, civil services, or trade, women are extremely under-represented.

Women's empowerment and their due status in the society is a responsibility that should be shared by all of us. The women have been provided equal rights as men on the paper everywhere in the society, but somehow there are social dilemmas that have sent them aback. For real empowerment, what is necessary is that our policy-makers should guard against any further alienation and marginalisation of women in the course of socio-economic and political development in the country. Besides, there should be specific programmes and measures to improve the condition of women in respect of issues where women are lagging behind the men and have been deprived of basic human rights. Among these issues are education, employment, equal wage rate, medical care, food and nutrition, political participation, economic independence and the programmes relating to the enhancement of gender sensitiveness. With regard to the violence and crimes committed against women, stringent panel provisions and honest application of such laws seem to be the real remedy.

If we want to empower the women of our country to play an effective role in shaping and modeling India's society and destiny, we must ensure that their human rights are properly honoured, protected, and that they should not be treated as inferior or subordinate human beings and as second category sex. Their contribution to family and to the society is appreciated not just by paying lip service to their goodness, but respecting their human rights. To halt the process of declining sex ratio resulting in the phenomenon of missing girls we have to change the mindset of doctors and members of our society. To stop general discrimination we have to convince doctors, clients, state and civil societies that "daughters are not to be slaughtered". Hence, we should make every effort to empower women in all the fronts so that a stronger society could be built.

Finally, we can say that economic reforms could not impact women empowerment in positive direction and women of our society failed to exploit the benefits of economic reform, as they should have had.

References

Bajpai, U.N. (2005), "Women Status in the Indian Society," Published in *Health for Million*, April-June Vol. 31, No. 1.

Bihar Insight, 3/2005.

Bishnyi Deepak (2005), IT New Mantra for Women's Empowerment Published in *Social Welfare*, Vol. 52, No. 5, August.

Das, Jogendra Kr. (2003), "Reflection on Human Rights and the Position of Indian Women," Published in the *Indian Journal of Political Science*, Vol. 46, Nos. 3-4, July-December.

—— (2005), Different Issues of *Economic Times*, June-July.

Mahendra Verman, P. (2005), "Impact of Self-Help Groups on formal Banking Habits," Published in *Economic and Political Weekly*, April 23.

Mathur, Ritu (2005), Skewed Sex Ratio in India. The Beginning of A Nightmare, Published in *Health for Million*, Vol. 31, No. 1, April-June.

Narain, Yogendra, S.N. Sahu and L. Lakshmi, (2005), "Political Empowerment of Women," Published in the *Indian Journal of Public Administration*, Vol. LI, No. 1, January-March.

Narasairah M. Lakshmi, "Mainstreaming Women for Political Progress" (2005), Published in *Social Welfare*, Vol. 52, No. 5, August.

Pattnaik, Dr. Satyanarayana and Trupty Mayee Pradhan, (2005), "Empowering Women by Ending Gender Violence, Published in *Social Welfare*, Vol. 52, No. 5, August.

Report of Tenth Five-Year Plan, Vol. II, Planning Commission of India.

Sahay, Sushma, "Framework for Measurement of Women's Empowerment: Difficulties and Challenges", Published in *Indian Journal of Social Development*, Serials Publication, N. Delhi.

Sharma, Dr. B.R. and Dr. Manish Gupta, 2005, "Violation of Women Human Rights" Published in *Social Welfare*, Vol. 52, No. 5, August.

Singh, Preeti, Anu Pandey, (2005), "Women in Call Centres," Published in *Economic and Political Weekly*, Feb. 12.

Sinha, Niroj, Women in Indian Politics; Empowerment of Women Through Political Participator, Gyan Publishing House, N. Delhi.

Usha, K.B. (2005), "Political Empowerment of Women in Soviet Union and Russia: Ideology and Implementation Published in *International Studies*, Vol. 42, No. 2, April-June, *Journal of the School of International Studies*, JNU, New Delhi.

9

Empowerment of Women in Bihar

RAM NARESH THAKUR

The paper is an attempt to analyse various aspects of demography of Bihar which is counted as one of the most backward states with least literacy level. Datas collected in various Censuses tell the gloomy story of the state. The literacy rate is low and lower in case of females. It has direct bearing on the fertility rate, population growth, orthodoxy, and other related issues. These are the major hurdles in achieving the goal of "Women's Empowerment". The analysis of district wise figures of different parameters say only the plight of women in Bihar. The paper is an eye-opener and it is high time, all concerted efforts should be made to improve the status of women. The sooner it is done the better for the state in general and for the overall "empowerment of women" in particular.

Economic Reform and New Economic Policy enunciated by the policy of globalization has affected the economy in independence different ways. The year 1991 is a landmark in the post-planned economic development in India. It brought several changes in different sectors and sections of the economy in general, and also to the downtrodden and weaker sections viz. women in particular. Bihar is itself a very backward state in many respects including; education, literacy, enrolment, health facilities, and increased school drop-out rate in general, but to the women in particular. Economic Reform has brought the women on to the lowest ladder of development, especially in education and employment, in searching ways and sources of income. The education guarantee has lapsed along with the guarantee and opportunity of income and employment for women in Bihar. The economic reform has reduced the opportunity of jobs and employment for the women. Women had to choose part time, muster roll jobs in place of full-fledged, full time, regular and full salary jobs. Their social status has been reducing due to different reasons.

In 1985 there came 'The international women's conference' at Nairobi which opened the eyes of the women to conceive the concept, 'empowerment of women' as a re-distribution of social power and control of resources in favour of under privileged (including 'women'). The 'programme of action 1992' has broadly conferred the following measurements of empowerment for them. They are:

(a) To enhance self-esteem and self-confidence in women;
(b) To develop in them an ability to think critically;
(c) To foster decision-making and action through collective process;
(d) To ensure equal participation in the developmental process;
(e) To provide information, knowledge and skill for economic independence; and
(f) To enhance access to legal literacy and information to their right and entitlement in the society with a view to increase their participation on equal footings in all areas.

These parameters of empowerment are multi-faceted and multi-dimensional for the real upliftment of the down-trodden and weaker sections of the society, particularly women.

TABLE 1

Features of Population of Bihar, 2001 Census (Provisional)

1.	Total Population	8,28,78,796
	(a) Rural.	7,41,99,596
	(b) Urban	86,79,200
	(c) Male	4,31,53,964
	(d) Female	3,97,22,832
2.	Annual Exponential Growth Rate	2.53 %
3.	Density of Population	880/sq km
4.	Literacy Rate Total	47.53 %
	(a) Male	60.32 %
	(b) Female	33.57 %
5.	Sex Ratio	921/1000 Male
6.	Percentage of Urban Population	10.47%
7.	Percentage of Rural Population	89.53 %

Sources (a) *Economic Survey*, 2001-02, Govt. of India; (b) *Census of India*, 2001, Provisional Population Totals.

There are many aspects of women's empowerment viz. economic, social, political, academic, and psychological, etc. Here we see the case of women's population in respect of men, its increase or decrease, sex ratio, the trend of changing this ratio and literacy of women of Bihar during the reform period. For this I have compared the census figures of 1991 and that of 2001 for comparing the status and empowerment of women.

Population

The population of Bihar according to 2001 Census was 8,28,78,796 consisting of male population 4,31,53,964 and female population 3,97,22,832. Thus, male-female ratio(sex ratio) is 921 as, against 933 at all India level. Whereas this ratio was 907 in 1991 Census against 927 at all India level. One has to consider the fact the female population decreased not only an all India level but also at the state level (Bihar), but it is alarming that it is decreasing in almost all the districts of Bihar. There is not a single district in Bihar where female population increased during the two Census periods, i.e., between 1991 and 2001 Census and also during the period of economic reform i.e., between 1991-2001 (a decade). It is due to the various factors going adversely against the women in Bihar, viz.:

TABLE 2

District-wise Population Growth in State of Bihar

District	*Population 2001*			*Decadal Growth Rate*		*Percentage Share of District*		
	Total	*Males*	*Females*	*1981-91*	*1991-01*	*Total*	*Males*	*Females*
1	2	3	4	5	6	7	8	9
Bihar	82,878,796	43,153,964	39,724,832	23.38	28.43	100.00	100.00	100.00
W. Champaran	3,043,044	1,600,853	1,442,191	18.30	30.40	3.67	3.71	3.63
E. Champaran	3,933,636	2,072,350	1,861,282	25.46	29.27	4.75	4.80	4.69
Sheohar	514,288	271,261	243,027	27.34	36.16	0.62	0.63	0.61
Sitamarhi	2,669,887	1,410,149	1,259,738	23.13	32.58	3.22	3.27	3.17
Madhubani	3,570,651	1,837,361	1,733,290	21.73	26.08	4.31	4.26	4.36
Supaul	1,745,069	908,855	836,254	23.45	29.95	2.11	2.11	2.11
Araria	2,124,831	1,108,924	1,015,960	26.69	31.50	1.56	1.55	1.58
Kishanganj	1,294,063	666,910	627,153	22.20	31.50	1.56	1.55	1.58
Purnia	2,540,788	1,325,794	1,214,993	23.76	35.23	3.07	3.07	3.06
Katihar	2,389,533	1,244,943	1,144,590	27.77	30.91	2.88	2.88	2.88
Madhepura	1,524,596	796,372	728,324	22.16	29.45	1.84	1.85	1.83
Saharsa	1,506,418	788,585	717,833	25.54	22.03	1.82	1.83	1.81
Darbhanga	3,285,473	1,716,640	1,568,833	25.04	30.85	3.96	3.98	3.95
Muzaffarpur	3,743,836	1,941,840	1,802,356	25.30	26.74	4.52	4.50	4.54
Gopal Ganj	2,149,343	1,072,151	1,077,192	25.12	26.11	2.59	2.48	2.71
Siwan	2,708,840	1,332,218	1,376,622	22.04	24.78	3.27	3.09	3.47
Saran	3,251,474	1,654,428	1,597,046	23.44	26.37	3.92	3.83	4.02

(*Contd.*)

TABLE 2 (*Contd.*)

District-wise Population Growth in State of Bihar

1	*2*	*3*	*4*	*5*	*6*	*7*	*8*	*9*
Vaishali	2,712,389	1,412,276	1,300,113	29.08	26.39	3.27	3.27	3.27
Samastipur	3,413,413	1,771,249	1,442,164	28.35	25.63	4.12	4.10	4.13
Begusarai	2,342,989	1,226,057	1,116,932	24.61	29.11	2.83	2.84	2.81
Khagaria	1,27,677	675,501	601,176	28.44	29.32	1.54	1.57	1.51
Bhagalpur	2,430,331	1,294,192	1,136,139	20.67	27.24	2.93	3.00	2.86
Banka	1,608,778	843,061	765,717	24.44	24.47	1.94	1.95	1.93
Munger	1,135,49	604,662	530,837	17.79	20.34	1.37	1.40	1.34
Lakhisarai	801,173	416,727	384,446	21.08	23.94	0.97	0.97	0.97
Sheikhpura	525,137	273,468	251,669	19.84	24.96	0.63	0.63	0.63
Nalanda	2,368,327	1,336,467	1,131,860	21.73	18.64	2.86	2.87	2.85
Patna	4,709,851	2,514,949	2,194,902	19.84	30.17	5.68	5.83	5.53
Bhojpur	2,233,415	1,175,335	1,058,082	20.86	24.58	2.69	2.72	2.66
Buxar	1,403,462	738,239	665,223	18.63	29.03	1.69	1.71	1.67
Kamur (Bhabhua)	1,284,575	673,556	611,019	24.20	30.64	1.55	1.56	1.54
Rohtas	2,448,462	1,382,655	1,166,107	21.77	27.71	2.95	2.97	2.94
Jahanabad	1,511,406	783,960	727,446	19.43	28.64	1.82	1.82	1.83
Aurangabad	1,004,960	1,035,757	969,203	24.49	30.19	2.42	2.40	2.44
Gaya	3,464,425	928,638	880,787	23.70	33.08	2.18	2.15	2.22
Nawada	1,809,425	928,638	880,787	23.70	33.08	2.18	2.15	2.22
Jamui	1,397,474	728,812	668,662	21.90	32.90	1.69	1.69	1.68

Source: Same as Table 1

(a) Teasing and harassment of women is increasing.

(b) Women are paid very low wages compared to men.

(c) Women and girl labourers are forced to work as labourers.

(d) The poor girls and children are burning into beggars or pick-pockets or child labourers.

(e) Land disputes involving women are decided against item by the affluent society which marginalish them.

(f) Reservations for women in jobs is marginal or nil. Reservations for the women in Assembly and Parliament is in doldrums. But at lower level, at the panchayati Raj level where reservation had been implemented, they are doing well and are given recognition in the society.

(g) Women are generally neglected in different kinds of appointments and promotions to various jobs. Bureaucrats and policy-makers are reluctant help them.

(h) Women deserve the same respect and honour like men in the society, but they do not receive the same. It has became worse particularly in the reform period.

(i) In the family and social life humiliation and reluctance in almost all affairs plague the women. Thus, women have to face negligence every where, particularly during the market economy and consumer culture of the reform period.

(j) Female foetus murder is rampant practice spreading rapidly in Bihar. It is clear that reduction in the population of women will be soon evident.

(k) Due to the lowest female literacy rate in Bihar, the women are conservative, orthodox and traditional. They are pressurised by their family members and join with them in female, foetus murder, in burning and killing of women due to dowry or for other reasons.

(l) Health facilities and medical treatment for women is very poor. Prenatal and postnatal deaths occur everyday. Per capita health expenditure is very low and particularly for women. Deaths during be maternity period are not reported. Women's health and treatment are neglected by the government as well as by society.

In the reform period due to reduction in incomes and expensive sector, women have suffered much.

TABLE 3

Age-wise Distribution of Female Population in Bihar

Age Group		*Population of Females (Bihar)*
0-9		12,03,034
10-14		47,86,831
15-19		32,88,984
0-24		34,32,965
25-29		32,19,063
30-34		30,01,538
35-39		25,15,689
40-44		20,84,847
15-44		1,75,43,076
45-49		16,74,837
50-80		57,36,596
All age		4,11,72,374
Sex-Ratio		
Census	*Bihar*	*All India*
1991	907	927
2001	921	933

Source: Same as Table 1.

(m) The number of prostitutes or sex-workers is increasing by leaps and bounds in Bihar.

(n) In the constitution, women had been kept on an equal footing with men. There should be no difference or inequality on the basis of sex (along with other things also like religion, creed, caste, language, place, colour etc.). Equality will be maintained between men and women without any consideration of sex along with all other requisites. The Indian Constitution has granted women the same democratic rights viz. some to vote, to be elected, to get a job, etc. But there had been reluctancy in implementing the policies and therefore women had been kept in the margin or they lead their lives in isolation and thus every where women are left behind.

Thus it is seen that women are going behind the scenario. The state shows a rising masculinity with the proportion of women in the total population gradually falling. This is very shocking and alarming for the process of economic development.

Age-wise Distribution of Female Population in Bihar

When the age wise distribution of female population in Bihar is analysed, it is found that the number of population under age (0-14) is 59,89,865 i.e., (Adolescent Population). The teenagers (15-19) are 32,88,984 (under teen). The number of 'Active working age group' population (15-44) is 1,75,43,076. The number of age group 49-49 is 16,74,837 and 50-80 is 57,36,596.

Thus it is seen that like male population in female population also there are large levels of dependence. Thus the dependency ratio in the economy has been very high due to:

(a) Persistency of high fertility, and
(b) Declining mortality rate.

From beginning till 1941, the state had more females than males (except 1931-sex ratio 995). In 1951 the sex ratio became equal (1000). Then the sex ratio declined sharply in this state (Table 4). Declining trends maintained till 1991 (except 1961-sex ratio 1005).

TABLE 4

Sex Ratio in Bihar and India: 1901-2001

Census Year	*Sex-ratio in Bihar*	*Sex-ratio in India*
1901	1061	972
1911	1051	964
1921	1020	955
1931	995	950
1941	1002	945
1951	1000	946
1961	1005	941
1971	957	930
1981	948	934
1991	907	927
2001	921	933

Source: *Economic Survey*, 2001-02, Govt. of India, *Census of India*, 2001, Series II, Bihar Provisional Population Total, Delhi.

As per the current Census (2001), the sex ratio increased. In 1991, it was 907 females per thousand males. This increasing trend means this ratio depends on migration. Due to migration so many Bihar people (generally workers and labourers) migrated from state and reached Delhi, Punjab, Kolkata, Gujarat etc. for their livelihood.

At the district level sex ratio in Bihar as per the 2001 Census, only two districts of the state, Gopalgunj and Siwan have more females than males. It is 1005 and 1033 females per 1000 males respectively. In 1991 Census only Siwan district had recorded more male-female ratio, i.e., 1017. both these districts are border districts. The trend of large scale male has been witnessed migration in different parts of the country. Further, there are seven other districts—Patna, Bhgagalpur, Munger. Khagaria, Sitamarhi, Sheohar, and East Champaran where the sex ratio remained less than 900. Among them Patna district had the lowest sex ratio of 873. The Reason behind it is that the Patna is capital city and so it is attracting the male people from different parts of the state. Bhojpur is only district in Bihar where sex ratio decreased during 1991-2001, it was 904 in 1991 and later came to 900 in 2001.Vaishali is also a strange case where sex ratio remained unchanged in Census 1991-2001; it was 921. All these symptoms show the fall in women's empowerment in Bihar.

First of all Census 1991 contributed the concept of 'Child Sex Ratio' and tabulated it separately for the age-group 0-6 years. In 1991 child sex ratio of India was 945 female children per thousand male children. In 2001 child sex ratio has declined from 945 to 927 in 1991. The child sex ratio in Bihar declined from 953 female children per thousand male children in 1991, to 938 female children in 2001. The district wise variation has been negligible from 974 in Nawada to 885 in Darbhanga district. Though it is hoped that the figure of 'child sex ratio' (Infant Sex Ratio) of Bihar has remained more than (>) the 'adult sex ratio' (male female ratio) which is an encouraging sign for future increase in the female population. But the rate of increase will be very low. In Bihar as per 2001 census, 'child sex ratio' is 938 (decreasing from 953 in 1991), but at all-India level this ratio is 927 (2001 census) (decreasing from 945 to 927 in 1991). Both the 'sex ratio' as well as 'child sex ratio' are pessimistic figures for the women's empowerment in Bihar and in India too.

TABLE 5

District-wise Sex Ratio of Bihar State

Districts	*Sex Ratio*	
	1991	*2001*
Bihar	907	921
W. Champaran	877	901
E. Champaran	883	898
Sheohar	876	896
Sitamarhi	884	893
Madhubani	932	943
Supaul	904	920
Araria	907	916
Kishanganj	933	940
Purnia	903	916
Katihar	909	919
Madhepura	885	915
Saharsa	884	910
Darbhanga	911	914
Muzafrarpur	904	928
Gopal Ganj	968	1005
Siwan	1017	1033
Saran	963	965
Vaishali	921	921
Samastipur	926	927
Begusarai	989	911
Khagaria	968	890
Bhagalpur	864	878
Banka	893	908
Munger	856	878
Lakhisarai	880	923
Sheikhpura	896	920
Nalanda	898	915
Patna	867	873
Bhojpur	904	900
Buxar	884	884
Kaimur (Bhabhua)	884	907
Rohtas	894	909
Jahanabad	919	928
Aurangabad	915	936
Gaya	922	927
Nawada	903	917

Source: Computed from Census 1991 and 2001.

TABLE 6

Ranking of Districts in Sex Ratio

Rank in 2001	*Districts*	*Sex Ratio*		*Rank in 1991*
		2001	*1991*	
1.	Siwan	1033	1017	1
2.	Gopalganj	1005	968	2
3.	Saran	965	963	3
4.	Nawada	948	936	4
5.	Madhubani	943	932	6
6.	Kishanganj	940	933	5
7.	Gaya	937	922	8
8.	Aurangabad	936	915	11
9.	Muzaffarpur	928	904	15
10.	Jehanabad	928	919	10
11.	Samastipur	927	926	7
12.	Lakhisarai	923	880	31
13.	Vaishali	921	921	9
14.	Sheikhpura	920	896	22
15.	Supaul	920	904	16
16.	Katihar	919	909	13
17.	Jamui	917	903	18
18.	Purnea	916	903	19
19.	Araria	916	907	14
20.	Nalanda	915	998	20
21.	Madhepura	915	885	25
22.	Darbhanga	914	911	12
23.	Begusarai	911	898	21
24.	Saharsa	910	884	26
25.	Rohtas	909	894	23
26	Banka	908	893	24
27.	Kaimur	907	884	27
28.	Buxur	901	884	28
29.	West Champaran	901	877	32
30.	Bhojpur	900	904	17
31.	East Champaran	898	883	30
32.	Sheohar	896	876	33
33.	Sitamarhi	893	884	29
34.	Khagaria	890	868	37
35.	Munger	878	856	34
36.	Bhagalpur	878	864	36
37.	Patna	873	867	35

Source: Census of India, 2001, Series II, Bihar, Director of Census Operations, Bihar.

Child Sex Ratio

Census	*Bihar*	*All-India*
1991	953	945
2001	938	927

TABLE 7

Child Sex Ratio in Bihar, 2001 (0-6 Age Groups)

District	*Sex Ratio/000 Male*	*District*	*Sex Ratio/ 000 Male*
Bihar	938	Samastipur	945
Pashchim Champaran	942	Begusarai	940
Purbi Champaran	934	Khagaria	942
Sheohar	919	Bhagalpur	966
Sitamarhi	896	Banka	938
Madhubani	938	Munger	915
Supaul	921	Lakhisarai	955
Araria	967	Sheikhpura	959
Kishanganj	941	Nalanda	941
Purnia	968	Patna	948
Katihar	966	Bhojpur	938
Madhepura	918	Buxar	936
Saharsa	900	Kaimur (Bhabua)	940
Darbhanga	885	Rohtas	947
Muzaffarpur	925	Jehanabad	909
Gopalganj	961	Aurangabad	932
Siwan	927	Gaya	957
Saran	941	Nawada	974
Vaishali	933	Jamui	964

Source: Computed from Census 2001.

Literacy is such a parameter which indicates the index of economic development and human development of the state or country. Bihar is on the last ladder of the literacy rate of parameter as well as female literacy rate parameter in the country. In 2001, the literacy rate in Bihar remained 47.53 per cent against 65.38% at an all India level) and female literacy rate 33.57 (male literacy 60.32%) against 54.3 per cent at all India level. Kerala is on the peak where literacy rate is 90.9 per cent and female literacy is 87.9 per cent. No state in India records lower literacy rates or lower female literacy rates other Bihar. The most disturbing feature of population growth trend in Bihar is its low level of literacy. Thus, lowest social infrastructure in Bihar keeps the women in the lowest place in the field of empowerment.

Only about 13.5 per cent people were literate in Bihar in 1951. Since 1951 the rate of literacy has been continuously

TABLE 8

District-wise Child Population (0-6 years), Percentage Share of State and Child Sex Ratio

Age group 0-6	*Child Population*		*Total Bihar Population*		*District-wise Distribution of Child Population of Bihar*		*Sex ratio*	
Districts	*Persons*	*Males*	*Females*	*Males*	*Persons*	*Males*	*Females*	*Males*
Bihar	16,234,539	8,375,532	7,859,007	82,878,796	19.59	10.11	9.48	938
W. Champaran	805,238	325,203	306,209	3,043,044	20.75	10.69	10.06	942
Sheohar	101,630	52,954	48,676	514,288	10.76	10.30	9.46	919
Sitamarhi	539,288	284,369	254,919	2,669,887	20.20	10.65	9.55	896
Madhubani	699,906	361,075	338,831	3,570,651	19.60	10.11	9.49	938
Supaul	364,701	189,821	174,880	1,745,069	20.90	10.88	10.02	921
Araria	449,343	228,476	220,867	2,124,831	21.15	10.75	10.39	967
Kishanganj	280,498	144,501	135,997	1,294,063	21.68	11.17	10.51	941
Purnia	536,851	272,748	264,103	2,540,788	21.13	10.73	10.39	968
Katihar	514,326	261,630	252,969	2,389,533	21.52	10.95	10.58	966
Madhepura	320,359	167,034	153,325	1,524,596	21.01	10.96	10.06	918
Saharsa	306,253	161,190	145,063	1,506,418	20.33	10.70	9.63	900
Darbhanga	627,897	333,061	294,836	3,285,473	19.11	10.14	8.97	885
Muzaffarpur	718,298	373,238	345,060	3,743,836	19.19	9.97	9.22	925
Gopalganj	417,061	212,641	204,420	2,149,343	19.40	9.89	9.51	961
Siwan	532,447	276,274	256,173	2,708,840	19.66	10.20	9.46	927
Saran	619,872	319,229	300,443	3,251,474	19.06	9.82	9.24	941
Vaisahli	522,714	270,420	252,294	2,712,389	19.27	9.97	9.30	933
Samastipur	695,995	357,866	133,129	3,413,413	20.39	10.48	9.91	945

Begusarai	464,176	239,209	224,958	2,342,989	19.81	10.21	9.60	940
Khagaria	269,582	138,821	130,761	1,276,677	21.12	10.87	10.24	942
Bhagalpur	456,956	232,399	224,557	2,430,331	18.80	9.56	9.24	966
Banka	323,329	166,872	156,457	1,608,778	20.10	10.37	9.73	938
Munger	197,144	102,928	94,216	1,135,499	17.36	9.06	8.30	915
Lakhisarai	160,210	81,944	78,266	801,173	20.00	10.23	9.77	955
Sheikhpura	106,335	54,278	52,057	525,137	20.25	10.34	9.91	959
Nalanda	444,749	229,109	215,640	2,368,327	18.78	9.67	9.11	941
Patna	795,842	408,453	387,389	4,709,851	16.90	8.67	8.23	948
Bhojpur	406,343	200,650	196,693	2,223,415	18.19	9.39	8.81	938
Kaimur (Bhabhhua)	258,460	133,238	125,212	1,284,212	20.12	10.37	9.75	940
Rohtas	463,050	237,841	225,209	2,448,762	18.91	9.71	9.20	947
Jehanabad	282,774	148,160	134,614	1,511,406	18.71	9.80	8.91	909
Aurangabad	378,774	148,160	134,614	2,004,960	18.89	9.78	9.11	932
Gaya	666,327	340,443	325,884	3,464,983	19.23	9.83	9.41	957
Nawada	346,564	175,549	171,015	1,809,425	19.15	9.70	8.45	974
Jamui	264,768	134,841	129,927	1,397,474	18.95	9.65	9.30	964

Source: Same as Table 1.

TABLE 9

Intertemporal Trends in Sex Ratio in India: A State-wise Composition

	1901	*1911*	*1921*	*1931*	*1941*	*1951*	*1961*	*1971*	*1981*	*1991*	*2001*
All India	972	964	955	950	945	946	941	930	934	927	933
Bihar	1061	1051	1020	995	1002	1000	1005	957	948	907	921
Jharkhand	1032	1021	1002	989	978	961	960	945	940	922	941

Source: Same as Table 1.

increasing. But this is not a matter of great happiness for us. We have entered 21st century but even now more than 52 per cent, Biharis use their thumb-impressions or they are merely thumb-printers. What a sorry state it is. The condition of women is the worst in this regard because 67 per cent of our women do not know even how to read and write. The problem becomes more heart-rending when we compare the literacy rate of Bihar with that of other states and the national average.

Female Literacy and Population

The rising population levels of the country is a great problem. Due to lower literacy rates and particularly of females the population of a country is being adversely affected. Due to this it increases very rapidly and *vice-versa*. Its remedy is also possible through the expansion and extension of literacy and education. In India those states, which have as lowest level of female literacy and education levels, have higher fertility rate. It is evident that Bihar is at the top in this respect (having female literacy rate at the bottom).But those states, which have higher level of literacy and education, have lower fertility rate. Bihar, U.P. and Rajasthan having least female literacy rate, are in the category of such states having most fertility rate. Kerala, T.N. and W. Bengal have higher female literacy rates, thus those states have less fertility rate. The present Union U.P.A. government has assured in its manifesto that it will increase the education expenditure by up to 6 per cent of G.D.P., increasing from current 3.2 per cent. In 2003-04 the total G.D.P. of the country was more than Rs. 25 lacs crores, of which 6 per cent becomes Rs. 1.5 lacs crore. When the union and state govt. made expenditure over education Rs. 80,779 crore only being combined together. It means if the union government fulfils its promise of education, it has to spend on education at least Rs. 70,000 crore additional expenditure.

In 2001 Census, literacy rate of India was 65.4 whereas female literacy rate was 54.3 per cent In 1991 Census, literacy rate of India was 51.6 per cent, whereas female literacy rate was 39.3 per cent. In Bihar 1991 Census recorded 37.49 per cent literacy rate whereas male literacy rate was 51.37 per cent and female literacy was 21.99 per cent. But as per the 2001 Census, literacy rate was 47.53 per cent; male literacy rate is 60.32 per cent, and

TABLE 10

Trends of Literacy: Child Population and Sex Ratio in Bihar

Districts	*Percentage of Child Population*				*Literacy Sex Ratio*				
	Population	*Decadal growth child*	*%age of urban population*	*%age of population*	*Sex ratio*	*%age literacy rate*			
					Total	*Child*	*Total*	*Male*	*Female*
Bihar	828787796	28.43	19.59	10.47	921	938	47.53	60.32	33.57
W. Champaran	3040344	30.40	20.75	10.17	901	942	39.63	51.91	25.85
E. Champaran	3933636	29.27	20.47	6.39	898	934	38.14	50.14	24.65
Sheohar	514288	36.16	19.76	4.15	896	919	37.01	45.54	27.43
Sitamarhi	2669887	32.58	20.20	5.74	893	986	39.38	51.02	26.35
Madhubani	3570651	26.08	19.60	3.48	943	938	42.35	57.26	26.56
Supaui	1745069	29.95	20.90	5.04	920	921	37.80	53.23	21.02
Araria	2124831	31.84	21.15	6.24	916	967	34.94	46.50	22.14
Kishanganj	1294063	31.50	21.68	9.97	940	941	31.02	42.80	18.49
Purnia	2540788	35.23	21.13	8.74	916	968	35.51	46.16	23.[illegible]
Katihar	2389533	3091	21.52	9.13	919	966	35.29	45.51	24.03
Madhepura	1524596	29.45	21.01	4.46	915	918	36.19	48.87	22.31
Saharsa	1506418	33.03	20.33	8.23	910	900	39.28	52.04	25.31
Darbhanga	3285473	30.85	19.11	8.12	914	883	44.32	57.18	30.35
Muzaffarpur	3743836	26.74	19.19	9.30	928	925	48.15	60.19	35.20
Gopalganj	2149343	26.11	19.40	6.07	1005	961	48.19	63.81	32.81
Siwan	2708840	24.78	19.66	5.45	1033	927	52.01	67.67	37.26
Saran	3321474	26.37	19.06	9.17	965	941	52.01	67.81	35.74
Vaishali	2712389	26.39	19.27	6.88	921	933	51.63	64.00	38.14

Samastipur	3413413	25.63	20.39	3.62	927	945	45.76	57.83	32.69
Beguasari	2342989	29.11	19.81	4.58	911	940	48.55	59.71	36.21
Khagaria	1276677	29.32	21.12	5.97	890	942	41.56	52.02	29.62
Bhagalpur	2430331	27.24	18.80	18.59	878	966	50.28	60.11	38.83
Banka	1608778	24.47	20.10	3.50	908	938	43.40	56.28	29.10
Munger	1135499	20.34	17.36	27.88	878	915	60.11	70.68	47.97
Lakhisarai	801173	23.94	20.00	14.68	923	955	48.21	60.97	34.26
Sheikhpura	525137	24.96	20.25	15.48	920	959	49.01	62.56	34.13
Nalanda	2368327	18.64	18.78	14.92	915	941	53.64	66.94	39.03
Patna	4709851	30.17	16.90	41.80	873	948	63.82	73.81	52.17
Bhojpur	2233415	24.58	18.19	13.98	900	938	59.71	74.78	42.81
Buxar	1403462	29.03	18.66	9.18	901	926	57.49	72.82	40.36
Kaimur (Bhabhua)	1284575	30.64	30.12	2.23	907	940	55.57	70.57	38.90
Rohtas	2448762	27.71	18.91	13.34	909	947	62.36	76.54	46.62
Jehanabad	1511406	28.64	18.71	7.40	927	909	56.03	70.90	40.08
Gaya	3464983	30.03	19.23	13.71	937	958	51.07	63.81	37.40
Aurangabad	2004960	30.19	18.89	8.42	936	932	57.50	71.99	42.04
Nawada	1809424	33.08	19.15	7.66	948	974	47.36	61.22	32.64
Jamui	1397474	32.90	18.95	7.38	917	964	42.74	57.10	26.92

Source: Census of India 2001, Series—Bihar: Provisional Population Totals, Paper-2 of 2001, Rural-Urban Distribution of Population, Director of Census Operations, Bihar, Annexures 3 to 5, pp. 75 to 112.

Low Level Literacy Rate:

Census	*Bihar*		
1991	Persons—37.49%	Male—51.37%	Female—21.99%
2001	Persons—47.53%	Male—60.32%	Female—33.57 %

TABLE 11

State-wise Literacy Rate in India

	Literacy Rate (%)	
	2001	*1991*
Andhra Pradesh	61.1 (51.2)	44.1
Assam	64.3 (56.0)	52.9
Bihar	47.5 (33.6)	37.5
Delhi	81.8 (75.0)	75.3
Goa	82.3 (75.5)	75.5
Gujarat	70.0 (58.6)	61.3
Haryana	68.6 (56.3)	55.9
Himachal Pradesh	77.1 (68.1)	63.9
Jammu & Kashmir	54.5 (41.8)	N.A.
Karnataka	67.0 (57.5)	56.0
Kerala	90.9 (87.9)	89.8
Madhya Pradesh	64.1 (50.3)	44.2
Maharashtra	77.3 (67.5)	64.9
Manipur	68.9 (59.7)	59.9
Meghalaya	63.3 (60.4)	49.1
Nagaland	67.1 (61.9)	61.7
Orissa	63.6 (51.0)	49.1
Punjab	70.0 (63.6)	58.5
Rajasthan	61.0 (44.3)	38.6
Tamil Nadu	73.5 (64.6)	62.7
Tripura	73.7 (65.4)	60.4
Uttar Pradesh	57.4 (43.0)	40.7
West Bengal	69.2 (60.2)	57.7
All-India (incl. others)	5.4 (54.3)	51.6# (27.8)
	25.7 (54.3)	65.4 (51.6)#

• Figures relate to population aged seven years and above, Figures in brackets show female literacy rate.

Excludes Jammu & Kashmir

Source: Statistical Outline of India, 2003-04.

TABLE 12

Literacy Rate in Bihar (1951-2001) (In percentage)

Census Years	*Person*	*Male*	*Female*
1951	13.49	22.68	4.22
1961	21.95	35.85	8.11
1971	23.17	35.86	9.86
1981	32.32	47.11	16.61
1991	37.49	51.37	21.99
2001	47.53	60.32	33.57

Source: Census of India 2001, 'Provisional Population Totals', Sahitya Bhavan, Agra.

TABLE 13

District-wise Literacy Rate of Bihar State

	Literacy Rate (In per cent)					
	1991			*2001*		
	Persons	*Males*	*Females*	*Persons*	*Males*	*Females*
Bihar	7.49	51.37	21.99	47.53	60.32	33.57
W. Champaran	27.99	39.65	14.41	39.63	51.91	25.85
E. Champaran	27.59	39.65	13.69	38.14	50.14	24.65
Sheohar	26.18	36.36	14.34	37.01	45.54	27.43
Sitamarhi	28.49	39.86	15.49	39.38	51.02	26.35
Madhubani	33.22	48.49	16.75	42.35	47.26	26.56
Supaul	28.11	40.96	13.74	37.80	53.23	21.02
Araria	26.19	36.99	14.01	34.94	46.50	22.14
Kishanganj	22.22	33.12	10.38	21.02	42.80	18.49
Purnia	28.52	38.92	16.80	35.51	46.16	23.72
Katihar	28.70	39.24	16.88	35.29	45.51	24.03
Madhepura	27.72	39.31	14.41	36.19	48.87	22.31
Saharsa	29.98	42.37	15.83	39.28	52.04	25.31
Darbhanga	34.94	48.31	20.09	44.32	57.18	30.35
Muzaffarpur	36.11	48.44	22.33	48.15	60.19	35.20
Gopalganj	34.96	51.62	17.75	48.19	63.81	32.81
Siwan	39.13	57.51	21.33	52.01	67.67	37.26
Saran	41.79	60.18	22.71	52.01	67.81	35.74
Vaishali	40.56	55.62	24.08	51.63	64.00	38.14
Samastipur	36.37	50.39	21.17	45.76	57.83	32.69
Begusarai	36.88	48.66	23.52	48.55	59.71	36.21
Khagaria	32.33	42.97	19.79	41.56	52.02	29.62
Bhagalpur	41.84	53.41	28.11	50.28	60.11	38.83
Banka	34.55	48.17	18.99	43.40	56.28	29.10
Munger	52.27	64.95	37.07	60.11	70.68	47.97
Lakhisarai	39.40	53.12	23.48	48.21	60.97	34.26
Sheikhpura	40.92	55.43	24.41	49.01	62.56-	34.13
Nalanda	46.95	61.95	—	53.64	66.94	39.03
Patna	56.33	69.07	41.35	63.82	73.81	52.17
Bhojpur	48.18	66.35	27.95	59.71	74.78	42.81
Buxar	45.54	62.94	25.74	57.49	72.82	40.36
Kaimur (Bhabua)	39.35	55.68	20.69	55.57	70.57	38.90
Rohtas	48.52	64.50	30.29	62.36	76.54	46.62
Jehanabad	45.83	63.11	26.81	56.03	70.90	40.08
Aurangabad	45.14	61.80	26.67	57.50	71.99	42.04
Gaya	40.47	55.22	24.20	51.07	63.81	27.40
Nawada	38.96	54.85	21.82	47.36	61.22	32.64
Jamui	33.41	48.48	16.41	42.74	57.10	26.92

female literacy rate is 33.57 per cent. Thus, it is seen that in 2001 census difference between male literacy (60.32%) and female literacy (33.57%) much higher. It was almost double. So it is evident that female literacy rate is very low in Bihar as against respect of male literacy rate. It is also the lowest in respect of female literacy rates of all the states of India. There is one encouraging fact that rate of female literacy in Bihar during the period 1991-2001 increased more rapidly than that of increase in male literacy rate. But in spite of that female literacy rate of Bihar is far behind the male literacy rate.

TABLE 14

	Female Literacy %	*% of Female Literacy*	*Workers' Population*	*Total Fertility Rate*	*Contraceptive Prevalence Rate (1997)*
	1991	*2001*	*1991*		
All India	39.3	54.2	22.25	3.3	44.10
Bihar	22.9	33.6	14.86	4.4	19.7
M.P.	28.8	50.3	32.68	4.0	46.5
Rajasthan	24.4	44.3	27.40	4.2	36.4
U.P.	25.3	43.0	12.32	4.8	38.2
Kerala	86.7	89.4	15.85	1.8	40.5
Punjab	50.4	68.1	4.80	2.7	66.0
Jharkhand	–	39.4	–	–	–

TABLE 15

Female Literacy and Fertility Rate

States Having Least Female Literacy	*Adult Female Literacy Rate (2001)*	*Total Fertility Rate*
Bihar	33.6	4.28
U.P.	43.0	4.73
Rajasthan	44.3	4.13
Kerala	87.9	1.80
T.N.	64.6	1.96
W. Bengal	60.2	2.44

In Bihar 17 district are such which record more female literacy rates in respect of its state level rate (i.e. 33.57%). The districts that are the following viz., Patna—52.7 per cent, Munger—47.97 per cent, Rohtas—46.62 per cent, Bhojpur— 42.81 per cent, Aurangabad—42.04 per cent, Buxar—40.36 per cent, Jahanabad—40.08 per cent, Nalanda—39.03 per cent, Kaimur (Bhabhua)—38.90 per cent, Bhagalpur—38.83 per cent, Vaishali—38.14 per cent, Siwan—37.26 per cent, Begusarai—36.21 per cent, Saran—35.74 per cent, Muzaffarpur—35.20 per cent, Lakhisarai—34.36 per cent, and Sheikhpura—34.13 per cent.

The Kishanganj district recorded the lowest female literacy rate, i.e., 18.49 per cent. This district records the lowest literacy rate 21.02 and male literacy rate 42.80 per cent also. This district is Muslim-majority district. Thus, the Muslim populated district (both male and female) has least rate of literacy. In this way the empowerment of women in Bihar is on the last step of the ladder of development.

References

Bose, Asis (1991), "Population of India", pp. 57-66.

Census (1991), Provisional Population Totals, Govt. of India.

Census (2001), Provisional Population Totals, Govt. of India.

'Economic and Political Weekly', (2002), No. 34, August 24-30.

Economic Survey (2001-02), Provisional Population Totals, Govt. of India.

Statistical Outline of India, (2003-04).

Thakur, R.N. (2004), "Empowerment of Poor People Under Panchayati Raj in Bihar", *Bihar Economic Journal.*

—— (2004), *Economy of U.P.—the Glorious Past and Gloomy Present,* 87th Annual Conference Spl. Lecture, I.E.A., B.H.U.,Varanasi.

—— (2002), "Economy of Kerala—Human Development", Social Progress and Economic Crisis, 85th Annual Conference, I.E.A., I.E.A. Spl. Lecture, Trivandrum.

—— (2002), *Empowerment of Indian Women-Challenges to Development,* Spl. Lecture in National Seminar in T.M. Bhagalpur University, Bhagalpur.

—— (2000), "Education and Political Status of Indian Women—Key to Economic Development", *Women and Development,* (ed.) A. Banarjee, R.K. Sen, Deep and Deep Pub., New Delhi.

—— (2002), "Women and Employment Strategy in India," *Women and Technology,* ed. S. Murthy, RBSA Pub., Jaipur.

10

The Dalit in India: Caste and Social Class

HARI NARAYAN PRASAD SINGH

Despite the far-reaching legislative and educational quotas for SCs and STs, and their benefits, dalits are still savagely attached to the Countryside. In urban areas, untouchability still knocks at the doors of institutions like arranged marriage, Caste Hindu temples, Classical music concerts, and the private sector. The cultural hegemony of 'dwija' remains intact and dalitness remains physical reality. Dalits as Pariah played crucial role in allowing the upper castes a monopoly on education and in certain pure trades.

The dalit or "Untouchable" is a government servant, the teacher in a state school, or a politician. He is generally never a member of the higher judiciary, an eminent lawyer, industrialist or journalist. His freedom operates in designated enclaves: in politics and the administrative posts he acquires because of state policy. But in areas of contemporary social change and culture, his "Untouchability" becomes his only definition. The right to pray to a Hindu god has always been a high caste privilege. Intricacy of religious rituals is directly proportionate to social status. The dalit has been formally excluded from religion, from education, and is a pariah in the entire sanctified universe of the "dvija" unlike racial minorities, the dalit is physically indistinguishable from upper castes, yet metaphorically and literally, the dalit has been a "shit bearer" for three millennia, toiling at the very bottom of the Hindu caste hierarchy. The word "pariah" itself comes from a dalit caste of southern India, the Paraiyar, "those of the drum" (papai) or the "leather people" (Dumont, 1980: 54).

At 150 million, dalits or "scheduled castes" and "scheduled tribes," form about 20 per cent of India's population (Census of India, 1991). Backward castes as a whole, taking dalits, tribes, and other Backward castes (OBCs) into consideration, form about 52 per cent of India's population. Today, widening policies on affirmative action have opened up government service and state education to dalits.

But areas of freedom are limited, largely to sectors that are under the aegis of the state, such as the civil service or state–owned enterprises. Exclusion from cultural and social networks emerges from the dalit's crucial exclusion from the system of castes (Mendelsohn and Vicziany, 1998: 39). The dalits pariah status derives its strength and justification from religious texts. In the Manusmriti, the dalit is described as "polluted," in the same way as a menstruating woman, a widow, or a person who has recently been bereaved is polluted. The dalit is "unclean" from birth. He violates, by his very existence, the brahminical obsession with hygiene (Dumont, 1980: 131). While the "untouchability" of the menstruating woman or the bereaved is temporary and he or she can escape the Untouchable condition after the period of "pollution" is past, the dalit can never escape his status: he is perpetually filthy. In a hymn from the purusasukta of the Rig Veda, the dvija are said to have been born from elevated parts of the unborn with no physical link with the supreme being. According to this hymn, from the body of Brahma come the four main categories of Hindu society, namely the four varnas (colors or castes): Brahmins (priests), Kshatriyas (warriors), Vaishyas (businessmen), and Shudras (servants). The priest is born from the mouth of the creator, the warrior from the arm, the businessman from the stomach, and the servant from the foot. Untouchables are born from outside the body of the creator, almost a different species of Brahma's children. Their entry into the divine body would be as unthinkable as the entry of an animal.

Today, the literary and scholarly efflorescence among dalits is set apart for caste Hindu society as a particularly dalit development. Dalit critiques of nation and society barely impinge on upper–caste nations of the social order, of the nation-state, and of modernity in general. The reasons for this are often attributed to the grafting of traditional caste networks into modern state institutions—for example, the upper-caste Seizures of Western education and the higher bureaucracy. The slide of the independent Indian nation-state into a landscape dominated by the brahmanical upper castes has meant that new ways have been found to effectively seal the dalit in his "democratic" prison (Nigam, 2000). As a result of legally reserved quotas in government and in state educational institutions, sections of dalits have emerged from agricultural poverty to become Middle Class. Yet the waters of modern opportunity flow along the fields of the upper castes.

Upper Castes were the main beneficiaries of the professional opportunities provided by colonialism and they also stand to gain the benefits of contemporary globalisation, such as opportunities in the Information Technology Sector or in the private sector. Thus, while dalit's political importance and militancy rises, at the same time, the dalit remains segregated from caste Hindu society by the invisible arms of caste. The word "dalit" or crushed "underfoot" or "broken into pieces" is the contemporary version of the Word "Untouchable." "Dalit owes its genesis to the Nineteenth Century writings of Jotirao Govindrao Phule as well as to the literature of the Dalit panthers, a political group formed in 1972 in the state of Maharashtra. British colonial census takers grouped together all those communities' neighbours considered "polluted" and called them "Untouchables," "Harijan," or "children of god" was Mahatma Gandhi's name for dalits. The word "Untouchable" is sometimes still used, but "harijan" is seen as an equivalent of "Uncle Tom," a paternalistic and condescending categorization of a group doomed to remain in perpetual bondage. Dalit leader Bhaurao Gaikwad observed in 1935 that "It is no use only giving Untouchables a sweet name. Something practical should be done to ameliorate their conditions" (Moon, 1987, Vol. 4: 230). Today most Untouchable castes would prefer to use the term "Dalit" as an assertion of identity. "The UN Conference against Racism, Racial Discrimination, Xenophobia, and Related Intolerance" held in Durban, South Africa, in September 2001 equated "racism" with untouchability; although this parallel has been systematically criticized, the word "dalit" has been interpreted by some activists as being equivalent to "Black." Dalits are the main targets of what are termed "caste-related crimes." Over 2000 dalits died in the three years between 1989 and 1991 as a result of atrocities against harijans. Hacking to death, massacres, and clopping off heads are the marks of a horrific bestiality inspired by the unshakeable taint of dirtiness.

It is the argument in this paper that despite the far-reaching legislative and educational quotas.for scheduled castes and scheduled tribes, and their undoubted benefits, dalits are still savagely attacked in the countryside.

In the Urban areas, untouchability still knocks at the doors of such institutions as the arranged marriage; the caste Hindu temple, the classical music concert, and the private sector. The cultural hegemony of the dvija remains virtually intact. Dalitness remains physical reality.

The idea of the polluted bonded servant is so ingrained in the sub-continental mind that the dalit remains at the bottom of the intellectual and emotional landscape of contemporary India, however far he may advance in a public career and agitate for change. Every child born into an upper caste Hindu family grows up with a mind's eye image of the *acchyut* (untouchable). The Imagined Untouchable is 'squalid in appearance and it is the religious duty of "pure" Hindu to consider' him perpetually inferior. The emergence of the Outcaste Pariah: The Dalit and the Brahmin; "If a kalash (vessel) of water comes into a bhangi's (Untouchable's) hand" sing the women of the dalit Vankar caste, "he'll drink and drink until his stomach bursts" (Franco, Macwan, and Ramanathan, 2000: 193). The poor Untouchable is so eager just for water, that when he gets it he drinks until his stomach bursts! An enormous body of scholarly work exists on the Indian system of castes. For Dumont (1980), Indian society has always been defined by the hierarchy of castes. Caste "is above all, a system of ideas and values, a formal comprehensible rational system [imbued with] the idea of hierarchy "Purity" and pollution "remain central to the caste system indeed, central to hinduism itself-and for the Brahmin, purification and hygiene are a necessity" (Dumont, 1980:52).

It is impossible to construct a uniform hierarchy of caste based on the notion of purity and pollution. No caste would acquiesce to its placement among the so-called "untouchables."

No caste would agree that members of other castes are made up of substances better than theirs. No caste would like its people to marry outside the community. No caste would like to merge its identity with any other caste.

No caste accepts that it has originated from a shameful act of miscegenation. Any suggestion of being half-breed is dismissed haughtily across the board by all castes (Gupta, 2000:33). However self-important, caste remains an invisible engine of Hindu society, creating, subtle social and political linkages, functioning as a closed enclave of common practice and thought and working as a lobby or pressure group that over the time creates monopolies over certain professions and businesses.

Caste is today, seen to have become secularised, that is, caste has become, a modern interest group, transformed into small monopolies of economic, political, and cultural interests. Caste steps out from the shadows every time a marriage is arranged or a child is born or a new professional or business opportunity emerges.

Caste is, at its very base, linked to production and occupation. It is a system of division of labour from which the element of competition has been largely excluded. Economic roles are allocated by right to closed minority groups of low social status; members of the high status 'dominant caste' to whom the low status groups are bound, generally form a numerical majority and must compete among themselves for the services of individual members of the lower castes (Leach, 1960, 5-6). The membership of a caste implies that a person becomes part of a person based social network that controls insider information about economic opportunities; transmits skills; and provides varied types of human and material support (Panin, 1996, 39).

Caste is by its very definition, exclusive and because of the manner in which particular castes channel themselves into particular occupations, it becomes virtually changeless. India's software industry, for example, is dominated by Tamil Brahmins and; the civil service by kayasthas from Uttar Pradesh.

In the pre-British period, the Jajmani system–by which the blacksmith, carpenter, potter, oilman, barber, washer man, and priest all became linked with the household of the upper–caste landowners and were paid in kind by the landholder for services rendered during the year–helped to ensure the durability of the caste system in the rural countryside (Srinivas, 1962; Leach, 1960). This principle of heredity and caste soon solidified into a family trade as well as an almost irreversible social category that was maintained as much by social taboos as by economic imperatives.

Thus the dalit, the caste that exists outside the caste system, is trapped by its own economic activities. The dalits pariahness begins with the untouchable castes becoming associated with those groups specializing impure tasks, such as cleaning out waste, skinning and cattle, working in leather, butchery, fishing, and supervising cremations. Leather workers, washerman, scavengers, toilet cleaners, toddy tappers, sweepers, and rural labourers were polluted because of their works. Their role in the caste based economic system meant that the modern dalits, descended from the professionals of impure tasks, are heirs to centuries old filth, professional as well as psychological.

Acchut! (Untouchable!)

Myriad practices existed and still exist to denote the pollution of the dalits. Not only could the dalit not enter a Hindu temple or drink water from temple tanks, but he had to live in segregated huts on the outskirts of villages. In parts of south India in the nineteenth century, dalit women were forbidden to cover their breasts.

Dalits had to beat a drum to signal their arrival so that Brahmin knew where to hide or how to protect his food. The Brahmin is the most vulnerable to pollution when he is eating, so if a shadow of a dalit fell on his food, the food too became untouchable. On occasions dalits had to wear a spittoon so that his spittle did not fall on his surroundings and he could never stand in the way of a wind that might carry his smell or breath to a Brahmin. In a Jataka story (377.III.154), a Brahmin cries, "curse you, ill omened candala dalit, get to leeward" (Omvedt, 1998).

Nonetheless, there are qualifications to untouchability.

Instances can be found of dalit midwives, local functionaries, and local soothsayers and saints who have been revered by all sections of society. There are also instances of dalits participating in caste Hindu festivals; sections of dalits have also sometimes engaged in upper-caste rituals.

Yet the dalit as pariah played a crucial role in allowing the upper castes a monopoly on education and in certain pure trades. Because of the divine sanction for eternal serfdom, the denial of education and thus opportunities for advancement, upper castes were able to successfully eliminate masses of people from the competitive economy that developed under colonial rule (Harrison, 1960).

Reform : from Buddha to Phule to Naicker
Choo-o, choo-o, na chee! O je chandalini'r jhi!
Noshto Bobe je doi, she kothajaano naki?

(Don't touch her don't touch her, ugh! She's the daughter of a Dalit woman! Your yogurt will get spoiled, don't you know?)

Song from Rabindranth Tagore's Bengali dance drama Chandalika. In Chandalika, Prakriti, a young dalit woman falls in love with a Buddhist monk, Ananda, who wins her heart by drinking water from her cup, even as she's shunned by the rest of the villagers.

Subsequently, Ananda leaves on pilgrimage and Prakriti is devastated. She forces her mother to use her powers of black magic to bring him back.

The witchlike mother brings Ananda back to Parkriti but he dies. In the process, the grief stricken girl is seen seeking the blessings of Ananda, who encourages her to take to Buddhism to escape the cycle of degradation.

The pollution of Prakriti and her mother is contrasted with the purity of Ananda. The mother, a sensual practitioner of black magic is revealed as ultimately powerless against the monk. Chandalika is not only a comment on the fate of the untouchable girl but on the new life promised to dalits by religions like Buddhism.

Indeed, Buddhism is easily the most famous of the innumerable reform movements within Hinduism that have been in progress since the fifth and sixth centuries B.C. The underlying impetus to change the dalit 's pariah status was provided by these reform movements and the innumerable voices that have been raised for centuries against orthodox Hindu practices.

The ascetic-led Buddhism and Jainism movements developed as alternatives to the ritual-bound and caste-dominated doctrine that Hinduism had become. The ascetic Buddha and Mahavira both sought to create egalitarian faiths based on companion, and simplicity, and provided theological foundations for subsequent protests.

The Bhakti movement that emerged in the Fourteenth and Fifteenth centuries, exemplified in the cults of popular "saints" like Kabir and Mirabai, tried to negate the power of the Brahmin clergy and questioned the Brahmin's chief weapon: purity and the power to dispense with untouchability.

It's all one skin and bone,
One piss and shit,
One blood, one meat.
From one drop, a universe. Who's a Brahmin? Who's shudra?

So sang kabir, the fifteenth-century Bhakti saint (Hess, 1983:25). Yet the Bhakti movements were unable to change the working of the caste system, primarily because these saints formed a sort of mystic fringe, spiritually intense alternatives to the main body of orthodoxy that, although popular and doctrinally seductive, were no threat to a 3,000-year-old faith.

However, the Bhakti movements, the impact of Western ideas during the colonial encounter, social reform movements of the nineteenth century, the Gandhian movement, and finally the dramatic dalit movement led by B.R. Ambedkar have combined to create a significant tradition of anti-caste reformism not only among educated elites but also among today's newly articulate voters.

In the Nineteenth Century, social reform emanated from the soul searching that had become part of the educated upper-caste elites once they came into contact with Western ideas of liberalism and rationality (Raychaudhuri, 1999: 60). There were campaigns to secure the rights of the widow, Bansati (the practice of widows immolating themselves on their husband's funeral pyres), and reject caste. This argument is opposed by, among others Dipankar Gupta, who argues that Dumont's idea oversimplifies caste and papers over regional particularities and transactions.

11

Impact of Economic Reform Policy on Weaker Sections and Dalits

S.K.L. Das

"Necessitous men are not free men"—said Franklyn Roosevelt in 1941. It is true to its word. A large number of people in Jharkhand and Bihar are living in abject poverty. As per the 2001 Census, there are 13.7 crore rural families in the country are living below the poverty line. About 4.5 crore people only in Bihar are living below the poverty line. They are the real necessitous men. These strata of the population are leading a life of economic insecurity.

Economic security matters because human freedom and dignity matter to every human being. Real freedom cannot exist unless a certain level of economic security is achieved. Basic security must encompass freedom from morbidity, freedom from fear, control of own development and sustainable self-respect. The weaker sections of the society lack basic security in themselves, in their families, in their workplaces and in their community tend to become socially irresponsible. Mass insecurities have forced them to the path of extremism and violence. The naxal activities in Jharkhand, Bihar, Madhya Pradesh and other parts of the country are the burning examples of such activities, where insecurity has made them to adopt the path of intolerance and violence.

Economic security is linked with labour market security, income security, job security, employment security, work security, social security, as well as political security. While employment security is protection against loss of income earning work, or it refers to the sense of attachment to a current enterprise, job security refers to the sense of attachment to a particular job. Work security is about working conditions that are safe and promote workers' well being. A good society is one that guarantees all its members equal basic economic security. This requires at least a minimal income to the weaker sections on which to survive in decency in the society.

The Indian government spends about 5.5 billion $ on poverty-reduction programmes. Apart from that 5 billion $ is spent by other government departments on poverty relief. But ironically this amount never reaches the poor or the downtrodden people of the society. Hence they become economically insecure.

Economic Reform Policies

Just after independence, for achieving self-sustained growth and self-generating economy, public sector was regarded as a panacea for all economic evils. But during the forty years of planned socialistic development the country had to face regressive development, galloping inflationary trends, deficit balance of payments, and heavy fall in foreign exchange rates, the political-*cum*-economic thinkers embarked on the roads of reforms in order to redeem the economy from the clutches of the economic crisis and to put the derailed economy on the road to rapid development. The reform policies comprising industrial policy, fiscal policy, trade policy, and monetary policy, were introduced in 1991 by the then Narsimha Rao led Congress government.

The important features of this reform policy are to liberalize the industry, trade and business ventures, privatisation and globalisation and shifting the emphasis from public to private.

Under the globalisation following eleven points have been chosen:

(a) International financial market liberalisation,
(b) Domestic market liberalisation,
(c) Trade liberalisation,
(d) Labour market flexibility,
(e) Secure individual property rights over physical and financial assets,
(f) Reduction in the size of and role of the public sector,
(g) Weak property rights over human assets,
(h) Taxation reform policy-taxes from capital to labour and subsidies from labour to capital,
(i) Independent banking system,
(j) Social safety net, and
(k) Privatization and liberalisation of social policy.

It is the belief that there has been a steady move away from what is known as the Westaphalian system, which granted states jurisdiction over their own territories, to the new liberal cosmopolitanism, whereby national sovereignty is limited by institutions of global order. This policy indicates that national government must accept less discretionary power over national policy-making and adapt to the dictates of a global model. The Washington-based international financial institutions can be described as the midwives of globalization, and the economic liberalization in particular. The International Monetary Fund (IMF), the World Bank and their regional associates have played a powerful role in making domestic policies through its policies of granting loans and grants as well as technical assistance. It certainly accentuates social and economic insecurity. It means the government of developing countries like India lost control over their policy-making.

It is said that New Reforms Policy or globalization is a paradigm of insecurity of the downtrodden people of the country. A large number of such events occurred in different parts of developing and poor countries in the world after embarking on the roads of economic reform policies made us to think in this way. The Brazilian financial crisis of 1999, the Russian debt default and economic plunge in 1998, the economic and political implosion in Argentina as well as central and eastern Europe and the Mexican crisis in 1994, has made millions of people into devastating economic insecurity.

Not only this during reform policy trade has become an important engine of economic growth. It also amplifies the impact of economic shocks elsewhere in the world. The East Asian economy such as Singapore and Taiwan had been badly affected during 2001-02 due to the huge cut back of information technology (IT) investment. Growing economic specialization may certainly affect the employment prospects of weaker sections, which are basically untrained labour force.

Globalisation has been associated with a massive increase in foreign capital flows. Large surges of capital to developing countries can be problematic. The flows are volatile, with outflows as much as 50 per cent of inflows. The type and composition of the flows may not be what the developing countries want or need. It also creates a substantial increase in factor payments abroad. The burning example in this regard is the Asian crisis. Other feature of FDI is the multinationalisation of production. This potential mobility has given their representatives enhanced power in their dealings with national and local governments. FDI has become an increasingly important source of investment for developing countries. But it is more volatile than domestic investment and depends on decisions taken in its own interest rather than the interest of the developing nations.

Prof. Joseph Stiglitz said: "One of the main dissatisfactions with globalisation is precisely that it tends to deprive LDC of the freedom to apply policies that can protect their economies and their citizens. It seems that special interests in industrilised countries have precedence over broader interests."

There may be considerable financial market integration, which almost definitely impinges on the autonomy of national policy-makers. It is observed that global foreign exchange transactions and short-term financial flows have soared, while financial markets increasingly move together in response to the same events and shocks. Due to financialization of corporations, a large nubmer of major corporations, including household name-manufacturers, have devoted large increasing proportions of their financial resources to speculative investments. Many ran into difficulties following the stock market plunge in 2001-02, leading to retrenchment and divestments. It is detrimental in long-term productive strategy or the employment and income security of workers.

Privatisation cannot sensibly be separated from liberalisation. Essentially, the conventional wisdom is that public enterprises are both inefficient and contrary to free markets. So governments have moved to mixed provision, allowing an increasing element of private competition where the public sector was once the sole provider. Now the condition has completely changed. Due to reform policy external pressure builds up to allow foreign as well as national firms to enter the market and the WTO's GATS may then be used to make the presence of foreign firms a permanent feature. There are several reasons for believing that privatisation and liberalisation are intensifying insecurity. Most worrying is when the state withdraws from a commitment to provide a social service or protection, leaving people to make their own arrangements. In that case those living below the poverty line will have to face a miserable life.

In developing country like India, the capacity to implement regulation is limited. In our country deregulaton has led to large price fluctuations and wipeouts, in which farmers who could previously have balanced poor and good harvests lose everything in the wake of a poor season. Reform of the factory acts, for instance, has weakened the position of regular wageworker in India. The era of globalisation has undoutbtedly been characterised by a greater increase in capital mobility than labour mobility. Economic policy and regulatory changes have made capital mobility easier, While many barriers to labour mobility have been left or even strengthened. Some economists have argued that the rights of capital have been strengthened relative to the rights of labour.

It is a well known fact that a large number of people in India are living in rural areas. Most of them are deprived people and they are dependent on manual work. Due to adoption of economic reform policy, these untrained labour/dalit/weaker sections are facing difficulty in earning their livelihood. A large number of downtrodden people of Bihar, Jharkhand, Orissa, West

Bengal and UP, who were solely became dependent on Public Sector Units of Fertilizer Industry, have jobless as these units were closed down by the central government under the pretext of reform policy. In Jharkhand, due to closure of Sindri Fertilizer Factory in September, 2002 more than million people, who were from weaker section as well as tribals and dalits have been badly affected. Thousands of contract workers have become jobless over night. Their purchasing power has come down sharply. It has a negative cumulative effect on their purchasing power. The economy of nearby rural and tribal areas was shattered due to closure of industrial units, which is a fallout of reforms. Three industrial units have been closed down, thousands of workers, maid servants, tiny businessmen and others have become jobless. Entire township presents a deserted look. Similar is the condition of several other townships like Barauni of Bihar, Talcher of Orissa, Ramagundam of Andhra Pradesh which have faced same problems.

However, the economic growth rate of India is gradually increasing but due to rise in inflationary condition the economic health of the common people is badly affected. They are facing difficulty in meeting their daily needs. Except two or three developing countries, the growth rate of other less developed countries experienced the largest drop in growth from 5.5 per cent to 2.5 per cent annually. Even in The United States there was a decline in growth of GDP per capita. And in spite of remarkable performance of China and India, the per capita growth rate of in developing countries fell from 3.1per cent to 2.7 per cent.

It is evident that Economic Reform Policy has generated economic instability. The proponents of this policy have conceded that instability can be coped with through a social security safety net. But the growth record is at best unclear and financial liberalization could endanger economic stability. Generally economic reform policy has been associated with currency and banking crisis, which creates economic turbulence with drastic social consequences.

No doubt free trade promotes economic growth, while free capital mobility leads to lower growth and more economic instability and insecurity. The rapid growth in China and India has undoubtedly pulled large number of people out of desperate poverty. However, it may have increased insecurity as traditional ways of life and support systems have been disrupted.

In India two-thirds of workforce is directly engaged in agriculture for its livelihood and nearly 80 per cent of India's population below the poverty line lives in rural areas and is directly or indirectly dependent on agriculture. The current globalisation started in 1991 during a financial crisis in the country. A new government stabilised the economy, simplified investment in the country, removed many trade barriers, and reformed the tax-system. On account of this liberalization of the economy, direct foreign investment in the country increased more than ten-fold between 1991 to 2004. But this financial blessing evidently happened only for the relatively rich farmers. The fate of the poor did not improve. This reform policy made the rich farmers access new hybrid of seeds; such system cost much than the traditional varieties. Only the rich can have capacity to buy them.

Intellectual property rights in agriculture is another danger for the agriculturists. Similarly biotechnology firms present another aspect of the dangers of the current globalisation. This phenomena also indicates a disturbing abdication by the state of its duty to protect the most vulnerable sections of the population.

After a lapse of 14 years of reforms, condition of rural India has not improved. Every night 300 million people go to bed hungry, about 4.5 lakh people die of tuberculosis every year and half a million people who suffer from diarrhoea everday. Market-oriented economy has caused incredible number of job losses, land alienation, food riots and tension of economic disparities leading to rising organised crime, degeneration of public support system, and environmental degradation.

The weaker sections and dalits, who are living below the poverty line die because they do not have enough to eat and have no access to essential medical treatment. As per the Human Development Report 65 per cent of population has no access to essential medicines. These people live in sub-human condition and go through unutterable indignities because of the accident of their births in dalit castes. Despite living miserable lives they cannot not articulate their grievances as they live in an unorganised way.

Besides health, illiteracy, among these people, are the other problems. Such illiterate masses have become the tools of the mafia raj. The votes of uneducated people can be manipulated with the help of castes and creeds as well as muscle power.

Out of 700 million people living in villages only 210 million are functionally literate despite the government expenditure of Rs. 30,000 crore on primary education. The Entire country is marching towards total failure. Corrupt governance, ineffective judiciary and sick public sector—a clear road map to disaster. The great thinker and economist Karl Marx called for a Proletarian revolution to end all exploitation in this world and wanted to lay the foundation for the greatest human democratic society, where weaker sections and common man can improve their lot.

Survival of the weakest should be the norm of the economy. However Darwins theory of survival of the fittest is the maxim for the existence. Men are born equal. If given the same opportunities of health, education, and environment, their capacity to contribute would have become nearly equal. It is the society that we have created where these opportunities are not equally distributed thereby leading to a differency between men and men.

With survival of the weakest as the maxim, the people at the bottom rung of the economy would get more purchasing power along with better health and education facilities. This would not only make a huge difference in the quality of human capital in the country but would also satisfy the most important criterion for the growth of Indian industry by becoming the part of the consumer market. The market will no long comprise of a hundred million people but one billion people because it is the purchasing power of the markets that determines the long-term growth of any economy. Hence, an economy that wants to survive and not be swept off its feet by the giant corporations should place their faith on the survival of the weakest.

Hence, globalisation with a human face should be the basic norm at this juncture. Social development can only change this system. But condition is otherwise. The impact of the reform policies in terms of unemployment revealed that there is large scale retrenchment of workers. The fertilizer industrial units and the National Textile Corporation have retrenched about one lakh workers. Voluntary retirement has been pushed in a large number of public sector units. Thus both the public sector on the plea of overstaffing and redundancy, and private sector on the plea of modernisation and technological upgradation, workers are gradually being retrenched or forced to accept voluntary retirement scheme. It is really distressing for the large number of weaker sections who are living in different type of insecurity situations in the reform era. The image of a large rural population surrounding cities and towns is giving way to one of an increasingly urbanized world, which will create further social and economic insecurity for the weaker sections of the society. Basic economic security should become a human right. Hence, new policies will be needed to reduce the insecurity of the weaker sections as well as the large number of dalits, who are living a life of misery and destitute.

REFERENCES

Economic Security For A Better World: ILO.
Economic Survey, Various years. Government of India.
Growth, Employment and Poverty—D.T. Lakdawala.
Rural Employment: Facts and Issues by M.L. Dantwala.
Rural Non-Farm Employment—T.S. Papola.
The Indian Economy: Problems and Prospects by Bimal Jalan.
World Bank: Global Economic Prospects and the Developing Countries.

12

Problems of Child Labour Under Globalisation

SUKHMANI DAS AND MEERA RANJAN LAL

It is well recognised that child laboures are one of the important vulnerable groups in Indian society. The country has probably the largest number of child labourers in the world. The Convention on the Rights of the Child recognizes that every child should have a right to education. In other words, many children in India are being deprived of this right. In this context, it may also be noted that neglect of primary education is one of the biggest failures of Indian development policies. The 52nd Round of NSS shows that there are about 230.8 million children in the age group 6-14 in 1995-96. Around 61 per cent of these children were attending school. In other words 39 per cent of the children in the age group were out of the school. In absolute sense, 90 million children are out of school in India in 1995-96. In recent years, the issue of child labour has acquired more prominence because of discussions on the relationship between international trade and labour standards in the context of World Trade Organization (WTO).

Children are the future hope of society and are destined to

play a important role in shaping the destiny of the nation. But unfortunately they are suffering a lot and are subjected to endless toil and hard work without having the corresponding opportunities to grow. The following remark sums up the sad plight of child labour: "It is really sad to note that children in most of the developing countries are living miserable, cheerless lives, toiling endlessly to ward-off starvation totally deprived of all comforts and opportunities for self growth and development."

The phenomenon of child labour robs the child of his youthful life, restricts the prospects of education, which can enable him to reach a higher level at a later stage of life, on the one hand, and ultimately, it harms the progress and prosperity of the nation. It has been correctly stated: "Starve a child of food, of affection, of freedom of education and you produce an adult who is stunted as an individual and holds back progress what is towards development rather than accelerate it". This is exactly happening in our country. When put to work at a tender age, it reduces physical growth and ultimately their ability and thereby nation's growth in future. Thus, child labour is economically unsound, psychologically disastrous, and physically as well as morally dangerous and harmful. It is inefficient utilization of labour power at the lowest productivity level, which precludes full development of children's potentialities, and ultimately harms economic development.

Poverty is undeniably a major factor leading to child labour because children from poverty-stricken families are compelled to join labour force but equally important is the exploitative nature of the system. Due to poverty 'parental authority' is misused. In this context Marx said: "It was not the misuse of parental authority that created the capitalistic exploitation of children's labour, but on the contrary, it was the capitalist mode of exploitation which by sweeping away the economic basis of parental authority, made its exercise degenerate into a mischievous misuse of power". There are many who view the problem in this way and link it with exploitive capitalist mode of production and working of the capitalist system. It has been opined: "Child labour more truly mirrors the character of the society and policy, including the nature of transition, than any other set of indicators". Thus, the exploitative capitalist order perpetuates the problem.

The roots of the problem lie in the exploitative systems prevailing not only at the national level but also at the international level. At the national level the lopsided development process in the background of socio-economic structure results in marginalisation of the poor, who are left with no option but toresort to emplay their children as child labouers use child labour as a survival strategy. At the international level, the need for foreign exchange, on the one hand, and stiff competition for markets in the developed world on the other, encourage the producers of export industries in the Third World to use cheap and vulnerable child labour. Also, powerful multi-national corporations choose child labour directly or indirectly, to minimize the cost of production and to maximize profits.

The Experience of the European countries as analyzed by Klaus Voll, Ester Kostal *et. al.* shows that child labour has been an integral part of the early stages of the development of the capitalist mode of production, and for a considerable extent its incidence depends on socio-cultural and religion-based values of the society. Indira Hirway regards the phenomena of child labour as both a consequence as well as cause. The existence of child labour reduces the level of employment of adults, which has a dampening effect on their wage rate. The resulting poverty in turn, encourages parents to send their children out to work for the survival of the family. The vicious circle is further strengthened through the limited access of the poor to nutrition, health, and education. The poor access reduces the productivity as well as wages of adults, which again forces them to make their children work for the family's survival. The child labour system is thus used as a tool by the vested interests to strengthen their own position further and to maintain and sustain the poverty of the poor. Thus, the child labour problem has complex dynamics having its dimensions within the precinct of national boundary and also extending upto international level. The exploitative system both within and outside sustains and supports this child labour exploitation.

Rodgers and Standing employ useful categories to classify child labour. These are: (a) domestic work; (b) non-domestic and non-monetary work; (c) bonded labour, and (d) wage labour. In the first category are included household works like those of maidservants, domestic servants, etc. Children are employed in time consuming activities such as child care, cooking, cleaning, washing clothes, etc. The examples of second category are commonly found in the form of grazing of cows, goat, pigs, etc.

where children of five to six and especially female children have to bear the burden. These children may be engaged in family activity or may be a type of self-employment. In spite of ban on bonded labour in the countryside, examples are not uncommon where parents pledge their children to employ both in rural agricultural and urban unorganized sectors against loans taken by these families. The children so pledged have to work for a pittance. Children are also employed as wage labour, though their wages are often very low. Thus, they perform as unpaid workers in homes or in their own fields as helpers and as paid labour on other's fields or in factories.

The concentration of child labour is to be seen in agriculture as cultivators and agricultural labourers. Children work as helpers in different agricultural operations such as sowing, weeding, harvesting, and threshing. They are also engaged in road construction, digging of wells, and house-building. A large number of them are employed in plantations. We see their concentration in agriculture and unorganized sector due to lack of enforcement of child protection laws there and partly due to the legal restrictions put on employing them in organized sector. Children are found commonly in wayside restaurants, small hotels and dhabas, tea stall and sweets shops.

They are engaged in casual work where there is no provision of holidays, social security, or other permissible allowances which completely absent and they have to work in hazardous, and adverse working conditions affecting their health and efficiency. As they start work at a very young age they are deprived of education, training (vocational or otherwise), which ultimately limits their earnings, and restricts upward mobility.

Besides, child labour creates many social and psychological problems. Due to their misuse for illegal, immoral works, viz. smuggling, prostitution, etc. their personality development is impaired. They grow as stunted ill-mannered citizens. This psychological deprivation (due to lack of care, free life, and freedoms) harms millions of children, and, so not only individual or family suffers, but, ultimately society suffers, leading to many adverse also social problems.

Thus, the fears that globalization will increase the incidence of child labour do not seem to be realistic given the decline that is being induced by the falling proportion of children in the vast majority of states (ILO, 1997). However, the need to continue the pressure on national governments, multinational corporations, and domestic companies through civil society can be hardly over-emphasised. The role of the ILO in this context becomes far more significant in the era of globalization in that it should use all opportunities to elicit commitments from the nation-states, MNCs, and other stake-holders for enhanced commitment to family planning, child development, and the elimination of child labour.

REFERENCES

Hirway, Indira (1991), "Eradicating Child Labour or the World: Some Basic News," *Towards Eradicating of Child Labour* (eds.) Hirway Indira, Cottyn. J. *et. al.* Oxford Publishing Company, New Delhi.

John, Grun (1979), UNICEF SCARU, Health and Basic Services, New Delhi, as quoted in *Child in Third World*, Peoples Publishing House, 1979.

Pati, R.N. (1991), "Rehabilitation of Child Labour in India," p. 268, Ashish Publishing House, New Delhi. Singh, Bhagwan Pd. and Mohanty, *"Children at Work,"* p. 64.

Rodgers, Gerry and Standing Guy (1981), *Child Work, Poverty and Underdevelopment*, ILO, Geneva, pp. 2-8.

Shandilya Tapan Kumar, Nayan Kumar and Navin Kumar (2006), *Child Labour Eradication*, Deep & Deep Publications Pvt. Ltd., New Delhi.

Shandilya, Tapan Kumar (2003), *Child Labour: A Global Challenge*, Deep & Deep Publications Pvt. Ltd., New Delhi.

13

Economic Reform and Child Labour

BIRENDRA KUMAR JHA

There are a large number of vulnerable groups in India which, it is feared, may have to bear the costs of globalisation and liberalisation and child labour is one of such vulnerable groups. Child labour is not the domain of the developing countries alone though they constitute lion's share of all such forces i.e., 78 per cent or above. The number of child labourers in the world has been calculated to be 210 million and thus, the magnitude of child labour had decreased by almost 25 per cent since 1995 (from 250 million to 210 million) resulting in child labour incidence of 20.2 per cent compared to 24.7 per cent five years earlier. On the basis of estimates in 2000, the ILO concluded, India is said to have the largest number of World's working children followed by Pakistan, Bangladesh, China, Nigeria, Kenya, and Egypt. India has 307 million children upto 14 years and 8 per cent of them is categorised as child labourers. Thus, India has 25 million child labourers which is 10 per cent of the 250 million child labouers in the world.

PROLOGUE

The preamble to the constitution resolved to secure to all its citizens social, economic and political justice, and equality of status and opportunity. There is provision in the constitution for promoting these objectives through fundamental rights and a set of directive principles of state policy. The accomplishment of these objectives warranted a number of specific duties which can be grouped into two broad categories. The first is related to the aspects of welfare comprising livelihood and conditions of work, health and nutrition, education, social security and equal access of all to law. Where the second identifies certain disadvantaged sections of the society like weaker sections, in particular the SCs and STs, women and children and youth, as requiring the special care and protection of the state. In any policy or strategy adopted for economic development these objectives need to be accomplished on a priority basis. India's aspiration to achieve higher economic growth rate may be possible if sufficient investments are made in the human capital and so the issue of the welfare of children who are the citizens of tomorrow being one of the major dimensions of human development deserve special attention. It is beyond imagination that a country can move forward with half of 16 million children undernourished, stunted, anaemic and illiterate. Denial of opportunities to children for their development and education is an issue of serious nature. Child labour is bad for the child as its natural development is impaired resulting in adverse repercussion on the economy. The process through which child labour adversely affects the economy is by way of lower human capital formation because if children start working at an early age, they would not be in a position to acquire human capital that is necessary for their own well-being *vis-a-vis* the economy. It needs hardly to be emphasized that, "The process of development is no more conditioned by Harrod-Domar's technical coefficients and the rate of physical capital alone, human capital is already surging ahead to replace physical capital as the sole mover of the growth process," (Chadha, G.K., 2002). Perhaps this is the reason for taking the issue of child labour seriously all over the world. About 191 countries in the world are legally obliged to respect and ensure all the rights set forth in the CRC for each child within their jurisdiction. Child labour is a universal phenomenon and its prevalence is more or less seen in all periods of time. However, the Declaration of 1979 as International Year of the Child in this paper is my focus to see what is happening to the child labourers in the post-reform era?

There, never was a period before 1991, when India did not face one crisis or another but never before had the country to contend with the convergence of such serious crisis, both internal and external as it faces in the very beginning of the last decade of the 20th century. Two terrifying crises of fiscal and balance of payments left no scope for the then government with Narasimha Rao as Prime Minister and Manmohan Singh as Finance Minister to go on with business as usual. To save country from the total collapse of international confidence in the fiscal and economic system drastic steps like adoption of economic reforms had to be taken. It is but true that the foreign exchange reserves were reduced to a dangerously low level, capable of meeting only a few weeks of imports and nearly 25 per cent of export earnings were needed for meeting external debt servicing obligations. Export earnings were only 50 per cent of the value of imports. Instead of the revenue surplus of the first three decades, during the 1980s the surpluses turned into deficit recording Rs. 45,000 crores and the total trade deficit in this period was Rs. 65,700 crores. The risks of runaway inflation and default on interest payment to foreign creditors persuaded the government to borrow from the International Monetary Fund (IMF) and the World Bank on condition of prudent fiscal and economic behaviour implying deflation, devaluation, decentralisation, and deregulation. These four Ds entail a shift away from the model of accumulation based on the domestic market at prices that did not discriminate between Imports and exports (Deshpande, Sharma, Karan, Sarkar, 2004). Undoubtedly, in the post-reform era the country appears more prosperous than ever before, For instance, the economy is expected to grow at a rate close to 8 per cent during 2003-04. There has been appreciable increase in the growth of exports and the country's foreign exchange reserves are in a comfortable position with more than 100 billion dollars. (Sharma, A.N., 2004) Dr. Manmohan Singh as a Finance Minister had expressed his optimistic outlook in these words, "We are creating a macro-economic environment in which industries speed ahead with a growth rate of 12 per cent or more, generate more jobs and higher levels of wages and incomes through increased productivity." The rationale of the introduction of reforms cannot be doubted. However, very often apprehensions have been expressed over the adverse effects of LPG model on livelihood, poverty, employment, and human development. There are a large number of vulnerable groups in India which, it is feared, may have to bear the costs of globalisation and liberalisation and child labour is one of such vulnerable group.

MAGNITUDE OF CHILD LABOUR

Child labour is not the domain of the developing countries alone though they constitute lion's share of all such forces i.e., 78 per cent or above. Child labour is also found in the developed countries like U.S.A., U.K., Japan and so on. As regards the developed countries, where a large number of school-age children are involved in part time work, they are working for their pocket money and usually are engaged in non-hazardous jobs. On the contrary, in the developing countries the children work for family survival even in hazardous situations. However, a much lower proportion of the children is working part-time in these countries, for example, less than 5 per cent in India (Cigno and Rosati, 2002). The number of child labourers in the world has been calculated to be 210 million and thus, the magnitude of child labour had decreased by almost 25 per cent since 1995 (from 250 million to 210 million) resulting in a child labour incidence of 20.2 per cent compared to 24.7 per cent five years earlier on the basis of estimates in 2000, the ILO concluded (Lieten, 2004). The problem of child labour is global in nature but it is more alarming in the developing countries particularly in India. The magnitude of this problem gets reflected in the fact that India is said to have largest number of world's working children followed by Pakistan, Bangladesh, China, Nigeria, Kenya and Egypt. India has 307 million children upto the age of 14 years and 8 per cent of them are categorised as child labour. Thus, India has 25 million child labourers in the world. The National Sample Survey (NSS) data in India suggests that India had 22 million child labourers in 1983, 17 million in 1987, 13 million in 1993, and 10 million in 2000 (Lieten, 2004) while the Census of India estimated it to be 13.7 million children. The Planning Commission says that it is likely to around 20 million by the year 200 (Kumar, V. and Prasanna, K., 1999). The wide variation in estimates is also due to the fact that there are varying perceptions with regard to the definition of child labour. It is not possible to have an exact estimate of child labour in India due to the informal and unorganised nature of labour market and such a scenario makes the figure of children working anywhere for payment in kind or money vary from source to source. It is but natural because they are more guess estimates than estimates. Whatever may be the estimates there is no denying that the magnitude of child labour is alarming in India, although this phenomena had also existed in one form or another in all historical periods. It existed in the form of child slaves. There is little evidence of the employment of children for wages, but if child slavery could be regarded as that, existence of child labour in ancient India cannot be denied. But even in ancient times the first reforms in the field of slavery came when Kautilya realised that children were not physically fit for doing noble work, and sought to bring about this idea in the form of imposition of a ban upon the sale of children as slaves. However, the economic practice of child labour in India, dates back to the Industrial Revolution in the country. Since then the demand of industry for cheap labour grew so rapidly and the poverty of the masses became so acute that the tendency to exploit child labour among the employers increased in an unprecedented manner. It is but very ironical that at a time when children should be enjoying their childhood days they are sweating it out in factories, agriculture fields, and in the process earning a paltry sum to support their poverty stricken families. It is worth-noting that earlier the jobs for children were confined to agriculture and plantations where they were involved in sowing and reaping, havesting, threshing, etc. besides taking care of the cattle and fodder but with industrialisation, their employability stretched to jobs involving harder and harsher physical labour. Hence, the problem attracts attention.

BIHAR'S SCENARIO

The problem of child labour emerges out of the socio-economic conditions prevailing in the country. And there is variation in the nature of child labour both state-wise and sector-wise. Agriculture and allied activities account for more than 4/5ths of the working childre; half of them working as agricultural labourers and the other half engaged as cultivators and in plantations, livestock, forestry, fishing, etc. The remainder that is less than 1/5th of child labour, is engaged in manufacturing, processing, servicing, trade, and commerce, construction, transport, storage, communication, etc. Bihar is an agriculture, dominated rural economy having about 85 per cent rural population and it is obvious from the above that child labour is prevalent more in the rural areas than in the urban centres. According to the latest NSS 55th round, 80.6 per cent of the total rural workforce is engaged in agriculture and allied activities. The state with 58 per cent rural poverty ratios witnesses the fact that an overwhelming majority of rural households live of a subsistence level. Bihar is one for the four BIMARU states, having unmanageable size of population, high density of population, high birth rate, high infant mortality rate, high dependency on agriculture, low age of marriage, low percentage of urban population, low literacy rate, low student enrollment rates, high dropout figures and above all strong caste-class nexus. The state is at the lowest rung of the literacy ladder. According to 2001 census, the percentage of literates is 47.5 per cent of the total population. This seems to indicate that children are not enrolled in school and thus, their poor educational status is one of the critical indicators of the prevalence and magnitude of child labour.

Whatever was found in the case of Ghana in the study conducted by the World Bank, is also applicable in the case of this backward state. The World Bank observed, that the high cost of schooling increases the probability of child work. This is because as children find that they cannot afford school, they are pushed into working in order to enable them to attend school, or it may just completely prevent them from going to school and participate in household enterprises. The PROBE (1999) report calculated that an agricultural labourer in Bihar with three children in school, for example would have to work for 40 days per year just to pay for educational costs. Ninety per cent of parents interviewed by the PROBE team quoted the direct costs of education as the main reason for not sending their children to school. In fact, there is evidence that many children work in order to pay for their own schooling or that of their sibling. (ILO, UNICEF 1997) Besides these, many parents feel frustration to see that many school leavers cannot find jobs and so they refuse to bear the costs of sending their children to school. As a result, the very state of education system often drives children away from school into work (Meir, 2002). Undoubtedly, when the type of education available is not very useful for to the occupations with which the children will have to be associated with in future, the parents may consider it to be a sheer wastage of time, energy, and opportunity to send their children formal education to any significant level. There is perhaps no reason in their view for bothering for the education of their children which only makes them misfit for jobs they will be compelled to take up when they grow up. Child labour is intricately connected with non-schooling of children. A large survey conducted in the year 1999-2000 in the six districts of Bihar by Piush Antony reveals the fact that 89.5 per cent of child workers have never had any schooling and 9.5 per cent have marginally attended schooling in primary education. A causal caste-class relationship in the contests of child workers is visible in Bihar when one finds that child workers belonging to the OBC, Muslim, SC and ST households have had no exposure to formal education. The illiteracy level among SCs/STs and Muslims is over 86 and 93 per cent respectively, while it is over 66 per cent among the forward castes. The state is still in the grip of a strong caste-class nexus and so the labour market segmentation in the state needs to be understood in terms of this nexus. Poverty, a key variable for explaining the magnitude of child labour in India and Bihar in particular, also emanates from this nexus. There is no denying the fact that the so-called lower caste groups still account for a major portion of the poorest of poor. Piush Antony in his microstudy of six districts in Bihar has found the highest concentration of child workers in households belonging to the categories of backward castes including Muslims as well as SCs/STs and the majority of child workers belong to either agricultural labour households or to families with marginal land holdings reflecting the caste class correlation. According to a study, child labour in Bihar constituted 1.28 per cent of the total population, 4.3 per cent of the total workforce, and 3.5 per cent of the total child population. The female child labour is more prevalent in the tribal areas of the state. In some parts of the state child labour is lured away by the carpet making industries in Mirzabad and Bhadoi belt in U.P. and also to work in brick industry. The grinding poverty in the lower castes in the rural areas forces the parents to send their children to work places rather than to the school. In Bihar, the unorganised sector accounts for a good portion of child labour engaged in various occupations such as; domestic servants, helpers or assistants in hotels, restaurants, road side dhabas, tea shop workers, news paper sellers, porters, shoe shine boys, sweepers, scavengers, in motor garages, book binding and paper cutting stores industries, stone crushing, loading and unloading of materials, beedi-making, carpet-weaving, etc. (R.K. Chatterjee and Arun Nandi in their article on child labour). Inter-state variations in rural India have rightly observed that "children in rural India compared to their urban counterparts are generally exploited and less tortured in their work place or in course of their work. They are often engaged in grazing cattle and collecting fuel and fodder. When they perform such types of job in a group. The work may give them some scope for relaxation and community enjoyment." Moreover, children working in their households where there is no guarantee of two times meals and facilities for entertainment in the form of T.V., feel somewhat better to work as servants in the high income group who are generally of upper class and where there is hundred per cent guarantee for two times meals and facilities for entertainment in their leisure period. It is true but at the same time it cannot be said less true that even children in urban sector feel not so bad working in hazardous condition because they have a kind of happiness to get rid of schooling which seems to them at that age worse job than any other. Besides this, they forget the hardship of their jobs when they receive their remuneration against their labour the joy of which is what extent harder that is as the mother who forget pain delivery after seeing the crying face of her child. It is but stark reality that Bihari children prefer work somewhere else to their home place where they feel some kind of pressure of guardians/parents. They like to go to Rajasthan, Punjab, Delhi or anywhere out of their home place because there they enjoy freedom to visit cinema, gamble and smoke cigarettes out of their meagre incomes received against their hard labour which is injurious to their health and hampers their all round development. Whatever amount they send to their parents after meeting all such types of expenses is an addition to their income and so they remain more or less satisfied and they feel that their children have freed them from bearing their cost of maintaining. Hesitation on the part of their children to go to school on the one side and on the other side their readyness to undertake their parent's job makes their parents indifferent to some extent in applying pressure on their children for going to school. And their parents feel satisfaction in taking their children's support in their jobs. This scenario is generally found in the case of middle income households. Where lower income households belonging to lower castes feel some kind of economic need to push their children in the labour market for getting economic support for maintaining their family having more children than that of ideal size of family i.e., only two children. In Muslims their religious dogma is more dominating factor than the cost benefit for having a larger size of their family. The percentage of nowhere children and street children is quite high in Bihar along with other poor states like Madhya Pradesh, Rajasthan, and Uttar Pradesh. Nowhere children are considered as potential child labourers who are nowhere because of lack of job opportunity. The incidence of nowhere children in the case of Bihar is 44.3 per cent next to Madhya Pradesh i.e., 44.4 per cent followed by Rajasthan and Uttar Pradesh having 44.0 per cent and 41.8 per cent respectively. On the contrary, the incidence of nowhere children is the lowest in Kerala having 8.5 per cent followed by Himachal Pradesh i.e., 12.4 per cent, Punjab i.e., 17.8 per cent, Maharashtra i.e., 18.3 per cent, Tamil Nadu i.e., 21.3 per cent and Andhra Pradesh i.e., 22.3 per cent. The sex-wise analysis reveals the fact that the percentage of nowhere girl-children is higher than for boys. Bihar witnesses 52 per cent nowhere boy children and 70.5 per cent nowhere girl children. Bihar is at the top so far as the percentage of nowhere children of both the sexes boys and girls separately is concerned, among the major states of the country. Bihar is followed by Uttar Pradesh, West Bengal, Rajasthan, Madhya Pradesh and Andhra Pradesh having 49.6 per cent, 43.8 per cent, 41.5 per cent, 38.2 per cent and 35.3 per cent nowhere boys children respectively whereas it is followed by Uttar Pradesh 68.6 per cent, Rajasthan 66.1 per cent, West Bengal 54.3 per cent, Madhya Pradesh 52.6 per cent, Orissa 49.2 per cent and Andhra Pradesh 48 per cent in the case of nowhere girl children. Once again Kerala is state having the lowest percentage of nowhere children recording only 12.9 per cent in both the sexes followed by Himachal Pradesh having 20.3 per cent and 26.7 per cent in boys and girls cases respectively. Thus, the highest percentage of children who are not working and not enrolled is a sufficient indication for having little job opportunities for such job-seeking children in the state and at the same it also reflects higher degree of bad habits which make these street children their victims.

Bihar is a state having 4.4 per cent and 1.6 per cent incidence of rural and urban child labour in the age groups 5-14 respectively and its ranking based on the incidence of child labour is fifth in rural case and fourth in urban case as per 1991 Census. Kerala is the state recording lowest incidence of child labour i.e., 0.6 per in rural case and 0.5 per cent in urban case and thus, it has got first ranking in both rural and urban cases whereas Andhra Pradesh has the highest incidence of rural child labourers that is 12.5 per cent and the incidence of urban child labourer is 3.1 per cent next to Karnataka. It is interesting to note down that child labour incidence is high in southern states like Andhra Pradesh, Karnataka, and Tamil Nadu whereas poorer states like Bihar, Uttar Pradesh, Madhya Pradesh, and Orissa have lower incidence comparatively. The lowest incidence of child labour is found in Kerala which reveals the fact that Kerala is a state where nearly 100 per cent literacy is found. Children from literate households are less oriented towards child labour as it is associated with the level of literacy. It is well known that parents who had themselves been in school are presumbly more likely to invest in education of their children. In a study of 'Part Time Labour Force Participation of Pakistan children' it was found that one additional year of education of father decreases the part-time work by 9.9 per cent whereas in case of mother's education one additional year of her education decreases the part-time work by 13 per cent. Thus, the impact of mother's education is stronger than that of father (Khan Ali and Ali Karamat, 2004). Here it is worth-noting that whatever is true for the part-time work is also true for full-time work, difference is only in percentage. Above all, a child living in a household containing a large number of children is more likely to be living in poverty than a child residing in a household with few children reflecting the intra-household resource competition so much so that children have to do part-time or full-time work to support their households' expenditure. Needless to say Bihar's economic backwardness exhibited by low employment opportunities, poverty, low literacy rate and inadequate infrastructural facilities are considered to be the prime cause of child labour.

IMPACT OF ECONOMIC REFORM ON CHILD LABOUR

In the post-reform era labour issue has attracted worldwide attention. In recent years this issue has acquired more prominence because of discussions on the relationship between international trade and labour standards in the context of World Trade Organisation (WTO). The international crusade against child labour waged by the world bodies like the ILO and the WTO is hardly guided by any ethical or humanitarian motive. The reality lies in the fact that in the shadow of human rights for children there is a *malafide* intentions on the past of the developed countries to protect their own industries, trade and agriculture. Their sole motive is to preserve the interests of the MNCs by depriving the labour-intensive export industries of LDCs of cost advantages in the international market. The WTO takes child labour in the developing countries as an excuse to restrict goods from these counties because the production of such goods employs cheap child labour. In such a scenario, the issue of child labour has become a trump card in the hands of the WTO and the ILO to serve the interest of the U.S.A., the U.K., and E.U., and thus, this becomes an explosive bone of contention between the developed countries and the developing counties like India. The developed countries have raised this issue for creating serious hurdles in the way of our export-oriented growth strategy. As a result, this issue raised by *malafide* intention of the developed countries in the name of new economic system has adverse repercussions on the economic health of our nation.

Some organisational observations (ILO and UNICEF) are unequivocal about poverty as the major determinant of child labour. Under the dictates of the IMF-World Bank prescriptions of the LPG strategy as a straight jacket solution for all, a large number of developing countries including India throughout the world had adopted such policies no doubt, but what has happened to poverty, unemployment and inequality in the post-reform era in India? The latest official statistics on poverty (1999-2000) suggest that nearly 26 per cent of our population is below the poverty line whereas non-official estimates are much higher. Whatever the figure this may be, it cannot be said to be comforting figure for a country which is aiming at poverty eradication for the last five decades or more. Apart from the relatively large proportion of households suffering from low income, rural households also suffer from deprivation in terms of education which works as a fuel to fire child labour and the most worrisome feature is the addition of the new poor among agricultural households due to different types of shocks e.g., disease and death of the earning member, loss of assets due to natural disasters or loss of livelihood or severe impact on the current income due to market induced factors. Of course, the last two shocks are by-product of LPG strategy directly or indirectly and thus, it results in increasing the scope for enhancement in the number of child labourer. Bihar is one of six states where a large concentration of the chronically poor, i.e. over 70 per cent is found. Besides Bihar, these states are undivided Uttar Pradesh, Madhya Pradesh, Maharashtra, West Bengal and Orissa. Among these three states, undivided Bihar, Uttar Pradesh and Madhya Pradesh account for approximately 36 per cent of the country's population but 48 per cent of the poor. Apart from the chronically poor a dampening effect on schooling because of cuts in education expenditure in the initial years of the reform era is also a shocking factor if we assume that quality of schooling is one of the determinants of child labour. No doubt, the globalisation process can reduce or increase the education expenditure depending on how the countries are successful in mobilising resources through tax and non-tax sources and the priority given to education but widening gap between the rich and the poor in the post-reform era leaves little scope for the latter to increase their expenditure on education. Moreover, education has become highly expensive and on the other side, the government has to import most advanced and expensive technology for reducing the cost of their domestic products to compete in the international market. This is the reason behind the curtailment of educational expenditure at least in the initial stage of economic reform because the meagre resources in the form of monetary income, in such developing countries cannot meet all the expenses at the same time to the desired extent. Fourteen years of economic reforms is reasonably a long-term to make its impact visible. Inspite of more than 6 per cent GDP growth rate after 1992-93 there was no reduction in percentage of population below the poverty line. Instead, there was an increase in poverty percentage. There is also decline in employment growth rate both in the organised and unorganised sector. There was an increase in the proportion of casual labour, indicative of a shift from secure and regulated employment to insecure and unregulated employment. If growing unemployment and inequality, growth of informal sector, modification of goods and services and lure of consumerism are considered as major determinants of child labour, we cannot hope to get rid of the problem of child labour. It is hoped that economic growth will generate productive employment and help to eradicate poverty and illiteracy but in vain. It is a paradox of the illiteracy development process that despite the alarming growth of unemployment in the developing countries which have failed to come to grips with the problem of unemployment while there exists high incidence of child labour, exploitative forms of child labour has crossed the level of reasonableness in society and has become a matter of disgrace particularly in India. The persistence of child labour is attributable not only to rise in its supply but also to rise in demand for it. They are in demand primarily because they can be substituted for adult labour. The displacement of adult worker can also increase the problem of unemployment. In fact, a series of factors, such as the payment of low wages, absence of trade unions, ease in handling, long working hours, less scope for job change and no necessity for compensation motivate the employer of substitute child labour for adults. (Mohanty and Mahapatra, 2000). In such scenario, how can the problem of child labour be solved? The reality lies in this fact that the situation has worsened with economic reforms where market is the temple and money is God.

CONCLUDING REMARKS

Amartya Sen in his lecture at ILO Geneva (1999) said, "It is often claimed that the abolition of child labour will harm the interests of the children themselves, since they may end up starving because of lack of family income and also because of increased neglect. It is certainly right that the fact of family poverty must be considered in dealing with this issue. There is no escape from that. But it is not at all clear why it must be presumed the aboliion of child labour will lead only to a reduction of family income and further neglect of children, without any other economic or social or educational adjustment. The case for a broader and more inclusive economic analysis and ethical examinations is very strong in all these cases. It is but true that child labour connot be abolished as long as there are widespread poverty, unemployment, illiteracy, inequality, low wage, larger size of family, etc. The problem of child labour is a socio-economic demographic problem and so it cannot be settled by mere legislation, better enactment of laws and by imposition of heavy penalty. A variety of remedial measures can be suggested for the eradication of this ill. Broadly based growth that reduces poverty along with increased, better adult employment opportunities may in the long-run be more conducive to alleviating the incidence of child labour, introduction of compulsory free education, mid-day meal scheme, etc. alongwith prohibition of use of child labour can be suggested for reducing he numbers of children working in rural areas and as part of family labour but fertility and population control policies are so significant in this concern that they cannot be ignored. There are countries like Japan, Republic of Korea, Singapore, Kuwait, and Saudi Arabia where both population below poverty line and child labour are now completely absent and so the process of economic development must accompany successful implementation of social sector reforms for eradication of this ill. But, our fourteen years experience of development paradigm is desirable to solve the problem of child labour along with other measures. The literacy ladder has recorded 47.5 per cent literates in 2001. This seems to indicate that children are not attracted to school and thus, their poor educational status is one of the critical indicators of the prevalence and magnitude of child labour. The high costs of schooling increases the probability of child work. The PROBE (1999) report calculated that an agricultural labourer in Bihar with three children in school, for example, would have to work for 40 days per year just to pay for educational costs. Ninety per cent of parents interviewed by the PROBE team quoted the direct costs of education as the main reason for not sending their children to school. There is evidence that many children work in order to pay of their own schooling or that of their sibling (ILO, UNICEF, 1997). The state is still in the grip of a strong caste-class nexus and so the labour market segmentation in the state needs to be understood in terms of this nexus. All the state level surveys confirm that food insecurity is concentrated largely among the lower castes and class groups and that in most cases size of family in the lower castes in the rural areas forces the parents to send their children to work places rather than to the school. Bihar is a state having 4.4 per cent and 1.6 per cent incidence of rural and urban child labour in the age group 5-14 respectively and its ranking based on the incidence of child labour is fifth in rural case and fourth in urban case as per 1991 Census.

In the post-reform era child labour issue has attracted a world-wide attention. The WTO takes child labour in the developing countries as an excuse to restrict goods from these countries because the production of such goods employs cheap labour. The issue of child labour has become a trump card in the hands of the WTO and the ILO to serve the interest of the U.S.A., the U.K., and E.U. The developed countries have raised this issue for creating hurdles in the way of our export-oriented strategy. Poverty, unemployment, and inequality are the major determinants of child labour. In the post-reform era, these problems become more serious and so there is no question of eradication of child labour. The most worrisome feature is the addition of the new poor among agricultural households due to different type of shocks. Some shocks are by-product of LPG strategy and, thus, it results in increasing the scope for enhancement in the number of child labourers. If we assume that quality of schooling is one of determinants, cuts in education expenditure in the initial years of reforms is also a shocking factor.

The problem of child labour is a socio-economic-demographic problem and so it cannot be settled by mere legislation. It cannot be solved as long as there is widespread poverty, unemployment, illiteracy, inequality, low wage, larger size of family etc. A pro-poor growth strategy as an alternative development paradigm is desirable for solving the problem of child labour along with other measures.

REFERENCES

Deshpande, A.N. Sharma, A.K. Karan and Sarkar (2004), "Liberalisation and Labour", IHD, New Delhi.

G.K. Lieten (2004), "Child Labour and Work Numbers from the General to Specific", Memorial Lecture, 46th Conference, Indian Society of Labour Economics.

N. Ramachandra, Lionel Massun (2000), "Coming to Grips with Rural Child Work", IHD, New Delhi.

—— (2004), *Indian Journal of Labour Economics*, Vol. 47, No. 2.

—— (2000), *The Indian Economic Association*, Conference Vol. 83.

Yojana, Government of India.

14

Economic Reforms and Child Labour

MD. REYAZUDDIN

The problem of child labour has been a worldwide problem; child labour is not new phenomenon to our age. What is new, however, is its perception as a social problem the world over. What seems to be realistic and pragmatic at the present stage of development is to develop such conditions in which children, instead of being forced to take up employment, may be able to go to school and pursue their studies effectively and in which those children who have unfortunately been driven to work, may also be able to start getting their education and to work in a healthy and congenial atmosphere, in such a manner that their involvement in work does not mar their proper personality development. Broadly speaking; widespread poverty, illiteracy, and ignorance of parents are the main causes for the rampant prevalence of child labour in our country.

Child labour is embedded in the fabric of our society and this is one of the serious problems facing the country as a whole. Now the basic question is, "can we identify" set of interventioist or a set of uniform programmes to effectively deal with the problem and need of working child throughout the country? Perhaps not. The reason is that the situation that makes a child to work varies so much, that it is difficult to suggest measures suited to all situations.

Concept of Child Labour

The term 'child labour' is used as a synonym for 'employed child' or 'working child'. It is very difficult to give a precise definition of child labour; however, child labour, can be defined as that segment of the child population which participates in work, either paid or unpaid. Any work by children that interferes with their full physical development, the opportunities for a desirable minimum of education and their needed recreation is called child labour (Stein and Davis, 1940). An All India Child Labour Sample Survey Commissioned by the Ministry of Labour in 1980-81, defined a working child as "that child who . . . falling within the five to fifteen age bracket . . . is at enumerated work, may be paid or unpaid . . . within or outside the family." Usually, the concept of child labour stands for the participation of children below 14 years of age in the labour force for paid or unpaid work. Now-a-days, child labour is a widespread phenomena. It is not only confined to work on family farm or in traditional family jobs and occupations but it has also extended to other fields. They work in agriculture and allied activities, unorganized small-scale sector and even in organized industries.

What is Child Labour?

It is difficult to determine who falls under the category of 'child labourer' since it is culturally a relative term. According to the ILO Convention 138—the standard setting instrument on child labour—the term refers to any child under a specifically defined age who is engaged in employment.

In an effort to arrive at clear definitions of child labour, many academics, policy-makers, and child advocates have begun to make a distinction between 'child work' and 'child labour'. Lieten (2001, p. 2) defines 'work' as any type of work being done in any mode of relationship. The concept of work serves as a description of the physical or mental involvement in the job. Labour, on the other hand, should be regarded as the production of goods and services that interferes with the normative development of children. This could also be the case when the child is doing strenuous household work that pre-empts schooling and leisure.

Many find the distinction between work and labour difficult to apply, since most of the work that children perform falls in the grey area in between these two extremes. White (1999) has developed a continuum that contains more gradations and that allows for more subtlety in assessing the nature of children's work. Rather than simply making a distinction between labour and work, the continuum makes distinctions between work that is intolerable, detrimental or hazardous, neutral or positive. The latter is the case when, for example, work is not harmful, contributes to self-esteem and provides useful skills (IWGCL, 1998, pp. 40-41). On the basis of this continuum, children's engagement in activities that are considered intolerable, detrimental or hazardous should be considered 'labour' and should generate concern and lead to intervention.

Why is Child Labour a Problem?

While not all work is harmful to children, there is a great deal of evidence that many children are engaged in labour that is detrimental to their well-being. The ILO therefore, refers to child labour as the 'single most important source of child exploitation and child abuse in the world today' and as 'a future denied' (ILO, 1996, p. 8). Child labour can damage child's health and psychological well-being, interfere with schooling and undermine his or her potential, and the potential of society at large.

Although there has been relatively little research on the conditions under which children work and the impact of work on their health, the studies that are available reflect clear evidence that children are more vulnerable to occupational hazards and are adversely affected by them. Children engaged in agricultural work, construction work or mining, for example, are exposed to dangerous chemical products and mechanical equipment and to unhygienic conditions. While these conditions are serious for the adults, they are even more detrimental to the children.

Childhood is the period of rapid growth and development and any insult or interruption in the process for a long period of time will cause life-long deficiency. Doctors and researchers agree that working children are at an increased risk of mortality and morbidity because of the incomplete maturation of their cells, organs and systems, and because of the higher proportion of surface area of some organs such as skin and lungs as compared to that of adults. Furthermore, young children's systems and tissues lack the plasticity and adaptability of the adults to irritants (Shah, 1996, p. 6). Moreover, children are, dependent on the care of others, cannot defend themselves easily, and are therefore, easy targets of exploitation and abuse. When they work outside the realm of their protected environments, they are vulnerable to ill-treatment, which can have adverse, long-term psychological effects (Stegeman, 2004).

Child labour is also detrimental because it interferes with a child's ability to attend school or concentrate in class. Today, lack of education is especially damaging because individual success increasingly depends on literacy, numeracy, and intellectual competence. Education is, perhaps, the most useful tool of self-realisation and social advancement. Children who do not attend school cannot develop the intellectual and social skills that in adulthood are linked with higher earnings, greater job security, and competitiveness in the labour market. This reduces the prospect of escaping the poverty trap into which most children who have to work are born. Education and training are the most effective social investment that the governments can make because of their significant 'multiplier effects'. Returns to individuals include higher incomes, lower fertility rates, improved health and coping skills and higher life-long productivity (Himes and Saltarelli, 1995, p. 228).

Another reason to be concerned is that a high incidence of child labour undermines that development of societies as a whole. The fact that work may harm children, and interfere with their education and obstruct national economic and social development makes child labour a matter of extremely poor economics. When children's physical and psychological well-being are damaged during childhood and they fail to get education, the potential contributions that they could make to economic and social development are lost. Child labour, thus, leads to a vicious cycle of individual poverty and under-development. Edwards (1996, p. 820) makes this point succinctly thus:

"Children are . . . once-and-for-all biological window of opportunity for investment in human beings. Losses incurred can never be made good and a failure to support children as children will have permanent effects on society's capacity to develop."

Development of Modern Concept of 'Childhood'

As noted above, it is very difficult to define child labour since the term is culturally relative. Nevertheless, childhood as experienced by children in the developed countries serves as a model that all societies strive to achieve. International standards on child labour reflect this model, which sees childhood as a period of growth and development, in which children should attend school, be provided for and be sheltered from the adult world of work.

The modern concept of childhood developed as a result of the Industrial Revolution. Before the Industrial Revolution, most children worked alongside their parents in agricultural areas. When at the onset of the Industrial Revolution, growing numbers of the rural population were displaced and had to seek a living in the factories of emerging urban areas children became wage earners alongside their parents to contribute to family earnings. There was at this time little concern that work might be harmful to children. In a world where mass education systems were not yet in place, the view prevailed that work would benefit them (Stegeman, 2004). As working class children became increasingly exposed to the rigours of working life, the lives of children of the growing bourgeois class became more protected (Lavalette, 1997, p. 220). The bourgeois children's experience of childhood inspired thinkers and writers to develop the image of children as passive, unformed and vulnerable beings and to reflect childhood as a period of happiness and dependency. This model of childhood was adopted as the norm, as the notion that parents should provide for their children, and send them to school. Not to rely on a child's work or income became a principle of social ethics.

Moral considerations helped fuel, but did not lead to, the development. It was made possible as a result of a general increase in income levels that enabled all parents to provide for their children and to send them to school. The general rise in wages was the result of technological developments and economic growth. This meant a decrease in demand for low skilled workers, including child labourers. As industry and the economy grew, trade unions became more powerful and demanded improvements in labour conditions. Workers also began to demand a 'family wage', whereby the male head of the household could earn enough to feed his family (Lavalette, 1997, p. 222).

These factors led the state to intensify efforts to implement legislation to limit children's factory work and to enforce compulsory school attendance. A broad spectrum of activities that children engaged in were left untouched by legislation: housekeeping, child-minding, helping and assisting adults for no pay on the family farm, in small enterprises and shops, domestic service, street-selling, running errands, etc. These activities were considered necessary for the livelihood of the family and remained morally unquestioned. Rather than being considered 'labour', these activities were defined as training, helps and socialization.

Around the turn of the century, standards already in place in most industrialized countries found their way into international legislation. Since its inception in 1919, the ILO has played a particularly important role in the field of child labour, devoting a major part of its standard-setting activity to abolition. Several months after it was created, the ILO adopted the Convention No. 5, which prohibits work by children under 14 years of age in industrial undertakings. This was the first of 20 Conventions and recommendations addressing the issue of child labour. In 1973, all the existing ILO Conventions regarding child labour were consolidated into the ILO Convention No. 138 and Recommendation No. 146. This Convention has come to be regarded as the standard setting instrument when it comes to child labour (Stegeman, 2004) However, relatively fewer states have ratified this Minimum Age Convention. As of mid-1997, only 63 countries ratified it (Stegeman, 2004).

Globalisation and Causes of Child Labour

Given the parallels that exist between the situation of children working in 'traditional' economies and children in pre-industrial Europe, it is easy to jump to the conclusion, that the answer to the problem of child labour lies in economic development. Child labour will be similarly marginalized when the developing countries industrialise and achieve economic growth along the lines of their Western counterparts.

Only a few developing countries, however, are experiencing considerable economic growth and technological change.

Conditions in the international political economy are making it very difficult for developing countries to achieve economic growth, with the ensuing increase in wages, decrease in demand for child labour and increase in demand for an educated workforce. The need for children to work is not likely to decline in the near future as the effects of economic competition, commodification, consumerism, and the growing gap between the rich and the poor are drawing children into the workforce.

Today, the international climate in which countries must achieve economic growth is highly competitive and volatile, with large differences in the resource bases of states and their 'competitors'. The developing countries also face the burden of having to repay debts, which reflects and outflow of money that could be spent on industrial and social development. The conditions under which the developing countries must achieve economic growth are also far from stable, since they depend largely on foreign investment and face the threat of investor 'bail out', when investors do not like the conditions as was recently experienced by countries such as, Thailand and Indonesia.

Production techniques in many agricultural regions remain poor and generate meager incomes. Incomes also remain low due to population growth which diminishes land availability and market competition. Poverty in rural areas may intensify because of mass manufacturing and the commodification of goods. Basic necessities, such as water, are becoming commodities and sold at marker prices. Under these conditions, more and more people are migrating to urban areas, where incomes are higher, even in the large informal sector. Here again, all family members must work to scrape together a living.

Since the price of labour is cheap, wages and remuneration for goods and services are so low that the only way the poorest families can survive is to enlist the labour of children who work within or outside the home to supplement the family income. Children in these countries often contribute the bulk of their earnings to their families (Stegeman, 2004).

The processes of globalisation are changing social expectations and altering cultural relations throughout the world by exposing societies to consumer culture, or to the demand for goods other than basic necessities. The social disease of consumerism has raised the need for additional money. Examples illustrate that children are being exploited not because of absolute poverty but as a result of relative poverty. Social status is often attained and reflected by ownership of consumer goods.

Consumerism is also enticing children and youth into the labour market, as they too want to earn money to purchase goods that represent participation in a universal youth culture and thereby higher social status. Youth throughout the world who want to be a part of this culture need money to buy the consumer goods that associate them with it. Ironically, this means that they must join the adult world and work (White, 1996, p. 830).

While poverty generates the need for children to work, the other side of the coin is that there must be a demand for labour. The developing countries have, as noted above, vast pool of unemployed or underemployed unskilled labour. Children are the cheapest workers of all. This makes them attractive to employers who otherwise might hire adults from the large pool of available labour (Gilbert and Gugler, 1992, p. 93).

Export or domestic industries that provide labour intensive and/or low cost and low quality goods survive by undercutting price of machine or foreign made products. Wages must, therefore, be as low as possible. Carpet loom owners in India, for example, work to such slim profit margins that they can as much as double their income by utilizing child workers (Stegeman, 2004). Eliminating child labour would, they argue, entail a serious drop in their profits.

It should be noted that expenses and profit margins are not the only reason why there is a demand for child labour. Many times children are employed because they are easy targets for those who seek to exploit the labour of others; they are less aware of their rights, less troublesome and more willing to take orders to do monotonous work without complaining (Lieten, 2001; ILO, 1996, p. 20). Children are also thought to be particularly useful in some activities and occupations because they are smaller, more agile, and can move faster than adults. Sometimes employers perceive themselves, and are perceived to be doing families a favour by employing children, since they provide families with a source of income, and children with the opportunity to learn a trade.

The enforcement of compulsory education in the countries that underwent early industrialization was instrumental in reducing child labour. These measures were effective because they were necessitated by and reinforced through changes in the production process. The developing countries, however, lack demand for highly skilled labour. Because of this, governments lack strong incentives to invest in the development of quality public education system. At the same time, parents and children lack the incentive to pursue it.

Education has additional attraction to parents and children if they believe that it leads to social and economic returns. Unfortunately, in many developing countries this perception does not exist. The material taught in schools may have little relation to children's experiences, as schools are often of bad quality, arbitrarily imposing strict discipline, and encouraging rote learning, thereby doing little to develop children's self-esteem and impart the most basic of skills. This may be one of the factors discouraging attendance. While school gives children the status of a dependent minor, work can provide children with rewards and give them status within the family and the community as a whole. Therefore, it gives children pleasure and self-confidence, even when the conditions are hazardous and long. Work also enables children to earn the global youth culture. Chinh has argued that many parents and children only pursue education if they believe it will lead to material benefits. In the wake of the transition in Vietnam from a planned to a market economy, education is no longer the only or secure path to material success, and many children and youth opt to work, rather than attend school.

The idea that people's social status is pre-ordained and that the poor have fewer rights than the wealthier members of society also persists amongst a number of social groups. Without a good public education system, which generates opportunities for upward mobility, it is very difficult to break away from such hegemonic ideas. Whereas poverty may seem the major underlying cause of child labour, inequality is a more important determinant. The result of a quantitative cross-country empirical study conducted by Ahmed (in Lieten, 2000, p. 2038) makes him conclude thus:

> "Contrary to expectations, our empirical results clearly confirm that poverty is only a minor explanatory factor behind the incidence of child labour. Poverty ranked last

> among the seven determinants of child labour in terms of their respective explanatory power . . . After accounting for the set of eight factors that influence child labour, it can be concluded from our multiple regression results that economies with very unequal income distribution and with a high dependence on agriculture have higher rates of employment of child labour."

Inequality reflects, by definition, that the resources that are available in society are not distributed in a fairly equitable fashion. Some poor areas have lower levels of child labour than their richer counterparts because the resources that are available are better distributed; all children can, for example, attend school and do not have to work full time. When countries in the North/West were industrialized, the labour movement in formal sectors of the economy gained power *vis-a-vis* the owners of capital to demand a more equitable distribution of resources. It is unlikely that greater equity can be achieved in the same way in the developing countries given the structures of today's political economy. As discussed earlier, formal sectors constitute just a very small part of the developing countries' economies and workers in these sectors have seen their bargaining power reduced. It is also very difficult to organize workers in the informal and agricultural sectors of the economy. Furthermore, since production structures have become increasingly complex and fragmented, it is also hard to determine and target the sources of inequality and exploitation, especially of those who are excluded from the formal economy.

CONCLUSION

Thus, the present paper is an attempt in defining nature and problems of child labour in the context of globalisation. Initiatives are being taken today to address the problem of child labour. Child labour is a social and economic problem. Since social and economic problems are global in nature, they require a global approach. Two new international human rights conventions, such as the ILO 182 and the CRC, have been developed in recent years to tackle the problem of child labour. These conventions have been designed to mobilize the governments and civil society to take action on eradications child labour.

Thus, child labour cannot be weeded out despite several welfare legislations enacted by the government from time to time.

It needs a change in our social attitude. Social awareness is also needed to discourage the practice of child labour. Besides this, the tightening of laws and activating enforcement machinery is needed badly to weed out child labour in its true perspective. Long-term and short-term measures are required to check this menace. This problem cannot be seen in isolation from other social changes. Besides, the role of Government and NGOs would be to play very effective roles in implementing the Government schemes for children's welfare. After all, children are the blooming flowers of the garden of our society. Therefore, it is every one's responsibility to protect these flowers from the damaging effects of excessive exposure to heat, cold, and rains. They should be put on the right track always as they are the seeds of future national growth.

REFERENCES

Edwards, M. (1996), "Policy Arena of Children in Development, New Approaches to Children and Development: Introduction and Overview," *Journal of International Development*, Vol. 8, No. 6, pp. 813-27.

Gilbert, A. and Gugler, J. (1992), *Cities, Poverty and Development: Urbanitiation in the Third World*, Oxford University Press, Oxford.

Himes, J. (ed.) (1994): *Implementing the Convention on the Rights of the Child: Resource Mobilisation in Low-Income Countries*, Martinus Nijhoff, The Hague.

ILO (1996), Child Labour: Targeting the Intolerable, 86th Session, Report VI (1), International Labour Organisation, Geneva.

IWGCL (1998), *Working Children, Reconsidering the Debates, International Working Group on Child Labour*, DCI and ISPCAN, Amsterdam.

Lavalette, M. (1997), *Child Employment in the Capitalist Labour Market*, Avebury Press, Aldershot.

Lieten, G.K. (2000), "Child Work and Education," I: General Parameters, and II: Field Work in two UP Villages, *Economic and Political Weekly*, Nos. 24 and 25, pp. 2037-43 and pp. 2171-81.

—— (2001), "Child Labour: Questions on Magnitude," in Lieten, G.K. and White, Ben (eds.), *Child Labour: Policy Options*, Aksant, Amsterdam.

Shah, P.M. (1996), "Physical and Mental Health of Working Children: Gaps in Our Knowledge and Challenge for Pediatricians," in Waal, F. De *et.al.* (eds).

Stegeman, I. (2004), "Child Labour in the Context of Globalisation" in *Working Children Around The World* (Edited by G.K. Lieten), Institute for Human Development, New Delhi and IREWOC Foundation, Amsterdam.

Stein, E. and J. Davis (eds.) (1940), *Labour Problem in America*, New York.

White, B. (1999), "Defining the Intolerable: Child Work, Global Standards and Cultural Relativism," *Childhood*, Vol. 6, No. 1.

15

Impact of Reforms on Child Labour

PASHUPATI RAY AND SHAMBHU PRASAD SAH

The phenomenon of child labour is a symptom of disease and is a consequence of exploitative system, operating at the national and international levels, lopsided development, uneven resource ownership correlating of large-scale unemployment and abject poverty among the nations. The practice of child labour in India or in any other country of the world is an age-old phenomenon. In pre-industrial agricultural society of India, children worked as helpers and learners in hereditarily determined family occupations under the benign supervision of adult family members. The work place was an extension of the home and work was characterized by personal informal relationships. The task and technology that work involved were simple and non-hazardous.

Globalisation is a fact of twenty-first century which cannot be overlooked. It is a process by which an increasing share of world production is traded internationally and the productive systems of different countries become more and more interdependent. Given that globalisation is unlikely to stop, it seems reasonable and desirable to understand the consequences and various dimensions of globalisation. There must be gainers and losers from the process of globalisation. Who are they? Are children among the latter or among the former? Is further liberalisation and privatization likely to raise the number of children engaged in labour? Is there a direct link between exposure to international trade and child labour? However, it must be remembered that globalisation is different from internationalization. While the latter refers to economic and social interactions that occur across national boundaries, the former denotes the expanding scale, growing magnitude, speeding up and deepening impact of inter-regional flows and patterns of social interaction. Globalisation process in not limited to economic dimension, it also involves a number of key non-economic forms of social interactions relating to culture and governance.

Moreover, globalisation has also changed the traditional economic thinking that countries with a relative abundance of labour i.e., the developing countries will export labour intensive products, while countries with a relative abundance of capital, i.e. the developed countries will export capital-intensive products. Since, within each country, an increase in trade raises the price of the abundant factor relative to that of the scarce one an implication of this thinking would be that 'globalisation', will make workers worse-off relative to capitalists in the developed world. This vision of the world has undergone a change over the last few decades, while the traditional theory equated economic growth with the accumulation of physical capital (buildings and machinery) per head of population; modern theory attaches much greater importance to the accumulation of human capital (knowledge and personal skills). The human capital is embodied in skilled workers. Further, globalisation does not simply mean more international trade in final goods. It also means more trade in intermediate goods. Falling transportation costs and advances in linkages and information technology, facilitating the co-ordination of dispersed production activities, are in fact favouring the segmentation of production process as also the location of different segments of the same process in different countries. Although the immediate beneficiary of this intra-industry trade expansion are developed industrial countries, the potential implications of such process for developing countries, in general and for child labour in particular, cannot be overlooked.

The impact of globalization on child labour in India becomes crucial because India is the home to the world's largest population of children. India, as a nation, has always proclaimed to follow a proactive policy in the matter of elimination of child labour. This is sought to be achieved through constitutional and statutory provisions combined with a range of development measures and policies. The strategy of the Government has been to eliminate child labour sequentially beginning with the most hazardous forms and subsequently moving towards the less hazardous forms. Since the Global Report on Child Labour, 2002, prepared by the ILO highlighted the close interlink between poverty and child labour, India is also trying to address the issue through the implementation of its national poverty eradication programmes and simultaneous sustained efforts at providing primary education to the children. Education for all children in the age-group of 6-14 years has been made a Fundamental Right by the 93rd Amendment Bill to the Constitution passed in May 2002 (86th Amendment Act).

Besides being a founder member of the ILO, India has ratified 39 ILO conventions. Out of which 20 are core conventions. The ratification by India of the UN Convention on Rights of the Child (CRC) in 1992, has set in motion a process of greater state initiative and public accountability. It has imposed a legal obligation upon the state to "undertake all appropriate legislative, administrative and other measures for the implementation of the rights recognised in the convention as well as its responsibility to submit to the committee on rights of the child periodical reports on the measures that they have adopted which give effect to the rights recognised and the progress made on the enjoyment of those rights."

The Constitution of India lays down that child labour in factories, mines and any other hazardous occupations should be prohibited (Art. 24), and that children below the age of 14 years should get free and compulsory primary education (Art. 45); because the tender age of children should not be abused and that they are not forced to enter avocations unsuited to their age and strength (Art. 39-C). The Constitution also states that children be given opportunities and facilities to develop in a healthy manner, and in conditions of freedom and dignity, and that childhood be protected against moral and material abandonment (Art. 39-f). Read together, the above constitutional provisions have a potential for laying down very comprehensive guidelines for total elimination of child labour.

Legislation pertaining to child labour has existed in India for over a hundred years. The enactment of the Factories Act, 1881, and the Mines Act, 1901, was to some extent, influenced by the ratification of ILO Conventions by British India. From the time of independence, India has committed itself against child labour. Guided by the provisions of Art. 24, Art. 39, and Art. 45 of the Constitution of India, India has sought to take care of its children and ensure the safety of workers. Bonded labour was sought to ended by the Bonded Labour System Act of 1976, while the Child Labour Act, 1986 'prohibits the employment of children who have not completed their 14th year in specified hazardous occupations and processes'. However, the Act does not fulfil the suggestion of ILO Convention No. 138 that the minimum age for employment should not be less than fifteen years. In 1994, the Elimination of Child Labour Programme was announced which pledged to end child labour for two million children in hazardous industries as defined in the Act of 1986 by the year 2000. But only about 4 percent of the five year estimated cost of eight and a half billion dollars was allocated for child labour elimination programmes in 1995-96.

The main cause of child labour is assumed to be poverty. Indeed, data reveal a negative association between income and child labour. Similarly, higher primary enrolment is associated with lower labour participation among children. The correlation cannot be perfect partly because work in informal or illegal labour markets is usually underreported, and partly also because a sizeable proportion of children combines, in some countries, work with school attendance.

It is important to keep in mind the fact that children do not normally choose to work. Mostly, the decisions are thrust upon them by their parents. Even in the case of the child who is expelled, or runs away from home, the reason for his or her working can be traced back to parental actions that made it impossible for the child to remain in the home. The only exception are children who are abducted, or who get lost or are separated from their families due to war, or some natural disaster. A cross-national study edited by on Giovanni Andree Cornia on "Harnessing Globalization for Children: A Report to Unicef" shows that, exposure to international trade does not appear to encourage child labour. On the contrary, higher foreign trade appears to be associated with a lower incidence of child labour. However, the existence of considerable national differences in the exposure to international trade and the incidence of child labour seems to indicate that the type of policies a country pursues shifts the relationship between child labour and globalization.

The study also concludes on the basis of data surveyed that there is no *prima facie* evidence that globalization will necessarily result in more child labour. Rather, it finds signs that suggest that international trade and economic integration offer governments the opportunity to reduce child labour. Since trade promotes economic growth, the opportunity could come in the form of higher income, or it could be that the relative wage changes brought about by international trade are conducive to lesser child labour. An important role is also played by the capital market and educational policy. If there is an increase in the remuneration of skilled, or just literate, adult workers and the opportunity-cost of time spent in education falls, it would reduce the labour force participation of each school-age child.

Studies reveal that there is no empirical evidence that globalization increases child labour. But it has been found that in a country that has a large uneducated workforce globalization raises the wage rate of uneducated workers. Therefore, unless the government takes steps to counter the reduction in the incentive to educate children, the net effect of globalization is likely to be an increase in child labour. However, in developing countries that have a larger number of workers with at least a basic education, globalization raises the wage rate of educated workers. Thus, developing countries can turn globalization into an opportunity to reduce child labour by spending more on education and public health.

To Sum Up

It is feared that in the developing countries, globalization and liberalization would also result in casualisation of workers, which would further add to the already large workforce in the informal sector in countries like India, which have more than 90 percent of their workforce in the informal sector. Therefore, employment generation and decent working conditions in the informal sector have to be our primary concern besides very strong anti-poverty programmes.

Consumer campaigns to insist that governments add a lable clearly stating that child labour has not been used in the making of the goods being sold can go long way in solving the problem of child labour and can make globalization a boon for the deprived and exploited children. It should be noted that till now, there are few organised boycotts of such products; however spontaneous action by consumers is forcing change. Therefore, the international community urgently needs to take the initiative to enforce labour standards around the world, because it has been seen that in no single case has child labour been eliminated voluntarily.

References

Aghion, P. and Williamson, J.G., *Growth Inequality and Globalization: Theory, History and Policy*, Cambridge University Press, U.K., 1998.

Burra, Neera, *"Born to Work: Child Labour in India"*, O.U.P., New Delhi, 1995.

Duranton, G., "Globalization-Productive Systems and Inequalities", Centre for Economic Performance, London, 1998.

Easterlin, R.A., "The Globalization of Human Developent," *Annals of the American Academy of Political and Social Science*, Vol. 570, 2000, pp. 32-48

Grootaert, C. and R. Kanbur, "Child Labour: An Economic Perspective," *International Labour Review*, 134, 1995, pp. 187-203.

Held, David and Anthony McGraw, "The Great Globalization Debate: An Introduction" in David Held and A. McGraw (Eds.), *The Global Transformation Reader*, Polity Press, Oxford, 2001.

16

Economic Reforms and Child Labour

UMESH PRASAD AND BINOD CHOUDHARY

INTRODUCTION

Economic reforms process have played a major role in pushing the issue of child labour as a priority issue in the international debates. The reason for this is that the impact of economic reforms on child labour is as contentious as the issue itself. Some perceive a direct negative impact in that it contributes to an increase in child labour because of intensified competition over wage costs. The fact that economic liberalisation leads to an increase in the incidence of child labour is not an unconvincing proposition. The opening up of a labour-surplus economy like India, may witness a shift to labour-intensive forms of production and into cheap labour that can minimize the labour costs to make them internationally competitive. And, in this order of things, child labour can form the first priority for a cheap, least demanding, and pliable labour force. In India, many empirical studies in the post-liberalisation period tend to substantiate this eventuality. Nevertheless, the counterpoint of this maintains that, child labour existed prior to globalisation in most of the developing countries, and increase awareness about and enhanced attention on the sources of 'unfair competition' in which informal women workers and child labour came into focus. Moreover, those who maintain this position argue, that there is a need to delineate the increase in the incidence of child labour and changes in its sectoral composition without necessarily increasingly the absolute number of child labourers in the country. The meagre attention received by the large proportion of child labour in the industrial informal sector is cited as a case in point. However, in India, the studies so far have been more in favour of the former course of events which is characterized by increased competition leading to cost reduction methods, and zones showing tendencies to absorb unprotected cheap labour such as child and women workers.

The recent trend in the global system is to evaluate the development of any country, not in terms of their military or economic strength or the splendour of their capital cities and public buildings, but also in terms of human development or the well-being of its people. Against this backdrop the existence and perpetuation of child labour has been one of the main limiting factors in the way of human development in almost all the Third World countries including India. The issue of child labour is a major human rights issue and at the same time it is a highly emotive one; these emotions tend to be coupled with very strong views both on what the child labour problem is and on what ought to be done for its elimination. Although the predominance of child labour has to be quite pronounced in all the developing and underdeveloped countries, it is a global phenomenon which exists in almost all the countries of the world and the difference, if any, is of degree only. The concept and practice of child labour being economically unsound, psychologically wrong, and socially disastrous has posed a big threat to peace and overall world development. Therefore, the gravity of the situation and pervasive nature of the problem has attracted the urgent attention of all-social, political organisations, social scientists, activist groups and governments of the world including India.

SOME HISTORY

In his seminal work on the Indian working class, Mukherjee (1995) provided some insights into the magnitude and the plight of child labourers in the subcontinent in the 1940s. In the Assamese tea gardens, he calculated that, children account for roughly 17 per cent of the labour force. At that time, child labour legislation was in place. The Indian Factories Act of 1881 had placed many restrictions on the use of child labour. The prohibition made child labour visible in public accounts, but at the same time sealed them off from public scrutiny. Children below the age of 15 years were prohibited to work in the mines, and official figures on the prevalence of children in the mines are not available, but as Mukherjee noticed that "children are found in the coal mines to help the parents in cart-pushing or loading or as shale pickers or coolies. In the mica mines also children of very tender age are found to work". That was also the case with stone quarries. Stone quarries are usually situated in the jungles and hill sides and are difficult to reach and difficult to escape from. Entire families were recruited from distant places, with written and oral agreements binding them for a term of 5 years. The very precise figures that we find in the official accounts of many industries; the tea gardens, the coal mines, the mica industry, the bidi industries, and the regulated and non-regulated factories have been carefully sifted and convey a picture of the reality in those days.

It is most probably a distorted picture, since it was based on deceptive official figures and on questionable definitions of what constituted child labour. The legislation that was in place was the benchmark for the assessment of the existence of child labour, but labour supervisors and surveyors already in the late nineteenth century had a tough job locating and counting the child labourers. They reported that when they entered the factories in Bombay, the owners were seen 'busily engaged in hustling all the smallest children they can meet with out of the mill' (quoted in Alexander, 2004). This happened one-year after the Indian Factory Act of 1881 had imposed restrictions on child employment. Children between 7 and 12 were allowed to work for only 7 hours a day, not before 5 a.m., and with a break of half an hour. If age certificates were issued, the system allowed for so much fudging that the children officially worked as half-timers and many children under 14 workers as full-timers had false certificates. Even then, an inspection of two factories in Bombay in 1881, registered that 23 per cent of the labourers were children.

It proved to be very difficult to establish how many children were working in the factories that come under the purview of official inspection. In all other trades and industry and in the agricultural and domestic sector, such accounting was altogether absent. Mukerjee, despite his undeniable skill as an historian and labour sociologist, worked within the official parameters of what constituted child labour and has left us with a distorted picture of history. Such distorted pictures of history are common. The overall picture that emerges from 19th century England is that of child labour as a widespread and ghastly by-product of capitalism, and many testimonies of those days described the factories as 'hellish institutions for the destruction of childhood', but as Nardinelli (1990, p. 3) argues, the advocacy reports assumed child labour especially industrial child labour, to be a more serious problem than it actually was. The advocacy statistics and reports helped to create a forceful public opinion which gradually, over a period extending over more than one century, by and large helped to do away with child labour in the now developed countries.

CONCEPT OF WORK AND CHILD LABOUR

The concept of work should be used as the generic term, and would refer to any type of work being done in any mode of employment relationship and for any purpose; it should serve as a description of the physical (or mental) involvement in a job. The concept of (child) labour on the other hand, should be restricted to the production of goods and services, including work in the household, that interfere with the normative development of children as defined the UN Convention on the Rights of the Child (CRC), 1989.

The distinction needs to be made since child labour has very much become restricted to the normative concept as bad, and since it has become a bad, one has to introduce another concept which refers to some work done by children which is a normal and even beneficial activity. This principle is likely to be accepted as an ethically correct attitude. Even the ILO (2002, p. 9) accepts such a position: "Millions of young people legitimately undertake work, paid or unpaid, that is appropriate for their age and level of maturity. By doing so, they learn to take responsibility, they gain skills and add to their families' and their own well-being and income, and they contribute to their countries' economies".

This is an important admission that the involvement in work can have positive aspects. Disagreements, however, will merge when this principle is applied to concrete cases. How to judge what is right and what is wrong? Article 32 of the CRC has put down a general case: "the right of the child to be protected from economic exploitation and from performing any work that is likely to be hazardous or to interfere with the child's education, or to be harmful to the child's health or physical, mental, spiritual, moral or social development."

Such a principle could lead to arbitrary judgements and a number of big players in the field, including some of the well-known NGOs, have actually argued that children should have a right to work as long as it does not harm them, contributes to their survival, teaches them skills, and socializes them in the cultural and artisanal traditions.

That, it seems to me, is a dangerous road to follow. There should be a general standard to adhere to. Such general standards apply to all types of social interaction: the legal system has ordained that all restrictions and obligations should apply to all persons, irrespective of their personal skills and capacities to do otherwise. The CRC has actually called for such legislation. In clause 2 of Article 32, it has stipulated that the governments shall take the relevant measures such as minimum ages and the regulation of hours, and conditions of employment.

Article 32 of the CRC is not a general principle open to discretion. It should be seen in combination with the ILO conventions. In a sense, the ILO could be considered more as representative of civil society than the UN system, since it is a tripartite of governments, business associations and trade unions. The ILO in its own way has clarified what child labour actually is. Conventions 138 (on the minimum age) and convention 182 (on the Worst Forms of Child Labour) provide a general framework for national legislation. For a long time, the ILO particularly Convention 138 of 1977, was setting the benchmark. That Convention was quite accommodative to conditions in developing countries. It stipulated various age limits: fourteen years of age as a full-time worker in developing countries, and fifteen in other countries, and respectively 12 years and 13 years for doing light work in the labour market. The distinction between light work and harmful work and therefore intolerable work was given firm shape with Convention 182 of 1999. It distinguished hazardous work, which no child under 18 should do; harmful work, which no child under 14 should do, and light work for which the age limit was 12 years in developing countries.

The ILO definitions are rooted, being based on the role of the child in the labour market, in the child's engagement in economic activities. Figures produced from this perspective may result in a serious undercount. Children spending many hours looking after the household or taking care of infants from the child rights' perspective (CRC 32) should be treated as child labourers, although they are not labourers in the proper sense of the word.

Child labour is to be defined neither by the form of the labour relationship nor by the type of activity, but by the effect the activity has on the child. The ILO struggles with this dilemma. The statistical organisation of ILO (SIMPOC) has the following definition of child labour: "Child labour is work performed by children under 18 years of age which is exploitative, hazardous and inappropriate for their age, and which is detrimental to their schooling, or social, mental, spiritual and moral development". That definition would exclude from the child labour category many instances of work done in and around the household: "Child labour does not include activities such as helping out, after school is over and schoolwork has been done, with light household or garden chores, childcare or other light work. To claim otherwise only trivializes the genuine deprivation of childhood faced by the millions of children involved in the child labour that must be effectively abolished" (ILO, 2002, p. 9).

The qualifications are of a general nature and are difficult to translate into exact measurable figures. In short, although the general principles underlying international and national regulation are unambiguous, the concrete application is full of loopholes. Child labourers, it is agreed, are those entering the labour market under hazardous conditions or for long hours, or those who work at home for too long and at too early an age. But then, how many hours should one work everyday and under which circumstances to qualify as hazardous, as harmful to the child and therefore as child labour. And child, labourers are also those who are involved in household work beyond a certain threshold without producing goods and services which can be added to the national accounting statistics.

The growing concern for child labour in the contemporary world also to no small extent has been fuelled by statistics, suggesting vast numbers of children working in dire circumstances. The statistics in the 1980s—the ILO estimated that 50 million children were economically active—were probably an undercount. They were more guesstimates than estimates. The warning came from the ILO Director General himself: "Statistics that try to capture in one number the manifold dimensions of a complex phenomenon can be treacherous. This is especially so in the case of child labour" (ILO, 1983, p. 6). Different notions of the meaning of child work and labour, he stressed, in addition to differences in social perceptions and the illegality of the phenomenon made counting a complex issue: "For such reasons, global figures purporting to demonstrate the extent of child labour are not very meaningful. They may have dramatic effect but they do not offer a basis for policy. In view of these reservations, I hesitate even to advance any figure. . . . At best, for the conceptual and methodological reasons outlined above, they are of a limited reliability. They are also of a limited utility. In themselves, they tell us nothing about the nature of the work children are doing or the circumstances and conditions under which it is being done".

The figure of 250 million, which the ILO projected in the mid-1990s, soon developed into an icon. The accuracy of the statistics was not the first concern. Statistics were appropriate in the realm of 'advocacy statistics' as Anker (2000) suggested. Accurate numbers were not looked for. On the contrary, an exaggeration of numbers was helpful for various reasons. I have suggested four explanations for the excessive accounts, which I shall mention briefly. The first three are of an instrumental and ideological nature. The fourth one relates to the essence of what child labour is and how it should be tackled.

In the first place, the high accounts have been useful in the debate on social clauses in international trade agreements. Particularly the US government has taken a strong stand on the inclusion of child labour as a social clause in international trade sanctions. The higher the figures of child labour, the more likely to expect that nimble and cheap fingers have been involved in production for export and the more convincing the argument that a developing country is engaged in 'unfair' competition. Trade policy initiatives banning child-labour tainted products are more likely to be endorsed by the public, if the idea is carried that developing countries make use of child labour on a massive scale, and thereby disrupt normal economic business in the developed world.

The high figures are possibly also related to unconscious forms of stereotyping and even of stigmatization. A high prevalence of child labour would help to stereotype developing countries and to confirm the negative image that people in the 'developed countries' generally have of the Third World and its governments. It helps to put the blame on governments, who are portrayed as being callous, and on parents, who are suspected of having more children in order to make them work and earn an income. Through the stigmatization of the other, one elevates one's own culture and one's involvement (intervention) to a righteous position.

A third ideological (and commercial) use is the marketing strategy of NGOs, whose financial income corresponds with the gravity of the problem. A basic characteristic of NGOs is that they move along with the changing fashion. Exaggerated figures would be helpful for all child-focused organisations whose income and importance depends on the seriousness of the problem that they are involved in. The higher the numbers of deprived and exploited child labourers, the more the willingness of funding agencies to contribute financially. These three factors help to explain why figures may have been kept artificially high.

There is, however, also a more fundamental reason as to why statistics vary so widely. The high figures are partially based on the inclusion, without discrimination, of all so-called 'nowhere children' or idle children in the workforce, i.e., the children who are not attending school and who are not engaged in a labour process as it is being defined for national accounting statistics. My argument shall be that all these categories shall have to be meaningfully separated for a sound analysis. In addition to the separate category of nowhere children, a crucial distinction could be made between child labour and child work.

MICRO STUDY

Child labour is a curse upon society, a malady wrecking the economic backbone of a country. Above all, a disgrace for the development of entire human civilization. There are no two opinions that children lack the facilities for developing themselves into a good citizens. The study so far reveals that children in India and elsewhere in the world have not been given proper attention and are being exploited by the people for the accomplishment of their selfish ends. They have been exploited more or less in all periods of history, though varied in its nature and dimension, depending on the existing socio-economic structure of the society. Although, the problem of child labour is a global phenomenon and it exists in almost all the countries of the world, the difference, if any is only of degree or form. But it is very saddening to note, that India is one of the nations in the world, which has the unique distinction of being the largest employer of child labour. Despite an array of child welfare legislations and judicial verdicts the problem of child labour has assumed dangerous dimensions in the country. There appears to be an improvement in the working condition of child labourers. They are deprived of education, proper health, and even basic amenities of life. In fact, the philosophy of independence and fundamental rights embodied in the constitution have no meaning to them. Poverty and illiteracy force the parents to send the children to seek employment for the survival of their poor families.

The present study is based on primary data made available through a questionnaire envisaging different aspects and to test the impact of socio-economic conditions of child labourers. As the study has been applied to examine the different variables of the problem of child labour and correlation among them, sampling is based on random samples. The study is based on answers received from the child workers themselves. We have designed questionnaire and have taken 50 male and 50 female child labourers aggregating 100 child labourers. Utmost care has been taken and respondents from all castes, categories and religions have been included in our sample. Hence, the source of information is based on primary data.

CAUSES OF CHILD LABOUR

The problem of child labour is a universal problem, but it is more prevalent in underdeveloped countries. On the one hand because of the poverty of masses, they send their children to work, and on the other hand due to the backward and labour-intensive technology in these countries, there is a search for cheap labour which is available in the form of child labour. In the absence of State sponsored schemes for family allowances, to enable parents to ensure their children's proper and adequate nutrition and living conditions, the poor parents are forced to send their children to work, and on the other hand, the lack of protective child labour legislation and the evasion of existing laws for the protection of child labour keep the child labour going and facilitates their exploitation. Besides these causes, sudden death of father, mother, or both parents in a poor or low middle class family, big size of family, ill-habituated father spending money on drinking, illegal children and sometimes the child's desire to work makes them workers during childhood. Children work because of one or more of these causes. The 100 working children surveyed gave the cause of working as shown in Table 1.

Table 1 shows that poverty is the most prevalent cause of child labour. Hundred per cent of the children said that they have to work because they are poor. Added to poverty, 30 per cent children have to work because of the death of one or both parents, whereas 68 per cent have work because of the big size of the family. More girls suffer due to this cause. The reason may be that in India, most of the big sized families have more girls, because if there is no son, the orthodox parents go on giving birth to children in the hope of a son. A total of 14 per cent working children are suffering because of ill-habituated father who spends money on drinking etc., and the children have to work to recoup this loss. In this survey, I did not come across any illegal child. Six per cent boys said that they want to work, so they are working though their fathers want them to go to school.

CONDITIONS OF CHILD LABOUR

These working children were asked questions about themselves, their families, their working conditions, job satisfaction, etc. The answers received give information as in Table 2.

Table 2 shows that the maximum percentage of child labourers in unorganised sector is in 8 to 12 years of age group.

TABLE 1

Cause of Working by Surveyed Child Labour

Cause of Working	*Girls*		*Boys*	
	Number	*Percent*	*Number*	*Percent*
Poverty	50	100	50	100
Death of Father	6	12	7	14
Death of Mother	13	26	7	14
Death of both parents	03	06	03	06
Big size of family	40	80	28	56
Ill habituated father	8	16	6	12
Illegality of Child	Nil	Nil	Nil	Nil
Child's desire to work	Nil	Nil	6	12

TABLE 2

Age of Surveyed Child Labour at the Time of Survey

Age Group	*Number*	*Percentage*
Below 4 years	Nil	Nil
4 to 8 years	08	08
8 to 12 years	72	72
12 to 16 yeas	20	20
Total	100	100

Table 3 shows that 88 per cent of the child labourers belong to Hindu religion, 10 per cent are Christians, and only two per cent are Muslims. There is no Sikh child working.

Table 4 shows that maximum number of working children belong to Scheduled castes and backward classes, their percentage being 51. Others are Kshatriyas, Brahmins and Vaishyas, respectively.

TABLE 3

Religion of Surveyed Child Labour

Religion	*Number*	*Percentage*
Hindu	88	88
Muslim	02	02
Sikh	Nil	Nil
Christian	10	10
Others	Nil	Nil
Total	100	100

TABLE 4

Caste of Surveyed Hindu Children

Caste	*Number*	*Percentage*
Brahmin	13	15
Kshatriya	19	22
Vaishya	10	12
Shudra	46	51
Total	100	100

Table 5 shows that 61 per cent children have both parents alive, 6 per cent have lost both parents, 20 per cent have only father alive, whereas 13 per cent have only mother alive. Thus most of the child labourers has to work inspite of the fact that both their parents are alive. Still there is 30 per cent child labour, which is suffering from the absence of at least one parent.

TABLE 5

Presence of Parents of Surveyed Child Labour

Status	*Number*	*Percentage*
Only father alive	20	20
Only mother alive	13	13
Both alive	61	61
Both dead	06	06
Total	100	100

Table 6 shows that most (37%) of the children belong to a family of 7 to 8 members, and a big number (27%) belong to a family of 9 to 10 members, followed by 4 to 6 members size family. Very small and very big families are comparatively less prevalent.

TABLE 6

Size of Family of Surveyed Child Labour

Size of Family	*Number*	*Percentage*
Below four	07	07
4 to 6	25	25
7 to 8	37	37
9 to 10	27	27
Above 10	04	04
Total	100	100

Table 7 shows that most of the fathers (52%) are working in factories, whereas most of the mothers (56%) are working in households. In both cases, the second place is occupied by construction workers who mostly work in building construction or road construction work. Other percentages are nominal. Only three per cent fathers are not working and only four per cent mothers are not working.

TABLE 7

Parents' Occupation of Surveyed Child Labour

Occupation of Parent's	*Father's*		*Mother's*	
	Number	*Percentage*	*Number*	*Percentage*
Agricultural Labour	05	06	03	04
Factory Labour	42	52	09	12
Construction Labour	21	26	15	20
Household Labour	01	01	41	56
Peons	05	06	01	01
Others	05	06	02	03
Not Working	02	03	03	04
Total	81	100	74	100

Thus most of the girls are working in households. They do such work as house cleaning, utensils cleaning, washing clothes, cooking, child keeping, etc. No girls are working in factories, construction work, hotels or shops. Most of the boys are engaged in shops and hotels. Some of them are working in households and construction work. A few are working on farms and other occupations.

TABLE 8

Type of Work of Surveyed Child Labour

Type of Work	*Girls*		*Boys*	
	Number	*Percentage*	*Number*	*Percentage*
Agricultural Labour	02	04	03	06
Factor Labour	Nil	Nil	Nil	Nil
Construction Labour	Nil	Nil	Nil	Nil
Household Labour	47	94	10	20
Hotel Work	Nil	Nil	12	24
Shop Work	Nil	Nil	15	30
Others	01	02	03	06
Total	50	100	50	100

Table 9 shows that the duration of the present job is generally 12 to 18 months for girls, and 6 to 12 months for boys. Boys are less consistent in their jobs in comparison to girls, no child is working at one place more than 30 months.

TABLE 9

Duration of Present Job of Surveyed Child Labour

Type of Work	*Girls*		*Boys*	
	Number	*Percentage*	*Number*	*Percentage*
Less than 6 months	08	16	12	24
6 to 12 months	12	24	20	20
12 to 18 months	18	36	15	30
18 to 24 months	07	14	03	06
24 to 30 months	05	10	Nil	Nil
More than 30 month	Nil	Nil	Nil	Nil
Total	50	100	50	100

Table 10 shows that most of the girls are working for six to eight hours, whereas most of the boys are working for 8 to 10 hours. Such children are generally household or hotel workers. The working hours of boys are more than that of girls. The reason may be that the girls have to work in their own houses also.

TABLE 10

Working Hours of Surveyed Child Labour

Working Hours	*Girls*		*Boys*	
	Number	*Percentage*	*Number*	*Percentage*
Below 2 hours	Nil	Nil	Nil	Nil
2 to 4 hours	07	14	Nil	Nil
4 to 6 hours	09	18	05	10
6 to 8 hours	15	30	10	20
8 to 10 hours	08	16	15	30
10 to 12 hours	06	12	11	22
More than 12 hours	05	10	09	18
Total	50	100	50	100

Table 11 shows that most of the girls are earning between Rs. 400 to Rs. 600 per month, whereas most of the boys are earning Rs. 800 to Rs. 1000 per month. Previously we have seen that the working hours of boys are also more.

TABLE 11

Earning of Surveyed Child Labour

Earning per month (in Rs.)	*Girls*		*Boys*	
	Number	*Percentage*	*Number*	*Percentage*
Below 200	07	14	Nil	Nil
200 to 400	09	18	05	10
400 to 600	15	30	11	22
600 to 800	08	16	14	28
800 to 1000	11	22	20	40
Total	50	100	50	100

TABLE 12

Percentage share of Working Children in the Earning of Families

Family earning per month (In Rs.)	*Share of Girls (%)*	*Share of Boys (%)*
Below 1000	40	32
1000 to 2000	30	28
2000 to 3000	22	18
3000 to 4000	08	12
4000 to 5000	Nil	10

Thus the share of working children in the earnings of their families is between 8 to 40 per cent. As the earning of the family goes up, the share of working child goes down. It goes down faster in the case of girls.

Table 13 shows that more girls get tea casually or regularly. The boys who are working in hotels or are full time household servants get tea and food regularly. Some girls, who are full time household servants, get morning food but they go back to their homes in the evening. So they do not get evening food. Most of the girls get old dresses but the boys working in hotels, or doing full time household work get about two new dresses every year. Other perks include cinema ticket once in a while for boys.

TABLE 13

Perks to Women Children

Perks	*Girls*	*Boys*
Tea casually	16	05
Tea regularly	15	15
Food one time	10	15
Food two times	Nil	15
Dresses old	40	07
Dresses new	05	15
Others	Nil	03

Besides the above, some general questions were also put to the working children about their job liking, job satisfaction, master's behaviour, etc., the replies can be classified as represented in Table 14.

TABLE 14

Job Satisfaction Surveyed Children

Question	Girls				Boys			
	Yes		No		Yes		No	
	No.	%	No.	%	No.	%	No.	%
Do you like to work?	30	60	20	40	35	70	15	30
Are you satisfied with your work?	27	54	23	46	30	60	20	40
Are you satisfied with your master's behaviour?	27	54	23	46	30	60	20	40
Do you feel exploited?	23	46	27	54	20	40	30	60

Table 14 shows that most of the working boys and girls like to work but boys have more liking for their work. Most of the boys and girls are satisfied with their work, but boys are more satisfied. Almost half of the boys and girls are satisfied with their master's behaviour, while about half are not satisfied. Those who are not satisfied with their master's behaviour, also feel that they are being exploited.

CONCLUSION

The institution of child labour is a global phenomenon and is quite pervasive over time and space. However, it is more concentrated in poor developing countries as compared to rich developed countries of the world. The incidence of child labour is poorly, though positively, correlated with the level of poverty. It is strongly correlated with the level of illiteracy and the overall work participation ratio. The incidence is more in those areas, which are not well developed both socially as well as economically. Hence, the continuation of child labour is essentially a case of underdevelopment, economic as well as social.

Questions were also asked about the studies of these children; 22 per cent boys and 19 per cent girls of these working children are going to schools. They are all going to government schools because of fees exemption there. No one is going to private school. 100 per cent working students said that they are not able to clear any class in one year because they do not get enough time to read. They are hardly present for half the days in the schools. Though all the SC and ST students are getting scholarships, still they are not able to purchase all books and stationery required, but 10 per cent of them do purchase. These working students adjust their schools time according to their work time, and not their work time according to their schools time. For them work is of primary importance and studies come at the second place.

Thus the story of working children is multi-dimensional but not colourful.

SUGGESTIONS

Economic reform has created winners and losers. But majority of the child labourers are the losers. In our country implementation of adjustment programmes has lead to deterioration of child labour conditions.

In the process of economic reform, there has been decline in real wages for the child labour. Uncontrolled contracting out of jobs has lead to employment externalization all over the world through payment of lower wages and reduction of job security. The problem is more serious in India and poor children work in small business units with low wages have poor working conditions. On the basis of the study we drawn following conclusion:

(i) Globalisation is not a new phenomenon but is rather a historical feature, which tends to expand and contract over time.

(ii) In the last wave of globalisation, migration was an important instrument for reducing the supply of potential adult and child workers. This enhanced the possibility that labour standards could be raised.

(iii) The current wave of globalisation differs significantly from its predecessor in terms of global governance and the potential for the movement of labour.

(iv) The incidence of child labour (only for the age group of 10-14 years) has followed a pattern similar to that of the demographic transition. As the proportion of children in a population declines so too does the activity rate. This implies that the magnitude of the supply of potential child workers impact on the incidence of child labour.

(v) The decline in the proportion of children in population and the labour force is greater with a higher Human Development Index (HDI) value.

(vi) Child labour as a core labour standard is likely to be made effective with a successful demographic transition. Hence, the ILO should include family planning as an additional instrument in its campaign against child labour.

(vii) The high rates of growth that can potentially be generated by the globalisation process will need to be accompanied by perceptibly adequate instruments of social protection and the meeting of basic needs if the globalisation process is to be sustained. But it is important to note that the characteristics of India economy will not allow to easily chalk out the process. So that globalisation process in a country like India is not suitable as a development module for future.

SOME MAJOR EFFECTIVE SUGGESTIONS

The suggestions regarding child labour can be framed at two levels, long-term and short-term. The long-term policies should be aimed at improving the conditions of the society as a whole to such an extent that ultimately child labour is completely eliminated. Whereas, the short-term policies have already been suggested by different authors or committees.

The purpose of the long-term policies is to bring about a gradual standstill to the problem of child labour i.e., the complete elimination of these short-term policies have already been suggested by different authors or committees through the measures like eradication of poverty, spread of education, public awareness, welfare services, health and nutrition, working conditions, housing, etc.

Today the problem of child labour has assumed the most challenging and alarming proportions in India. It is directly related to human resource development of the country. This human problem has closed the future development of the country. The concept and practice of this phenomenon is economically as unsound psychologically disastrous and morally wrong. Despite several legislations on child labour, it continues unabated. It may wreck the back-bone of the economy, and above all it may threaten peace and even national security. Hence, the above study will be open new doors in controlling the menace of child labour.

REFERENCES

Gupta Manju, "Child Labour in India," 1997, p. 2.

Hirway, Indira, Cottyn, J., *et.al.* (1991) (Eds.), *Towards Eradication of Child Labour*, Oxford and IBH Publishing Company, New Delhi.

J.C. Kulshrestha, Child Labour in India, Ashish Publishing House, New Delhi, 1978, pp. 46-47.

Mihaly Simai, "Situation of Children in New Global realities in the year 2000" New Perspectives: *Journal of the World Peace Council*, Vol. 9, 6/1979, p. 34.

Ministry of Labour, *Report of the Committee on Child Labour*, Government of India, Dec. 1979, p. 17.

Musafir Singh, V.D. Kaura and S.A. Khan, *Working Children in Bombay—A Study NIPCCD*, New Delhi, 1980, pp. 152-55.

N. Mitra, "The Slave Children of Mandsour," *Sunday*, 8, 19 Dec., 1980, pp. 10-17.

Padmini Sengupta, "Children Work to Live," *Social Welfare*, April 1975, p. 11.

Pati, R.N.; *Rehabilitation of Child Labour in India*, p. 144.

Prasad, Umesh, "Socio-Economic Problems of Child Labour: A Case Study," *The Hindustan Review*, Vol. 9, No. 7, Jan.-April, 2002.

Shandilya, T.K. and Khan, Shakeel Ahmad, *Child Labour: A Global Challenge*, Deep & Deep Publication, New Delhi.

Shandilya, Tapan Kumar (1977), '*Child Labour in India*,' Dr. Ambedkar Journal of Social Sciences, MOHW (M.P.).

Shandilya, T.K., "Child Labour At Work: A Case Study," *The Hindustan Review*, Vol. 9, No. 7, Jan.-April, 2002.

17

Reforms and Child Labour

JAGDISH PRASAD AND RAJESH KUMAR

It is not an exaggeration to say that the children are the blooming flowers of the garden of society and so, it is our duty to protect these flowers from damaging effects of excessive exposure to heat, cold and rain. It is quite imperative to give vent to the thought of Hon'ble Justice Mr. Subba Rao who has rightly observed: "social Justice must begin with children. Unless tender plant is properly tended and nourished, it has little chance to growing into a strong and useful tree. So, first priority in the scale of social Justice shall be given to the welfare of children."

PROBLEMS OF CHILD LABOUR

Prevalence of child labour is historically nothing new, nor in this respect India is the only culprit in the world. Child labour problem manifested in various forms, is now-a-days a challenging and contentious issue in all the Third World countries. The widespread use of child labour can be traced back to the early days of Industrial Revolution in England and elsewhere. In the aftermath of Industrial Revolution, however, the exploitation of children also received considerable outcry and this gradually led to the awareness effects of child labour. In a large and vastly populated country like India, even though children are employed in a wide variety of occupations, many, however, focus on the children working in hazardous industries-like fireworks factories, glass factories, mines, etc. It may be recalled here that the Constitution of India in its chapter on "Directive Principles of State Policy" (Art. 14) declares that "no child below the age of 14 years shall be employed in any factory or mine or engaged in any other hazardous employment." However, actually the problem of child labour received some serious attention only after the U.N.O.'s Declaration of 1979 as the International Year of the Child. It is surprising that while the Indian Constitution was adopted as far back as in 1950, it was only in 1986 that the Child Labour (Prohibition and Regulation) Act was promulgated. Despite the constitutional law and the enactment of the 1986 Act, a large multitude of children in India continue to be involved in various hazardous and non-remunerative occupations.

Abolition of child labour in our country is not an easy job and mere enactment of child abolition laws will not guarantee the attainment of the desired goal. There are a host of other factors that can easily render the existing laws blunt and ineffective. A fundamental problem relates to the definitional aspect of child labour. On the other hand, the poor parents, having no other assets, themselves treat children as assets rather than liabilities as hinted at the outset. Rather than sending their wards to schools, they prefer to associate the children in whatever income-earning activities that may be available before them. In most cases, these activities turn out to be petty income earning and/or niggardly paid activities. Often the rate of payment is not the parents' concern; the absolute income earned by the children is the major deciding factor.

ROLE OF NGOs AND GOVERNMENT

Of late, both the Central and the various State Governments have woken up to the problems of child labour in the country. Various NGOs are especially waging a battle in favour of child labour abolition. Even at the global level, some developed nations have hardened their stance on this issue. These developed countries are threatening to ban exports from developing countries, which rely on utilization of cheap child labour. These countries are trying to stick to the clause that some particular exports from developing countries must come with a certified declaration from the appropriate authority that the products have no child labour content.

At the national level, apart from passing relevant acts, the central and state governments have attempted to lure children from work places to schools by making primary education free and introducing mid-day meal scheme at the schools. In the states like West Bengal, along with free primary education, books, etc. are being distributed free of cost at the primary school level. A large part of credit for forcing and inducing the governments in initiating steps against widespread use of child labour is due to some NGOs. In recent years, a number of NGOs have undertaken a crusade against the evils of child labour and have been largely responsible for spreading campaign on the issue among the masses.

The pertinent questions on this issue are: (i) can and should child labour be stopped altogether, and, if so, (ii) how can it be stopped? The first of these two is reeled in some normative considerations. Obviously, the first best and ideal world is the situation where the phenomenon of child labour is totally absent. But given the existing socio-economic condition in India, mainly that of the rural masses and of the vast low-income population, first best solution overnight is ruled out. A more pragmatic approach would be to strive to mitigate the plight of the child labourers in the immediate short-run and to get rid of the vice in the long-run, if not possible in the near future. For this, however, it is imperative to set a deadline—say 8-10 years horizon from now on and work sincerely towards attaining a child labour free society.

Simply passing of laws and making primary education free, obviously cannot ensure the emancipation of child labour. In fact, we have observed that what is truly lacking is presence of quality education at Primary level. Because of this, families are forced to seek private tuitions for their children, which they cannot afford. Naturally, free primary education scheme fails to serve any meaningful purpose. The entire question needs to be addressed in a general equilibrium framework and within the ambit of present socio-economic parameters. It can safely be presumed that the current parametric configuration is not conducive to improved well-being of the child workers simply based on legal intervention. The economic conditions of the poor families needs to be improved coupled with the general awareness—about the long-term benefits of education as well as of family planning among the low income people. Economic condition of the poor families cannot just be improved by some stopgap, *ad-hoc* measures and measures like minimum wage laws. It is interesting, and ironical too, to learn that Prof. Kaushik Basu in a recent work has even come up with the piquant situation where adult minimum wage laws actually encourage child labour-parents reduce their labour hours as a result of higher minimum wage, while inducing their wards to work longer.

It will perhaps be worthwhile to contemplate an India free from the vice of child labour by the year 2010. A specific deadline like this must be adhered to, which the governments (Central and State), various agencies, NGOs and all other must accept as unalterable. Unless and until a rigid time frame is adopted, the total abolition of child labour may well remain an elusive goal. If we can undertake such programmes like 'Polio free India', 'Drinking water for all', etc. (set to be achieved within a given time), then why can't we achieve the same thing in case of child labour? A few things however must be borne in mind. First, given the present dimension of the problem, the initiatives on the part of the Central and State Governments along with a vigorous media campaigns, alone would not suffice; what is needed is active involvement of various NGOs in making people aware of the ill-effects of child labour. The NGOs possibly will be able to act as watchdog as well as to monitor the progress towards a child labour free society. The NGOs should therefore, be armed with adequate legal powers so that they are able to play a much more effective role in arresting, if not eliminating, the growth of population of working children. Given the existence of large, unorganised, and scattered nature of child labourers in the country, there will always be problems arising out of asymmetric information. In other words, even if any government tightens its child labour laws and attempts to plug the existing lacunae in the laws, it will still prove to be extremely costly to successfully implement these laws. The NGOs usually work at grassroot levels and accordingly, they possess much more and reliable information on the uses and abuses of child labour. Second, the political leadership at the grassroot level also needs to be thoroughly motivated in seriously taking up the challenge of abolition of child labour.

TO SUM UP

Thus, it is an undeniable fact that the long-run solution of the problem requires radical reforms in property relations. This issue is now all the more important because the current phase of economic reforms has been pushing a large majority of population, who mostly reside in rural areas, on to the brink. Encouraging free market forces, coupled with globalization and open-door policy, and/or elimination of subsidies in many key sectors are going to hurt these people severely. This is likely to accentuate the problem of child labour since the poor parents or families will be forced to rely more on child labour than before. On the other hand, if the child-labour-related laws are made more stringent, the children of the poor families may well be forced to earn their livelihood from underground and undesirable activities, like, drug-trafficking, child-prostitution, etc. (e.g. drug-Mafia's often find it easier to rely on children as 'carriers' as they may be usually unsuspecting). Therefore, creating ample opportunities for gainful employment among the masses is extremely urgent. Serious and honest land reforms along with sufficient provision of credit and other infrastructure facilities are very much essential. In other words, the total effacement of child labour phenomenon in India in the long-run can be possible under a comprehensive policy package, and not simply by enactment of laws (i.e. reforms in property relations, reforms in primary education, reforms in legal structure, etc.).

REFERENCES

Lieten, G.K., Srivastava, Ravi and Thorat, S. (eds.) (2004), "Small Hands in South Aisa," *Child Labour in Perspective*, Manohar, New Delhi.

Mukherjee, Radhakamal (1951), *The Indian Working Class*, Hind Kitab (3rd edition), Bombay.

Nardinelli, Clark (1990), *Child Labour and the Industrial Revolution*, Indian University Press, Bloomington.

Ramachandran, Nira and Massun, Lionel (eds.) (2002), *Coming to Grips with Rural Child Work: A Food Security Approach*, Institute for Human Development, New Delhi.

Roselaers, Frans (2004), "Foreword", in Lieten, G.K. *et. al.* (eds.), pp. 7-13.

18

Female Child Labour and Economic Reforms

MRIDULA KUMARI

INTRODUCTION

Children are the budding resources and the future citizens of any Nation. The government of India in its National Plan of Action for the International Year of the Child (1979) acknowledged the importance of children, "A nation's children are its supremely important asset and the nation's future lies in their proper development... A healthy and educated child of today is the active and intelligent citizen of tomorrow." But even after a lapse of two and half decades since this resolution was passed by the government, the situation has not changed much, rather it has deteriorated.

As we come to terms with child labour the first question that arises is who are the child labourers? How and when did it come into existence?

When children join the labour force to support family income they are called child labourers. In almost all the families, in all communities and in every economic class children do perform some work but it does not come under the purview of child labour. A child who starts working for family or for self-support before attaining certain specific age and who is physically and mentally not mature enough to bear the hazards of work is called a child labourer. Engagement of a child as worker certainly hampers his/her physical and mental growth and education opportunities which lead to loss of opportunities of training and distorted adulthood. It is a social as well as an economic evil. This is a new dimension of the concept of child labour. In earlier days, the problem was not such a complicated one. Employment of children belonging to poor, under privileged class was thought to be a training for future responsibilities. Exploitation of children too did not receive any critical comments.

History of child labour dates back to the Industrial Revolution in Europe during the period from 1760 to 1840. In India seeds of child labour were sown during mid-nineteenth century by employing children in jute mills and mines.

The problem of child labour is found more or less every where in the world. Child labourers are generally required to work beyond their normal physical capacity. Long working hours without recreation and rest, low wages, and hazardous working conditions are the various forms of his/her exploitation. In the Indian context the form of child labour is more violent and hence a bit different. Children of school going age are seen working as coolies, rag pickers, domestic helps, in motor garages and road side *dhabas*. They have lost their childhood somewhere on the way. It becomes a matter of deep concern to find out ways and means which may put an end to the employment and exploitation of children who are forced to join the labour force.

DEFINING CHILD LABOUR

There is no universally accepted definition of working children. Child-labour has been defined by various agencies in terms of types of work and age. In fact, age criterion has become an universally accepted criterion. Various laws enacted by the governments have defined child labour keeping in views, the minimum age criterion. But the minimum age criterion differed from Act to Act and from work to work. The Indian constitution while providing for prohibition of child labour, states in Article 24, "No child shall be employed to work in any factory or mine or engaged in any other hazardous employment. Article 39(e) and (f) in the same constitution and Article 45 of the Directive Principles of State Policy provide that: The tender age of children should not be abused by economic compulsions to join such a job which is unsuited to their age and strength; and children should be given opportunities and facilities to develop in a healthy manner and in conditions of freedom and dignity, and that childhood and youth are protected against exploitation and against moral and material abandonment. The state shall endeavour to provide within a period of ten years from the commencement of this constitution for free and compulsory education for all children until they complete the age of the fourteen years.

Prohibition of employment and free and compulsory education to all the children below fourteen years of age as provided by the constitution is indicative of the minimum age of employment that is above 14 years. According to the International Labour Organization (ILO), "Child Labour includes children permanently leading adult lives working long hours for low wages under conditions damaging to their health and to their physical and mental development, sometimes separated from their families, frequently deprived of meaningful educational and training opportunities that could open up for them a better future.

According to the Operation Research Group, Baroda (India), "a working child is that child who was enumerated during the survey as a child falling within the 5 to 15 age bracket and who is at remunerative work may be paid or unpaid and busy any hour of the day within or outside the family."

It is now clear that exploitation and age are the two indicators through which child labour can be identified.

CAUSES OF CHILD LABOUR

Now the question that arises is why children at a very tender age instead of joining schools join labour force? There are various pushing and pulling forces behind it. Pushing or supply forces constitute large scale poverty, illiteracy, and ignorance, and high rate of unemployment in adults. Child labour and poverty are interrelated. Even after a decade of much talked about economic reforms 26 per cent of our population is still struggling for bare physical existence. Poverty forces poor parents to seek loans and mortgage their children's interests in lieu of loans. High rate of unemployment among adults and large sized families are other contributing factors. Unemployment rate in India was 7.29 per cent in 1990-2000, after a decade of (adoption of) economic reforms in 1991. In Bihar the rate of unemployment increased form 6.25 per cent in 1993-94 to 7.37 per cent in 1999-2000.

Another factor is that many poor parents feel that sending their children to school will not improve the child's employment opportunities in life. They do not think schools are a good alternative to work. Discriminating attitude towards poor, and irrelevant curriculum in preparing children for the job market are other important factors to keep children out of schools.

Demand side or pulling forces of the child labour is made up by the preference of employers to child labour, it being cheaper than adult labour and children unlike adult can not question the type of treatment meted out to them. Evidence indicates that the child's wage is one-third to one-half that of an adult for the same output with the child working for as many hours if not more than the adults.

MAGNITUDE

India has the largest number of child labourers which varies from 20 million to 100 million. The National Sample Survey data for the year 1991 shows 24.44 million child workers in the age group of 5-14 years. According to 1991 census, there were 11.28 million child workers in the country.

Bihar has a considerable number of child workers. The state's contribution to the child workers population is to the extent of about 8.35 per cent of the all India total.

An industrial category-wise distribution shows that 36.4 per cent of the total child workers of the state are engaged as cultivators and 54.9 per cent as agricultural labourers. Other sectors have only 2.6 per cent of the total Rural sector in the state has a major proportion of the child labour.

TYPE OF WORK AND CHILD LABOUR

By studying the type of work children are engaged in their problems can be understood with more clarity. The type of work suggests that majority of children are engaged in unskilled jobs. Another deciding factor is gender participation. There are some works where only girls are employed. Similarly, there are some works in which only boys are employed.

The problems of child workers in India have assumed alarming proportions in recent years. But the most suffering among them are female child workers. They not only bear the brunt of gender discrimination but also have to protect themselves from various types of physical insecurity. They are frequently denied entitlement to any societal resources. The girl child in India is denied her rights to dignity, health, and education.

Girl child as domestic help is the most invisible form of child labour. It is very difficult to estimate the number of the 'invisible or nowhere' category of girl child workers. The girl child domestic helpers are the most vulnerable lot, suffering worst forms of exploitation. Being in nowhere category they are not covered under any programme of intervention. They have never been a subject of concern for the government. The present study is with reference to the girl child domestic helpers in the slum area in Rajendra Nagar at Patna.

These children belong to the families that had migrated from rural Bihar in search of employment and desire to have a better deal in the gains of economic reforms. The process of economic reforms failed to create much employment opportunities particularly for the unskilled, and illiterate labourers in the state. It has rather reversed the path of development leading to shrinking employment opportunities. It is the children in these poor families who have to suffer the most.

Slum women and girls are the providers of cheap household services in the nearby areas. Male members of these slum-dwellers have a very flexible job pattern. They work as rickshaw pullers, vendors, or do some petty business such as pickle making and selling or remain idle for a major part of the year wasting time and hard earned money of the children and women in wine and gambling.

TABLE 1

Status of Girl Child Domestic Help

Status	*Number*	*Percentage*
Helping in family business	25	22.73
Working as domestic helps	85	77.27

Source: Primary Data.

TABLE 2

Age Profile

Age Group	*Number*	*Percentage*
8-10	07	6.36
10-12	18	16.36
12-14	45	40.91
14-16	40	36.37

Source: Primary Data.

They live in congested thatched huts sans any civic facilities and filth scattered all along. Some even live under the roof of polythene sheets fighting the odds of nature.

This study is based on the field survey in the said slum on 110 girl child domestic helpers aged between eight to sixteen years. Information was derived from them in informal talks regarding their age, education, hours of work, work type, income and expenditure pattern, etc. Information so obtained was categorized, tabulated, and analysed.

TABLE 3

Education

Educational level	*Number*	*Per cent*
Illiterate	15	13.64
Can Read and Write	70	63.64
Below Primary	20	18.18
Below Middle	05	4.54

Source: Primary Data.

More than three-fourths of the girls of poor destitute families work as domestic helpers in near by houses. Nearly 23 per cent help their own family in running their business of pickle making and in tea shops.

The age profile indicates that majority of the girl child domestic workers belong to the age group of 12 to 16 years. This is the most vulnerable age group of children being pushed into the work force. Girl children generally start working at a very tender age of 5 to 6 years in their families. They look after young siblings, bring water from the nearby wells or hand-pumps and do other household chores while their mothers are away at their work place. By the age of 12 to 16 they become full-time workers contributing to family income. Majority of the proverty stricken migrant families in urban areas present a similar scenario.

TABLE 4

Marital Status

Age group	*Number*	*Percentage*	*Total No. (married)*	*percentage*
12-14	45	40.91	8	17.78
14-16	40	36.37	25	62.5

Source: Primary Data.

TABLE 5

Occupation of Husbands/Fathers of the Girl Child

Occupation	*Number*	*Percentage*
Rickshaw Pulling	62	56.36
Vending	10	9.00
Pickle-making	15	12.73
Tea-Stalls	08	7.27
Labourers	06	5.46
Others	09	8.18

Source: Primary Data.

The educational status of girl children was found to be deplorably poor. About 7 per cent of them had never been to school. However about 64 per cent can be said to be literate because they could manage to read and write their names. About

23 per cent have been to school but had to leave it in between to join the labour force. By and large, the main reason to forgo education or to discontinue very early was poor economic condition, domestic duties, and parents strong preference for male education in lower income group. Opening up of Indian economy to the world has had its impact on consumerism but not on old biased attitude towards women.

17.78 per cent of the girl children in the age group of 12-14 years were married. In the age group of 14 to 16 years 62.5 per cent were married. Marriage at the tender age of 12 to 16 years has both physical and mental fallout. Causes for early marriage as cited by their parents were rising dowry with rising age and for physical security of the girls. Economic reforms had neither provided them economic security nor physical security.

TABLE 6

Reasons for Employment

Reasons	*Number*	*Per cent*
Poverty	99	90.00
Forced by husbands	05	4.54
Following mothers	04	3.64
Others	02	1.82

Source: Primary Data.

Occupational pattern of husbands/fathers of girl child domestic help is indicative of their poor deprived status and strong reason for their taking up jobs so early in their life. Fathers/husbands of more than 56 per cent girls are rickshaw pullers earning around Rs. 50 to Rs. 60 daily. Nearly 30 per cent have their fathers/husbands engaged in their own small business of vending, making and selling pickles and running tea-stalls or beetal shops. They are comparatively better off than others but this does not give girls of these families any respite as instead of going to work as domestic help they work as unpaid labourers in the houses to support the family business whatever it is.

Ninety per cent of the girl children from poor deprived familes had to work either as domestic help or as unpaid labourers in their houses due to abject poverty. Only about 2 per cent of them work due to other reasons.

TABLE 7

Working Hours (Daily)

Work hours	*Number*	*Per cent*
2.00-4.00	09	8.18
4.00-6.00	40	36.37
6.00-8.00	50	45.45
8.00-10.00	11	10.00

Source: Primary Data.

TABLE 8

Work Pattern

Work type	*Number*	*Per cent*
Sweeping and cleaning floor	106	96.36
Washing utensils	90	81.82
Washing clothes	70	63.64
Cooking	55	50.00
Looking after children	40	36.36
Others	11	10.00

Source: Primary Data.

Working hour patterns are indicative of the heavy burden of work load on the girl children. More than 80 per cent girl children work on an average for 4 to 8 hours per day to earn livelihood for their families. The working hours of the domestic help is on an average 2 hrs. in one house but since they work in more than one house, their average working hours per day goes up.

TABLE 9

Income Pattern

Income per month (in Rs.)	*Number*	*Per cent*
Nil	25	22.73
200-500	15	13.64
500-800	32	29.09
800-1100	38	34.54

Source: Primary Data.

In addition to their paid work they have to cook, wash utensils, look after young siblings or do other works in their own houses too. This way their working hours extend beyond 12 hours a day. They get hardly any time for themselves to relax.

Girl children whether working in their own houses or as domestic help in other houses have to do a variety of works from clearing and sweeping floor to washing clothes, washing utensils, taking care of small children, etc. More than 96 per cent do the work of cleaning and sweeping floors. 82 per cent do the work of washing utensils, 50 per cent of them also do the cooking at their work place. In addition to these works, many of them have to do other works too such as grinding spices, chutneys, making floor dough, bringing milk from milk booths, taking clothes to the washer man for ironing, etc. Although these works are not hazardous in any way it is monotonous and quite tiring, particularly sweeping and cleaning the floor. Children who help in their household business have to do each and every type of work. There is no respite from the hard work in their life time.

Income pattern of the girl children indicates that nearly 23 per cent do not get any income individually. These are those girls who do not go out to work but help in their household business, in addition to all the domestic works in their own houses. They do not get even a single penny for their hard work. These are the most deprived children being exploited by their very own parents and relatives. 34.54 per cent get an income of Rs. 800 to Rs. 1100 per month in lieu of about six to eight hours of hard work per day.

TABLE 10

Expenditure Pattern

Items of Expenditure	*Number*	*Per cent*
1. Taken away by parents/husbands	95	86.36
2. Spend on self	09	8.18
3. Save for future	06	5.46

Source: Primary Data.

TABLE 11

Exploitation

Type	*Number*	*Per cent*
Verbal abuse	38	34.55
Beating	20	18.18
Sexual abuse	12	10.91
Free from abuse	40	36.36

Source: Primary Data.

Although girl children put in their hard labour for 8 to 10 hours daily, they do not have any right over the fruits of their hard labour. In 86 per cent cases, their income is appropriated either by their parents or by their husbands. Only 8.18 per cent are free to spend their earnings in their own way and 5.46 per cent are wise enough to save for future. These girls also get some gifts or money on the occasion of festivals from their employers.

TABLE 12

Distribution of Workers (usual Status) by Category of Employment (Per cent of Total Worker)

	Self-employed	*Regular Salaried*	*Casual*
Rural			
1993-94	58.0	6.4	35.6
1999-2000	56.0	6.7	37.3
Urban			
1993-94	42.3	39.4	18.3
1999-2000	42.1	40.1	17.8
Total			
1993-94	54.8	13.2	32.0
1999-2000	53.9	13.9	33.2

Economic Survey, 2003.

On the question of abuse 64 per cent of the girls reported in affirmative. They were subjected to one or other type of abuse. But only about 11 per cent of them admitted that they were subjected to sexual abuse. It may be an underestimation because they feel inhibited to reveal the extent of abuse which they have to undergo at the work-place or within the four walls of their houses. Verbal abuse may have a temporary disturbance on the mental set-up of a girl child but physical abuse may threaten the physical security of the girl child.

CONCLUSION

This study is an attempt to know the status of girl child working as domestic help. They all belong to poor, deprived migrant families from rural areas. They live in slums sans basic facilities such as; drainage, drinking water and sanitation, electricity, etc. Their houses often fail to protect them from scorching heat of summer, chilling cold winds of winter and filth of rains.

A majority of the girls in these families never go to school because they have to work for almost the whole day as maids in nearby houses and apartments.

Most of the men in these families are rickshaw pullers vendors, etc. Women work as maids and earn about Rs. 500 to 1000 per month. The average family income of majority of families ranges between Rs. 1000 to Rs. 3000 per month. Generally, this income is not sufficient to feed a family of 5 to 7 persons. Hence the pressure on children to start earning at an early age increases.

Girl child domestic workers are generally in the age group of 8-16 years. Most of them have never been to school, although they have learnt to read and write from their employer's children. Nearly 1/3rd get married before the age of 16. Generally the age at the time of marriage of the girl child is between 16 to 18 years. Majority of them get married before the age of 18 which is the legal age for marriage. Early marriage leads to early motherhood and premature births which in turn may bring mental disorders. Long and arduous working hours and monotonous work does not leave scope for innovation.

The term reform means improvement or betterment in a situation. The final goal of any reform process, in any sphere is to increase the quality of life of the ordinary persons of the society and to increase the growth and prosperity of the nation. Although economic reforms have brought a lot of changes in our economic life but they have failed to increase the quality of life of the people at the lowest rung of the economic and social ladder. The GDP growth rate was 9.8 per cent in 2002-03. So per capita income also rose substantially but it is not distributed equally. Structural changes have lessened the employment opportunities in both urban as well as in agriculture sector. Employment opportunities have shrunk and casualisation of labour has increased during this period.

As adults cannot find jobs particularly among poor families the burden falls on children. Economic reforms should have widened the base of basic facilities necessary for development of human resources but findings in this study suggest that poorer sections and more particularly children of poorer sections of the society have felt the impact other way. Privatization has made the services such as medical education, etc. costly which in turn have debarred the poor from getting to it.

RECOMMENDATIONS

The Following recommendations may be made on the basis of the findings of the study to upgrade the status of girl child domestic help and get them liberated from the tentacles of poverty and gender discrimination.

1. They should be provided residential facilities with basic amenities such as: drinking water, drainage, toilets and electricity.
2. NGO's and government should come forward to persuade and pressurize parents to send their daughters to school. There should be a provision of school near the slums for these children.
3. The school curriculum should be such that it can create better chances for the job market after schooling.
4. Vocational training should be provided to children particularly to girl children so that they may become self-reliant, self-assured persons.
5. There should be a complete ban on children's employment in all services whether formal or informal till they complete the education up to secondary level.
6. Agricultural and Rural sectors should be developed to create more employment opportunities for adults to lessen migration of labourers in order to lessen the burden on children.

7. Adult members of these families should be guaranteed employment at least for some part of the year.

REFERENCES

M. Swapna, Sudarshan, M. Ratna, (eds.) (2003), Tracking Gender Equity under Economic Reforms: Continuity and change in South Asia, New Delhi, Kali For Women, 3.

Ruddar Dutt, *Economic Liberalization and its Implications for Employment in India in Globalised Indian Economy; Contemporary Issues and Perspectives*, Edited by P. Jegadish Gandhi.

Nadeem Mohsin (2002), *The Lost Innocence* (A perspective on child labour).

Dr. Pandey M., Dr. Dixit D. (1996), Child Labour Problem in India, *Kurukshetra*, Sept.

Dr. Mathur R. (1994), "Child Labour: Problem and Solution," *Yojana*, Nov.

Chander, Suresh (2004), *Child Labour in Informal Sector: A Sociological Study*, New Delhi, Sunrise.

N. Reddy (1993), *Street Children of Bangalore: A situational Analysis*, National Labour Institute, Noida, India.

UNICEF (1988), Background Paper Presented for the National Workshop on Street Children, UNICEF, New Delhi.

UNICEF (1997), *The State of the World's Children*; New York.

ILO (1998), UN System in India: Position Paper on Child Labour, New Delhi.

19

Child Labour in India: Dimensions, Issues and Policies

RAM KUMARI DEVI

INTRODUCTION

For centuries, child labour has been a way of life in India. In rural areas, children have always helped around the farm and in production of its various rich handicrafts. Even the epic Mahabharat relates how the God Vishnu in his incarnation as Krishna, spent his boyhood contentedly fending cows. However, during the period of 150 years of colonial rule, which saw impoverishment of the masses, millions of children worked to help their families to survive. Only the few privileged children could go to school, while the others remained without education, enough food, clothes, and shelter, generation after generation. During much of the post-World War-II era, it was considered good public relations for companies to brag about the "job opportunities" they provided to children. If a consumer complained to a match company about the quality of its matches, he might get a reply begging indulgence on behalf of the immature factory hands.

Mirzapur, a district west of the holy city of Banaras is a district where thousands of children work for making the country's most beautiful carpets. Mirzapur is the 'nimble finger capital' of India where children work from 6:30 a.m. to sunset seated in sunken earthen pits. The fact is that children in Mirzapur as in the glass factories of North India and the match factories of the far south work for as long as their adult supervisors tell them to. They are not much valued for their "nimble fingers" as the industry claims, but rather for their cheap labour and submissiveness. Even the ILO in one of its reports has said: "Their work is usually done less efficiently than if it was performed by an adult. If in fact the employer benefits economically from such work, it is because he pays even less for it than it deserves."

After independence, a spate of legislature acts were enacted and provisions such as Article 24 and Article 39 were adopted in the Constitution. These articles forbid employment of children below 14 and seek to protect children against exploitative practices. But, all these legislations remained on paper except in the case of organised industries.

Then came one more change in 1979, when the International Year of Child prompted several academic studies and numerous critical articles in the press about child labour. The country woke up to the fact that it had a problem. The government commissioned a study and it fine-tuned its child labour law in 1986. Factories were raided and trial child welfare programmes were set-up. But in eight years since the International Year of Child, the bureaucrats, the social scientists, and even the press have discovered that the problem of child labour is as complicated as it is large. Legislature is no good without enforcement and the government sometimes admits that it has not succeeded. Some people say child labour is just an offshoot of dire poverty and a child denied a job is a child who goes hungry. Others say that it is an argument for inaction.

Child labour in India can be broken into three groups: children legally working on land who account for 90 per cent of child workers; urban street children working as maids, bartenders and construction workers, the worst paid of the child labourers; and, those in factories of Dickensian squalor where the hiring of children is strictly prohibited but depressingly common. This last category has attracted most of the public attention because of the grim working conditions and the government's abdication of its own responsibility under enlightened laws. It is also this sector in which one encounters the most bizarre justification for child labour. Factory owners defend their employment of children by praising their 'nimble fingers' and evoking bucolic memories of India's past when children happily toiled alongside their parents. Some factory owners even say that children help them to compete against multinationals. The arguments may seem ludicrous to outsiders but in India they have become a kind of an accepted phenomenon.

Conventionally, a working child is defined as a child in the range of 5 to 14 years who is doing labour work, either paid or unpaid. Here one can distinguish between child labour and 'child work'. While child labour is a conventional definition's child work is a broader definition.

One can broaden the definition of child labour to child work by defining it as a child who is deprived of the right to education and childhood. The child population can be grouped into three categories: school going children, child labour, nowhere children (non-labour-non-school goers). According to NSS data, the last category of nowhere children forms about 35 per cent and they are potential child labourers. Therefore, the child labour problem should address not only the category of child labour but also the category of nowhere. In this study, we consider both the dimensions i.e., conventional and broader definitions.

INDIA AND THE OTHER REGIONS IN THE WORLD

The international statistics generally place child labour in the 10-14 age group. As in other regions, the incidence of child labour in India has been declining overtime. From this trend, one should not conclude that economic policies or liberalisation in the 1990s is responsible for the decline in child labour. It looks like the decline seems to be a long-term phenomena for many countries. The numbers presented for the age group 10-14 in Table 1 show that the incidence of child labour in India has declined from 21 per cent in 1980 to 13 per cent in 1997. India's incidence of child labour is close to that of the world average. The proportion is lower for India as compared to other South Asian countries except Sri Lanka.

The incidence of child labour in India (13%) or in South Asia (16%) is not that high as compared to Sub-Saharan Africa (30%)

in 1997. The absolute numbers are, however, quite high in countries like India.

TABLE 1

Incidence of Child Labour: 10-14 Age Group

(percentage)

Country/Regions	*1980*	*1997*	*Region*	*1980*	*1997*
Bangladesh	35	29	Sub-Saharan Africa	35	30
India	21	13	Latin America & Caribbean	13	9
Nepal	56	44	East Asia & Pacific	27	10
Pakistan	23	17	Middle East & North Africa	14	5
Sri Lanka	4	2	Europe & Central Asia	3	4
South Asia	23	16	World	20	13

Source: World Bank's Development Indicators, 1999.

A complete and separate analysis for incidence of rural-urban child labour may be made with the help of Table 2. It is a real fact that Child labour incidence is higher in Southern states like Andhra Pradesh, Karnataka and Tamil Nadu and lower in poor states like Bihar and Uttar Pradesh. There are significant regional disparities in the incidence of child labour. Table 2 provides the percentages of child labour across states from three sources (Census, NSS and NCAER).

NSS provides two types of estimates: one based on principal status and the other based on principal and subsidiary status. The work participation rates for children are high for the latter category. The NSS principal and subsidiary numbers for rural areas show that it was the highest in Andhra Pradesh (17.8%) and lowest in Kerala (0.76%). These two states have same ranks for urban areas also. The regional disparities are much higher for rural areas as compared to urban areas.

VARIOUS DIMENSIONS OF CHILD LABOUR

(a) Concentrated in Rural Areas

Estimates based on the NSS data show that there are 214 million children in the age-group of 5-14 years in 1993-94. Out of these 13.2 million are child labourers in the conventional sense in the same year. Table 3 provides estimates of incidence of child

TABLE 2

Incidence of Child Labour Across Indian States: 5-14 Age Group

	Rural				Urban		
	Census 1991	*NSS 1993-94*		*NCAER 1994*	*Census 1991*	*NSS 1993-94*	
		PSS	*PS*			*SS*	*PS*
Andhra Pradesh	12.5	17.8	15.3	9.0	3.1	6.8	5.7
Assam	–	2.6	1.7	2.6	–	3.8	3.6
Bihar	4.4	3.7	3.2	3.9	1.6	1.3	1.2
Gujarat	7.1	4.1	2.8	6.2	1.7	2.0	1.4
Haryana	3.0	2.6	1.3	1.9	1.1	2.4	1.9
Himachal Pradesh	4.8	13.2	3.2	0.8	1.3	2.4	1.5
Jammu & Kashmir	–	5.6	3.3	–	–	1.1	0.8
Karnataka	11.0	13.7	10.7	7.4	3.5	4.3	4.0
Kerala	0.6	0.8	0.5	0.4	0.5	0.6	0.5
Madhya Pradesh	9.9	8.4	6.4	3.5	1.8	1.5	1.1
Maharashtra	8.1	6.5	5.3	8.0	1.6	2.1	1.8
Orissa	6.5	7.4	5.5	5.1	1.9	2.8	2.2
Punjab	3.6	2.7	2.1	3.4	1.6	1.7	1.4
Rajasthan	7.8	12.2	11.4	1.2	1.7	3.2	2.6
Tamil Nadu	5.9	10.4	9.3	5.6	2.6	5.2	4.6
Uttar Pradesh	4.2	5.0	3.4	1.5	2.3	3.2	2.2
West Bengal	4.9	5.1	3.5	6.7	1.9	3.8	2.9
All India	6.4	7.2	5.8	4.3	2.0	3.1	2.5
CV Across States (%)	49.0	65.0	76.0	63.0	39.0	55.0	60.0

Sources: 1. Census 1991.
2. NSS 50th Round on Employment and Unemployment.
3. Duraisamy, M (2000) for NCAER Data.

labour from various sources. It is around 6.2 per cent according to NSS 1993-94 data, while Census gives 5.4 per cent in 1991. In rural areas also NSS based estimates are higher than those of Census and NCAER. The percentages in rural areas are two to three times higher to those for areas (Table 3). The difference between incidence for boys and girls is not much in both Census and NSS.

TABLE 3

Incidence of Child Labour from Different Sources (5-14 Age Group), All India

	Census 1991	*NSS 1993-94*	*NCAER 1994*
Total	5.4	6.2	–
Rural	6.4	7.2	4.3
Urban	2.0	3.1	–
Boys	5.7	6.3	–
Girls	5.1	6.0	–

Sources: Col. 2 = Decennial Census 1991.
Col. 3 = NSS on Employment and Unemployment 50th Round.
Col. 4 = NCAER Human Development Survey, 1994.

(b) Child Labour Incidence has been Declining Over Time

The NSS data during the period 1997-98 to 1993-94 shows that, the incidence of child labour has been declining over time in both rural and urban areas (Table 4). In rural areas, till 1987-88, the percentage of child labour for boys was higher than that for girls while in 1993-94, the percentages are same for boys and girls. In the case of urban areas, percentages for boys were always higher than that for girls.

TABLE 4

Trends in Incidence of Child Labour: 5-14 Age Group, NSS Data, 1993-94, All-India

	Rural Boys	*Rural Girls*	*Rural Total*	*Urban Boys*	*Urban Girls*	*Urban Total*
1977-78	14.4	11.6	13.1	6.1	4.4	5.3
1983	13.5	12.5	13.0	6.1	3.8	5.0
1987-88	10.1	9.6	9.9	4.4	3.3	3.9
1993-94	7.1	7.2	7.1	3.6	2.5	3.1

Sources: 1. Computed from NSS 50th Round data for 1993-94.
2. Visaria *et. al.* (1993) for 1977-78, 1983 and 1987-88.

(c) Incidence is high for SCs and STs and Agricultural Labourers

Among the social groups, SCs report the highest incidence of child labour followed by STs (Table 5). A micro-study on Andhra Pradesh (Reddy and Rao, 1999) also shows that scheduled castes report highest incidence of child labour in the study areas (Table 6). The same study shows that it is high for agricultural labourers and non-agricultural labourers as compared to that for cultivators.

TABLE 5

Incidence of Child Labour: Social Groups, 1993-94, All-India

	Rural Boys	*Rural Girls*	*Rural Total*	*Urban Boys*	*Urban Girls*	*Urban Total*
SC	11.9	13.8	12.8	4.4	6.2	5.3
ST	7.4	8.8	8.1	3.0	2.9	3.0
Others	5.9	6.5	6.2	3.5	2.6	3.1
All	7.1	7.2	7.1	3.6	2.5	3.1

Source: Computed from NSS 50th Round on Employment and Unemployment.

TABLE 6

Incidence of Child Labour: Social Group and Occupation Category: Micro-Study in Andhra Pradesh, 1995-96

(Percentage)

District	*Special Groups*				
	SC		*ST*	*BC*	*OC*
Mahaboobnagar	16.3		18.7	14.7	6.1
Kurnool	31.2		14.2	28.4	15.8
Anantapur	19.8		14.9	13.8	9.4
All	23.8		15.6	19.9	11.3
	Occupation				
	AL	*CULT.*	*NAL.*	*Others*	*Overall*
Mahaboobnagar	16.2	11.7	20.0	9.2	13.8
Kurnool	32.2	23.6	24.0	14.5	25.2
Anantapur	21.9	8.9	22.0	9.9	13.6
All	25.1	15.1	22.2	11.9	18.4

AL: Agricultural Labour; CULT: Cultivators; NAL: Non-Agricultural Labour.
Source: Reddy and Rao (1999).

(d) Child Labour is Concentrated in the 10-14 Age Group and in Agriculture, there is some Intolerable Exploitation in some sectors

The trends in the incidence of child labour for two age-groups show a decline for both the groups (Table 7). However, Child Labour is concentrated in the 10-14 age group (14% for rural areas and 5.6 per cent for urban areas). Child Labour is concentrated in agriculture in India (Table 8). Cultivators and agricultural labourers constitute around 78 per cent for boys and 83 per cent for girls.

TABLE 7

Trends in Incidence of Child Labour 5-9 and 10-14 Age Groups, 1993-94, All India

	Rural Boys	*Rural Girls*	*Rural Total*	*Urban Boys*	*Urban Girls*	*Urban Total*
			5-9 Age Group			
1983	2.5	2.6	2.5	0.8	0.7	0.7
1987-88	2.4	2.3	2.3	0.5	0.3	0.4
1993-94	1.1	1.4	1.3	0.5	0.5	0.5
			10-14 Age Group			
1983	25.3	24.0	24.7	11.3	7.0	9.3
1987-88	19.0	18.0	18.6	8.5	6.5	7.5
1993-94	13.8	14.1	14.0	6.6	4.5	5.6

Sources: 1. Computed from NSS 50 Round Data for 1993-94.
2. Visaria et al (1993) for 1977-78, 1983 and 1987-88.

TABLE 8

Child Labour by Sub-Sectors (1991), 5-14 Years Age Group (%) All-India

	Boys	*Girls*
Cultivators	37.9	30.8
Agricultural Labourers	39.6	51.9
Manufacturing in Household Industries	20.4	12.7
Others	2.1	4.6
	100.0	100.0

Source: Census, 1991.

ISSUES AND POLICY

There are several issues which need to be highlighted for the purposes of study and for the use of policy practitioners so that problem of child labour can be taken care of and government may take a healthy decision regarding eradication of child labour in India. Some policies and issues are discussed here:

(a) Economic Growth, Poverty and Child Labour

The policies that improve economic growth and reduce poverty certainly would help in reducing child labour. Increase in adult wages are important to reduce the supply of child labour. A micro-study by Swaminathan (1998) argues that economic growth alone is not sufficient to eradicate child labour. Her study examines features of child labour in an area of high economic growth in western India. Growth was associated with an increase in the number of child workers in over the last 15 years. The analysis shows that children who work repetitive manual tasks do not require long years of training or experience. The work is low paying, involving drudgery, is extremely and hazardous. Work forecloses the option of school education for most children. Thus, aggregate economic growth is not a sufficient condition for reduction in child labour.

(b) Going Beyond Poverty: Compulsory Education

The establishment of compulsory education for children is a necessary condition for the reduction and abolition of child labour. In a narrow sense, compulsory education is under-stood as a law making it compulsory for parents to send their own children to school and allowing for the punishment of parents who do not comply with it. In a broad sense compulsory education may be interpreted as, "(a) a compulsion on the state to provide adequate schooling facilities to all children, and (b) subject to that, an obligation of the parental community to send all children to school. Thus, understood compulsory education is a broad notion" (Dreze, 1997). The most important thing is that compulsory education would put much needed pressure on the state to expand schooling facilities. The argument against compulsory education is that it leads to official harassment of parents and poor families who lose their earnings from child labour. It may be noted that non-coercive means can be used for promoting compulsory education. The girl child is going to be particularly benefited from the establishment of compulsory education.

The 83rd constitutional amendment for India speaks of "the right to compulsory education." The compulsory education and right to education makes sense on the basis of two conditions: (a) adequate facilities being available at a convenient distance, and (b) education being free. [Introducing compulsory education before the horse (Dreze, 1999)].

(c) National Government and Child Labour

R.K.A. Subrahmanya's paper; "A Critical Evaluation of Policies and Programmes of the International Organisations" starts with quoting the declaration of the rights of the child by the UN General Assembly which accepts eradication of child labour as an important objective for the children of the world. Subrahmanya reviews the ILO's approach as reflected in various Conventions and Recommendations starting from the year 1919 to the comprehensive convention of 1973 which aims at elimination of child labour from all the major sectors of an economy. He argues that total eradication of child labour is not a practical proposition for Third World countries because a high incidence of poverty on one hand, and low level of political will of the national governments on the other hand, which will not allow an effective implementation of any such move. He therefore suggests, gradual move in the direction through expansion of schooling facilities, faster rate of economic development, etc.

(d) Issues Pertaining to Health and Education

Working children are prone to serious problems in the areas of health and education. These problems are highlighted by G.R. Ramachandran, S.H. Clerk and Kamala Srinivasan.

Ramachandran's paper gives a broad view of the problems of health and safety of working children. While using the various studies on these problems, the author observes that working children are likely to suffer specific problems of occupational health and safety, because: (a) the working conditions of these children are invariably poor, (b) machines on which they work are meant for the adults and are not meant for them, (c) their easy fatigability and lesser span of attention making them accident prone, and (d) children have a high susceptibility to specific toxics and chemicals, such as, lead and synthetic resins. He also adds that child labourers suffer from poor nutrition because of their low wages and the poverty at home, as well as poor psychological and social problems, originating from their deprivation of education and forced adulthood. Consequently, when they become adults, their health status is poor, education is nil or limited, and they are incapable of getting work with a reasonable level of remuneration. In fact, frequently these adults are thrown out of their old jobs. They are then forced to join the vast army of the unemployed.

(e) Voluntary Agencies and Child Labour

Though it is clear that voluntary agencies should play an important role in resolving the problem, what precise role can they play?

Vidyut Joshi defines the role of NGOs in the context of the concept of child labour. According to him, child labour is the labour put in by children which directly or indirectly comes into conflict with their opportunities for mental and physical development. These opportunities however are determined by the socio-economic background, institutional framework and political goals of a nation's society. Eradication of child labour therefore can be brought about not by legal action, but by the efforts of non-governmental agencies which try to change the social milieu in which child labourers work. Social activists can contribute significantly by organising child labour and by relating the issues of child labour to larger issues such as, the type of society and the level of technological and economic development they want.

NATIONAL POLICY ON CHILD LABOUR

Mere legislation however, is not enough to cope with the problem. Therefore, a National Policy on Child Labour has been framed by the government to take care of the administrative and welfare aspects. The main features of the National Child Labour Policy are as follows:

1. It will be ensured that the legal provisions pertaining to prohibition of child labour in hazardous employments,

regulation of their conditions of work in other employments, and provisions pertaining to health, safety, welfare amenities and other benefits are strictly implemented so that child labour does not live at the mercy of the employers under highly exploitative and inhuman conditions.

2. Ten specific projects will be undertaken in areas of concentration of child labour: (i) Ensuring that all the poor families from which child workers come, are covered by the income and employment generation programmes. This will enable them to cross the poverty line. In addition to the funds of the existing programmes additional funds will be spent in these areas, to cover all the families in three years. (ii) The programmes pertaining to education, vocational training, health and nutrition will be strengthened in the project areas. (iii) Special schools will be opened to rehabilitate the children removed from the prohibited employments and to provide welfare inputs to the children working in the permitted employments. The schools for rehabilitation of child labour will provide non-formal education, supplementary nutrition and vocational training, along with a stipend so as to compensate the loss of income to their family. The schools for the working children however will be part-time, running on holidays or after work hours, etc., and will not contain an element of stipend. The course for non-formal education and skill development programmes will have to be drawn up very carefully keeping in view the needs of the children, their aptitude and the local situation.
3. The programmes of education, health, medical care, supplementary nutrition, as well as of income and employment generation for the parents of child labourers are most relevant in the context of the problem of child labour. If these programmes are implemented well, the problem of child labour will be eliminated gradually.

LEGAL SAFEGUARDS

Although the parliament of India has passed several legislation to eradicate the child labour from Indian society but has not be proved useful. Article 24 of the Indian Constitution lays down that no child below the age of 14 years shall be employed in any factory or mines, or engaged in any other hazardous employment. Further, the Directive Principles of our Constitution urge that: (a) the government should see that health of workers including child workers and the tender age of children are not abused, and that citizens are not forced by economic necessity to enter a vocation unsuited to their age or strength; and (b) the childhood and youth is protected against exploitation and against moral and material abandonment.

The government of India has passed a number of legislations banning or regulating the working conditions of child labourers. The recent act, namely, Child Labour (Prohibition and Regulation) Act, 1986 however is a comprehensive act which prohibits employment of children under 14 yeas in specified occupations and processes, and regulates the conditions of work of children in employments where they are not prohibited from working. The Act also provides for a Child Labour Technical Advisory Committee to advise the government regarding banning child labour in different occupations and processes. The Committee is expected to examine all occupations and processes where children work and determine which are hazardous for children. After this exercise is over, child labour will be prohibited from all hazardous occupations. In the remaining occupations and processes, the working conditions will be regulated in a phased manner. The Act also provides for framing rules for the health and safety of the children employed in permitted employments and for severe penalties for their violation and for violation, of the relevant portions of the Factories Act, 1948, the Mines Act, 1950, the Merchant and Shipping Act, 1951, and the Motor Transport Workers Act, 1950.

SOME IMPORTANT RECOMMENDATIONS

In order to oversee the ban and make it possible to regulate working conditions, the first step necessary is to shift the units doing the hazardous jobs of polishing, electroplating, and spray painting from the city centre and the *mohalla* to an area like the industrial estate. To facilitate this shift, the government may consider offering plots of land at concessional rates to small entrepreneurs provided they do not employ children. Other incentives like cheaper electricity tariffs and subsidised raw materials could be given to the units not using child labour. Along with the carrot of such facilities, the stick of stringent penal action should be kept in readiness. Those units that continue to employ children in these processes should be severely fined and closed down, if necessary. Every unit must be registered, even if it is not getting any aid from the government and owners must not be allowed to engage even their own children in these obviously hazardous processes.

Keeping in mind the poverty of the children, we do not recommend complete banning of child labour in the short run. These children however should be employed in filing, assembling, and packing, which are not hazardous to their health. However, children should not be allowed to enter the factory, as it is difficult to control their work once they enter it. Such activities should be organised in outside centres where non-formal education, and feeding programmes also can be organised. To the extent possible, the small entrepreneur who just about manages to stay afloat should not be displaced. Sudden and drastic changes are likely to make child labour even more unregulated and exploited.

CONCLUDING REMARKS

It is very clear that the problem of child labour is a highly complex problem as it is a consequence of the system under which the national economies are functioning. The problem has so far defied all kinds of solutions tried out at various levels. Even in industrialized countries the problem is not fully resolved.

In addition to the legislative and administrative actions of the government, involvement of voluntary organisations, social groups and trade unions is absolutely indispensable. Also, the society in general will have to be conscious against the social evil. The recent amendment in The Child Labour (Prohibition and Regulation) Act 1986, banning the employment of children in all the hazardous units, has not made any difference except that it has enabled the authorities to collect more money from the owners of these units.

Hence, we strongly feel that imposing a complete ban on child labour without the attendant economic incentives would not be effective and could be counterproductive. It is, therefore, essential to tackle this issue simultaneously from all related angles, so that as a whole the impact is visible and useful.

References

Choudhary, D.P. (1997), "A Policy Perspective in India with Pervasive Gender and Urban Bias in School Education," *The Indian Journal of Labour Economics*, Vol. 40, No. 4.

Dev, S. Mahendra, "Child Labour in India: Dimensions, Determinants and Policies," *IEA Conference Volume*, 2000.

Dreze, J. and Amartya Sen (1995), *India: Economic Development Social Opportunity*, Oxford University Press, New Delhi.

Gerry Rodgers and Guy Standing, "The Economic Role of Children Issues for Analysis; in Gerry Rodgers and Guy Standing (eds.), *Child Work, Poverty and Underdevelopment*, ILO, Geneva, 1981, p. 10.

ILO (1996), Child Labour: Targeting the Intolerable, ILO Report VI(I) *International Labour Conference*.

Kulashrestha, J.C. (1978), Child Labour in India, Ashis Publication, New Delhi.

MV Foundation Annual Reports, 1996-97, 1997-98, 2000-01.

Swaminathan, M. (1998), "Economic Growth and Persistence of Child Labour: Evidence from an Indian City," *World Development*, Vol. 26, No. 8.

UNICEF, Patna, Child Labour in India, 1997.

Economic Reforms and Women Empowerment: A View Point

NAGESHWAR SHARMA AND ANIRUDDH KUMAR

OVERVIEW

The structural adjustment reforms (economically called "New Economic Policy") encompassing both macro-economic stabilization measures and the measures to restructure several sectors of the economy are being undertaken in India since July, 1991 on an evolving and ongoing basis, with experience based modifications being made periodically. These reforms have been announced mainly in the Budgets of the Central Government. These have been supplemented by the periodic policy documents of the concerned wings of the government for the relevant sectors (such as: for foreign trade; industry; banks; financial institutions; and the capital markets). The macro economic stabilization measures have been announced by the Finance Ministry mainly including the fiscal policy measures and the Reserve Bank of India monetary policy and exchange rate policy measures (Charan D. Wadhva, 1994).

The Policy of Economic Reforms, undertaken by the Government of India in 1991 is being called by different names. Some people call it as 'Manmohanomics', some as 'Raonomics' and some others as 'Rao-Mohanomics'. There is one more category of persons, particularly of political arena, who try to pit it against 'populonomics'. (G.S. Batra and R.C Dangwal, 2004) Whatever names, the economists and politicians may give to the policy of economic reforms, the fact is that it has become since qua non for the economy and the Indian economy has to go ahead with the policies of economic reforms.

WOMEN EMPOWERMENT

Human race is divided into two categories Men and Women. Women cover almost half of the total population. In India, the proportion of females is 933 per 1,000 males in 2001 (Census, 2001). As a matter of fact, women are the vital human infrastructure and their empowerment – economic, social, and political would hasten the pace of social development. The issue of women empowerment has been a subject of grave concern for political thinkers and social workers as they are of the view that a nation or a society can go ahead only through the contribution of all its members. Put the women into the backyards and the society itself will be dragged behind. This is because the perception of the government towards women has been showing a radical change especially in government programmes. The emphasis has gradually been shifted from women welfare, to women development, and at present to women empowerment.

The terms Women Empowerment, Women Welfare, Gender Justice are in limelight in the social and economic development analysis of both developed and developing nations. The debate on Women Empowerment/Women Welfare/Gender Justice was at the center stage in the international arena in the 1994 UN conference in Cairo; UN's Fourth International Conference on Women at Beijing in 1995 and UN's Social Summit Conference at Copenhagen in March, 1995. Empowerment of women also means equal status to women. Empowering women socio-economically through increased awareness of their rights and duties as well as access to resources is a decisive step towards greater security for them. Empowerment includes: higher literacy level and education for women; better health care for women and children; equal ownership of productive resources; increased participation in economic and commercial sectors; awareness of their rights and responsibilities; improved standards of living; and acquiring self–reliance, self–esteem and self–confidence (*Kurukshetra*, November 2005).

INDIA'S PLACE

Initially women's welfare was a part of the government programmes to improve the status of women in India. Later on, the emphasis shifted onto women development, and subsequently in recent years, the attitude of the government towards women has undergone a major change where women empowerment is made an objective in the programmes of the government. A recent UN report notes that India has improved its position in education, employment and per capita income of women, but it has however not achieved two third representation of women in parliament, removed their unequal wages or lessened their debt burden. The United Nations Development Programme (UNDP) Report on Human Development 2003 reveals that India's position is 127 out of 174 nations as per the Index of Human Development (HD). If it is viewed on the basis of 'Gender Development Related Index (GDI), ours is 99th place out of 130 nations. The data collected for selected countries with regards to GDI reveals that near gender equality exists in Norway, Canada, United States, United Kingdom, Japan, Mexico, Russian Federation, Malaysia, Venezualla, Philippines, Sri Lanka, China, Vietnam, and Indonesia. Countries with higher gender inequality are Saudi Arabia, Pakistan, Iran, India, Egypt, and Nigeria. This clearly indicates how the women are subjected to discrimination all over the world. India's position is worse than many countries.

Though India has improved its position from 138 in 1994 to 127 in 2001 (UNDP, HD Report, 2003) in HDI, still it is far behind as far as the status of woman is concerned. Attrocities on women, wife beating, bride burning for have become very common in India. A very startling fact is that women belonging to Scheduled Tribes, Dalits and downtrodden are alleged to be practitioners of witchcraft, and they are paraded naked and beaten by men and they are compelled to drink either urine or swallow. Several cases have come to the notice in S.P. Division of Jharkhand. This clearly shows that women are being subjected to suppression and exploitation and being marginalized in every respect.

IMPACT OF ECONOMIC REFORMS

The launching of economic reforms oriented towards a more open and more competitive market economy since July, 1991 in a framework of a democratic polity, has been a historical landmark, not only in the economic history of India, but of the entire developing world (Charan D. Wadhva, 1994). The main aspects of economic reforms policy are to privatize the economy and to open our economy for world and to remove licensing, MRTP, and FERA Act. This model of development is called L.P.G model of development. Thus, these policies are expected to eliminate unnecessary government inter-vention which hinders the free development of private institutions. Therefore, the withdrawal of government regulations are expected to create a favorable atmosphere for the private organizations to take decisions freely and to utilize the resources efficiently so as to maximize the quantum of output.

With this background, the present analysis aims at to assess the impact of economic reforms on the marginalized sections of the society particularly women. The information regarding the impact of New Economic Policy on women empowerment is scanty. However, it is desired to analyse the impact of this policy on women particularly in respect of Education, Health, and Employment.

Education

Education is an index of development. Accessibility of education to a particular class can be used as a yardstick to estimate the status of that class. From this viewpoint, it is an accepted fact that women are backward in this regard. Literacy rate of women in 1951, was 8.56 per cent. After four decades, i.e., in 1991 it has increased to 39.29 per cent. In 1991, the women literates without any formal education were 8.6 per cent. No doubt, things have improved. However, it is usually uncommon to send girl child to school. In 1993-94, only 55.2 per cent girls who are in the age group of 11-13 years could go to school. Further, dropout rate is relatively higher among female children. It is 39.05 per cent in 1993-94 and at the stage of secondary education it is as high as 74.54 per cent. The observation as to the university level education reveals that the number of female students per 100 male students is 64.7 per cent in Arts, 49.1 per cent in Sciences 36.5 per cent in Commerce, 12.5 per cent in technical courses including Engineering and 57.5 per cent in Medicine (T. Jyothi Rane and H. Girija Rani, 2004)

Jharkhand, a newly created state presents very grim picture. Literacy rate here is 54.13 per cent. Literacy rate of men in Jharkhand is 53.49 per cent. It is only 24.02 per cent in women (2001). It is in fact disappointing. Data regarding dropout rate in Jharkhand among female children is very high. In general category 37.45 per girl student takes admission in class V which comes down to 27.20 per cent in classes IX and X. Among Scheduled Tribes girl. The drop out rate is a bit higher. 35.56 per cent tribal girl takes admission between classes I to V which remains at 24.49 per cent reducing in classes IX and X. Female literacy rate among tribal women is 39.38 per cent. But it is less than 20 per cent in the three districts of Palamu, Godda & Pakur (Jharkhand, 2002). It is clear from the facts that disparities prevail between male and female education. In spite of the introduction of programmes like compulsory free primary education, formal and informal education, subsidy, mid–day meal scheme, girls are far behind in the sphere of education. Under these circumstances, withdrawal of government from the education in the name of liberalization policies, made the educational institutions comercialised and the commercialization of educational institutions made the education inaccessible to common man in general and women in particular.

Employment

Employment is also an index to measure the changes in the status of women. In India, female work participation rate in rural area in 1987-88 was 32.3 per cent, where as it was only 15.2 per cent in urban areas. The observation in regard to female work participation in agricultural sector reveals that in 1981 out of women employees, 2.3 per cent were in technical jobs, 0.1 per cent in managerial functions, 0.7 per cent in clerical jobs and 1.9 per cent in service sector (Census, 1981). According to 1991 census female workers participation stood at 81.09 per cent in the primary sector, while it was only 8.07 per cent in secondary sector and 10.84 per cent in tertiary sector (Census, 1991)

According to 1981 census, more women when compared to men can be seen in the activities of beedi-making, tobacco processing, cotton joining, cashewnut and fish processing works. Most of the women workers are seen as servant maids, mid-wives, nurses, teachers and the activities that are associated with the preservation of food grains. On the whole, it can be stated that mostly they are confined to formal sector. Women's presence is very small in the services sector. At present, their involvement is merely as temporary labourers both in rural and urban areas. As per the Census of India, 2001, statistics show that out of a total of 32.62 crores of economically active female population, only 6.03 crores i.e., 18.5 per cent is employed, where as out of 34.97 crores of economically active males, 23.63 crores, representing 67.6 per cent is employed in paid jobs. (R. Chinnadurai, November 2005) According to an estimate by the National Commission on Self Employed Women, 94 per cent of the female work force operates within this highly exploited sector.

The expansion of Private sector is the result of LPG policies. It is a well known fact, that the sole aim of private sector is to maximize profit which naturally lessens the employment opportunities in general. Moreover, they take measures to extract more amount of surplus labour by raising working hours and by work intensification. They do not prefer to take women employees as it requires the creation of certain facilities at the work place which incurs cost. It is clear that the liberalization policies will not improve employment opportunities in general and for women in particular. Rather, they lessen employment opportunities to hapless women and make them subjected to wage discrimation.

Health

Physical health of women particularly in India has emerged as a serious problem. The health of men will be determined only by economic factors, while the socio-economic and cultural factors play a decisive role in the case of women. It is because of the patriarchal societies. It is no wonder that least preference is given to women's health.

Keeping aside the availability of nutritious food, women live in the socio-economic environment where it is not possible at least to have enough quantity of food (irrespective of its quality) throughout their lives since their childhood. This reflects in their health condition. Usually they suffer from anemia and under–weight. Therefore, they are subjected to ill-health associated with bloodlessness. Family, society, and state recognize women to the extent of her reproductive functions. Furthermore, preference is being given to the child rather than to the mother. With this viewpoint, women welfare programmes have been formulated in India.

The small family norm is another important aspect of India's Population Policy. In the patriarchal society, it is quite natural for them to have a strong desire for male child. Therefore, they use the facility of Amniocentesis test and opt for abortion if it is a female fetus. It is unfortunate to note that MTP Act (Medical Termination of Pregnancy Act) is favourably used for this purpose. All this clearly indicates that the National Health Policy did not take into consideration the health needs of women.

The implementation of liberalized policies compels the government to reduce expenditure on welfare programmes particularly on health. Consequently, the government hospitals and infrastructural facilities available in them go waste. The liberalization policies transform them into useless entities. The situation compels the people to go to private hospital. This has been reflected in the enormous rise in the number of hospitals and super–speciality hospitals in the private sector. Every hospital, usually, will have its own disease diagnosing center. A mushroom growth can be seen in regard to number of such laboratories. In order to utilize the installed capacity of the hospital including laboratory to the full extent every patient is forced to undergo various tests. Consequently, disease diagnosis itself is becoming costly. In these conditions, health facilities will not be in the reach of the poor people in general and women in particular.

CONCLUSION

It is clear that three indices—education. employment and health determine the status of women in the society. But of all the three, employment contributes a greater degree of empowerment to women in the family. Educated but dependent women are in a very critical position. Hence, the women empowerment requires her emancipation from dependency. The implementation of liberalization policies lead to the continuous decline in the employment opportunities specially in the organized sector. This causes the displacement of women. They are compelled to depend upon informal sector where women are exploited in many respects. Decline in the educational opportunities naturally prevents women to enter into better jobs. Women will not have any opportunity to utilize their intellectual creative abilities. Similarly, deterioration in the health facilities make the women's lives more critical. Women, in the patriarchal society are already subjected to dependence. The factors that determine the status of women should be strengthened, so as to improve the quality of life of women. What will happen in the years to come? But the present situation is sufficient enough to confirm that the implementation of liberalization policies has weakened all the three indices—education, employment and health. Thus, the liberalization process which forms the most important part of our economic reform policies clearly move in the opposite direction in the attainment of women empowerment.

REFERENCES

Agrawal, Vinita (1994), Women Empowerment, Sept.

Batra, G.S and Dangwal, R.C. (2004), *'Globalisation and Liberalisation: New Development'*, Deep & Deep Publications Pvt. Ltd., New Delhi.

Bhagwati, Jagdish and Srinivasan, T.N. (1993), 'India's Economic Reforms', New Delhi.

Government of India, *Women and Men in India*, CSO, 1995.

Jharkhand (2002), *Readers Corner*, Frazer Road, Patna.

Sinha, U.P. (1995), 'Socio-Economic Status of Women in India', paper presented at the National Seminar.

State of Governance Jharkhand Citizen Handbook, *Centre for Civil Society*, K-36, Hauz Khas Enclave, New Delhi, 2006.

The Journal of Economic Issues, Published by Planning Form, University Department of Economics, T.M. Bhagalpur University, Bhagalpur, Vol. 1, March, 2002, and Vol. 2, March 2003.

Wadhva Charan D. (1994), *Economic Reforms in India and the Market Economy* Allied Publishers Limited, New Delhi.

21

Empowerment of Women after Fifty Years of Independence: Where do they Stand?

CHANDRA PRAKASH AZAD AND CHANDRA PRAKASH SINGH

In the Partriarchal Indian society, women have been subjected to exploitation, attrocities, male-dominance and gender-bias. The international organisations have been highlighting the empowerment of women as the surest way of making them partners of development. There have been governmental interventions but much has to be done in this direction. For this, quantitave as well as qualitive education, Panchayati Raj Institutions, economic independence of women and self-help groups should be promoted.

The Global Conference on Women Empowerment, 1988 highlighted empowerment as the surest way of making women "partners in development". The Food and Agricultural Organisation (FAO) has also emphasized on strengthening and motivating them to claim their rights particularly the women at the grassroots. These can be achieved by infusing them with strong traits of positive self-image, critical thinking, group cohesion, decision-making and equal participation.

Records of the past bear testimony to the fact that in most times and places women have been dominated by the males. Even the traditions that evolved during the course of time, have strong male bias. Women participation in public affairs and self-determination are facing opposition from the traditionalists. Consequently, the case of women participation in socio-political process became a significant matter of analysis in recent times. Democratization, education, urbanization, modernization and the like, have precipitated women's liberation movement in the west. In India too, in recent years' concerns have been expressed over the lower status assigned to the women in the society. Forward-looking women and their male emancipators are not satisfied with periodic voting or the opportunities available to them. Instead of 'Pseudo Participation' commonly offered to the women, they want some decisive say in the decisions that tend to affect their lives substantially.

The constitution of India pledges equality of status, opportunities and the dignity of the individual to men and women on an equal footing. These were to serve as instruments for achieving equality of status and opportunity in all spheres of life. In actual practice these rights have however helped to build an illusion, a semblance of equality which is far from reality. The widening gap between men and women in all-important spheres of life observed after independence indicates that somewhere we have moved away from the goals set before us by the makers of our constitution.

The World Development Report, 2000 suggests that conquering poverty requires, not just economic development, but also actions to expand poor peoples opportunities, empowerment, and ensuring their security. The empowerment of poor women in general and tribals in particular are the only means of poverty eradication. So any economic strategy of empowering these poor rural womens must make provision to link the nature of employment with the skills and training required for efficiently running it. The study has following objectives:

1. to observe the level of socio-economic differentials according to caste and class in women empowerment;

2. to find out determinants and respective role of each variable in determining women empowerment; and
3. to enquire and gather the views of women on various aspects reflecting their present and future empowerment.

The study covers the following heads:

1. Status of women after fifty years of-Independence;
2. Empowerment of women through Panchayati Raj Institutions;
3. Empowerment of women through Self Help Groups; and
4. Eradication of poverty through empowerment of women.

I. SOCIO-ECONOMIC STATUS OF WOMEN: PRESENT SCENARIO

In spite of an impressive line up of constitutional provisions, Acts and laws enacted for the protection, emancipation, and empowerment of women, they are being subjected to deprivation, brutality, and humiliation. The National Committee for Status of Women in India (1975) in its report pointed out, that there has been serious deterioration in the status of women. They have been marginalized in both the socio-economic spheres and the political mainstream. The women have also realized the complex and subordinate socio-legal status in the conventional patriarchal structure along with the rising aspirations in the environment of consumerism. Despite several laws a perceptive increase in dowry deaths, violence and abuse at home, incidence of rape, female infanticide, child marriage, denial of property right to women are widely prevalent. For the working women, another set of exploitation takes place at their work place, such as sexual harassment, rape, violence or its threat, teasing, discrimination in pay scales, etc. The police record provides details of reported cases of crimes against women. It is also however, true that much of these crimes go unreported. In fact it has been observed that, women often face violence at the hands of their protectors, be it the law enforcement agencies or their family members. Table 1 will give a detailed account of these crimes against women.

II. EMPOWERMENT OF WOMEN THROUGH SELF HELP GROUP (SHGs)

Empowerment of women through SHGs are the need of the hours. It is basically concerned with equality, participation, influencing decision and access to opportunity. It has been realized that organising of women groups is one of the most effective tools for involving women in the development process and this task can be fully performed by the involvement of Self Help Groups in women's empowerment.

The emergence of SHGs is a right step in the right direction. A SHG is a group of 10 to 20 people from a homogenous class who come together for addressing their common problems. It is usually an informal group whose members have common perception of need and importance towards collective action. A common base like caste, blood, and community link the members.

The SHGs provide the benefits of economics of scale, cost-effectiveness, alternatives for different financial services, collective learning, democratic and participatory culture, and a common platform. Moreover, the benefits of SHGs are based on co-operation rather than competition. Social mobilization through SHGs is inevitable for economic empowerment and poverty alleviation. The SHGs have been formed to enhance the equality of status of women as participant decision-makers and beneficiaries in the democratic, economic, social and cultural spheres of life.

A study was made by the NABARD to review the performance of SHGs. Some of the findings of this study are given below:

(a) The average net income per household has increased by about 33 per cent;

(b) Employment has increased by 18 per cent;

(c) SHGs activities has enhanced the self-confidence of the members;

(d) The feeling of active participation, self-esteem and communication with others has improved after association with SHGs; and

(e) The members of SHGs are in position to formulate plans, implement the plan and evaluate the plans themselves.

III. POLITICAL EMPOWERMENT OF WOMEN IN PANCHAYATI RAJ

The Panchayati Raj Institutions (PRIs) were established with two basic objectives; firstly of Gram Swaraj through decentralization of power down to the village level and secondly, by providing an effective instrument of rural development. The 73rd Constitutional Amendment Bill (1989) depicts that women's role in PRIs has been ensured by provision of reservation of one third seats for women at all the three tiers. These provisions are directly related to women's participation.

In practice women were virtually denied access to political power through the Gram Panchayats. From gender perspectives, the three-tier Panchayati Raj system was more pro-women than earlier local bodies. It is because the new system envisaged the co-option of women as functionaries of these institutions. However, these institutions failed to achieve the desired result due to other administrative, political and financial constraints. Even the government report accepted the reality that despite the rapid growth of informal political of women, their role in the formal political structures had virtually remained unchanged.

The National Perspective Plan for Women (1988-2000) examined all aspects relating to political participation and decision-making, and expressed concern about the insignificant role of women in the formal political decision-making process.

It is true that the recent constitutional amendments have significantly enhanced the status and importance of Panchayati Raj Institutions (PRIs) as instruments of development and augmented their strength as institutions of paramount significance for the political empowerment of women. Due to poor female literacy rate, poverty, ignorances and other cultural and social barriers, the present level of participation of women in the political field has been quite insignificant.

The women's Bill seeking reservation of 33 per cent of seats in the Lok Sabha and the State Legislatures is not favoured by some of the political parties and hence the said Bill is still pending in the Parliament.

The success of the process of political empowerment of women will depend on organizational and policy changes for revitalization of PRIs, electoral reform, sustained drive for political education, gender sensitization campaign and male enlightenment about the importance of gender equality and justice.

IV. ERADICATION OF POVERTY THROUGH EMPOWERMENT OF WOMEN

It is becoming more evident that the majority of the poor in both the developed or even developing countries are women. Poverty among rural women is growing faster than among rural men. The number of women in absolute poverty rose by 50 per cent as against 30 per cent for rural men. The trend of this process strongly indicates that the gender composition of the poor is veering towards a greater share for women.

Analysis of women's poverty suggests that its main causes stem from the perpetual disadvantage of women in terms of their position in the labour market, access to productive resources and income for the satisfaction of basic needs. This also demonstrates that poor women possess exceptional resourcefulness, initiative, and entrepreneurial spirit, and that they show tenacity and ability of self-sacrifice in trying to take a long-term view of their poor economic conditions and in safeguarding their livelihood. For the last twenty years, the eradication of poverty among the growing proportion of poor women is the single most important issue before the policy makers.

The Earth Summit in Rio, the Human Rights Conference in Vienna, the Population Conference in Cairo and the Beizing Conference, etc., all were milestone events in terms of advancing our understanding of the crucial role of women in development and focusing the attention of the international community on the issues concerning the role of women in the work place and in society. All of them drew attention to women's full and effective participation in development.

V. GOVERNMENT POLICIES AND PROGRAMMES FOR EMPOWERMENT OF WOMEN

The STEP programme, which was launched in 1987, seeks to provide new upgraded skills to poor and assetless women in the traditional sectors of agriculture, sericulture, handicrafts, fisheries, dairying, poultry, etc. for enhacing their productivity and income generation.

The Norwegian Agency for International Development (NORAD) extends assistance for training and skill development, and promotion of self-reliance through income generation for women in non-traditional trades in the country upto 1999-2000. About 81 projects have been sanctioned to benefit 6,805 women. The National Commission for Women (NCW) was set-up in 1992 for safeguarding women's rights and promotion of their empowerment. The Commission works for review of laws, intervention in specific individual complaints of atrocities and sexual harassment of women at work place and remedial action to safeguard the interests of women. A National Credit Fund, Rastriya Mahila Kosh (RMK) was set-up in 1993 to extend credit facilities to poor and needy women in the informal sector. The scheme of Balika Samridhi Yojna was launched in 1997, with the specific objective to change the community's attitude towards the girl child, encourage enrolment and promote retention of girl children in schools.

The National Policy for Empowerment of Women would prescribe strategies and action points to bridge the gap between the equal dejure status and unequal defecto position of the women in the country. It would seek to guide action at every level and in every section of mainstreaming gender perspectives into all laws, policies, programmes, regulations, and budgetary allocation of the government. Five National Awards of Rs. 1 lakh each to be known as Stree Shakti Puraskar, have been instituted in the name of eminent women personalities in the Indian history namely, Devi Ahilya Bai, Rani Lakshmi Bai, Mata Jeeja Bai, Rani Gaidinlee Zeliang, and Kannagi. The awards will be given to women who have triumphed over difficult circumstance and have fought for and established the right of women in various fields.

CONCLUSION

The above analysis amply describes that the dream of empowerment of women is still a far cry. It can be achieved only after the women themselves develop positive self-image, self-confidence, and knowledge of human values, rights and privileges. Only this would enable them to take part in decision-making and to have access to information and resources.

Sustainable development can be achieved only if women's potential is also utilized. In short, we can say that women can be empowered through four processes i.e., (a) access, (b) conscientisation, (c) participation, and (d) decision-making.

REFERENCES

Gangopadhyay, S. (2004), "Gender Sensitization," *Third Concept*, March, 2005, Vol. 18, No. 205, pp. 33-36.

Manimekalai, K. (2005), "Women and Management," *Third Concept*, March, 2005, Vol. 19, No. 217, pp. 50-51.

Narasaiah, M.L. (2005), "Womens and Poverty," *Third Concept*, March, 2005, Vol. 19, No. 217, pp. 53-55.

Rachandran, S. (2004), "Growth and Development of Women," *Third Concept*, March, 2004, pp. 29-31.

22

Empowering Women Through Legal and Government Based Approaches in India

MANOJ SHANKAR GUPTA

INTRODUCTION

The Preamble to the Constitution of India promises, "to secure to all its citizens, justice—social, economic and political; liberty of thought, expression, belief, faith and worship; equality of status and of opportunity; and to promote among them all fraternity assuring the dignity of the individual and the unity of the nation". While improvement in the status of the women was a pledge made by the Constitution-makers and admitted by the national Government at the very outset as one of the major tasks facing the country, no comprehensive review of the achievements in this direction has been undertaken thus far (Prabhakar, 2004).

Some laws, attempting to embody the principles underlying the Constitution had, from time to time, passed through the Legislature. Attempts were made to introduce the programmes of development, aimed at enabling women to play their role in our national life in an effective manner. Partly as a result of these various measures and partly because of the general processes of social change, which have speeded up since independence, the status of women in our country has undoubtedly undergone considerable change. It is felt that while these changes have been considerable in the urban areas, problems continue to remain virtually unchanged in most of the rural areas. Further, with the changing social and economic conditions in the country, various new problems relating to the advancement of women, which had not been visualized by the Constitution-makers and the Government in its earlier days have manifested themselves.

The objective of the present study is to examine the status of women, privileges provided under the Constitution, legislative provisions through various Acts, Government based initiatives, programmes and special schemes related to women empowerment followed by some effective measures which will definitely be a landmark in filling the gap between needs and deeds.

STATUS OF WOMEN

The women of India have been exposed to greater insecurity, to poverty, illiteracy, casteism, orthodoxy, unhealthy living conditions, traditionalism, backwardness, corruption, criminalization and male dominance in most of the fields. They have been affected by lack of opportunities and facilities owing to the innate discrimination prevalent in the society. In the last 20 years, there has been a global effort with a strong support from the United Nations to understand the discrimination and restore status to women of the world. The slogan has been equality, development and peace.

The United Nations General Assembly declared the International Year of Women in 1975 followed by the International Women's Decade and organized three world conferences—Mexico in 1975, Copenhagen in 1980, and Nairobi in 1985. The Nairobi conference decided strategies for the advancement of women up to 2000 A.D. The world has consciously marched forward with various instruments for eliminating discrimination against women during the last 20 years. The fourth world conference on women held in Beijing in 1995, focussed on the structural changes that are necessary in the society. It emphasized that no enduring solution to societies most threatening social, economic and political problems can be found without the full participation and empowerment of the women. India's strategies and action plans are geared to eliminate all discrimination against women; remove the chasm between legal status and de facto status; create an environment of harmony and partnership between men and women.

There are countries like Sweden, Finland and Norway where women make up almost half of the national legislatures. Stories of smooth succession of power from husband to wife are in plenty. Commenting on how widows and daughters have been thrust into power by dynastic imperatives in Asian countries like Philippines, India and Indonesia, Rounaq Jahan, a Bangladeshi political scientist had observed, "They think that they can manipulate these women but every time they were surprised that once in power, women handled the men and mastered old style politics."

But behind most successful women leaders in India, there has been the hidden hand of a man. Just as Jawaharlal Nehru groomed Indira Gandhi, M.G. Ramchandran did for his screen partner Jayalalitha and Kanshi Ram is doing for his acolyte Mayawati. Even Laloo Prasad Yadav is not far behind these veterans in propping up his wife Rabri Devi, who confidently faces the camera today instead of taking shelter in her kitchen. There may be a sharp variance in their lifestyles, levels of political sophistication, in their dress sense, but they have one thing in common, that is, valuable grooming in a political career by their mentors. Grooming includes training in developing their ethos, political issues and marketing them to their selected audience (voters). Many of them would be raw, without a political or famed godfather to lend support. Like one-third reservation for women at rural and urban local bodies, 33 per cent quota may help women in increasing their numerical strength to 181 in the Lok Sabha. It certainly may not be enough in attaining empowerment in the real sense, which would still remain a far cry. After all the road to empowerment is circuitous, attaining political power may not mean enjoying or utilizing it for the betterment of the country or her constituents, till they are trained to cross the rough and tumble of Indian politics.

Therefore, the present political scenario and demand for women's quota have generated a need for starting grooming courses for women politicians in India just as the path of empowerment became easy for the American women by mastering political skills. The Indian women can also attain empowerment if only they are groomed well. For women in the West, there are no reservations on the road to political empowerment. But they have the 'primaries' and other sundry opportunities to make themselves hard enough for the long grind in the political arena. Strangely, the idea has not struck us, where women advancement in the political domain is just a matter of time. A politically ambitious woman in our country is just thrown in the thick of things, to fend for herself. As more and more women get into the thick of things, there is an urgent need to evolve a system that will prepare them for this opportunity. Though there are many examples of women who have come through the system, they are seasoned and experienced. But they have never been to any finishing school. What they have learnt is through sheer experience. There are no caucuses and no primaries where they can cut their political teeth in effect, they have to behave, react and act as a politician from the word go. It is not an easy task. There are few women in public offices because few of them run for elections. The reservations in panchayats and municipalities will gradually bring more and more women into the political field. They will gather experience at a level, which will teach them the indispensability of a plural society. Among the women at the local institution level, those who want to adopt politics as a full-time career will move up to the bodies in course of time and their male colleagues will regard their ascent as a natural and legitimate progression. The training institutions or organizations will teach these political women not only the finer things of decision-making and use their power properly, but also the awareness, understanding the outer world, public dealings and if required, literacy, can also be taught to them. Such a process will not cause any political or social upheaval. The benefits of empowerment would also come in due course without the element of confrontation with other groups. At present, like other Asian countries, there is very slow rise in the percentage of Indian women in Parliament, central cabinet, administration, higher education, and technical Institutions.

The Union Government obviously thinks this is a call for affirmative action as is evident from its decision to introduce the Constitution (81st Amendment) Bill in the Lower House. If passed, by Parliament, the amendment will have a third of the seats reserved for women in the Lok Sabha and the state assemblies. In this situation, the need for grooming institutions becomes very relevant. Mohini Giri wrote, "the country is facing, as never before, a torrent of crime due to various socio-economic reasons not to speak of infiltration of illegal migrants, besides other state sponsored terrorism . . . much of these kinds of heinous crimes and atrocities have their roots in the drug mafia, foreign patronage and other country strategies to destabilize civilian population". Criminalisation is a big problem as most Asian cities are unsafe to live in despite the economic growth in the region. Compared to them, the law and order situation in Indian metros is better. The crime rate in Bangalore and Delhi is much lower than that in Seoul or Tokyo.

Apart from this situation, women's status in Asia is clearly in a flux. Democracy seems to have helped by creating an environment, in which autonomous women's groups could form networks and develop some political influence. Progress in terms of formal political representation of women has been much more gradual in most Asian nations. The practice of reserving parliamentary quotas for women seems to be spreading, although this obviously is a lengthy process. Women in Asia, therefore, face substantial political challenges with significant, but limited resources at their disposal.

Fortunately, in recent times, women have awakened to the fact that in order to break gender-barriers and overcome social bias, women's participation in the political process is essential. Though women constitute nearly half of the total population, politics has all along been men's domain. A February 1997 report on inter-Parliamentary unions says that Indian women hold only 7.2 per cent seats in the Lower House and 7.8 per cent seats in the Upper House. This can be called as token representation.

The percentage of women M.L.As. in state assemblies is also not very encouraging. Though in comparison to 1952, the percentage in the years from 1993 to 1998 has certainly increased but still it is insignificant. The truth is that except for mouthing political platitudes during elections, men are not prepared to give political space to women. One must realize that advancing the status of women is not only a moral imperative, but women's presence at the decision-making level is *sine qua non* for strengthening democratic traditions and fighting against injustice and oppression.

However, laws alone do not lead to social transformation unless followed by resolute action and society's awareness of the wrongs that have been perpetuated on women from time immemorial. But first of all, there should be a revolution of consciousness in the minds of women in the way they thought about themselves. Women must realize that gender deprivation is inconsistent with the basic human rights of women. They must realize that they have constitutional rights to equality, health care, economic security and access to education, employment opportunities, pay equity and political power. As India has celebrated more than fifty-eight years of her Independence, this is a historic opportunity to invest in India's future for when a woman thrives, her family thrives, when family thrives, communities flourish and the nation reaps the benefits (Prabhakar: 2004).

CONSTITUTIONAL PRIVILEGES

Indian women are the beneficiaries of various constitutional privileges in the same manner as Indian men. Some of the major constitutional privileges are mentioned below:

Article 14—Equality before law for women.

The state shall not deny to any person/citizen equality before law or equal protection of the laws within India.

Article 15(i)—Prohibition of discrimination on the basis of religion, race, sex or place of birth.

The state shall not discriminate against any citizen on grounds of religion, race, sex and place of birth or any of them.

Article 15(ii)—Nothing in this article shall prevent the State from making any special provision for women and children.

Article 16—There shall be equality of opportunity for all citizens in matters dedicating to employment or appointment to any office under the State.

Article 16(ii)—No citizen shall, on grounds only of religion, race, caste, descent, place of birth, residence or any of them, be ineligible for, or discriminated against in respect of any employment or office under the State.

Article 39(a)—The State to direct its policy towards securing for men and women equally the right to an adequate means of livelihood.

Article 39(d)—The State is to direct its policy towards securing equal pay for both men and women.

Article 39A—To promote justice, on a basis of equal opportunity and to provide free legal aid by suitable legislation or scheme or in any other way to ensure that opportunities for securing justice are not denied to any citizen by reason of economic or other disabilities.

Article 42—The State shall make provision for securing just and humane conditions for work and for maternity relief.

Article 46—The State to promote with special care the educational and economic interests of the weaker sections of people and to protect them from social injustice and all forms of exploitation.

Article 51(A)(e)—To promote harmony and the spirit of common brotherhood amongst all the people of India and to renounce practices derogatory to the dignity of women.

Article 243D(3)—Not less than one-third of the total number of offices of Chairpersons in the Panchayats at each level to be reserved for women.

Article 243T(3)—Not less than one-third (including the number of seats reserved for women belonging to the Scheduled Castes and Scheduled Tribes) of the total number of seats to be filled by direct election in every municipality to be reserved for women and such seats to be allotted by rotation of different constituencies in municipality.

Article 243T(4)—Reservation of offices of chairpersons in municipalities for the Scheduled Castes, Scheduled Tribes and women in such manner as the legislature of a State may by law provide.

LEGISLATIVE PROVISIONS

The State has enacted legislative measures to support the constitutional directives intended to ensure equal rights to counter social discrimination and various forms of violence and atrocities and to provide support services especially to working women. The crimes that are directed against women are characterized as

'Crimes against women'. These are broadly classified under two categories:

The Crimes Identified Under the Indian Penal Code (IPC)

(i) Rape (Section 376),
(ii) Kidnapping and Abduction for different purposes (Sections 363-373),
(iii) Homicide for dowry deaths or their attempts (Sections 302/304-B),
(iv) Cohabitation caused by a man deceitfully inducing a belief of lawful marriage (Section 493),
(v) Marrying again during lifetime of husband or wife (Section 494),
(vi) Enticing or taking away or detaining with criminal intent a married women (Section 498),
(vii) Torture, both mental and physical by husband or relatives of husband (Section 498-A),
(viii) Molestation (Section 354),
(ix) Sexual Harassment (Section 509), and
(x) Importation of Girls (up to 21 years of age).

Code of Criminal Procedure, 1953

This code contains some provisions, which specifically relate to women. The relevant sections are 51(2), 98, 125 to 128 and 416. Section 51(2) provides that whenever it is necessary to cause a female to be searched, another female shall make the search with strict regard to decency. Section 98 provides that upon complaint made on oath of the abduction or unlawful detention of women or a female child under the age of 18 years for any unlawful purpose, a District Magistrate, Sub-divisional Magistrate or Magistrate of the first class may make an order for the immediate restoration of such women to her liberty or of such female child to her husband, parent, guardian or other person having the lawful charge of such child and may compel compliance with search order, using such force as may be necessary. Sections 125 to 128 relate to provisions for maintenance of Wives, Children and Parents. Section 416 provides that if a woman's sentenced to death is found to be pregnant, the High Court shall order the execution of the sentence to be postponed and may; if it thinks fit; commute the sentence to imprisonment for life.

Other Laws Regarding Special Provisions to Safeguard Women

In order to safeguard the various constitutional rights, the State has enacted many women-specific and women-related legislations. All laws are not gender specific. However, the provisions of law affecting women have been reviewed periodically and amendments carried out to keep pace with the emerging requirements (GOI, 2001). Some of the important Acts, which have special provisions to safeguard the interests of women, are mentioned below:

Employees State Insurance Act, 1948

According to the provisions of the Act, an insured woman will be entitled to periodical payments in case of confinement or miscarriage or sickness due to pregnancy, confinement, premature birth of child or miscarriage, such woman being certified to be eligible for such payments by an authority specified in this behalf by the regulation.

Hindu Adoptions and Maintenance Act, 1956

This Act has been promulgated in 1956 to amend and codify laws relating to adoption and maintenance amongst Hindu's. Section 18 and 19 of this Act describes specific provisions regarding maintenance of wife and widowed daughter-in-law while Section 23 relates to stipulations regarding amount of maintenance.

Indian Succession Act, 1925 and Hindu Succession Act, 1956

The two Acts relate to succession of property in India. Under the provisions of these two Acts, rights have been conferred upon women in general and the Hindu women in particular especially under the Hindu Succession Act regarding inheritance of the property on the demise of husband and parents.

Laws Relating to Marriage and Divorce

Women are also privileged to secure rights and benefits under the provisions various Acts relating to marriage and divorce. The various Acts may be categorized as follows:

(a) The Special Marriage Act, 1954,

(b) The Hindu Marriage Act, 1955,
(c) The Indian Christian Marriage Act, 1872,
(d) The Indian Divorce Act, 1869,
(e) The Parsi Marriage and Divorce Act, 1936,
(f) The Dissolution of Muslim Marriage Act, 1939, and
(g) The Child Marriage Restraint (Amendment) Act, 1979

Maternity Benefit Act, 1961

This Act was passed in 1961 aiming at regulation of employed women in various establishments/organizations before and after childbirth under the provisions of maternity. Some States' Acts also provide for additional benefits such as free medical aid, additional rest intervals, maternity bonus and provision of crèches, etc. The Act has been extended to whole of India and is applicable every factory, mines or plantation and an establishment irrespective of number of employees wherein ten or more persons are employed or were employed on any day of the establishment either industrial, commercial, agricultural or otherwise. However, the Act does not apply to such factory/ establishment to which the provisions of the Employees' State Insurance Act are applicable.

Medical Termination of Pregnancy Act, 1971

The Parliament has passed this enactment to provide for the termination of certain pregnancies by registered medical practitioner and other maters connected with such termination. The Act consists of 8 sections dealing with various aspects like the time, place and circumstances in which medical practitioners may terminate a pregnancy legally.

Under this Act, termination of pregnancy can take place only on medical ground that too when the registered medical practitioner has formed the above opinion in good faith. It a pregnancy in alleged to be caused by rape, the anguish caused by such pregnancy is presumed to constitute grave injury to mental health of pregnant woman. Similarly, if the pregnancy is caused as a result of failure of any family planning device used by any married woman or husband, the anguish caused by such unwanted pregnancy is presumed to constitute grave injury to the mental health of the pregnant woman. Therefore, a pregnancy caused by rape or which is unwanted may be medically terminated under a section of the Act. Therefore, it becomes clear that the Act of 1971 is a welfare legislation aimed at protecting the physical and mental health of a pregnant woman and also of the child being carried in the womb of the mother.

The Immoral Traffic (Prevention) Act, 1986

This Act contains 25 sections. Those provisions are supplemented by Rules framed by various State governments. The Act underwent two major Amendments in 1978 and 1986, which introduced radical changes in the scope of the legislations, the persons covered thereunder and the definition of prostitution etc. The Act also contains a number of penal provisions which aim to punish those who keep or manage a brothel, who procure, induce or take a person for prostitution and (who carry on prostitution in the vicinity of a public places etc.)

The purpose of the Act was to inhibit or to abolish commercial vice, namely, traffic in women men and children for the purpose of prostitution as an organized means of living. The aim was not to render prostitution 'per se' a criminal offence or punish a woman merely because she prostitutes herself. What is punishable under the Act is sexual exploitation for commercial purpose, or to make a living thereon. The provision found in sections 7 and 8 of the Act however makes the practice of prostitution in or in vicinity of certain places such as places of public religious worship, educational institutions, hospitals, etc. punishable. The Act deals with not only a social but also a socio-economic problem. Therefore, the provisions of the legislation are more preventive than punitive.

Equal Remuneration Act, 1976

This Act provides for payment of equal remuneration to men and women workers for same or similar nature of work. Under this Act no discrimination is permissible in recruitment and service conditions except where employment of women is prohibited or restricted by or under any law.

Family Courts Act, 1984

The Family Courts Act, 1984, was enacted with a view to promoting conciliation in and securing speedy settlement of disputes relating to marriage and family affairs and for matters connected therewith. This is a Central Act, which is enforced in different states except the State of Jammu and Kashmir by issuing notifications from time to time.

The Indecent Representation of Women (Prohibition) Act, 1986

This Act has been enacted to prohibit indecent representation of women through advertisements or in publications, writings, paintings, and figures or in any other manner and for matters connected therewith or incidental thereto. Section 3 of this Act provides for prohibition of advertisements containing indecent representation of women and Section 4 provides for prohibition of publication or sending by post of books, pamphlets, etc., containing indecent representation of women with certain conditions. Section 6 provides for penalty for the violation of this Act. Any person who contravenes the provisions of section 3 or section 4 shall be punishable on first conviction with imprisonment of either description for a term, which may extend to two years, and with fine which may extend to two thousand rupees, and in the event of a second or subsequent conviction, with imprisonment for a term not less than six months but which may extend to five years and also a fine not less than ten thousand rupees but which may extend to one lakh rupees.

The Commission of Sati (Prevention) Act, 1987

This Act has been enacted to provide for more effective prevention of commission of sati and its glorification and for matters connected with it. Under section 3 of this Act whoever attempts to commit sati and does any act towards such commission shall be punishable with imprisonment for a term, which may extend to one year or with fine or with both. However, in this section there is a provision that the Special Court trying an offence under this section shall, before convicting any person, take into consideration the circumstances leading to the commission of the offence, the act committed, the state of mind of the person charged of the offence at the time of he commission of the act and all other relevant factors. Section 4 of this Act provides that if any person commits sati, whoever abets the commission of such sati both directly or indirectly, shall be punishable with death or imprisonment for life and also be liable for fine.

National Commission for Women Act, 1990

This Act was enacted to constitute National Commission for Women and to provide for matters connected therewith or incidental thereto. The function of the Commission has been stipulated in Section 10 of the said Act which inter-alia makes provision relating to investigation and examination of all matters relating to the safeguards provided for women under the Constitution of India and other laws; presenting to the Central Government, annual and such other times as the Commission may deem fit, reports upon the working of those safeguards, looking into complaints and take *suo moto* notice of matters relating to deprivation of women's rights, non-implementation of laws enacted to provide protection of women and also to achieve the objective of equality and development.

Pre-Natal Diagnostic Techniques (Regulation and Prevention of Misuse) Act, 1994

The Parliament has realized the grave implications arising out of the misuse of the pre-natal diagnostic techniques and intended to regulate the same only for certain medical purposes. The Government felt that abuse of techniques for determination of sex of the foetus leading to female foeticde is discriminatory against the female sex and also affects the dignity and status of women. This realization led the Parliament to pass the above Act, which came into force from 1.1.1996. The legislation seeks to attain the following objectives:

- (a) Prohibition of the misuse of pre-natal diagnostic techniques for determination of sex foetus, leading to female foeticide;
- (b) Prohibition of advertisement of the techniques for detection or determination of sex;
- (c) Regulation of the use of techniques only for the specific purposes of detecting genetic abnormalities or disorders;
- (d) Permission to use such techniques only under certain conditions by the registered institutions;
- (e) Punishment for violation of the Act; and
- (f) To provide deterrent punishment to stop such inhuman acts of female foeticide.

Dowry Prohibition Act, 1961

The system of dowry in connection with marriage is a deep-rooted social evil in our country. The dowry death is a burning social problem (Ghosh, 2001). In this context, Dowry Prohibition Act, 1961 was enacted by the Parliament to restrict dowry and commit offences under this Act. The giving and taking of dowry at or before or at any time after marriage is an offence with imprisonment or fine or both in terms of Sections 6 and 4 of this Act. Even an agreement regarding dowry will be an offence under section 5 of the Act. The crucial provision in the Act relates to definition of the term 'dowry'. The definition is very wide and taking into consideration the aspects of giving and taking of property or valuable security as consideration for marriage.

Government Based Special Programmes and Schemes for Women's Empowerment

With the objective of empowerment and welfare of women, a number of government programmes and schemes have been implemented. Women lag behind men in different soico-economic spheres, therefore special programmes and schemes for women's empowerment are required. For the development and empowerment of women innovative programmes in the areas of welfare and support services, training and gender sensitization play a complementary role in support of these programmes. The objectives of all these efforts are to ensure eugenic and sexual empanelment of women.

Some of the important initiatives that have been undertaken by the government for the enlistment of women labourers are as follows:

Short Stay Homes for Women and Girls (1969)

The programme has been in existence since 1969 to protect and rehabilitate those women and girls who are facing social and physical danger due to family problems, mental strains, social exploitation, or other causes. The services extended in these homes include: medical care; psychiatric treatment; occupational therapy; education-*cum*-vocational training and recreational facilities. During 1998-99 a provision of Rs. 4 crores was made available to maintain 272 homes with 8,160 beneficiaries.

Development of Women and Children in Rural Areas (DWCRA)

The objective of this plan is to provide self-employment opportunities to women of poor households according to their skill, aptitude and local conditions so as to enable their organized participation in social development and economic self-reliance. There is also an indirect feature to develop poor children. It is implemented in all the districts of the country. Groups of 10-15 women members each from poor households are formed at the village level for delivery of services like: credit, for skill, training, cash and infrastructure support for self-employment. To facilitate the implementation of the scheme, one post of Assistant Project Officer (W) and one additional Gram Sevika have been provided in the District Rural Development Agencies and block level respectively. And viable activity can be taken up taking care of backward and forward linkages. All women who are living below poverty line in rural areas are eligible for the scheme. Eligible women desiring assistance under DWCRA are to form a group and approach DRDA through Gram Sevika for starting income generating activities.

Integrated Rural Development Programme (IRDP, 1980)

The main objective of this programme is to enable the identified poor families to cross the poverty line. It is a centrally sponsored scheme. Both Centre and states share 50:50 percentage funding responsibility. The target under IRDP consists of small and marginal farmers, agricultural and non-agricultural and free bonded laborers. In this scheme 50 per cent of the target group should be from the SC and ST categories. Forty percent assistance is given to women.

Setting of Employment-cum-Income Generation-cum-Production Units (NORAD, 1982-83)

A Programme called Training-*cum*-Production Centre (popularly known NORAD) was launched in 1982-83 with the assistance from the Norwegian Agency for Development Cooperation to improve the lives of young women/girls especially school drop-outs and semi-literates, by extending training in non-traditional trades like electronics, watch assembling, computer programming, garment making, secretarial practice, community health work, embroidery, weaving, hotel management, fashion technology and beauty culture, tourism, bakeries, office management, etc. Under NORAD as many as 1365 projects benefiting 1.99 lakh women have been approved since 1982-83. From 1996-97 assistance received under NORAD has been supplemented with domestic resources. Out of the total outlay of Rs.18 crores during 1998-99, Rs.13 crores was raised from domestic resources. Up to December 1998, the Department of Women and Child Development has sanctioned 81 projects to benefit 6,805 women.

Women's Development Corporation (WDC, 1986-87)

The WDC aims at promoting the development of women entrepreneurs. It provides consultancy services, facilities availability of credit, promotes marketing of products, promotes and strengthens women's cooperatives and arranges training facilities.

Jawahar Rozgar Yojana (JRY, 1989)

The JRY aims at gainful employment for the unemployed and the underemployed rural women and men by strengthening the rural economic infrastructure. In this programme, target group consists of people below poverty line, especially those belonging to Scheduled castes and Scheduled Tribes and free bonded labourers. Thirty percent benefit of this programme is ensured for women.

The National Plan of Action for the Girl Child (1991-2000)

The Plan of Action was to ensure survival, protection and development of the girl child with the ultimate objective of building up a better future for the girl child.

Reservation of Women in Local Self-Government (1992)

The 72nd and 73rd Constitutional Amendment Acts passed in 1992 by Parliament ensure one-third of the total seats for women in all elected offices in local bodies whether in rural areas or urban areas.

Mahila Samriddhi Yojana (MSY, 1993)

The main objective of this programme is to enable poor women in rural society to exercise greater control over household resources by redressing sender biases in production. It is a central sector plan scheme, which operates through rural post offices. It encourages women to open MSY accounts in post offices. Women can deposit money in instalments. The Department of Women and Child Development is the nodal institution for MSY's implementation.

Indira Awas Yojana (IAY, 1993-94)

The objective of this programme is to provide free of cost housing facility to people below poverty line, especially to poor women. It specifically extends to SC/STs and free bonded labourers. Main features of this programme are: (a) it extends help to people affected by earthquakes and other natural calamities, (b) house allotment is made in the name of the women or, at times, it is in joint ownership of husband and wife, (c) the beneficiaries have freedom of constructing their own house and choosing either hired labour or their own family labour, and (d) IAY builds houses in clusters so as to provide common facilities.

Rural Women's Development and Empowerment Project (RWDEP, 1998)

A centrally sponsored scheme of Rural Women's Development and Empowerment (RWDEP) was launched in 1998 for a period of five years in the states of Uttar Pradesh, Madhya Pradesh, Bihar, Haryana, Karnataka and Gujarat with an estimated outlay of Rs. 186.21 crores. A revolving fund for giving interest-bearing loans to beneficiary groups during their initial formative stages is being set-up with an investment of Rs. 5 crores. The overall objective of the project is to strengthen the process for creating an enabling environment for empowerment of women by establishing Self-Help Groups (SHGs) with 15-20 members each, which will improve the quality of their lives, through greater access to, and control over resources.

Standing Committee on the Empowerment of Women (1997)

An important monitoring machinery to oversee women's

empowerment in India was set-up by Parliament in the form of a Standing Committee on the Empowerment of Women in March, 1997. The function of this Committee include examining and reporting on the measures that should be taken by the Union Government for improving the status/condition of women and considering the reports submitted by the National Commission for Women.

Swayamsidha

This is an integrated project for the development and empowerment of women through Self Help Groups (SHGs) with emphasis on covering services, developing access to micro-credit, and promoting micro-enterprises. The most important component of the programme is formulation, implementation and monitoring of block specific composite projects of four to five years' duration through Project Implementing Agencies (PIA), which may be any appropriate government or non-government agency, nominated by the State Governments. So far 52,016 SHGs have been formed under the project out of 650 blocks allotted so far (GOI, 2004).

Swa-Shakti Project (1998)

Earlier known as the Rural Women's Development and Empowerment Project, it was sanctioned in October, 1998 as a centrally sponsored scheme to be implemented in the states of Bihar, Chhattisgarh, Haryana, Jharkhand, Karnataka, Madhya Pradesh, Uttranchal and Uttar Pardesh for duration of five years with an outlay of Rs. 186 crore. An additional amount of Rs. 5 crore has been provided in the project for facilitating, setting up of reviving funds for giving interest-bearing loans to beneficiary groups, primarily during the formative stages. The project aims at enhancing women's access to resources for better quality of life through the use of drudgery and time reduction devices, health, literacy and imparting skills for confidence enhancement and income generating activities. So far 17,647 Self Help Groups have been formed under the project against the target of 16,000 SHGs. The project is supported jointiy by the World Bank and the International Fund for Agricultural Development (IFAD).

Support to Training and Employment Programme for Women (STEP, 1978)

The programme STEP was launched in 1978 and seeks to provide updated skills and new knowledge to poor asset less women in eight traditional sectors of employment, namely, agriculture; animal husbandry; dairying; fisheries; handlooms; handicrafts; Khadi and village industry; and sericulture. The scheme is being implemented through public sector organization, state corporations, cooperatives, federations and voluntary organizations, which have been in existence for a minimum period of three years. Eleven projects were sanctioned during 2003-04, which is estimated to benefit 16,350 women (GOI, 2004).

Swalamban

The objective of this scheme is to provide training and skills to women to facilitate them to obtain employment or self-employment on a sustainable basis. Some of the trades where training is imparted include: computer programming, medical transcription, electronic assembling, consumer electronics repairs, radio and television repairs, garment making, handloom weaving, handicrafts, secretarial practice, community heakh work and embroidery. During 2003-04, 463 proposals were approved, benefiting 71,240 women (GOI, 2004).

Crèches/Day Care Centres for the Children of Working and Ailing Mothers

This scheme aims to provide day care services to children (0.5 years) of parents whose income does not exceed Rs.1,800 per month. The facilities provided to children under the scheme include sleeping and day care facilities, supplementary nutrition, immunization, medicine and recreation. The scheme is being implemented through the Central Social Welfare Board and two other national level voluntary organizations namely, the Indian Council for Child Welfare and the Bhartiya Adim Jati Sevak Sangh all over the country. About 33.11 lakh children were benefited under the scheme during 2003-04.

Hostels for Working Women (1972)

The scheme of assistance for construction and expansion of

hostel buildings for working women, with day care centers, is being implemented since 1972. Under this scheme financial assistance is provided to NGOs, cooperative bodies and other agencies engaged in women's social welfare, women's education, public sector undertakings, women development corporations, local bodies, universities and state governments for construction of buildings for working women hostels. The scheme envisages provisions for safe and affordable accommodation to working women (single working women, women working at places away from their hometowns, working but husband out of town, etc.), women being trained for employment and girl students studying in post-school professional courses. During 2003-04, thirteen new hostels were sanctioned under the scheme, benefiting 1,188 women (GOI, 2004)

Swadhar (2001-02)

This scheme was launched in 2001-02 as a central sector scheme for providing holistic and integrated services to women in difficult circumstances such as: destitute widows deserted by their families in religious places like Vrindavan and Kashi; women prisoners released from jail and without family support; women survivors of natural disaster who have been rendered homeless and are without social and economic support; trafficked women/ girls rescued or run away from brothels and other places or victims of sexual crimes who are disowned by family or who do not want to go back to their respective families for various reasons. The package of services made available under the scheme include: provision of food, clothing, shelter, health care counseling and legal support; social and economic rehabilitation through education, awareness generation, sill up-gradation and behavioural training. The scheme also supports a helpline for women in distress. Presently 31 projects are being funded under the scheme (GOI, 2004).

Rashtrya Mahila Kosh (RMK, 1993)

This programme is also known as the National Credit Fund for Women and was set-up as a registered society under the Societies Registration Act, 1860 on March 30, 1993 with a view to facilitate credit support or micro-finance to poor women to start income generating activities such as in dairy, agriculture, shop-keeping, vending and handicrafts, in 2003-04, and Rs. 25 crore was sanctioned through RMK benefiting about 32,765 women (GOI, 2004).

Sarva Shiksha Abhiyan (SSA, 2000)

Sarva Shiksha Abhiyan launched in November, 2000 as an umbrella programme, continued to be implemented to support and build up on other primary and elementary education projects. The programme aims to ensure five years of primary education for all children including girls in the age group 6-14 years by 2007 and eight years of schooling by 2010. The programme has been implemented in partnership with the States (GOI, 2005).

Mahila Samakhya (1989)

Mahila Samakhya scheme was started in 1989 for education and empowerment of women in rural areas, particularly those from socially and economically marginalized groups. It focuses on enabling a greater access to education, generating a demand for education, building capabilities and strengthening women's abilities to effectively participate in village-level processes for educational development. The scheme is being implemented in nine States: Andhra Pradesh, Assam, Bihar, Gujarat, Jharkhand, Karnataka, Kerala, Uttar Pradesh and Uttranchal. The programme covers over 12,000 villages in 59 districts (GOI, 2004).

National Programme for Education of Girls at Elementary Level (NPEGEL, 2003)

This programme has been approved by Government of India in 2003. This programme is amendment to the existing scheme of Sarva Shiksha Abhiyan for providing additional support for education of underprivileged or disadvantaged girls at the elementary level. The scheme is implemented in Educationally Backward Blocks (EBBs) where the level of female literacy is below and the gender gap is above the national average (GOI, 2005).

National Commission for Women (NCW, 1991)

The Government constituted NCW as a statutory body to study and monitor all matters relating to the safeguards provided for women. Major functions of the Commission are: (a) to investigate, examine and review matters relating to constitutional safeguards for women, (b) review of women-specific legislations, (c) suggest amendments, and (d) facilitate redresses of women's grievances, etc.

Kasturba Gandhi Balika Vidyalaya (KGBV, 2004-05)

Apart from NPEGEL, a new scheme KGBV has been approved for launching during 2004-05 for setting up 750 residential schools with boarding facilities at elementary level for girls belonging predominantly to SC, ST, Other Backward Castes (OBCs), and Minorities in difficult areas. A provision of Rs. 489 crores has been made for Tenth Plan (2002-07) involving an amount of Rs. 123.03 crores for the year 2004-05 (GOI, 2005).

It is also important to note that during 2001, the Women's Empowerment Year, the Department of Women and Child Development has reviewed five Acts with which it is administratively concerned with a view to make the provisions more stringent and to remove the lacunae. These Acts are: (a) The Indecent Representation of Women (Prohibition) Act, 1956, (b) The Immoral Traffic (Prevention) Act, 1956, (c) The Dowry Prohibition Act, 1961, (d) The Commission of Sati (Prevention) Act, 1987 and (e) The National Commission for Women Act, 1990.

The National Commission for Women is authorized to review the existing provisions of the Constitution and other laws affecting women and recommend amendments. It has till date, reviewed and suggested remedial legislative measures in 22 Acts.

CONCLUSION

It is evident from the above study, that besides the Constitution of India, there are many enactments in our country, most of which we have enumerated above, making provisions to secure rights, benefits and securities of women. But it is unfortunate that in spite of the existence of so many laws majority of women are being deprived of their rights and benefits and their securities are in jeopardy and the offences against women in various fields are on the rise. Some of the reasons for such a sorry state of affairs are: (a) lack of awareness and consciousness of women about their rights, interest and benefits provided in the existing laws; (b) inefficiency and lack of sincerity and seriousness of the authorities concerned who have been entrusted with the responsibilities for administration and enforcement of the said laws; and (c) the tardy and costly process in our existing legal system.

Another dark area where, perhaps enactment of legislation is overdue is the case of domestic workers. Domestic work is one of the major spheres of work, employing women in unorganized and informal sector. This is one of the most exploitative areas of work for women workers in India (Pathare, 2000). Domestic workers' are amongst a group of workers, which are the most exploited by their employers and the least protected by law. Therefore, there is an urgent need to create an environment where domestic workers may enjoy their rights and interests like other segments of the mainstream workers. This is possible only when legislation is enacted in this regard.

It is also important that economic empowerment of women is the most important way of emancipation of women folk everywhere in the world. Empowerment in other spheres of life would more or less automatically follow economic empowerment. Poverty has remained an intractable problem with inevitable consequences for human rights, especially for rural women who are among the porest of the poor and discriminated in terms of access to education, health, water, sanitation, food, globalization and information and communication technology. Much effort is still required in order to increase the number of women in decision-making at all levels, along with gender-sensitization of leaders and politicians and to study the importance of electoral systems for women's participation in politics. Lack of women's participation in policy-making is said to be one of the factors in countries currently having "hundreds of laws discriminating against women" (Jafri, 2001). Therefore, women's legal literacy and legal aid should be strengthened.

It may be suggested, that since women constitute a disproportionate number of poor and have increasingly been obliged to undertake agricultural activities for a livelihood, equal access to land and other resources for women, including by suitable changes in inheritance law, where possible, is necessary (Das, 1998). In some states in India, inheritance laws do not discriminate against women, but in some other states, poor women have few legal safeguards, and sometimes face legal obstacles, with regard to access to land.

The major approach for the future should be to bring in holistic approach for women's development. This underscores harmonization of various efforts in different fronts-social, economic, legal, political and cultural. This calls for consolidation of various programmes and efforts in different sectors of the Government and their integration in logical fashion to converge various services and facilities required by women. A Sub-Plan approach to package all relevant resources and benefits for women's development will be laid down to ensure their systematic focus on women. The thrust in the future should be on identifying traditional sectors of employment that are shrinking due to technology changes or market shifts, and retrain the women to take up jobs in the new and expanding areas of employment.

Keeping in view the aforementioned experiences, the following specific prorammes could be considered for adoption in future: (i) Expansion of education and training programming among women; (ii) Provision of child-care support facilities for men and women workers so that either parent can avail of this facility at the work place and not make it a cost on women's employment; (iii) Provision of hostel and residential facilities to enable women take up employment away from home; (iv) Special employment and placement services which should seek to promote employment of women in non-conventional sectors through dissemination of information, counseling, etc.; (v) Legal protection and legal aid services; (vi) Promotion of women workers' organizations through voluntary effort; (vii) Protection against flexibility. Considering the new trend towards economic liberalization such protection cannot be ensured through statutory means and should, therefore, be attempted through negotiations and collective efforts. The State, the employers as well as the workers must have separate layers of protection against loss of employment; (viii) Introduction of flextime, multi-entry, conducive personnel policy on leave, transfer and promotion and training opportunities, to help women retain their jobs or move to new and higher areas of work; (ix) Conducive credit policy to access credit to women through appropriate organizational and institutional mechanisms including, self-help groups; and (x) Improvement of the bargaining strength of women workers by encouraging their participation in trade unions (Das, 2004).

Thus, it can be concluded that empowerment has many

facets. It allows for political empowerment, economic empowerment, legal empowerment, human resource development or capacity building and beyond. It covers the right-based approach as well as the programmatic approach because it invites the active intervention by the human agent not just to claim one's rights within existing resources but also to develop one's potential. It can provide the core around which all our other concepts and resolutions can cohere or coalesce. At the risk of hyperbole, holistic view of empowerment is a concept that can capture the spirit of the project of the women's movement of our age.

REFERENCES

Das, Asha (1998), "Statement to the Commission on the Status of Women", General Debate at United Nations, March 6.

Das, Asha (2004), "Empowering Women in India" in *Women in Panchayati Raj Institutions* (Ed. Ashok Kumar Jha), Institute for Sustainable Development, Lucknow and Anmol Publications, New Delhi.

Ghosh, Kalipada (2001), "Laws Relating to Rights and Securities of Women in Our Country—A Brief Discussion", Nayabichar, (Organ of Legal Service Centre for Women), Bulletin No. 1, Published by Nirmalendu Mukherjee, Calcutta.

Government of India (2001), *Economic Survey*, Ministry of Finance, Economic Division, New Delhi.

Government of India (2004), *Economic Survey*, Ministry of Finance, Economic Division, New Delhi.

Government of India (2005), *Economic Survey*, Ministry of Finance, Economic Division, New Delhi.

Jafri, Talat (2001), "Legislative Responses to Violence Against Women – Issues and Priorities", UNIFEM http://www.afppd.org/workshop/paper2page1htm.

Pathare, Suresh (2000), "Struggle for Legislation Protection: A Case Study of Domestic Workers", *Women's* Link, October-December.

Prabhakar, V. (2004), *Women in Rural India*, Dominant Publishers and Distributors, New Delhi.

23

Economic Empowerment of Women

PADMINI PRASAD

When a girl child sees the light of this world, she is blessed with the power to endure the poignancy of her sex in the form of injustice, violence, abuse and exploitation. Millions of young girls have the courage to dream of a bright and prosperous future and yet never realizes, it just because they are crushed at the very nip. Suppressing one needs and desires becomes a habit with them as they silently accept the social norms irrespective of their education.

Within the family, poverty strikes women disproportionately hard. Women are entrusted with the responsibility of home management in the absence of resources and entitlement to meet the basic minimum needs for the survival of the family.

The 50 per cent of our working force is women who perform for 60 per cent of total working hours but they receive only 10 per cent of the total income. This paints a very dismal picture of condition of women.

WOMEN IN INDIA

The majority of Indian women residing in rural areas and urban slums are leading a hand to mouth existence and for this they depend on agriculture and they form the informal sector with little or no legislative protection and trade union support.

Rural women in our country suffer from being both economically and socially invisible. Economic invisibility comes from the perception that women are irrelevant to the wage and market economy. Social invisibility is the result of the general status of second-class citizens. The National Perspective Plan for Women (1988-2000) made an objective analysis of the impact of developmental plans and programmes for the Indian women with special reference to rural women.

There exists continued inequality and vulnerability of women in all sectors—economic, social, political, educational, legal, health care and nutrition. As women are oppressed in all spheres of life, they need to be empowered in all walks of life. Women need to be empowered for gaining collective strength. Collective strength is necessary for building solidarity and support among themselves to achieve empowerment. The solutions to overcome women's poverty can only come from steps taken by women's groups and such other organizations. Individuals cannot solve the problem of their powerlessness. This can only be done through action.

In the society, we are mutually dependent on each other. Only an interaction society can improve the quality of one's life. Women as a group can establish their identity and face the challenges in this social system. Women identify their common interest and establish their worth and change their roles with men. When a poor woman is influenced to participate, she gains a new sense of dignity and confidence to overcome her problems. Hence, they move towards economic independence.

OBJECTIVES FOR THE WOMEN

- Awareness of legal rights and legal access,
- Improve literacy,
- Development of leadership qualities,
- Building self-confidence,
- Increasing social awareness,

- Improved status of women in the family and society,
- Improvement in health and family welfare, and
- Development of strong cohesive self-help women's groups.

ECONOMIC DEVELOPMENT

- Increasing individual income;
- Developing habit of savings;
- Control over income and better income management;
- Access to market, choice of activities;
- Alternative credit delivery system; and
- Management of common funds for the benefit of community.

NEED FOR ECONOMIC EMPOWERMENT

Without economic empowerment, the development of women would be at its lowest level. Plans, policies and legislation provide only the blue print for directing the progress of society. These plans would be successful only when women receive economic powers. Once they get economic powers, the status of women would be uplifted immediately with economic independence.

The main season for a woman's subordination is her economic dependence. This condition brings them to a social crisis where a woman is unable to express or decide for herself mainly because she has no means to support herself and her children. It is precisely because of this that many women development programmes emphasize on the income generating activity so that there is money available for her and she can move towards economic independence. This makes her first step towards her empowerment.

Rural women in a state of acute poverty have become one of the important areas considered as consumers and not producers. They have no occupation, property, education, or skill. A majority of women are at a disadvantage in gaining professional training because of unequal access to education at preparatory levels. As a result, they hardly get into the formal sector of employment. To uplift the status of poor women, some of the self-employment schemes are introduced by the Social Welfare Department giving them training in cottage industries such as a sericulture, plantation of medicinal herbs, making candles, palm leaf articles, bamboo, Madhubani Painting, applic work, soft toys, craft and coir products.

If women have to become successful entrepreneurs, the programmes would also include training women to develop self-confidence, assurance and strength. They should be encouraged to believe in their own capabilities.

CONCLUSION AND SUGGESTIONS

The following points suggest income generating activities of women's group:

- To run the income generating activity successfully;
- The credit intervention definitely boosts the self-image and confidence;
- The proximity can be further increased by bringing the bank officials into counsel and guide the women in selecting and implementing profitable income generating activities; and
- Both the government and non-government organizations bring forth new schemes for their development.

If these measures are followed properly, rural women could maximize their contribution to the economy and enhance their physical and mental well-being which would promote their competencies to excel and reach top level positions.

REFERENCES

Choudhury, R.C. and Rajakully (1998), *Fifty Years of Rural Development in India: Retrospect and Prospect*, National Institute of Rural Development, Hyderabad.

Lolitha Rani, D. (1996), *Women Entrepreneurs*, A.P.H. Publishing Corporation, New Delhi.

Pamecha, Suman (2002), *Women on Economic Front*, Agrotech Publishing Academy, Udaipur.

24

Empowerment of Muslim Women

MD. IMETEYAZ HASSAN

INTRODUCTION

Women as a group have in particular always been at the receiving end of various crimes and injuries perpetrated by the society on their psyche. It is a pleasant yet a largely acceptable belief that discrimination against Muslim women in one form or the other is greater than the other societies. Despite a number of laws being passed to ameliorate their condition, significant improvement cannot be expected in their status, till the muslim women become aware of their social, economic and educational rights.

Most of the problems that the Indian Muslim woman faces today arise out of her ignorance of the law as well as lack of will power to assert her rights. It seems pertinent perhaps to look into the psycho-sociological aspects of problem of discrimination of Muslim women in Muslim society. In one context or the other, problems of women at large are related to the family. Muslim women do not seem to be subordinate in any manner. Adam and Eve sinned together and God drove them both out of the garden of Eden (Garden of Eden).

WOMAN IN ISLAMIC PERSPECTIVE

The first appearance of women in the Quaranic horizon came as an associate to keep company for man in heaven and to make it possible for him to lead a full life. On earth, she establishes a home for him. She guarantees the continuity of race; as a partner she wields such fateful influence on man. The significance of the sexes is emphasized by the fact that the Qur'an specially refers to God's creation of the male and female as of no little import. Morally at par with man, woman is the metaphysical necessity of his life. We have only to listen to the Qur'an to comprehend the almost incomprehensible mystery of life as it is revealed in the difference of the sexes in the human plan of existence.

The question that now irks is why should Muslim women then bear an oppressed status in society? The probable answer is because of illiteracy, ignorance and stigma attached to them by the society.

FEW GRIM TRUTHS

Who are to be blamed or held accountable for the backwardness or the suppression of Muslim women? It seems deliberate silence pervades as far as research on Indian Muslim women in concerned.

It is also felt that academic enquiries into the area of backwardness of Muslim women have been hampered by the political and psychological pressure on Muslim men which suggests that the orthodoxy within the Muslim society has suppressed the identity of Muslim women either to uphold the cultural distinctiveness of Muslims or the male chauvinism feels threatened that the education and modernization of Muslim women might question the position of a Muslim male in the family and in turn, the society. Queries and observations on this problem have also revealed that girls in Muslim families are not allowed to study at higher levels because after attaining the same, they might not get a suitable match. The parents, thus, try to get them married at an early stage due to the ostentations of the society and the Muslim community at large.

While linking up the psychological aspects of the discrimination of women in Muslim society with the tendencies of frustration and aggression among the Muslim women, suggests that the feeling of alienation experienced by the women appears to be the result of prejudice against her by the men of the same community. When prejudice leads to discrimination and does not accord Muslim women equal treatment to all the members of a society, it is violating the norms of justice.

'Prejudice' according to Ganguli may be a failure to abide by the norms of rationality when it occurs in the form of hasty judgment or pre-judgment, thinking in stereotypes, etc.

Harding writes: "It seems most useful to us to define prejudice as a failure of justice or a failure of human heartedness in an individual's attitude towards members of another ethnic group."

Women considered as minority within the Muslim community have been together with the men and the awareness of the fact that they are a minority reveals itself through the ideas, attitudes and values of the Muslim culture itself. Once the norms become established, the women learn willingly or unwillingly to surrender to the established rules of their community or culture.

Muslim women have been denied access to education for centuries and socio-religious environment has supported the maintenance of this prejudice. It is this aspect that has entitled them as the backward minority of Indian society.

Education has been one of the basic social factors in the formulation and reconstruction of any society. Education thus becomes an essential pre-requisite of a desirable society.

In spite of the limitation of the environment, culture and the society, Muslim women are capable of expressing themselves at a creative level equal to their male counterparts and females of other communities.

It is time that the oppressed Muslim woman comes out of the webs of isolation that the social norms have woven around her. Only then will they become powerful assets to the society. Those who are educated are the privileged among Muslim women and enjoy a status equal to the men in the society. It is our duty to fight for the less privileged women so that concrete results emerge from our endeavour. It is important to assess the level of education and employment among the Muslim women from a cross-section of economic levels to identify those factors affecting the educational attainments of women and their progress at large.

This, as a matter of fact, will only be possible if every Muslim woman realizes her potential. Female education among Muslims has yet to receive adequate support and planned community action to achieve meaningful results.

The Muslim community requires preparation to absorb (adequately) the benefits of available educational provisions. This preparation must come from the few fortunate women who have pioneered the path, by breaking social barriers. Supported by the foresighted and those holding authority, female education ought to be promoted among the members of the Muslim community by harnessing all available government and private resources

Islam, as it is claimed, has tremendous power of assimilation, adjustment and accommodation. "Allah never changes the conditions of people, unless they themselves change it," is one of the major admonitions of the Qur'an. It is not that the Muslim society in India is static anymore. The day is not far when Will Durant's (the well known writer of *The Story of Civilization*) words will prove true: "If in imagination, we place ourselves in the year 2000 and ask what was the outstanding feature of human events in the first quarter of the Twentieth Century, we shall perceive that it was not the great war nor the Russian Revolution but the change in the status of women.

CONCLUSION

To meet the challenge of ameliorating the oppressed status of Muslim women in India, efforts should be made by the women themselves towards their own education and also of the women and daughters of their families. Efforts should be made to increase the relevance of education content in the curriculum in rural areas.

Opportunities for secondary schooling for girls should be extended wherever they are lacking. It is time, Muslim women uphold their self-esteem, raise their voices for their rights in the fields of education, services, and the Muslim and Indian society at large. No longer will their status remain oppressed in India then.

REFERENCES

Bagal, Jogesh Chandra (1956), *Women's Education in Eastern India*, Kolkata, World Press Pvt. Ltd.

Ganguli, H.C. (1985), Prejudice and Its Social Consequences, *Indian Journal of Social Work.*

Mutahhani, Murtada (1981), *The Rights of Women in Islam*, Tehran, World Organization for Islamic Services.

Saiyed, V.V. and Saroj Narain (1990), "Problems of Education of Muslim Women in Delhi" Paper presented during seminar on Muslim Women —Problems and Prospects, A.M.U.

Vahiduddin, S. (1996), The Place of Woman in the Qur'an, Islamic Culture, LXX1-6.

25

Empowerment of Dalits: A Socio-Political Analysis

M. ALAMGEER

Dalits are a group of people who faced social discrimination in worst form, i.e., including untouchability. They are placed in the scheduled-caste categories in our Constitution. The term dalits was for the first time used by a great dalit leader Jyotiba Phule in the 19th century. It was first popularly used by Dalit Panthers in 1970s. It has been currently replaced by the category of Harijans or Scheduled Castes. Dalit movement raised issues of caste-based discrimination, economic inequality, and raised struggle for social justice. The issues that dalit movement are self-respect, harassment of women, payment of wages, forced labour, dispute of lands, implementation of reservation policy, promotion in jobs, denial of democratic rights and disrespect to Dr. Bhim Rao Ambedkar. This paper attempts to analyze the socio-political dimensions of empowerment of dalits. The empowerment as a concept was introduced at the International Women's Conference in 1985, at Narobi: The conference defined empowerment as "a re-distribution of social power and control of resources in favour of under-privileged." The programme of Action 1992 has comprehensively given the following parameters of empowerment:

(i) Enhance self-steem and self-confidence in women;
(ii) Develop in them an ablity to think critically;
(iii) Foster decision-making and action through collective process;
(iv) Ensure equal participation in the developmental process;
(v) Provide information, knowledge and skill for securions economic independence; and
(vi) Enhance access to legal literacy and information to their rights and entitlement in the society with a view to enhance their participation on an equal footing in all areas.

This is clear from the above mentioned agenda that empowerment needs a multi-dimensional approach to enable the down-trodden to have a share in the political-economy of the country. To name a few, they are legal and constitutional empowerment, economic empowerment, political empowerment, educational empowerment, and above all psychological empowerment. Dalits, who are at the lowest rung of the caste order have always been subjected to exploitation and injustice. It is a historical fact, that the caste system is at least 3000 years old, and discrimination and barbarity towards the dalits are an equally old phenomenon. The dominant castes consider that it is their privilege or birthright to beat, torture and butcher the dalits and downtrodden. Since the dalits silently suffered every detestable and barbaric crime committed against them, the dominant castes did not engage in excessive any physical aggression. But now the dalits have begun to raise their head against the atrocities. Hence the dominant upper castes are engaged in vicious repressive measures to silence any form of dissent arising among the dalits. Significantly it is not upper castes alone who abuse dalits, but the backward castes too engaged in the exploitation of dalits". Caste practices and caste discrimination are ingrained in the very foundations of the Indian society, 'Indian culture, Indian political economy and finally in the very Indian mind-set'. Any crime committed against the dalits is an act perpetrated by an anti-social element. Caste discrimination and caste related violence are the logical outcomes of the historic hatred and social abhorrence of the upper castes and the upper classes towards the dalits. This long standing animosity in the day-to-day life gets converted into anger and the anger takes the form of outrageous crimes. These horrendous crimes have disastrous and dreadful effects on the dalits.

The problem of untouchability was, therefore, bound up with that of a basic socio-economic reconstruction of the Indian society. For the creation of a prosperous national economy, the change in the existing economic and social relations which would elevate the material conditions of the people, including that of the untouchables. The expansion of education, and the enactment of positive legislation would regardless of the opposition of orthodox opinion, sweep away all disabilities that were imposed on the Dalits. Social reform movements had limited success. It generally could not go to the economic roots of the social evil. As such, it usually yielded partial and unstable results. In north India only a very small number, engaged as scavengers or doing unclean work, are considered untouchable. Fa-Hisen tells us that when he came the persons who removed human faces were untouchable. In South India this group is much larger. How they began and grew in such numbers is difficult to say. Probably those who were engaged in occupations considered unclean were so treated; later landless agricultural labour may have been added.

The process of dalit empowerment started during the freedom struggle itself. At the national level, Gandhiji and Dr. B.R. Ambedker attempted to take up the problems of dalits, Gandhi Ji found untouchability as a corrupt form of Hinduism and suggested that it can be solved by moral reform of Hindus. He coined the term Harijan to say that dalits were also people of God like those of the higher castes. Earlier movements like Brahmo Samaj, Pararthna Samaj, Arya Samaj, etc. also advocated the removal of untouchability. Phule, Naicker and Sri Narayan Guru organised the lower castes and spearheaded the movement of dalit empowerment.

Even the framers of the constitution of India were well aware of caste oppression and exploitation in the society. Hence, they on the one hand formulated legal provisions for the protection of the rights of dalits and on the other enforced special provisions for their development. Implementation of the universal adult franchise, abolition of untouchability, making provisions for equality before the law, for reservation in educational and political institutions and in jobs and promotions, are measures taken by the Government of India to ensure their empowerment and a rightful place in the society to further their upliftment and well-being. On the other hand, there are also negative injunctions enacted to protect the rights of the dalits and the downtrodden in this country. Article 15(2) of the Constitution declares that no citizen shall, on the grounds only of religion, race, caste, sex, place of birth or any of them, be subject to any disability, liability, restrictions or conditions with regard to (a) access to shops, public restaurants, hotels and places of public entertainment; (b) the use of wells tanks, bathing ghats, roads and places of public resorts maintained wholly or partly out of state fund or dedicated to the use of the general public.

The Indian constitution forcefully and fiercely oppose any form of discrimination. The first amendment of the Constitution Act, 1951 enjoins upon the ruling dispensation the following positive discrimination: Nothing shall prevent the state from making any special provision for the advancement of socially and educationally backward classes of citizens or for the schedule castes and schedule tribes. To reduce the inequality in the economic field the government has taken some measures for the specific benefits of the depressed classes. These reforms of progressive nature are important legal instruments to and social inequality. Article 46 of the constitution says that the state shall promote with special care the educational and economic interests of the weaker sections of the people particularly the SCs and STs. In fact, the prevailing social conditions characterized by extreme type of inequality necessiated the adoption of the policy of discriminative protection by the government. Not being content with all the above provisions, the government passed the Scheduled Castes Scheduled Tribes [prevention of atrocities] Act 1989 to ensure further protection of life, honour, and property.

Protection in this special manner is available to these people in the three fields, viz. education, government services, and political representation. These measures are often *criticized* on various grounds but it is a fact that these special provisions meant for the elevation of the socio-economic conditions of the scheduled castes have led to a considerable improvement among them so that they have come to occupy some positions of prestige, wealth and power unheard of in the history.

Since, the national leadership involved in the freedom struggle considered bonded labour to be inconsistent with human dignity and liberty, with the advent of independence, provisions were made in the new constitution against imposing of labour duty without consent. Inspite of this, the powers of the state were never invoked against the system. The report by the Commissioner for the Scheduled Castes and Scheduled Tribes testifies to the fact that the practice continues in one form or the other in a number of states. Tears were shed on the sad, plight of the bonded labourers in both the houses of parliament during 1973, but merely the words of sympathy and platitudes are no substitutes for real action. Realisation of the seriousness of the problem is one thing and doing something about it is quite another.

The most important step taken to abolish the system was undertaken in 1975. The abolition of bonded labour constituted one major item in the 20 point programme of the Congress government. On October 25, 1975 an ordinance was promulgated by the Union Government declaring the practice of bondage to be illegal and its violation was made a cognizable offence. Prior to this in her broadcast to the nation Mrs. Indira Gandhi the then Prime Minister of India said: "The practice of bonded labour is barbarous and will be abolished. All contracts or other agreements under which services of such bonded labourers are now secured will be declared as illegal." Since the subject fell within the Concurrent List in the seventh schedule of the Constitution, a Central enactment was necessary. This new enactment prevailed over the previous one, plugged the existing loopholes and ensured uniformity. The majority of the benifeciaries of this legislation were dalits as 52 per cent of the total agriculture labourers and 25 per cent of total farmers are dalits.

So far as the empowerment of dalit is concerned, the role of

B.S.P. in Uttar Pradesh is very important. The rise of the B.S.P. in U.P. has been the most striking feature of dalit identity and politics in India. It has been able to lead the government in U.P. thrice with a dalit woman as Chief Minister. She introduced special policies for dalits. The most important among them are, Ambedkar Village Programme consisting of special programmes for the welfare of dalits and naming of the public institutions after the low caste historical personalities.lt took strong and prompt action against those involved in atrocities against dalits. The rise of the B.S.P. has imparted a sense of pride and confidence among dalits in the country. In Bihar the landloards formed their caste senas or armies which most of the time indulged in crimes against dalits. Jagdish Mahto made first attempt to mobilise the dalits in Arrah district. He started a paper called; 'Harijanistan' (Dalit Land). He raised issues of low wages to the landless workers, protection of *izzat* of dalit women, and social honour. Dalit mobilization in Bihar got momentum again in 1980s following a spate of attacks by private armies, they formed "Lal Sena," Liberation, Party Unity, in Patna and Jahanabad districts, respectively. Party Unity also set-up Kisan Mazdoor Sangram Samiti and Bihar Pradesh Kisan Sabha in 1981. In 1983, the Liberation group formed another Public Front the Indian People's Front which also contested the 1985 elections.

A large number of constitutional provisions and legal texts exist to abolish the practice of untouchability and to protect the members of scheduled castes. Social, and educational policies have been adopted to improve the situation and to protect them from abuses widespread immunity of those who abuse them points twoards the limited effects of these measures. Even the Annual Reports of Scheduled Castes and Scheduled Tribes Commission—a statutory body of the Indian government to the fact that atrocities are still committed on dalits. It is important to look at both *de-jure* and *de-facto* segregation. In that sense, whereas *de-jure* discrimination against dalits has disappeared, *de-facto* segregation remain particularly at the social level specially in rural areas.

References

Desai, A.R. (1989), *Social Background of Indian Nationalism*, Popular Prakasan, Bombay, p. 272.

Lal, A.K. (1977), *Poles of Poverty: A Study of Bonded Labour*, Chetna Publications New Delhi, p. 92.

Nehru, Jawahar Lal (1946), *Discovery of Indias*, Oxford University Press, p. 254.

Prakash Louis (2001), *Mainstream*, July 21, p. 27.

University News, 39[9] Feb. 26, 2001, p. 13.

26

Bihar in a State of Despair

S.K. JHA AND NAND KUMAR

The division of Bihar has left the economy of Bihar hapless and helpless. Bihar is today condemned as the most backward state of the country and its present day problems are almost endless.

The economy of Bihar is dominated by agriculture. The process of occupational transformation away from agriculture has been in the reverse direction, i.e. the percentage of the workforce dependent on agriculture instead of coming down, has gone up from 77.12 in 1961 to 84.20 in 1991. Hence, in development of agriculture lies the major solution to the problems of poverty and overall economic emancipation of these poor but in terms of agriculture potentially rich state. This is not only because agriculture constitutes the largest sector of economy of Bihar and hence has to make its due product contribution in the process of economy growth but also because most of the poor in the third world, including those in India and Bihar, are rural-based who derive their means of livelihood from agriculture by working as landless agriculture labourers, marginal/small farmers or as petty rural artisans (Todaro, it is the value of agriculture output per worker which emerges as the key variable explaining the spatial (interstate) variation in the incidence of rural poverty (r=0.72) in

India. As most rural poor are engaged in agriculture, they stand to gain directly by way of higher income, wages and employment as agriculture affects even those who are not directly engaged in agriculture. They rely on non-farm income and employment which are dependent one way or the other on agriculture. Agriculture growth is particularly effective in reducing rural poverty because of demand spillover to local market in which non-farm rural poor have a large stake. Increased farm income is mostly spent in rural areas, especially on consumption of goods and services produced by the rural poor.

Very few countries have experienced rapid economic growth without agriculture growth either preceding or accompanying it. Agriculture has acted as the lead sector in the rapidly growing East Asian economies like Taiwan, South Korea, China, Thailand, and Malaysia. A review of the East Asian Economic growth experience since the 1950s clearly indicates the catalytic role of agriculture in generating economic growth and reducing poverty (Perpinstrup-Anderson & Rajul Pandya-Lorch). Thus, in addition to the rate of economy's growth it is the regional and sectoral composition of growth that affects the national rate of poverty reduction. If growth bypasses poor regions, growth may lead to rising inequality and poverty. On the other hand, if growth is concentrated in sectors from which poor people are more likely to derive their income, such as agriculture, growth can be associated with declaiming income inequality and reduced poverty, consistence with cross country evidence for developing countries. Indian states tell a similar story of the importance of rural growth in poverty reduction. As within rural areas, growth in agriculture and services has been particularly effective in poverty reduction, while industrial growth has not (World Bank, 2000-01).

The rural economy of Bihar is in the grip of massive poverty, unemployment, inequalities of income and enormous population. In the field of agriculture and rural industries incidence of rural poverty has been very high in Bihar. There has been only a slight decline in 1989-90 when it came down to 52.4 percentage. It reached its lowest mark in 1990-91 when it declined to 46.3 per cent from 61.1 per cent, as a result of it Bihar today is the poorest state in the country. Among the rural poor, the worst sufferers are agriculture labourers and daily wage earners.

Rural industries in any country of the world are an important component of the rural economy. These produce non-agricultural products and process agricultural produce, give non-farm employment, and generate income for many. However, these are not in good health in the state and they need to be developed properly as part of the state economy, so that these will help in the industrial sector of rural Bihar.

It is true that Bihar has no mines and minerals at present but it is a folly to think that this is permanent deprivation. There is even possibility of petroleum and gold in the bowels of the earth in Banka and South Munger. Many other minerals such as bauxite, mica etc. are buried in the entrails of mother earth in regions, which border Jharkhand, Bhagalpur and Munger areas. It needs exploitation and *prospecting* large scale efforts and endeavors in this direction which are sure to be amply rewarded.

CONCLUSION

We can say that state is endowed with fertile land, ample water resources, good climate and abundant manpower which, if properly harnessed can bring about a sea change in the rural scenario in Bihar, i.e. from one of poverty and hunger to that of affluence and good health. The harnessing of these natural and human resources, however, is critically dependent on an active role of the state in terms of massive public investments in irrigation, flood control and rural electrification to give a big push to its rural agriculture economy. The actual development during the 1990's however hs been just in the reverse direction, i.e. public investments in these fields, instead of going up have gone down drastically in real terms from those in the preceding decade, i.e. in the 1980s. This disturbing trend needs to be completely reversed if the otherwise stagnant agriculture economy of the state is to be brought out of its morass of under-development and the fate of masses dependent on agriculture is to be improved.

It is the need of the hour that all efforts should be made in improving integration between the agriculture rural industry and rural poverty. Linkages between agriculture development and rural poverty need to be strengthened through rural industrialization. Rural development in real sense of the term can only be achieved through by increasing agricultural growth and shifting of labour force in non-farm activities. Improvement in dry land technologies, more investment in rural infrastructure, adoption of modem farming technology, development of horticulture, proper and speedy execution of land reforms is essential for fast agriculture growth in the state.

Bihar must take special care to set afloat location specific projects. Maize complex can be started in Samastipur and Naugachhia. Makhana units can be initiated in Darbhanga and Madhubani. Mango units can be launched in Bhagalpur and *litchi* units in Muzaffarpur, pineapple at Araria, Jute complex can be inaugurated in Purnea and Katihar. Kishangang area may be developed as tea garden complex; Bihar Shariff can sustain potato units. The commercial banks must come out with prouse funds and unify these agro-based industries james, jellies, pickles, etc. which are demanded internationally. In an era of globalization, international division labour shall be extremely fruitful and Bihar must specialize in processing and preserving fruits and vegetables. All poverty alleviation and employment programmes of the government should be implemented sincerely and effectively. If the current crop of the government's employment-oriented programmes and targeted programmes is any indication, it is almost certain that any large-scale Employment Guarantee Programme, given the current mode of government's functioning would open a black hole in to which government expenditure would be sucked in. It would not result in the hoped for employment, but would, of course, generate vast rents.

Even there transfer-oriented programmes (such as pension for widows and old) has been that except in certain states, like Kerala and possibly Karnataka and West Bengal the leakages are very large.

A special programme for the poor makes sense in a rich society where the poor are few in number and similarly, a programme for employment guarantee when most are employed. After more than half a century of development and planning, we still have 20 per cent in abject poverty, the people in worthwhile jobs, less than a third of the work force and with vast disguised employment. Nothing illustrates this better than the fact that despite agricultures, share of GDP having fallen to 26 per cent or so, it continues to employ as much as 60 per cent of population, if not more. Agriculture inevitably is a reservoir of those who cannot find meaningful employment. Therefore, going by employment distribution, India is where England in 1810 or Japan in 1895! [*The Financial Express*, Fe Insight-Sebastian Morris]. Here, NGO's role may be significant. However, the objective of rural development cannot be achieved fully without bringing other social changes in the state. Fair and full utilization of all the funds meant for rural development should be made. Strong political will is needed to develop the economy of Bihar. Without it, the problems are bound to linger and deepen. Even today, if the Left and Right can come together on land reforms, capitalist employment-creating growth at rates in excess of 9 per cent would be possible. Imagine if agriculture were to grow average rates in excess of 5 per cent! The industrial growth rate that this could make possible is in excess of 12 per cent. That is the potential inherent in land reform.

References

Bhalla, G.S. and Chadha, G.K., *Green Revolution and the Small Peasants*, Delhi, Concept Publishing House, 1993.

Bhalla, G.S. and Tyagi, D.S., *Patterns in Agricultural Development: A District Level Study*, Delhi, 1989.

Guleti, Ashok and Pursell Garry, "Trade Policies, Incentives and Resource Allocations in Indian Agriculture," *World Bank* 1991, Mimeo.

Morris, S., "Employment Guarantee Scheme is a Still-born Child; Try Land Reforms"; *http://www.financialalexpress.com*.

Per Pinstrup-Anderson and Rajul Pandya-Lorch, "The Role of Agriculture to Alleviate Poverty," Agriculture Plus Rural Development, DLG-Verlogs-Gmbh, Eschnorner, Landstrabe, 122, 60489 Frankfertam Main, Germany, Vol. 6, No. 2, p. 53.

Prasad, K.N. (1987), *Bihar Economy Through the Plans*, Northern Book Center, New Delhi.

Sharma, I., "Rural Poverty in India: A Study Regional Dynamics," *Bihar Economics Journal*, Conference, Vol. 1998, p. 39; World Bank, World Development Report, 2000-01, p. 53.

Todaro, Michael P., *Economic Development in Third World*, Second Edition, Longman, New York and London, 1981, p. 131.

27

Child Labour in India: An Emerging Issue

SHEELA SHARAN SINGH

INTRODUCTION

It is well recognised that child labour is one of the important vulnerable groups in Indian society. Globalisation processes have played a major role in pushing the issue of child labour as a priority issue in the international debates. The reason for this is that the impact of globalisation on child labour is as contentious as the issue itself. Some perceive a direct negative impact in that it contributes to an increase in child labour because of intensified competition over wage costs. The fact that economic liberalisation leads to an increase in the incidence of child labour is not an unconvincing proposition. The opening up of a labour surplus economy like India may witness a shift to labour-intensive forms of production and into cheap labour that can minimize the labour costs to make them internationally competitive. And, in this order of things, child labour can form the first priority for a cheap, least demanding, pliable labour force. In India, many empirical studies in the post-liberalisation period tend to substantiate this eventuality. Nevertheless, the counterpoint of this maintains that child labour existed prior to globalisation in most of the developing countries, and increased global competitiveness has not accentuated its incidence.

Millions of children world-wide are engaged in labour that is hindering their education, development and future livelihoods; many of them are involved in the worst forms of child labour that cause irreversible physical or psychological damage, or that even threaten their lives. This situation represents an intolerable violation of the rights of individual children, it perpetuates poverty and it compromises economic growth and equitable development. The effective abolition of child labour is an essential element of the International Labour Organisation's goal of achieving decent work for all women and men.

A future without child labour, the third Global Report under the follow-up to the ILO Declaration on Fundamental Principles and Rights at Work, shows how the abolition of child labour has become a global cause for the new millennium. It explores the ever-changing manifestations of child labour throughout the world, and how girls and boys are affected differently, and it presents new data on the scale of this stubborn problem, and it sheds new light on its complex, interlined causes. It charts the growth of a global movement against child labour, reviewing the various types of action being taken by the ILO, its tripartite constituents (governments, employers' and workers' organisations) and other actors at international, national and local levels. The Report concludes with proposals for a three-pillar approach to strengthen the action of the ILO in this field, building upon the wealth of experience gained by the International Programme on the Elemination of Child Labour (IPEC) in the decades since its establishment.

The discussion in India unfortunately has confounded the different categories of children. By adding up all the children that, in one way or the other, are not attending school full-time or are attending school but are engaged in some 'working activity' on the other, the incidence of child labour has been blown out of proportion. Some sources claim that India indeed has more than 100 million working children (see e.g. Weiner, 1991 and Human Rights Watch, 1996).

The large number of working children is induced by a definitional deception. Neera Burra, an author whose writings have helped to focus the public attention on child labour (see Burra, 1995), explicitly writes that a working child is 'basically a child who is deprived of the right to education.' What makes this definition important is that it makes it unambiguously clear that all out-of-school children are child labourers in one way or another (Burra, 1997, p. 8). Mahendra Dev and C. Ravi (Ramachandran and Massun, 2002, p. 193) also consider a broadening of the definition 'by defining a child labourer as one who is deprived of the right to education and childhood'.

A policy to liberate children from forced or unforced labour and incorporate them into the educational stream requires a specific approach. If, on the other hand, we want to know the reasons why children are 'nowhere', i.e., neither in school nor in a work place, the explanatory factors need not be related to the factors that are at the root cause of children applying their labour power in exchange for a direct or indirect income.

The definitional clarity on what 'child labour' implies is helpful to clear the fog around the approximate quantity of child labourers in India (10 million or 100 million?). More importantly, however, it will allow us to question the usefulness of the various learned multivariate probit and regression analysis exercises. Independent correlates in such exercises are calculated to have a positive or negative impact on child labour. Conclusions then often suggest that poverty, nutritional poverty, indebtedness, literacy, work participation, the number of children and the size of cattle herd are important factors to be considered.

The problem with these exercises, however, is that 'child labour' is not a segregated category by definition. The variable 'mothers' literacy' may have a different impact on girls working in the household and on boys working on the family farm after school time or during school time, on the one hand, and on boys and girls working in stone quarries, in restaurants, in workshops, etc., on the other hand. While the former set of activities fall under child work, and can be considered as a valuable aspects of socialization, the latter are directly related to the sale or hire of labour power and may interfere with the normal physical, intellectual, psychological and emotional development of the child. The clubbing of all these different types of 'labour' together in econometric model (using the Census of NSS data) is unlikely to produce sound results or explain much of the mechanism that perpetuates child labour.

Since 'child labour', as it has been defined for most statistical exercises, tends to be concentrated in agriculture, it would be reasonable to expect that the more 'backward' a region, i.e., the less it has diversified; the lower its literacy rates and the lower its development infrastructure, the higher would be the incidence of child labour in the region. But that apparently is not the case. Bihar, a state that is usually referred to in derogatory terms as backward, feudal and under-developed, has one of the lowest child labour ratios in the country. On the other hand, Tamil Nadu and Andhra Pradesh, states which are doing fairly well in terms of economic development and human development indicators, have an incidence of child labour that is among the highest in all India states.

CHILD LABOUR POLICY

After independence India adopted many child related policies in conformity with the guidelines of ILO. It is widely accepted that four major reinforcing factors generate a vicious spiral resulting in the pervasive and high rates of illiteracy and non-participation in school education; static and inferior technology attempting to survive in the face of technical progress and unequal trade partnership with weak backward and forward linkages; and indifferent or inappropriate public policies dealing with social infrastructures. The exact opposite of a vicious spiral is a virtuous spiral. This is characterised by; faster demographic transition; a unimodal and universal school education strategy with rising participation rates in school education and literacy; dynamic technology rendering employability of children inefficient and uneconomic; strengthened backward and forward trade linkages generating specialization and dynamic comparative advantages and proactive social infrastructures; and policies of the state reduce gender, regional and social inequality.

In consonance with this, many scholars as well as international agencies have identified human resource development including school education, investment in production assets and infrastructure (social and physical), trade and the development-oriented socio-economic government policies as the main determinants of success (Castle, Chaudhri and Nyland, Nielsen and Dubey, Rustagi). However, it is lamented that these efficient solvents of child labour are not yet fully understood for their linkages (Lieten). Therefore, an attempt is made to develop a holistic perspective on these factors for evolving child labour regulations and prohibition policies for the Government of India.

In the context of child labour, the vicious spiral operating in some states of India can be reversed through the policy of a big push so as to trigger its reversal to the virtuous spiral. Although the big push is unlikely to yield visible short run effects, once a critical minimum has been accumulated and a tipping point reached, the change can be expected to be dramatic and fast. The most preferred instrument to combat the problem of child labour by international and national policy-makers is compulsory school education upto the minimum acceptable age of entry into the labour force, which is 15 years in the case of India. While this is being repeatedly emphasised, the other two essential accompaniments for this measure, namely, technology, and labour market regulations are rarely emphasised. However, the role of demographic transition is slowly getting recognised. A significant point here is that concerted efforts on all these fronts would trigger the tipping point, while any of these factors alone may not do so.

In terms of the specific policies, it is strange that with respect to the issues of child labour and education, the policy was formulated after the law was enacted instead of the policy document preceding the law. Therefore, the law lacks direction and with respect to child labour, the policy gets its 'vision' from the law! The main features of the two national policies, namely the National Policy on Education (1986) (hereafter referred to as the NPE) and the National Policy on Child Labour, (1987) (hereafter referred to as the NPCL) can be analysed using the following parameters—firstly, what is the perspective or understanding of the problem as reflected in the policy; secondly, what have been the choices exercised by the State with respect to these problems; and thirdly, what strategies have been drawn up to address the problems.

INCIDENCE OF CHILD LABOUR

We are made to accept that in all states there is 'a strong inverse correlation between rural literacy rates and the incidence of child labour', and that 'a strengthening of rural literacy programmes would lead to nearly a 50 per cent decline in the incidence of child labour' (V.V. Giri National Labour Institute, 2000). These correlations, in a statistical sense, may indeed exist, but a quick look at the cases selected in Table 1, informs us that there are significant differences, within states and particularly between states.

There is obviously an observable (and calculable) correlation. For example, Jhabua (Madhya Pradesh) has a child labour incidence of 25.5 per cent and a total literacy rate of 13.4 per cent. The figures for Durg, on the other hand, are 5.5 per cent and 50.4 per cent respectively. But some districts have a high child labour incidence under conditions that are not necessarily worse than conditions in other districts and in other states. Why should Mahboobnagar and Kurnool (Andhra Pradesh) have a child labour incidence of 14.6 per cent and 14.1 per cent respectively? They have a total literacy rate of 25.3 per cent and 33.3 per cent respectively. Why should Saharsa (Bihar) have a child labour incidence of only 5.9 per cent (while its rural literacy rate is 26.9 per cent) whereas Kalahandi in Orissa has a comparable literacy rate and a much higher incidence of child labour. Periyar (Tamil Nadu), on the other hand, has a child labour ratio that is comparable to Dumka in Bihar but it has almost double the rural literacy levels of the latter. In respect to the variables, 'agricultural orientation' and 'overall development', similar 'anomalies' can also be found.

The incidence of child labour can be witnessed through Table 2 which represents state-wise incidence of child labour.

It is significant to note, as we have indicated earlier, that the states with the highest child labour incidence (child labour as an ill-defined category) are also states with a high per capita state domestic product. These states (Andhra Pradesh, Karnataka, Himachal Pradesh, and Tamil Nadu) have a much higher (female) work participation rate than for example Bihar, Assam, Uttar Pradesh and West Bengal.

The data in Table 2, which clearly shows that (female) work

TABLE 1

Example of Child Labour-prone Districts

Districts	*Child Labour Literacy Rate*	*Incidence (%) in Agriculture*	*% Total Rural RID*	*% Workers*
Jhabua (Madhya Pradesh)	25.2	13.4	90.4	84
Surguja (Madhya Pradesh)	11.1	24.98	4.3	46
Durg (Madhya Pradesh	5.5	50.4	70.0	80
Kurnool (Andhra Pradesh)	14.1	33.3	75.2	83
Mahboobnagar (Andhra Pradesh)	14.6	25.3	83.4	53
Saharsa (Bihar)	6.0	26.9	91.0	24
Dumka (Bihar)	7.9	31.5	85.5	32
Kalahandi (Orissa)	12.5	27.9	85.6	51
Koraput (Orissa)	12.7	17.4	84.7	54
Periyar (Tamil Nadu)	8.5	53.8	75.4	128
Kamarajar (Tamil Nadu)	8.9	55.7	52.7	115
Dharampuri (Tamil Nadu)	8.1	43.3	80.8	79

Note: RID (Rural Development Index) is derived from a weighted combination of various indicators such as the importance of industry, the spread of bank services, literacy, etc.

Source: V.V. Giri National Labour Institute, 2000 (various booklets).

TABLE 2

Child Labour, Literacy, Income and Work Participation Across States

State	*Child Labour (%)*	*Per capita Domestic Product (in Rs.)*	*Female Literacy (%)*	*Work Participation (%)*	
				All	*Female*
Andhra Pradesh	17.8	7006	24.8	81.0	72.4
Karnataka	13.9	7242	34.6	74.9	61.3
Himachal Pradesh	13.6	6896	51.5	79.9	72.9
Rajasthan	12.2	5315	15.0	77.6	67.2
Tamil Nadu	10.4	8051	42.8	74.8	64.7
Madhya Pradesh	8.7	5516	22.1	76.5	63.0
Orissa	7.4	4662	30.5	65.3	45.7
Maharashtra	6.5	12010	39.7	77.7	70.5
West Bengal	5.1	6247	40.7	58.9	28.5
Uttar Pradesh	5.0	4794	22.9	61.9	34.7
Gujarat	4.1	9054	36.1	73.2	57.9
Bihar	3.7	3417	19.7	56.6	26.9
Punjab	2.7	12934	43.9	58.7	32.4
Assam	2.6	5520	52.1	54.5	23.9
Haryana	2.6	12934	43.9	58.7	32.4
Kerala	0.8	6524	81.7	53.4	32.5

Note: Domestic Product in Rs., the other column in Percentages.
Source: NSS 50th Round in Dev and Ravi, 2002.

participation has a strong influence on the prevalence of child labour. In general, one observes a positive correlation between the two indicators. The two *outliers* are Maharashtra and Gujarat. The states with the lowest child labour incidence, are also states with reasonably low female work participation. Kerala, Haryana, Assam, Bihar, and Punjab, despite showing stark differences in other variables, also have a low child labour incidence. The inference is in line with the theory of labour market segmentation and complementarily stated above: under conditions of a high demand for labour in the lower segments of the labour market, poor families will be tapped for additional labour power; after the adult male and adult female labour power, the child labour power will also be pulled into employment.

A separate study for incidence of rural-urban child labour may be made with the help of Table 3. Child labour incidence is high in Southern states like Andhra Pradesh, Karnataka and Tamil Nadu and low in poorer states like Bihar and Uttar Pradesh. There are significant regional disparities in the incidence of child labour. Table 3 provides the percentages of child labour across states from three sources (Census, NSS and NCAER).

The NSS provides two types of estimates: one based on principal status and the other based on principal and subsidiary status. The work participation rates for children are high for the latter category. The NSS principal and subsidiary numbers for rural areas show that it was the highest in Andhra Pradesh (17.8 percent) and lowest in Kerala (0.76 percent). These two states have same ranks for urban areas also. The regional disparities are much higher for rural areas as compared to urban areas. The coefficient of variation given in Table 8 shows the regional disparities in the incidence of child labour are much higher for NSS data as compared to that of Census data. The CV is 76 percent for principal status workers while Census data shows that it was 49 percent in rural areas. It is interesting to note that poorer states like Bihar, Uttar Pradesh, M.P., and Orissa have lower incidence as compared to Southern states. The NSS data for Himachal Pradesh needs some explanation. If we take principal and subsidiary status, Himachal Pradesh showed one of the highest incidence percentages in rural areas (13.6%). On the other hand, if we take principal status, the participation rate was low (3.2%) in the state. One of the reasons could be that many children might

TABLE 3

Incidence of Child Labour Across Indian States: 5-14 Age Group

	Rural (%)			*Urban (%)*			
	Census 1991	*NSS 1993-94*		*NCAER 1994*	*Census 1991*	*NSS 1993-94*	
		PSS	*PS*			*PSS*	*PS*
Andhra Pradesh	12.5	17.8	15.3	9.0	3.1	6.8	5.7
Assam	—	2.6	1.7	2.6	—	3.8	3.6
Bihar	4.4	3.7	3.2	3.9	1.6	1.3	1.2
Gujarat	7.1	4.1	2.8	6.2	1.7	2.0	1.4
Haryana	3.0	2.6	1.3	1.9	1.1	2.4	1.9
Himachal Pradesh	4.8	13.2	3.2	0.8	1.3	2.4	1.5
Jammu & Kashmir	—	5.6	3.3	—	—	1.1	0.8
Karnataka	11.0	13.7	10.7	7.4	3.5	4.3	4.0
Kerala	0.6	0.8	0.5	0.4	0.5	0.6	0.5
Madhya Pradesh	9.9	8.4	6.4	3.5	1.8	1.5	1.1
Maharashtra	8.1	6.5	5.3	8.0	1.6	2.1	1.8
Orissa	6.5	7.4	5.5	5.1	1.9	2.8	2.2
Punjab	3.6	2.7	2.1	3.4	1.6	1.7	1.4
Rajasthan	7.8	12.2	11.4	1.2	1.7	3.2	2.6
Tamil Nadu	5.9	10.4	9.3	5.6	2.6	5.2	4.6
Uttar Pradesh	4.2	5.0	3.4	1.5	2.3	3.2	2.2
West Bengal	4.9	5.1	3.5	6.7	1.9	3.8	2.9
All-India	6.4	7.2	5.8	4.3	2.0	3.1	2.5
CV Across States (%)	49.0	65.0	76.0	63.0	39.0	55.0	60.0

Sources: 1. Census 1991. 2. NSS 50th Round on Employment and Unemployment. 3. Duraisamy, M. (2000) for NCAER Data.

be working in a subsidiary status apart from attending school. In the case of Rajasthan, it is not clear why the NCAER data shows a very low level of incidence (1.2 per cent) as compared to NSS and Census data. On the other hand, Gujarat has lower incidence under NSS as compared too that for Census and NCAER. Madhya Pradesh has lower incidence while West Bengal has higher incidence under NCAER source as compared to other sources.

CHILD LABOUR AND LEGAL SAFEGUARDS

The government has framed many laws to protect the children from their exploitation. There is a wide gamut of legislation in India to tackle the complex problem of child labour. The country's commitment to the welfare of children is reflected in Articles 15, 24, 39, and 45 of its Constitution. Apart from these Constitutional rights/provisions, a number of Acts have been passed that have a bearing on child labour. The efforts and pressure from various quarters to eliminate the practice of child labour culminated in the enactment of the Child Labour (Prohibition and Regulation) Act, 1986 (CLA) in 1987. The CLA is considered to be a comprehensive Act, which takes into consideration the economic and social aspects of the problem of child labour. Specifically, it (a) bans the employment of children, i.e., those who have not completed their fourteenth year of age, in specified occupations and processes; (b) prohibits the employment of children in 13 "hazardous" occupations and 57 processes; and (c) regulates the employment conditions in other occupations/processes. However, many child labour activists and researchers feel that the Act is neither adequate nor effective in tackling the problem. The word "hazardous" has many connotations. Also, family-based work and recognised school-based activities are outside the purview of the CLA, whereby children working as part of family labour remain outside the purview of the law. Moreover, most of the children working in the informal sector are also not covered by child labour legislation.

In 1996, the Supreme Court of India, in the *M.C. Mehta* Vs. *State of Tamil Nadu* case passed a landmark judgement concerning child labour that has had wide ramifications covering child workers in all hazardous occupations including the carpet industry.

HISTORIC JUDGEMENT OF SUPREME COURT ON CHILD LABOUR

The Supreme Court of India delivered a historic judgement on the issue of child labour on 10th December, 1996. A three member bench of the Court delivered its verdict on the petition (No. 465 of 1986) of noted environmentalist M.C. Mehta, that sought to involve the Court's power under Article 32 of the Indian Constitution towards gross violation of Article 24 by the match factories of Sivakasi, which are infamous for the employment of children. The court observed, "By now (child labour) is an all-India evil, though its acuteness differs from area to area. So, without a concerted effort, both of the central government and various state governments, this ignominy would not get wiped out. We have, therefore, though it fit to travel beyond the confines of Sivakasi." Amongst the other industries identified by the Court for priority action was the handmade carpet industry in Mirzapur-Bhadohi, Uttar Pradesh. The major points of the verdict are as follows:

- An alternative source of income shall have to be provided to the family of child labour.
- Employers of child labour shall have to pay a compensation of Rs. 20,000 as per the provisions of the Child Labour (Prohibition and Regulation) Act, 1986, for every child employed. This would be deposited in the Child Labour Rehabilitation-*cum*-Welfare Fund.
- The State shall have to provide employment to an adult in the family in lieu of the child working in a factory or mine or any other hazardous work.
- In the absence of an alternative employment, the parents/guardian have to be paid the income earned on the Corpus Fund, the suggested amount being fixed at Rs. 25,000 for each child. The payment will cease if the child is not being sent for education. In the case of non-hazardous employment, the employer will bear the cost of education.
- The State's contribution/grant is fixed at Rs. 5,000 for each child employed in a factory or mine or any other hazardous employment. The sum shall be deposited in the aforesaid fund.

INITIATIVE TO ELIMINATE CHILD LABOUR

India adopted the power of economic reform in 1990. With the adoption of economic reform process the importance of empowerment of vulnerable groups got momentum. In the series of vulnerable groups, issue of child labour also became the centre point for discussion because the child labour belong to the poor or even BPL families. Hence, India as well as International Organisations like ILO showed their grave concern for the elimination of child labour particularly since the era of globalisation. In India mainly two kinds of initiatives have been taken for elimination of child labour: (1) State Initiative, (2) Other initiative which includes civil society organisations (CSOs) that are popularly known as non-governmental organizations.

INITIATIVES BY THE STATE

Although various legislations have been enacted by the government of India, some of them going back to even the pre-Independence period, the repeated failure of the state in implementing national legislations and formulating policies in tune with the Constitutional requirements is evident from the indifference with which the state government received the Child Labour (Prohibition and Regulation) Act, 1986. However, it is important to mention at this point that certain sections of the state administration recognised that the traditional tool of labour legislation calling for either a blanket ban or restrictions on child labour have been unable to deal with the problem of child labour. Also, believing that to fructify the objectives of the various legislations including the latest (Child Labour Prohibition and Regulation Act, 1986), it is necessary to have a plan of action involving several concerned ministries. The state launched a "State Programme of Action for the Child" for the first time in 1994. In terms of direct action, there are two types of interventions in the state—one, which looks at child labour as a "labour problem" and the other which believes that the abolition of child labour is inextricably linked with compulsory primary education. The Labour Commission rate and to a lesser extent, the Department of Women and Child Welfare belong to the former category. The Department of Education belongs to the latter category and it, at least on paper, believes that introduction of compulsory education will result in the reduction and finally, elimination of child labour and has therefore, launched a number of education-related programmes.

OTHER INITIATIVES

Other initiative includes civil society organisations that are popularly known as non-governmental organisations. The majority of NGOs use a combination of strategies in their efforts to eliminate child labour or ameliorate its effects. However, many have a distinct philosophy and consequently, a clear entry point, and area of emphasis. To take a few examples: Sankalp—an NGO working with tribals in the mining belt of Shankargarh-aims to secure the income and employment of parents as a prior condition to eliminating child labour. The MV Foundation, on the other hand, denounces the importance of poverty as the prime motivating factor, and focuses on changing deep-seated mindsets and attitudes about child labour and education in the entire community in villages of Andhra Pradesh. Rugmark—a labeling scheme for carpets made without the use of child labour-approaches this issue from the standpoint of international consumers, whereas CREDA, also located in the carpet belt of Mirzapur and Bhadohi, uses education as the entry point for weaning children away from the looms. CINI—Asha, working in the urban slums of Calcutta, takes a similar stance by providing bridge courses and after school tuition classes to enable working children to join the formal school system and stay there. A radically different standpoint and philosophy is to be found in the work of Concerned for Working Children (CWC), located in Karnataka, whose members believe that work is part of the reality of some children's lives and is not necessarily harmful for them. Consequently, they aim to give a voice to working children and to organize them so that they can demand better working conditions for themselves.

The following strategies are most frequently used by the NGOs: Mobilising and creating awareness, Providing education, Providing pre-school education, Facilitating child participation, Developing income compensatory strategies, Assuring work and income security for parents, Facilitating intra-household adjustments, Social labeling, and Advocacy for legal and institutional reform.

CONCLUSION

It is obvious from the above analysis, that multilateral organisations and national governments need to focus the greater part of their efforts on the children most at risk, i.e. those in morally and physically hazardous occupations. National government must focus more on agriculture and home-based occupations in the informal sector which account for a large amount of reported and unreported (nowhere children) child labour.

We need to explain the paradox that in areas where one can expect more push forces because of poverty and illiteracy, child labour incidence is lower than in areas where levels of poverty and illiteracy are considerably lower. Our suggestion is that an explanation can be provided by a specific labour market segmentation, a low reward for labour power and higher levels of employment under conditions of social, economic, and political submissiveness. Children, if not protected either by family adults or by public institutions, may end up in an abject dependency relationship with employers who may go to various extremes in exploiting the young children up to the hilt.

REFERENCES

Chandrasekhar, C.P. (1997), "The Economic Consequences of the Abolition of Child Labour: An Indian Case Study," *The Journal of Peasant Studies*, Vol. 24, No. 3, April.

Deshpande, Sudha (2000), "Girl Child Labour in India," Paper presented at National Seminar on Child Labour: Realities and Policy Dimensions, Organised by V.V. Giri National Labour Institute, Indian Society of Labour Economics and Institute for Human Development, NOIDA, U.P., December.

Dev, S. Mahendra, "Child Labour in India: Dimensions, Determinants and Policy," Published in Indian Economic Association, Conference Vol. 2000.

Gayatri, V., "Situational Analysis of Child Labour in Karnataka," Published in the *Indian Journal of Labour Economics*, Vol. 45, July-September 2002.

Lieten, G.K., "Child Labour and Poverty: The Poverty of Analysis," Published in the *Indian Journal of Labour Economics*, Vol. 45, July-September 2002.

Popola, T.S. and Alakh N. Sharma (eds.) (1999), *Gender and Employment in India*, Vikas Publishing House, New Delhi.

Raman, Vasanthi (2000), "Politics of Childhood—Perspectives from the South," *Economic and Political Weekly*, Vol. 35, No. 46.

Sharma, Alakh N., Sharma, R. and Raj, Nikhil, "Child Labour in Carpet Industries: Impact of Social Leveling in India," Institute for Human Development, New Delhi.

Supreme Court Judgement Case No. 465 of 1986.

Weiner, Myron (1991), The Child Labour and the State in India, Oxford University Press, Delhi.

28

Women's Empowerment Through Panchayati Raj Institutions: Some Problems and Prospects

SABITA KUMARI AND SURESH KUMAR

INTRODUCTION

In India, the policy approach to women's development has undergone significant shifts. These changes have occurred primarily in response to the concerns raised all over the world by the academia and women activists over the discrimination of women in the family, society, and polity. During Seventies, there was a markable shift from family centered welfare programmes to programmes for enhancing women's employment opportunities. Late Eighties and Nineties witnessed a drastic change in understanding women's issues in terms of gendered power relations and subsequently the empowerment of women became the catchword across the board.

It is in this backdrop, the decentralised planning programme attempted a gender planning exercise in the local self-governments. Massive training programmes were conducted for gender sensitisation of women elected representatives of local governments. Efforts were also made to ensure the participation of women in all the levels of the local level planning process.

The recent decade has witnessed a growing awareness of the importance of the roles to be performed by women in the public sphere and their impact on the process of development and establishment of good governance. Studies have adequately demonstrated the correlation between the women's participation in governance and decision-making, and the delivery of services to the people for their livelihood security and economic development. More specifically, the World Bank's studies confirm a strong correlation between low levels of female involvement in public life and high levels of government corruption (World Bank, 2001). Barriers prohibiting women from access to resources, jobs, education, and participation in governance inhibit a nation's economic viability. Gender inequality will result in greater poverty, slower economic growth and lower quality of life.

By involving women, delivery of services in the sectors of education, health, credit, and governance will become effective. Enhancing women's rights, access to resources, and participation in decision-making will not only benefit the women's segments but also the whole community. It is recognized throughout the world that grassroots women's groups are redefining governance and development in their orbit of action. They significantly alter the process of administering development. By their local action significant progress and changes are made in the life of communities which, in turn, draw the attention of the academics, administrators and the media. After seeing the implications of women's involvement in governance throughout the world, steps have been taken at the grass-roots level to build their capacity and skill, sharpen their leadership, and forge alliances with varied partners to project the emergence of the alternative governance. Grass-roots women deal with everyday survival and livelihood issues from their own perspective and with the most ingenious solutions as they have a knowledge base which is local in character (Huairou Commission, 2002).

The inception of Panchayati Raj institutions intended to translate the Gandhian dream of village self-governance (Gram Swarajya) to reality and making them as an effective tool of rural development and reconstruction. The new Panchayati Raj

TABLE 1

Women's Representation in Panchayati Raj Institutions

State/UTs	*Gram Panchayat*		*Panchayat Samiti*		*Zila Parishad*		*All Three Tiers of Panchayat*		
	Women	*%*	*Women*	*%*	*Women*	*%*	*Total*	*Women*	*%*
1	*2*	*3*	*4*	*5*	*6*	*7*	*8*	*9*	*10*
Uttar Pradesh	120591	15	13865	23	634	24	862458	135090	16
Gujarat	21351	17	1275	33	254	33	128045	22880	18
Assam	5469	18	669	26			33769	6138	18
Tamil Nadu	31548	25	2295	35	225	35	132999	34069	26
Rajasthan	33566	30	1740	32	331	32	1194419	35637	30
Haryana	16704	31	858	35	82	36	57002	17644	31
Madhya Pradesh	156181	33	369	35	338	33	484484	159688	33
Himachal Pradesh	6015	33	558	34	84	33	20177	6657	33
D & N Haveli	46	34		4	25	151	50		33
Maharashtra	101182	33	1174	33	857	33	308831	102943	33
Orissa	27036	33	1754	33	284	33	87191	29074	33
Tripura	1809	33	67	34	24	34	5687	1900	33
Andhra Pradesh	78000	34	5420	37	363	33	246266	83783	34

(*Contd.*)

TABLE 1 (*Contd.*)

1	*2*	*3*	*4*	*5*	*6*	*7*	*8*	*9*	*10*
A & N Island	229	34	—	10	33	697	—	239	34
Goa	468	37	—	—	—	1316	—	468	36
Manipur	555	36	—	—	22	36	1617	557	36
Punjab	26939	36	—	—	—	—	75437	26939	36
West Bengal	17883	36	2997	35	243	34	58461	21123	36
Sikkim	326	37		—	28	30	965	354	37
Kerala	3883	38	563	36	104	35	12117	4550	38
Lakshadweep	30	38	—	—	8	36	101	38	38
Daman & Diu	25	40	—	—	5	33	78	30	38
Karnataka	35305	44	1343	40	335	36	84886	36983	44
Bihar	9020	45	850	40	81	40	22573	9951	44
Total	694161	27	38597	30	4046	30	2744763	736804	27

Source: Ministry of Rural Development and Employment, 2000, Mathew, C.A. (ed.) 2000. Tamil Nadu (26), Rajasthan (30) and Haryana (31).

institutions, however, have assured the vibrant grass-root democracy through the 73rd constitutional amendment. This constitutional amendment clearly speaks of the meaning of the decentralised governance. Decentralization of economic power to the grass-root level, therefore, becomes essential not only for the sake of ensuring people's democracy, but also for ensuring higher growth and equity.

Decentralised Planning and Associated Devolution of Powers to the Villages

Panchayats are the new institutional arrangements which can be effectively utilised to meet the needs of rural people in changing environment.

After enacting the 73rd and the 74th Amendments to Constitution of India, the legitimately created space for women in the orbit of governance has raised a question about whether the women who have come to power at the grass-roots can achieve what they have to achieve. It is obvious that the entire public space was occupied by men for five decades but no question was raised as to the ability of those leaders. It is understandable that the women who have come to power with different kinds of disabilities have to perform the task assigned to them. The task assigned to them is not easy. Since the state and Central governments have failed in solving many of the nation's problems, they are being entrusted to the grass-roots institutions. Unless the newly recruited leaders equip themselves with skill, capacity, and capability to manage the people, the bureaucracy, the resources, and the Panchayats, they cannot deliver the goods.

After passing the 73rd Amendment Act most of states have passed the Panchayati Raj Act in their states in conformity with the Constitutional Amendment Act, such as Andhra Pradesh Panchayati Raj Act, 1993 and Bihar Panchayati Raj Act, 1993. With the passage of the 73rd and 74th Amendment, a new era has dawned on the process of democratic decentralization and strengthening of the people institution as well as empowerment of women at grass-root level.

EMPOWERMENT OF WOMEN THROUGH PRIs

In spite of the diversity of caste, religion, language, and

thought etc., India adopted Panchayat Raj system which has become a grass-root the level feature in India society. The 73rd and 74th Amendment in Indian constitution has strengthened the root of democracy in India and the amendments have provided ample opportunity to people to participate grass-root level democracy. Participation here is referred to as consultation, involvement, and empowerment of the people. It implies that people participate in the decision-making, design, formulation, implementation, evaluation, and monitoring of various programmes and development projects. It cannot control and manage the resources. It manifests equity, as there is complete involvement of each and every individual, including women.

With the enactment of Amendments the marginalized sections of society, viz., Scheduled castes, Scheduled tribes and women got the opportunity to enter public life through contesting elections to these local bodies. The 73rd Amendment made it obligatory to reserve not less than one-third of seats in favour of women including the number of seats reserved for women of Scheduled Castes and Scheduled Tribes communities.

The constitution in Article 243 (D) provides for reservation of seats to members as well as of chairpersons for Scheduled Castes and Scheduled Tribes as well as in the Panchayats at the villages, block, and district levels. Article 243 (D) (1) mentions that seats shall be reserved for the Scheduled Castes and the Scheduled Tribes in every Panchayat and the number of seats so reserved shall bear, as nearly as may be, the same proportion to the total number of seats to be filled by direct election in that Panchayat as the population of the Scheduled Castes in that Panchayat area or of the Scheduled Tribes in that Panchayat area bears to the population of that area and such seats may be allotted by rotation to different constituencies in a Panchayat.

Article 243(D)(2) also provides that not less than one-third of the total number of seats reserved under clause (1) shall be reserved for women belonging to the Scheduled Castes or, as the case may be, the Scheduled Tribes.

Article 243(D)(4) further mentions that offices of the chairpersons in the Panchayats at the village or any other level shall be reserved for the Scheduled Castes, the Scheduled Tribes and . . . as nearly as may be, in same proportion in the total number of such offices in the Panchayats at each level, as the population of the Scheduled Castes in the state or of the Scheduled Tribes in the state bears to the total population of the state:

(a) Provided further that not less than one-third of the total number of offices of chairpersons in the Panchayats at each level shall be reserved for women; and
(b) Provided that the number of offices reserved under this clause shall be allotted by rotation to different Panchayats at each level.

Article 243(D)(6) also authorizes the state governments to make any provision for reservation of seats in any Panchayat or the offices of the chairpersons in the Panchayats at any level in favour of backward classes. More than one-third of village panchayats throughout the country are now headed by the people of weaker sections and women including the women of weaker sections. This is a kind of silent social revolution taking place in the entire country including the feudal dominated state like Rajasthan. Though this leadership is new, unskilled, and untrained, yet they continuously raise citizen's voice in the meeting of gram-sabha and other meetings.

Recently held elections of local bodies in Bihar shows the better performances of weaker sections of society. The 143 candidates of S.C. and S.T. without reservation have been elected for Mukhiya; the women have shown better performance in this election. They constitute 81 Mukhiyas, 55 Pramukhs, 126 Deputy Pramukhs, 9 Chairman of Zila Prishad, and 11 Deputy Chairmen of Zila Parishads and they have been elected without any reservation.

Women are now expected to be active participants in election politics from village level to higher level though the provisions of 33 per cent reservation. Women from each social group has got wider scope of seeking election against reserved seats which creates the craze for public offices among themselves. They have already become competitive in the matter of contesting elections as was evident from the number of contestants. Distribution of positions among different castes in Bhagalpur district according to population ratio is given in the table below:

Table 2 clearly depicts the women representatives in Panchayat Raj Institutions in a backward but landlord mentality dominated or feudal state like Bihar. In the present stage of economic reform, the constitutional amendment has proved to be a landmark in the history of women's empowerment.

TABLE 2

Caste-wise Distribution of Membership among Women in Bhagalpur PRIs

	SCs	*STs*	*OBCs*	*General*	*Total*
Gram Panchayat Members	115	32	664	318	1129
Panchayat Samiti Members	11	2	62	30	105
Zila Parishad Members	1	1	6	3	11
All	127	35	732	351	1245

Source: *Bihar Economic Journal*, Conference Volume, 2004, p. 322.

While on one hand, women through PRIs are making the state sensitive to issues concerning poverty, inequality, gender injustice, on the other hand, they are also helping the women to change their perception about themselves. They have infused confidence and inculcated a sense of empowerment by enabling them to exercise control over resources, officials, and the greatest by challenging male authority and monopoly. Women have endeavoured to bring about the changes by raising the issues such as: health, sanitation, education, water scarcity, alcohol, and domestic violence. Women's entrance to PRIs is laced with power and authority has given them not only the opportunity to mobilize their struggle but also the strength to fight for the cause at the local level where it is most required knowing fully well that their march towards these powerful positions is not a cake walk but a troublesome path full of woes and agony from not only ego problems of male dominated society but also from their own family members. Still their march continues irrespective of their illiteracy, and lack of practical training, and operational modalities involved in the administrative functioning.

PROBLEMS FACED BY ELECTED WOMEN

Elected women have to face a number of problems in the course of discharging their duties. So some sort of training is also essential to them. To empower women, first, elected women representative have to be trained by building their skills capacity, and support structures. In this process, it is essential to understand the problems faced by women-representatives while performing their roles and functions, and to evolve solutions to these problems to the extent possible.

Women representatives elected to grass-roots-level institutions have been facing numerous problems, within their families as well as in their social, political, and administrative settings, where administration of these bodies would be done by women leaders. They do not have a common platform to express their grievances and get them redressed. Experiences from capacity-building exercises conducted in various parts of the state have enthused us to prepare an action programme for empowerment of women leaders at the grassroots level. We thought that this could be done by forming an association of women representatives, and federating it with similar associations of women representatives in local government in different parts of the country, and making them articulate their issues on their own.

In the Indian context, empowering women is a Herculean task, as social and cultural moorings have established strong roots in the belief system of the people. As a result, there has always been a significant disparity in the upbringing of women and men. All social reconstructions take place only through political activities, that too through political systems. Democracy provides enough scope for such reconstructions through polity. Hence, every social segment is moving towards power. Yet, women hesitate to take part in politics as if it is a male space. In order to break this barrier at the micro-level, a new device has been worked out through the 73rd Constitutional Amendment Act. Women had been made ineffective in administration since they came to these institutions as freshers, but there are instances of women having achieved a great deal of success in managing panchayat responsibilities.

Women leaders in Panchayats are engaged in a constant struggle. Many leaders are insensitive to their own and gender issues in general. They have been oriented to lose their identity and only serve as instruments to operationalise certain process for others. This process has made them sink in localism and become voiceless. As a result, their space is still severely limited.

The following are the main problems which should be solved for further empowerment of women:

(i) Women Workload

The moment the women filed their nominations for election to grass-roots level institutions, their workload doubled and so did the constraints. No woman representative from the rural areas reported that her workload on the home front decreased due to her work in the public space. In a joint family system, attention to routine work cannot be reduced. At every stage, the elected women representatives have to tackle problems of the family carefully, otherwise they court trouble. The family burden, coupled with the workload in the Panchayat, created a stressful situation for these women in their office. Their efficiency could neither be exhibited nor improved, as they had no time.

(ii) Illiteracy

Everybody knows that there is only 54.16% literacy among Indian women, while it is only 33.57% among women of Bihar. So, illiteracy is a basic problem among newly elected women representatives. They are not able to read and write, but they are allowed to file their nomination. After they are elected to positions, they feel frustrated about their inability to read and write. They want to be literate and are prepared to undergo training, but their husbands prohibit this since many of them operate the Panchayat on behalf of their spouses. Wherever the elected women representatives establish contact with NGOs, they are properly oriented and trained to manage institutions on their own. To maintain the required 31 records as a representative of Panchayati Raj Institutions, everyone requires adequate skill. The training programme is intended to impart skill in the art of management of Panchayat Institutions, for which literacy is a prerequisite. Nearly nine per cent of the participants lack this skill. Hence, they have to rely on others for managing Panchayats.

(iii) Male Dominated Society

It is clear from the experience of these elected women representatives that their capacity has not been recognised by the males of their families. After their election, women representatives have been attending meetings and training programmes, where they have learnt several things. Initially the men in the family, in the guise of helping them, accompanied the elected women representatives to offices and public places. Over a period of time, the women learnt the art of administration through interaction and training. But males would not accept that women of their families, have equipped themselves to manage institutions. It is an irony that though elected women representatives feel that they can manage the affairs of the Panchayat on their own without the help of any male from their families, they cannot say so. Further, elected women representatives face problems in Panchayats when the men of their families interfere in administration. In the absence of such interference, trouble from male representatives would be minimal and negligible.

(iv) Negatives Attitude of Officials

Elected women representatives find it difficult to deal with officials in government offices as the latter have a poor opinion of women representatives. They feel that these women are in position simply because of the reservation policy and that they do not have any opinion or vision of their own, and assume that all women representatives are ready to accept whatever advice they give. Consequently, women representatives who go to offices with aspirations and expectations feel frustrated.

(v) Ill-treatment by the officials

It is a sorry state of affairs in government offices where elected women representatives with high social and economic background get respect while poor elected women representatives, especially Dalits and OBCs face ill-treatment.

(vi) Information Blockade

There are several hurdles and barriers to the process of women's empowerment. Information blockade is the most powerful weapon used by officials to disempower women. Generally, women do not have access to newspapers. Moreover, all government information is transmitted from one department to another only among officials. They circulate information booklets and details only among men and not among women. Elected men representatives are not willing to share their knowledge with women representatives.

(vii) Caste Politics Dominated Panchayats

Traditional caste Panchayat leaders are yet another barrier to elected women representatives as they impose conditions and restrictions on them. If the elected women representative belongs to the caste of the traditional Panchayat leaders, they extend all support to her to remain in power but not to attend to the work on her agenda. The traditional Panchayat leaders expect that the elected woman representative should adhere to their advice. She is expected to carry out her work based on the agenda of the traditional Panchayat. If she belongs to any other caste, particular if she is dalit or OBCs, she would not be allowed to do any work at all. Invariably, she has to be under the control of the traditional Panchayat leader or else she has to face problems.

(viii) Lack of Communication Skills

Communication skills are very important for the success of any leader in the modern era. Elected women representatives have hardly any experience of public speaking and hence they lack communication skills. They have to manage the council and the public with effective communication skills. Since they feel that they lack such skills, they cannot achieve what they want.

(ix) Poor Economic Status

There are elected women representatives from the working class who have to rely on their daily wages. Though they have been entrusted with many responsibilities and duties, there are no means of reimbursing their loss of wages. This deprives them of their livelihood and hence some are forced to use proxies in their office.

(x) Exploitation of Women

When elected women representatives meet officials with men of their family, the officials talk to the men and not to the representatives. Even reserved seats are offered to their husbands and other male members of their family and not to them. Initially, they felt humiliated, but gradually they started taking these insults in their stride. However, in local politics, muscle and money power have an upper hand. Hence, all activities are planned in the context of managing muscle and money. In order to overcome this problem, women have to rely on the family, caste or party leader. At a later stage, whoever comes to the rescue of the woman representative comes to the Panchayat for personal favour and obligations. When such obligations are denied, women representatives are criticized and castigated.

CONCLUSION

No doubt, the 73rd and 74th Amendments have brought significant change in the status of women. These Amendments have bought empowerment to women in the liberalized era. But some sort of training programme is needed to achieve the final goal of empowerment of women.

Women need orientation, sensitisation, capacity building, specialised information, and counseling continuously, through organisations. The ongoing experiments and experiences suggest that periodical training; orientation and sensitisation make women leaders perform their assigned role in a better way. When women leaders respond to socio-political challenges, they need to be supported by organisations and institutions that work for their empowerment. Wherever such interventions are available, the achievements of women leaders are substantial and impressive. The government will respond to the needs of these women leaders only when they are supported by organisations well known for their credentials and are to be reckoned with as a force.

REFERENCES

Azad, Chandra Prakash, Pandey, Kanak K. and Laheri, Vandana, "Women's Participation in Panchayati Raj Institutions: A Study of Bhagalpur District," Published in *Bihar Economic Journal*, Conference Volume, 2004.

Batliwala, Srilatha, 1995, 1996, 'Empowerment of Women's Autonomy: Proceedings of a Consultation of Women's Health and Rights—Rethinking Population', HIV/AIDS Technical Report Series, 1 (14).

Deshmukh, Neelima, "Women's Empowerment Through Panchayati Raj Institutions: A Case Study on Wambori Gram Panchayat in Maharashtra," Published by the *Indian Journal of Public Administration*, Vol. LI, No. 2, April-June, 2005.

Government of India, 1975, Towards Equality: Report of the Committee on the Status of Women in India, New Delhi, Centre for Women's Development Studies.

Kumari, Ranju Ranjan and Yadav, K.N., "Panchayati Raj Institutions and

Decentralised Governance," Published in *Bihar Economic Journal*, Conference, 2004.

Ministry of Rural Development and Employment, 2002, Methew, C.A. (eds.), 2000, Tamil Nadu (26), Rajasthan (30), and Haryana (31).

Palanithurai, G., "The Empowerment Process: Women Representatives in Grass-roots Institutions in Tamil Nadu," Published by *Indian Council of Social Science Research*, Vol. 1, Jan.-Feb. 2004.

Thampi, Binitha V., "Decentralized Planning and Economic Empowerment of Women in Kerala," Published by Labour & Development, Vol. 10, No. 2, December, 2004, V.V. Giri National Labour Institute.

Women Representatives in Local Bodies, Gandhigram, Rajiv Gandhi Chair for Panchayati Raj Studies.

29

Impact of Economic Reforms on Dalits

ANIL KUMAR THAKUR, ASHWANI KUMAR
AND K.B. PADAMDEO

INTRODUCTION

Dalits are a very distinct social group. While belonging to a broad class of have nots, they suffer from an additional disability of social oppression. Economically, most of them are still the poorest of poor. The social dis-advantage suffered by the Dalits in India was taken note of in the Constitution of India, which was drafted under the chairmanship of Dr. B.R. Ambedkar—a person who had spearheaded the movement of the depressed classes. It provided the Dalits with many safeguards, viz.:

(i) Social, educational, cultural, and religious safeguards,
(ii) Economic safeguards,
(iii) Political safeguards, and
(iv) Safeguards for employment.

The free market ethos unleashed by the reforms, conceptually can neither conform to the democratic spirit of the Indian constitution of "one vote, one value," nor can it coexist with the system of positive discrimination embodied in these safeguards. For the market grants moneyed person more value, and overtly believes in the "Jungle law of 'might is right'." To a large extent, the primary motivation behind these constitutional provisions was liberal democratic aspirations that characterized the freedom movement. However, these aspirations and the initial ideological zeal of the founding fathers withered away in no time and what survived was its utilitarian dimension for the electoral politics. The sorry state of the executive compliance with the constitutional provisions amply bears out the fangs of the intrinsically iniquitous Indian society. The reforms will provide a kind of legitimacy to this attitudinal resistance of the upper castes and classes to the movements for change by the downtrodden. The safeguards will stand eroded as the reforms gain in momentum. Influence of the reforms is bound to be all pervasive.

The statistics indicate that Dalits have made significant progress on almost all parameters during the five post independence decades; the relative distance between them and non-Dalits seems to have remained the same or increased. More than 75 per cent of the Dalit workers are still connected with land, 25 per cent being the marginal and small farmers and balance over 50 per cent are the landless labourers. In urban areas, they work mainly in the unorganized sector. Out of the total Dalit population of 138 million, the number of Dalits in services falling in the domain of reservations does not exceed 1.1 million, a mere 0.8 per cent.

As per the Human Development Reports (HDRs) published annually by the U.N.D.P. since 1991, India has consistently improved on the human development front and is grouped among the countries with medium human development. But some components of human development indicators for health and education continue to lag behind the improvement in income and India's rank in terms of Human Development Index (HDI) and Gender Development Index (GDI) which continue to be low compared even to some countries of our region. India is ranked 127 in HDI for 2002 (same rank as in 2001) out of 177 countries, and 103 in GDI out of 144 countries in HDR 2004 (Table 1). Even today India is predominantly an agrarian economy, with over

65 per cent of its population living in villages. No statistics moreover can adequately capture the heinous socio-cultural inequality that is an abiding part of the Indian reality. It has acute inequalities not only in economic terms but also in the socio-cultural terms. However, only a few issues of importance to the Dalit masses have been picked up for discussion here.

TABLE 1

Percentage Representation of Dalits in Government Offices as on 1st January

Service Group	*1965*	*1970*	*1975*	*1980*	*1984*	*1992*
A	1.64	2.36	3.43	4.83	6.92	9.7
B	2.82	3.84	4.98	8.07	10.36	11.6
C	8.88	9.27	10.71	11.54	13.98	15.8
D	17.75	18.09	18.64	19.16	20.2	20.9

RESERVATION POLICY

The benefits of the reservation policy to the Dalit community have been more indirect than direct. Directly it benefited a few but indirectly it has created hope for advancement in the entire Dalit population. This hope is already faded even when not much of privatization has happened so far. Their ideological armour is proving insufficient to resist it. There is a visible alienation, hopelessness, and dejection setting in among them, which is getting manifested in increasing lumpenization and criminalization of Dalit youth. This trend portends doom not only for the Dalits but also for the entire oppressed people thirsting for some radical change. For, no radical change is possible in this country without Dalits participation. The Dalit consiciousness formed over centuries of struggle is getting obliterated by the contemporary compulsions created by the reforms. This phenomenon will catapult Dalit masses back on to the vicious spiral of backwardness and fortify reactionary regimes in the similar proportion. This loss would prove expensive to the Dalits.

While privatization might set in slowly, the free market ethos that it engenders much before could hit the Dalits really harder through the legitimacy it grants to the base instincts against any emancipation project. For, the likely victims of the privatization are still a miniscule part of the Dalit population but the impact of these social ethos should engulf the entire Dalit population. Howsoever base the individual conviction might have been, the ethos of yesteryears had nearly forbidden them from surfacing openly. But, now the emergent free market ethos is not only permitting but also promoting the vilest and venomous discourse against the Dalits and the minorities. The venhemence with which the reservations or any kind of subsidies or any type of positive discrimination which are derided today have a qualitatively distinctive edge. It is interesting to note that there a Dalit voice has not yet been raised against this fascist hegemony. It would indeed be difficult for the Dalits to resist this onslaught. The emergence of right wing politics to national prominence is merely a corollary or consequence of this transformation.

Social consequences of the economic miseries associated with these reforms are indeed ominous for the Dalits. On one side, they shall be subject to increasing pauperization and on the other, stand in competition with the multitude of masses in the job market. Increasing tendency of businesses to downsize, virtual abolition of the reservation system through privatization, the strategies of flexibilization and informalizaton of labour; corporatization and de-peasantization of farming, etc. will release vast numbers of people to the job market. The resident caste prejudices in such situations will certainly get activated to the detriment of the Dalits.

RESERVATION FOR DALITS IN EDUCATIONAL INSTITUTIONS

Reservation in the educational institutions and the financial assistance in the form of scholarships and freeships constitute perhaps the most important factor in the development scheme for Dalits. For, it is the primary responsiblity to make the basic input of education available and affordable to them. Without education, all the constitutional safeguards including the reservation in services would be in fructuous. Under this scheme, the Dalit students whose parental income is below a specified level, get freeship, reservation in admissions to all the colleges, getting grants-in-aid from the government, and scholarships. Without this assistance, even today, it would be difficult even for the second-generation educated Dalits to send their children to school.

The reforms have already resulted in freezing the grants to many institutions and in stagnating, if not lowering, the expenditure on education. The free market ethos has entered the educational sphere in a big way. Commercialization of education is no more a mere rhetoric; it is now the established fact. Commercial institutions offering specialized education that signify essential input from utilitarian viewpoint, have come up in a big way from cities to small towns. Their product-prices are not only based on the demand-supply consideration in their market segment but also are manipulated by their promotional strategies. In a true spirit of globalization, many foreign universities are invading the educational spheres through hitherto unfamiliar strategic alliances with non-descript commercial agencies, of course at hefty dollar equivalent prices. Many elite institutions like IIMs and IITs, suddenly facing fund crunch had to resort to raising their fee structure and other prices many fold. They were already beyond the reach of the Dalits. When they eventually turn self-financing, their prices would be bench-marked against their international counterparts, which any way would be affordable to the same top market segment that constitutes the focus of all the reform-talk. As the job markets become acutely competitive, owing to a sharp decline in job opportunities, the polarization between the elite and commoner would also sharpen. Various kinds of price barriers would be erected to thwart the entry of downtrodden to the portals of development.

Even the sphere of primary education the coverage of which has been so miserably inadequate as to leave out multitude of children in villages as illiterate, could not remain unaffected, notwithstanding its already existing divide between the vernacular and English schools. Corporatization has entered this arena, transforming the education into an enterprise for profits. The quality of input these expensive schools will provide will benchmark the products in the contracting job markets. Even today, because of preponderance of the English language in business circles, the divide between village and towns is almost complete in the field of education. It is so difficult for a village student; educated in vernacular medium to compete with his convent educated (now an understatement!) counterpart in cities and towns. If this is the situation of general village population, the plight of the Dalits who besides being the poorest of the village population carry the additional burden of social discrimination, is indeed a worrisome matter. Despite several kinds of state assistance, the Dalits are plagued with alarming rate of school dropouts. This may be explained out as much by the need for Dalit children to supplement their meagre family incomes for making the two ends meet as also by the erosion of their faith that education could be the instrument to change the pathetic course of their lives. This sense of alienation is going to grow with the progress of the reforms, giving rise to increasing lumpenization and criminalization of the Dalit youth.

The government policy of reservations in employment sphere has undoubtedly played an important role in the process of advancement of the Dalits. The policy broadly envisages representation of the Dalits in proportion to their population in all the public services, which includes the governments, the public sector, autonomous bodies, and other institutions that receive grants-in-aid from the government. A cursory glance at the figures of this representation is enough to discover the pathetic state of implementation of this policy.

However, unsatisfactory the results of implementation may be, see in Table 2, 3 and 4. As could be evidenced by the organized private sector, where it would be difficult to find a Dalit employee (save of course in scavenging and lowliest of the similar jobs), without reservations the Dalits would have been totally doomed. The importance of reservations thus could only be assessed in relation to situations where they do not exist. Whatever be their defects and deficiencies, they have given certain economic means of livelihood and some social prestige to the sons and daughters of over 1.5 million landless labourers. Whether they get real power or not, over 50,000 Dalits could enter the sphere of bureaucratic authority with the help of reservations. More importantly these tangible benefits to few have instilled a hope in their entire Dalit people to strive for their betterment. This hope predominantly manifests in the form of spread of education among them. Their emotional bond with the nation and its Constitution despite heaps of injustice and ignominy they bear every moment of their life may also be significantly attributable to the Reservation Policy.

TABLE 2

Percentage Representation of Dalits in Public Sector Undertakings (as on 1st January)

Service Group	*1974*	*1975*	*1980*	*1981*	*1983*	*1984*	*1985*	*1992*
A	1.19	1.44	2.9	3.18	3.56	3.93	4.12	6.69
B	2.96	3.02	5.11	6.12	5.52	5.38	5.5	9.92
C	13.18	13.73	18.08	18.15	16.09	18.23	18.34	16.82
D	26.7	26.29	22.36	20.89	34.28	27.27	27.2	23.25
E			64.69	81.62				71.91
Total	16.89		18.35		20.01	18.08		17.76

TABLE 3

Percentage Representation of Dalits in Nationalized Banks

Year	*Officers*	*Clerks*	*Junior Staff*
1975	0.58	4.34	11.13
1979	2.44	11.51	19.45
1980	2.98	12.11	20.98
1981	3.88	12.77	21.37
1983*	4.64	12.96	22.35
1984*	4.05	13.48	22.95
1985*	5.72	13.83	23.79
1992	11.12	14.31	21.97

* Figures are for 34 banks. For the rest figures are for only 14 banks.

ECONOMIC REFORM AND DALITS

The economic reforms have already shaken the very foundations of reservations. The reforms clearly envisage the minimalist state. Wherever the reforms patterned on the Structural Adjustment Programme (SAP) of the World Bank were carried out, de-nationalization and privatization of the public sector have come in a big way. Being a late starter, India has not reached the scales achieved by others, say, and the Latin American countries. However, the start has not been any less impressive. Within a short time, almost all the sectors of economy stand opened up for private investment. The disinvestments in existing public sector companies has already been allowed up to 49 per cent by the policy. The public stake being more than 50 per cent, the 'public sector' as such has not yet dismantled the policy. It continues to be the State as before, and hence attracts application of the reservation policy. However, the reform package has already endangered, if not abolished, the reservations through numerous back doors.

In the name of preparing the public sector undertakings (PSUs) for global free market regime, the PSUs are being allowed/ encouraged to have strategic alliances with private companies from India and abroad. As such, over the last five years, many profit-making PSUs have formed the joint venture companies (JVC). Most of the PSU investments continue to be channeled through the JV route despite repeated failures of the joint ventures. These JVCs are strategically structured so as not to fall in the ambit of the PSU-framework. The typical equity stake for the PSU and private could be 49.51. There appears to be a great deal of receptivity for this scheme in the government circles. There are no policy barriers on the business to be pursued by these JVCs. Theoretically, an existing PSU can hire off its business divisions into private JVCs and transform itself into a financial holding company, with a Board of Directors and skeleton staff. Even if such an entity technically remains a PSU and follows the reservation policy sincerely, it would still have little or no scope to absorb the Dalits in its staff. Whatever may be the strategic considerations, the fallout of this process practically amounted to shutting the doors of these new age companies to the Dalits and to potential neutralization of the reservation policy.

The policy of limited disinvestments of the PSUs not being in conformity with the spirit of the reforms, is bound to be relaxed in favour of privatization any time. But still, all the PSUs may not get privatized at once. The better ones would be gobbled up by the bigger sharks. The worst ones may be closed down or distress-sold. And the middle ones may for quite some time, continue to be the relic of their past whatever the scenario, the residual structures of the 'reformed' PSUs are never going to be the same, as far as the Dalits are concerned. The ethos of privatization and the excuse of global competition, superimposed on the traditional caste prejudice, will never allow reservations to happen, any more.

Other public services are also bound to slip out of the reservation policy. Most of the sectors, which were the traditional domain of the government investment, have already been released for the private investment.

Reservation policy that represented the strategic response of liberal bourgeoisie to the aspirations of the Dalit movement not quite unlike that of the colonial state at the time of its inception, was never swallowed by the civil society as rightful share of the Dalits. Its response initially reflected feudal magnanimity but once the first generation of the Dalits started pouring out of the university portals into the job markets and claimed their share of pie, caste dominated State apparatus was evident in full measure in the manner the circulars proclaiming this policy were issued. Their convoluted language facilitated the unwilling bureaucracy to thwart it to the possible extent and judiciary to be labour for over several years on what should have been so clearly evident. The broad statistics on the implementation of this policy are enough to reveal the extent of prejudice of the state machinery as well as the civil society. One of the provisions of the policy states that a Dalit candidate qualifying without any concession should not be placed in the reserved seat, implying thereby that the percentage representation of the Dalits in services or the educational institutions would be more than its prescribed value. But, over the five decades of implementation of the reservation policy, it refuses to reach even the prescribed levels confirming the casteist notion still prevalent in society that the Dalits are intrinsically an inferior species. Despite this vile attitude of the establishment, the reservations by far have been the sole contributors to advancement of the Dalits. Privatization is meant to directly hit it.

With regard to impact of the economic reforms on the caste system, the optimists and protagonists rely upon an old rhetoric of contradiction between feudalism and capitalism. The problem of annihilation of castes subsumes the change in the economic structure of the society in favour of the Dalits and simultaneously a massive cultural movement to cleanse the minds of people of the caste notions and implant in its place the attitude of scientificism and virtue of liberty, equality, and fraternity. Having seen that far from striving for economic equality, the reforms are going to accentuate the existing inequalities, we can just examine its attitude towards the caste system. Will the reforms promote the cultural movement for social equality? Does it have the wherewithal or motivation to catalyse struggle against the case system? The answers to these questions will also have to be in negative. The old rhetoric that capitalism will completely displace feudalism evokes positive expectations in some people about the prowess of the reforms to annihilate castes. They would argue, that the unbridled capitalism inherent in the reforms is not compatible with any feudal structure and hence implementation of the latter should remove these last blots of the caste system. This simplistic thumb rule does not seem to be entirely validated by the developmental experience in India. The capitalism in India did not have to sprout through the bedrock of contradiction of feudalism as in Western Europe. It was planted in the fertile soil of the Indian feudalism. It has grown here on its nutrients. The caste institution has defied the classical mould of feudalism by possessing many unique features, the most important being its resilience and adaptability. What we experience in the mysterious growth of casteist politics today in India is precisely this ability of caste to adapt to changing times. The vast army of unemployed created by the developmental dynamics of the economic reforms will need appropriate instruments for being controlled. The history bears ample testimony to the fact that whenever the people tended to come together with a common identity, the ruling classes have deftly used the time-tested weapon of castes to divide them. Caste with its divisive potential will never be abandoned by any iniquitous regime. Its resilience may diffuse its contours but in its essence the caste would coexist with the reforms.

Privatization and free market components of the reforms are certainly impacting very adversely on the job situation as seen in details above. Many resources for public consumption shall also be scarce, as they would be produced in private enterprises for profits. They would be beyond the reach of common people. The impact of the reforms in terms of increasing inequality has been established beyond doubt. Therefore, it can be inferred that the reforms are potentially incapable to alleviate the pain of Dalit masses. In sum, the atrocities on the Dalits not only shall continue but may also increase on account of the reforms.

CASTE ATROCITIES AND DALIT LIFE

The caste atrocities are an integral feature of the Dalit life. The government machinery keeps on collecting their statistics year after year and issues it in a report of its Commissioner for the SCs and the STs (now the National Commission for the SCs and the STs). There are at least three Articles (15, 17, and 23) in the Constitution of India, which seek to mitigate the evil. To give effect to these constitutional provisions, the following Acts also have been in operation:

1. The Untouchability (Offences) Act, 1955, later amended and re-titled as the Protection of Civil Rights Act, 1955, and
2. The Scheduled Castes and Scheduled Tribes (Prevention of Atrocities Act), 1989 and The Bonded Labour System (Abolition) Act, 1976.

Despite this, the statistics of the registered atrocities reads like a balance sheet of a blue chip company with consistent rise every successive year (Table 5). It is pertinent to remember that owing to the dependency relationship of the Dalits with the perpetrators of atrocities, not every occurrence of the atrocity gets registered. Rather, it can be safely assumed that behind each registered atrocity over ten atrocity cases go unreported. As per the latest statistics, every day nearly 50 cases of atrocities are registered all over the country. Over three Dalit women are raped and six are disabled on each day round the year. The National Commission analyzed the causes of each of the atrocities in a sample of 45 cases. The analysis shows that out of 45 cases 13 are clearly attributable to the economic reasons. The balance can also be explained out to be some kind of weakness of the Dalits. Coupled with the weakness of the Dalits, their growing assertiveness and the refusal to submit to the casteist dictates of the village lords, rebellion ethos assimilated through dictates of the village lords, rebellion ethos assimilated through the Ambedkarian struggle and the process of general awareness, also cause atrocities to increase.

TABLE 5

Atrocities on Dalits

Year	*Murder*	*Riots*	*Rape*	*Arson*	*Others under IPC*	*Total*
1989	556	1630	830	703	12080	15799
1990	584	1691	885	599	13908	17667
1991	610	1706	784	602	3944	17646

Atrocities are basically a rude reassertion of power over the powerless by the powerful in the wake of threat. It is thus an expression of insecurity by the powerful who perceive power slipping from their hand. In the pre-colonial closed loop production system of a typical village, since everyone followed his or her calling under the divine authority of religion, there were no atrocities of the kind we experience in the saner age of globalization today. If any one questioned or defined this system, the religious code provided for the punishment. In this scheme, it was more important to fortify the religious control on populace than physically taming them to comply. Although, the emphasis was on enslavement of mind, physical punishment did exist as a contingency measure. Atrocities on the Dalits today are in essence a physical punishment for their act of forsaking the bondage. The physical punishments or atrocities presuppose material power in the hands of perpetrators of atrocities. Not only that the Dalits lit the fire of anger in materially powerful upper castes by defying their notion of caste authority but also they added fuel to it by entering the competition for partaking scarce resources. The emergence of the land owning middle of the existing castes during the post-independence development process who at the one end replaced the traditional upper castes and wore their mantle of superiority but who at the other end found themselves in competition with the Dalits for resources like education and employment, moreover led to accentuation of atrocities. These middle castes lacked the cunning and sophistication of the upper castes and enraged themselves into physical response on slightest provocation. They could not stomach the Dalits who were utterly dependent on them in the village setting asserting their human rights or competing with them on an equal platform for scarce resources and eventually winning them away in some cases with the help of reservations. This commonplace experience is amplified by the vested interests of the ruling classes. Thus, the essential ingredients for atrocities on the Dalits can be identified as: the existence of material power in the hands of perpetrators of atrocities; enduring sense of social superiority; increasing scarcity of resources; and growing pauperization of the masses. The directional impact of the reforms on the atrocities on the Dalits therefore can be inferred from the effect it would have on the existing dependency relationship in the villages that the Dalits are engaged in with the powerful middle castes; on the caste system itself; on the availability of certain critical resources like jobs; health care, education, etc.; and on the income distribution to the people.

Atrocities are seen to occur where the dependency relationships are more pronounced. Villages, where the Dalits for their livelihood and where the traditional caste equations have a potential to yield economic surplus to the latter, provide an ideal setting for atrocities. What impact would the new regimes have on the socio-economic setting of an Indian village? In the face of it, this relationship cannot be altered till the Dalits get land. Can the new regime afford this economic empowerment of the Dalits? Can it, for instance, grant them land? The answer to all these questions will be in negative. Instead of talking about land reforms, the new regime will promote depeasantization of Indian agriculture and consolidation of their holdings to start corporate farming. The capital influx in the rural areas will have a natural ally in the rich farmers who have hegemonic hold over their areas. These sections will be the main beneficiaries of the improved terms of trade and capitalist development in the rural areas. The form that the new system may take will have the corporate structure of management and beneath the local vendors to provide various inputs and services. While the rich farmers may assume the roles in this organizations as big or petty capitalist, the erstwhile landless labourers, marginal and small farmers shall together constitute the vast army of job-seekers. Although in national terms the Dalits might get rid of the old relationships, in reality they will still be dependent on their upper caste employers and certainly far more vulnerable than before.

CONCLUSION

The state has intervened in favour of Dalits in a variety of ways since independence. These include: (a) an array of constitutional and legal provisions; (b) protective discrimination in government jobs as well as in elected representative bodies; (c) budgetary support through the special component plan (SCP) approach; (d) special programmes of health and education; (e) priority in all rural development, slum improvement; and anti-poverty programmes; etc.

No doubt that these wide ranging measures have succeeded in improving the socio-economic conditions of the Dalits, yet the Dalits continue to suffer from poverty, caste prejudice, untouchability, and atrocities in large parts of the country. Thus, the state must intervene in alleviating the plight of these people with a view to erase the lingering scars of an age old exploitative social order.

From July, 1991 onwards the Indian government has initiated a series of economic reforms. The whole package is commonly known as the 'new economic policy' (NEP). The NEP is logically more coherent, holistic, and marks a significant departure from the past. The long cherished principles of growth with justice; social responsibility and accountability, equity and self-reliance have been rendered obsolete with the new slogans of liberalization, privatization, globalization, efficiency, and competitiveness.

Needless to say that these reforms are not going to affect different social groups and sub-groups uniformly. While some groups—usually the richer sections—tend to gain as a result of the economic reforms large sections-usually the poor ones-suffer during the structural adjustment programmes.

Various studies have shown that the poor bear the main burden of these reforms. Adjustment programmes have shown that there is a rise in unemployment, inflation rates, shift in income distribution in favour of the rich and adversely affected the living conditions of the poor sections.

It seems that the economic reforms will increase the socio-economic inequalities everywhere which will definitely result in increasing social tensions in our society. It seems once again that a major portion of the population, Dalits in this case, who are ill-equipped to participate in a competitive world would be left out of the development process.

Evidently, the NEP, the SAP and the GATT have considerably weakened the ability of the state to impose its own policies and to regulate social and environmental degradation. The Indian state as an autonomous economic and political entity will be threatened by the globalization of capital and the consolidation of neo-imperialism. Economic liberalization threatens the interests of organized industrial labour because in a labour surplus economy such as that of India, liberalization would allow employers to hire and fire laborers at will. The real wages of the farm workers have been, by and large, stagnating for the last several years. Hardly one or two per cent of the farm workers are organized. As the NEP has inflated the prices of food items, the farm workers, largely belonging to the Dalits and OBCs, and the other poor people, will have to face a formidable crisis of survival and social reproduction.

The tribals will suffer the most from the NEP. Agro-forestry, fishery, tourism, and domestic big business houses will displace them from their habitats in large numbers.

Unemployment and poverty are endemic in the country, and the NEP will aggravate them further. Leaving the public sector to fend for itself, the private sector will thrive where reservations of employment will have no room. The Dalits fear that when they manage to get reserved jobs in the government, economic liberalization and privatization were introduced (under NEP package) to reduce the number of jobs in the government and public sector enterprises. Needless to say, the liberalization and privatization will have adverse impact on the Dalits.

References

Bhaduri, Amit, and Deepak Nayyar (1996), *The Intelligent Person's Guide to Liberalization*, Penguin Books, New Delhi, p. 100.

—— (1993), Entrepreneurship Development Institute of India (1993): Research Report on Impact of New Economic Policies on Small and Tiny Industrial Sector, Ahmedabad, November.

—— (1993), National Council of Applied Economic Research (NCAEF) and Friedrich-Nauman-Stiftung (1993): *Structure and Promotion of Small Scale Industries in India: Lessons for Future Development*, New Delhi, December.

Bhattacharya, M. (1994), Impact of Liberalisation on Small Scale Sector, Office of the Development Commissioner, India, New Delhi, *EPW*, p. 1312.

Deshpande, Ashwin (1995), 'Rethinking Strategy for Global Debt Crisis', *Economic and Political Weekly*, May 27, p. 1247.

Dev, S. Mahendr (1995), 'Economic Reforms and the Rural Poor', *Economic and Political Weekly*, August 19, p. 2085.

EPW Research Foundation (1994), Three Years of Economic Reform in India, *EPW Research Foundation*, Bombay, pp. 6-9.

Ghose, A.K. (1992), "Economic Restructuring, Employment and Safetv Nets: A Note" in ILO-ARTEP, *Social Dimensions of Structural Adjustment in India*, New Delhi.

Gupta, S.P. (1995), "Economic Reform and Its Impact on Poor," *Economic and Political Weekly*, Vol. XXX, No. 22.

Gupta, S.P. and Raman, P.S. (1992), "Economic Liberalization and Its Social Impact," Indian Council for Research in International Economic Relations, New Delhi.

Johansen, Frida (1993), "Poverty Reduction in East Asia: The Silent Revolution", World Bank Discussion (papers, 203).

Joshi, Vijay and I.M.D. Little (1996), *India's Economic Reforms: 1991-2001*, Oxford University Press, Bombay, pp. 238-39.

Kishwar, Madhu (1996), "A Half Step Forward: The Thwarting of Economic Reforms in India," *Manushi*, January-April.

Kurien, C. T. (1996), "The Real Impact", *Frontline*, February 9, 1996, p. 97.

—— (1996), "Development and Marginalization: Global and National Scenario," Key Note paper presented at the Conference on "Towards a People Centered Development' organized by TISS, Mumbai, November.

—— (1996), Economic Reforms and the People, Madhyam Books, Delhi.

Mundale, S. (1992), "Employment Effects of Stabilisation and Related Policy Changes in India, 1991-92 to 1993-94" in ILO-ARTEP, *Social Dimensions of Structural Adjustment in India*, New Delhi.

Mundle, Sudipto (1993), 'Unemployment and Financing of Relief Employment in a Period of Stabilization: India, 1992-94', *Economic and Political Weekly*, January 1993, p. 173.

Pathy, Jagannath (1995), "The Consequences of the New Economic Policies on the People of India: A Sociological Appraisal," *Sociological Bulletin*, Vol. 44, March.

Randive, Joy, R. (1994), "Gender Implications of Adjustment Policy Programme in India," *Economic and Political Weekly*, April, 30.

Research Unit of Political Economy (1994), 'The Warped Logic of Globalization', Aspects of India's Economy (No. 14), July-September 1994, pp. 14-18.

Singh, Ajit Kumar (1993), "Social Consequences of New Economic Policy," *Economic and Political Weekly*, February 13.

—— (1994), "Social Consequences of New Economic Policies," *Economic and Political Weekly*, April, 30.

Teltumbde, Anand (1996), *Aarthik Sudhar Ani Dalit Sosit* (in Marathi) Prabuddha Bharat Publications, Aurangabad.

Index